Contemporary History in Context Series

General Editor: **Peter Catterall**, Lecturer, Department of History, Queen Mary and Westfield College, University of London

What do they know of the contemporary, who only the contemporary know? How, without some historical context, can you tell whether what you are observing is genuinely novel, and how can you understand how it has developed? It was, not least, to guard against the unconscious and ahistorical Whiggery of much contemporary comment that this series was conceived. The series takes important events or historical debates from the post-war years and, by bringing new archival evidence and historical insights to bear, seeks to re-examine and reinterpret these matters. Most of the books will have a significant international dimension, dealing with diplomatic, economic or cultural relations across borders. In the process the object will be to challenge orthodoxies and to cast new light upon major aspects of post-war history.

Titles include:

Nigel Ashton
KENNEDY, MACMILLAN AND THE COLD WAR
The Irony of Interdependence

Oliver Bange
THE EEC CRISIS OF 1963
Kennedy, Macmillan, de Gaulle and Adenauer in Conflict

Lawrence Black
THE POLITICAL CULTURE OF THE LEFT IN AFFLUENT BRITAIN, 1951–64
Old Labour, New Britain?

Christopher Brady
UNITED STATES FOREIGN POLICY TOWARDS CAMBODIA, 1977–92

Roger Broad
LABOUR'S EUROPEAN DILEMMAS
From Bevin to Blair

Peter Catterall and Sean McDougall (*editors*)
THE NORTHERN IRELAND QUESTION IN BRITISH POLITICS

Peter Catterall, Colin Seymour-Ure and Adrian Smith (*editors*)
NORTHCLIFFE'S LEGACY
Aspects of the British Popular Press, 1896–1996

James Ellison
THREATENING EUROPE
Britain and the Creation of the European Community, 1955–58

Helen Fawcett and Rodney Lowe (*editors*)
WELFARE POLICY IN BRITAIN
The Road from 1945

Jonathan Hollowell (*editor*)
TWENTIETH CENTURY ANGLO-AMERICAN RELATIONS

Simon James and Virginia Preston (*editors*)
BRITISH POLITICS SINCE 1945
The Dynamics of Historical Change

Harriet Jones and Michael Kandiah (*editors*)
THE MYTH OF CONSENSUS
New Views on British History, 1945–64

Wolfram Kaiser
USING EUROPE, ABUSING THE EUROPEANS
Britain and European Integration, 1945–63

Keith Kyle
THE POLITICS OF THE INDEPENDENCE OF KENYA

Adam Lent
BRITISH SOCIAL MOVEMENTS SINCE 1945
Sex, Colour, Peace and Power

Spencer Mawby
CONTAINING GERMANY
Britain and the Arming of the Federal Republic

Jeffrey Pickering
BRITAIN'S WITHDRAWAL FROM EAST OF SUEZ
The Politics of Retrenchment

Peter Rose
HOW THE TROUBLES CAME TO NORTHERN IRELAND

L. V. Scott
MACMILLAN, KENNEDY AND THE CUBAN MISSILE CRISIS
Political, Military and Intelligence Aspects

Paul Sharp
THATCHER'S DIPLOMACY
The Revival of British Foreign Policy

Andrew J. Whitfield
HONG KONG, EMPIRE AND THE ANGLO-AMERICAN ALLIANCE AT WAR,
1941–45

Contemporary History in Context
Series Standing Order ISBN 0–333–71470–9
(*outside North America only*)

You can receive future titles in this series as they are published by placing a standing order.
Please contact your bookseller or, in case of difficulty, write to us at the address below with
your name and address, the title of the series and the ISBN quoted above.

Customer Services Department, Macmillan Distribution Ltd, Houndmills, Basingstoke,
Hampshire RG21 6XS, England

The Political Culture of the Left in Affluent Britain, 1951–64

Old Labour, New Britain?

Lawrence Black

Fulbright-Robertson Visiting Professor of British History
Westminster College, Missouri, USA

Published by
PALGRAVE MACMILLAN
Houndmills, Basingstoke, Hampshire RG21 6XS and
175 Fifth Avenue, New York, N.Y. 10010
Companies and representatives throughout the world

PALGRAVE MACMILLAN is the global academic imprint of the Palgrave
Macmillan division of St. Martin's Press, LLC and of Palgrave Macmillan Ltd.
Macmillan® is a registered trademark in the United States, United Kingdom
and other countries. Palgrave is a registered trademark in the European
Union and other countries.

ISBN-13: 978–0–333–96836–9
ISBN-10: 0–333–96836–0

This book is printed on paper suitable for recycling and made from fully
managed and sustained forest sources. Logging, pulping and manufacturing
processes are expected to conform to the environmental regulations of the
country of origin.

A catalogue record for this book is available from the British Library.

Library of Congress Catalog Card Number: 2002072615

Printed and bound in Great Britain by
CPI Antony Rowe, Chippenham and Eastbourne

Contents

General Editor's Preface

Consumption has always occupied an awkward place within the ideology of the British Left. Arguably, it ought to have been able to secure some kind of pride of place, stemming not least from the Rochdale pioneers of 1844 and the cooperative societies they gave rise to, which by the early twentieth century had come to occupy a key place in the domestic economy of the working classes. It could even feature prominently in left-wing programmes such as the ILP's 1926 *Socialism in our Time*, which drew attention, in a proto-Keynesian manner, to the problem of under-consumption. Yet, as Lawrence Black points out here, the Left were to be much discomforted by the rise of consumer society in the 1950s. Cooperative consumption to deal with insufficiency, or the stimulation of consumption to mop up unemployment, were all very well. But the Left had never had to think, until this point, too deeply about consumption in and of itself, whether it was a public good, or how it fitted in with visions of a more just society. Traditional visions of the latter had seen socialism as a means somehow of distributing social goods more equitably. Socialism was also an ethical ideal, requiring a better society, if not better human beings, to be realized. Quite how that fitted with consumer choices and desires, however, had never been effectively addressed, let alone explicated.

The resulting perplexity is effectively delineated in this, the first full-length study of the Left's attempts to come to terms with these difficulties. In the process, as Black demonstrates, the Left – whether Communist or within the Labour Party – added to its own problems through its own self-image, and its view of the people it sought to represent. A powerful myth of the forward march of Labour contributed to considerable cognitive dissonance as it began to dawn that the forward march had halted. Like Thatcherites in the 1990s, convinced of the essential popularity of their cause, rather than its contingent electoral success in the particular circumstances of the 1980s, many on the Left resisted all attempts to unveil to them the mind of the electorate. Instead, in a piece of cod-Gramscism, they found that the only way they could explain the failure of the people's party to prove the people's favourite was to resort to lamenting the ways in which the Tories had duped the voters with their false white goods paradise. Thus

Macmillan's banal observation in 1957 that 'Most of our people have never had it so good' was played up as a paean to consumerism, rather than as the warning against inflation which was at the forefront of his concerns both in that speech and throughout that year. Macmillan, as a politician, is perhaps fair game for this kind of distortion. However, behind it, as Black shows, was a rather patronizing attitude to the electorate. Contemporary studies showed that the voters did not necessarily switch parties as they changed washing powders, or unceremoniously dump one for the other when they acquired a new television. Nevertheless, Black argues, Labour anxieties on this score, and the way in which they were articulated, may have helped to put off potential supporters.

To be fair, however, a view that there existed a solid working-class Labour vote which was in danger of bleeding away through embourgeoisement was by no means confined to activists on the left. More sophisticated variants of this view continued to be a dominant theme within British psephology during the Thatcher decade. Perhaps it is doomed to reappear whenever the Conservatives enjoy a lengthy spell in power? Evidence that voters could choose to acquire washing machines but cling to their socialist faith tended to bounce off such adamantine convictions. Black argues that Wilson's electoral successes did not so much show that he had come to terms with this evidence, but skirted round it through promising not white goods but 'white heat'. The corporatist nature of many of Wilson's policy prescriptions would seem to support this view. It is Tony Blair, in discovering Mondeo man in the aftermath of Labour's disappointment in 1992, who is supposed to have uncovered the elixir for resolving this problem. Aspirational voters were not to be treated with 1950s-style disdain. Instead of waiting for the state to deliver socialism, electors were now to be the recipients of targetted services and wealth redistribution. The rhetoric was different, and continually repackaged, even if the content bore a greater resemblance to the past. In the process, however, socialism (or whatever it is Blair thinks he has been elected to deliver) really does become 'whatever a Labour government does', as Morrison famously put it, rather than an ethical ideal for which the left was simply, as late as the 1950s, as Black shows, a somewhat flawed vehicle. And if that government fails to deliver, the consumer as voter can always elect someone else.

Peter Catterall
London, January 2002

Acknowledgements

For support, advice and encouragement at various stages in the research, writing and publication of this book thanks are due to Peter Catterall, Mark Donnelly, Steve Fielding, Nina Fishman, Harriet Jones, Mervyn Jones, Cameron Laux, Pat Thane, Richard Toye, Louise Tracey, Richard Weight and Dominic Wring. I owe much to archivists and librarians – notably at the Modern Records Centre, the National Museum of Labour History and the British Library. I also owe much to various history departments and academic institutions: London Guildhall University (as was), St Mary's University College, Kingston University and the Institute of Contemporary British History at the Institute of Historical Research. Thanks are also due to the Department of Historical Studies and Faculty of Arts at the University of Bristol for granting me a research fellowship, which greatly aided the book's completion and otherwise provided a stimulating research environment.

I would like to thank Andrew Thorpe for first sparking my interest in the history of the British left. Special thanks are reserved for Peter Mandler who supervised the thesis for which much of this research was originally undertaken and who has been a constant source of good, critical counsel since; for Nick Tiratsoo, always a font of awkward questions, useful sources and insightful ideas; and for Leo Zeilig, critic and comrade *par excellence*. Above all, thanks to my parents, Ken and Felicity.

Abbreviations

AIC	Advertising Inquiry Council
ASA	Advertising Standards Authority
BBC	British Broadcasting Corporation
BLPES	British Library of Political and Economic Science, LSE
BJL	Brynmor Jones Library, University of Hull
BMRB	British Market Research Bureau
CA	Consumers' Association
CLP	Constituency Labour Party
CND	Campaign for Nuclear Disarmament
CPGB	Communist Party of Great Britain
CPV	Colman, Prentis and Varley
ITA	Independent Television Authority
ITV	Independent Television
LLOY	Labour League of Youth
LPACR	Labour Party Annual Conference Report
MML	Marx Memorial Library, London
MRC	Modern Records Centre, Warwick University
NEC	National Executive Committee (Labour Party)
NMLH	National Museum of Labour History, Manchester
NSA	National Sound Archive, British Library
THMOA	Tom Harrisson Mass Observation Archive, Sussex University
TUC	Trades Union Congress
YCL	Young Communist League
YS	Young Socialists (Labour Party)

1
Introduction

This book traces the attitudes of the political left towards social change in the 1950s and specifically to the changes involved in what was known (particularly after J. K. Galbraith's 1958 study) as the 'affluent society' – ranging from popular prosperity and consumerism to television and youth culture. As in the 1980s, the left encountered 'New Times' that it found not only unfavourable electorally, but which it feared were in a deeper sense deleterious to socialism. Affluence threw socialism's customary ways of thinking, its language and aspirations into doubt.[1]

The title of this book is by way of analogy with New Labour, but is primarily a peg on which to hang debates about the relationship between politics and social change. As more recently, the 1950s raised the issue of whether social change had undermined and outdated the left's appeal or whether this required more effective articulation. Also at issue is how historians connect political parties and social change, and in Labour's case the notion of 'old' and 'new'. Indeed a subtitle like 'Good Labour, Bad Britain (or Britons)' would convey the book's flavour just as well. Whilst this book is mainly about the Labour Party, it ranges across the British political left of which Labour was the major part.

Still, the 1950s are a site on which New Labour has affirmed the shortcomings of 'Old' Labour. Pollster Philip Gould has used memories of the 1950s as a pretext for New Labour. He relates how he learnt his politics not in 'great Northern cities, the Welsh valleys or crumbling urban estates', but 'an unexceptional suburban town' (Woking, Surrey), and argues this was 'the land that Labour forgot':

> my party was to betray the people who lived here: ordinary people with suburban dreams ..to get gradually better cars, washing

machines and televisions ...holiday in Spain rather than Bournemouth ..Labour had failed to understand that the old working class was becoming a new middle class: aspiring, consuming, choosing what was best for themselves and their families. They had outgrown crude collectivism and left it behind in the supermarket car park.[2]

Contrary to Gould, this book shows that more often the attitude of the 1950s left towards these social changes was less that Labour had betrayed the people, than that the people had betrayed socialism or fallen short of the potential of 1945.

The left struggled to either resist or meet the demands of affluence. They were equivocal not only as to how, but even whether, to come to terms with affluence. Richard Crossman, a sort of weathervane of socialist thinking, buffeted about by affluence, ventured in 1960 in *Labour in the Affient Society* that the Labour Party should hold itself in reserve, refusing in any way to come to terms with the affluent society.' That socialists who engaged affluence less equivocally were titled revisionists or the New Left, testifies to the unease with which socialism encountered modernity in the 1950s. 'Affluence', Kenny has suggested, was à metaphor for the inability of socialism to come to terms with the post-war world.' For Vernon Bogdanor, the years of affluence were years of disaster for the Labour Party.'[3]

This study relates the left's difficulties in addressing the altered contours of modern Britain to the characteristic values, morals, ways of performing politics and even ways of living, sustained by its political culture. The concept of political culture is a slippery one. Formisano has indicated its multiple usages: symbolic, comparative, anthropological, dispositional, not simply an upshot of politics but causal also. It regards politics as a culture. In accord with Drucker's contention that Labour's ideology embodies both doctrine and ethos', political culture is broadly defined, encompassing ordinary and elite political activity, activists and spectators. The potential for investigating the ethos of political life has been shown in Samuel's evocation of the Lost World' of British Communism (CPGB). Capturing it as it crumbled in the 1980s, Samuel revisited the dense, exclusive world in which CPGB activists lived. Since the spectre of Blairism similarly haunts 6ld' Labour culture, historical notice might soon be served on a lost world' of labourism.[4] Political culture, this study suggests, is as much constituted of informal, instinctive and ethical impulses, as of more formal or explicitly ideological reasoning. Such as it was in the 1950s, the book endeavours to scrutinize what amounted to a way of thinking, a 'socialist gaze.' This was not far removed from what historians and political scientists have termed 'labourism' since the 1960s. Desai describes this as denoting the untheorised reflexes embodied in the Labour movement – its culture and institutions.' 'Labourism' was always a term of political critique more than historical analysis that came (for Stedman Jones) to 'stand-in for a history of the Labour Party.' Taken up in the New Left's explanation of why Labour had never amounted to much in terms of socialist theory, Nairn despaired Labour had developed 'not ... in response to any theory about what a socialist party should be; it arose empirically, in a quite piece-meal fashion.'5 Seen in terms of political culture, these same reflexes can be seen as ideologically loaded, shaping the way socialists viewed social change.

Assessing political culture sheds new light, rendering the history of socialism more transparent. Certainly the intuitive suspicion many socialists felt towards commercial TV, advertising or commercial 'mass' culture, and the effects of such ethicalism on their audience in the 1950s, is not clearly disclosed by a reading of party manifestos, parliamentary machinations and such stuff as has constituted the conventional diet of the political historian. Not that research into ideas and policy-making is unnecessary – this book attempts to supplement rather than supplant it. Indeed Catherine Torrie's work on Labour's ideology argues differences between 'left' and 'right' were less clear-cut than standard accounts of this period assume. And whilst her case that Labour emerged in 1959 with a considerably more sophisticated understanding of the ways .socialism could be applied in the Britain of the 1950s' begs the question of why this did not translate into greater electoral success (or why it shifted tack to 1964), it might further suggest the key answers lie in examining political culture.6

Rather, the book looks to local party publications and literature, and addresses social change and those experiencing it to understand the ways in which socialists perceived their audience in the 1950s. Journals such as *Labour Organiser*, the Wilson Report (1955) into Labour's constituency organization, the campaign against commercial television, the dismissive comments passed on youth culture, the language in which they understood the consumer, their instinctive suspicion of television in politics and simply the way they themselves lived, disclose as much about the political, social and cultural assumptions within which socialists worked as more formal declarations. Equally, new light can be shed on the traditional sources of high' politics by approaching them in new ways, as Martin Francis has shown.[7]

The book's approach is also informed by the 'new political history'. In redefining the category of 'the political', by seeing it as a more diverse activity and setting it in a wider context, this recognizes what has been termed the 'relative autonomy of politics'. [8] This stresses that politics can't be reduced to other determinants – it is not solely or even primarily an expression of socio-economic changes or of class and popular 'interests'. It regards politics not as a barometer of social change and popular opinion, not as simply responding and trying to attune to an *a priori* social context, but as integral to the making and understanding of these. As Lawrence and Taylor argue in *Party, State and Society*, voters' interests and identities are not pre-existing and parties attempt to define these and 'construct *viable* forms of social and political identity'. Parties make their own history by building constituencies of support. It focuses on language in the assembling of support, but also scrutinizes political culture – party life, traditions and values and how these conceive of the electorate; on how political discourses are constructed, but also how they are conveyed and received. How effectively politics is delivered to an audience bears upon its reception quite as much as how viable its message proves.[9]

This approach lends itself to analysis of cultures and mentalities (and the flavour of popular politics) and also to structural aspects like organization, finance and political technology. It is questionable how new it is, but the focus on how parties build support links 'high' and 'popular' politics and is useful in exploring the role of local activists. In the 1950s this evinces activists' importance in convening support (perceived to be under threat from TV, advertising and polling), but also tensions in the dialogue between socialists and their audience. Activists (and leaders too) could be as responsible for a party's demise as its rise.[10]

Parties then play an active role in their own fate. The left did not necessarily suffer because of the social changes of the 1950s. The assumed causal relationship between social change and political fortunes has tended to be the standard view. Writing in 1970 Bogdanor concluded the social base of the Labour Party has become eroded. And with the erosion of the social base, the politics became eroded too.' Rather *Old Labour, New Britain?* argues that the left's fortunes were contingent upon how it understood and described these changes and communicated with those experiencing them. As Stedman Jones argues, neither politics in general, nor the Labour Party in particular can be regarded as a passive victim of social change.' Social changes are only endowed with particular political meanings so far as they are effectively articulated through specific forms of political discourse and practice.'[11]

Politics is not unshackled from the social' by the new political history'. It is not (although it often seems close to) a re-assertion of the primacy of the political' [12] nor a supplanting of a social by a linguistic interpretation of politics. Rather, relations between political and social change are re-thought (both in terms of their ordering and proximity) and historians alerted to how this relationship is itself fluid and renegotiated, and more unstable than histories of both high' and popular' politics have suggested. Effective politics then relates to existing terms of experience or plausibly organizes it. Situating it more broadly within society is an acknowledgement that politics was often a discrete presence in the wider culture. Its apartness and difference from, rather than pivotal place in, everyday life is salient. This is vital to this study, where discussion of socialist perceptions of apathy and of popular activities (consumerism, leisure and culture) emphasizes the disjunctions as much as continuities between socialist politics and popular interests.

This proposes an alternative to the main analytical frameworks of popular political behaviour. Turner outlines these as the expressive' or electoral sociology approach, familiar in studies that relate Labour's fortunes and character to (primarily) the industrial working class, according to which parties express the socio-economic or other identities of voters. And secondly as the instrumental' or rational choice approach in which voters choose parties on the basis of their governing performance or policies. What both suppose is a clear and direct relationship between politics and the people, rather than one that is constantly being renegotiated and redefined or that is rather more distant.[13]

But if politics and party fortunes are more slightly connected to social reality than is often supposed, can much political importance be read into the left's distaste for affluence. This study proposes that it can in the general and informal impression formed of the left (and Labour in particular) – generated by itself and opponents too. The relative autonomy of politics suggests that how political parties and activists perceive social change and imagine the people is as central to explaining political fortunes as what historians can perhaps show to have been actually' happening. What a party says about social change tells as much (if not more) about that party as about social change. Votes are probably the best, but at best a weak, guide to how effectively a party's version of events is received, since many voters have an imperfect knowledge of parties and their vote cannot be read as a full endorsement of everything a party stands for. Votes are not a direct index of popular attitudes. The quite partial perception of party activists and leaders of what social, cultural and economic change is occurring and means was at least as decisive a factor in the political process as 'objective' change itself.

Labour historians too have often neglected to portray politics in a wider frame – as Fielding points out, since the socialist movement was the provenance of many, they have aped its assumptions. This has tended to produce inward-looking accounts in which politics is the be-all and end-all of life; socialism's basic efficacy and affinity with its audience is unquestioned and the focus is on ideological shortcomings or conflicts between 'right' and 'left' in the movement (reflecting a continuing belief in Labour's forward march' or socialism's inevitability).[14]

Symptomatically, the 'standard books' on Labour in the 1950s deal with the Gaitskellite and Bevanite 'wings' of the party. Indeed since Thorpe notes that work on Labour in the 1950s is 'relatively thin on the ground', this might signal the importance of political culture to understanding the left's history in this period.[15]

Such an insular approach requires revision – mainly because of its 'critical failure .to step outside the interpretative frameworks of its subjects.' The narratives and categories historians have used to understand post-war Britain,' Vernon and others have suggested, 'were also those of their subjects.' Likewise the 'Crisis in Labour History' has arisen partly because 'much of the literature devoted to the subject reflects positions held within the party itself.' In other words, avenues of enquiry not readily recognized in activist language were closed to historical exploration.[16]

Yet such faculties were all the more potent for defying catagorization. Thus, when Drucker came to consider *Doctrine and Ethos in the Labour Party*, one of the few accounts to pay due regard to 'the traditions, beliefs, characteristic procedures and feelings which help to animate members of the party', it was because he found the party was 'marching to tunes which none of the writings had yet scored.'[17] It is this score which this study aims to transcribe.

Besides an exercise in the history of political culture, this study suggests the partialness of familiar themes, such as consensus or decline, in post-1945 historiography. Consensus appears remote to evidence such as the contested politics of television. Rather than relative economic decline, parties were faced with relative popular economic prosperity. Newer accounts increasingly posit shifting identities of consumption and gender as key in understanding post-war British politics.[18]

A more cultural history of politics also, then, bypasses the familiar polarity of 'left' and 'right' in histories of socialism. In this context of the wider society and popular attitudes, it is the resemblance and generic qualities shared by 'right' and 'left' and different traditions within socialism that impress. Nor is this simply due to a new perspective, although exploring 'political culture' does enable (and oblige) a range across the 'right' and 'left' within Labour and to the CPGB and New Left beyond: it is borne out by research. Reviewing Newton's *Sociology of British Communism*, Hobsbawm found Communist activists were 'very like the Labour Party activists' – an elite of self-educating, respectable workers, of the sort who had, by and large, always formed the cutting edge of radicalism.[19]

Socialists were something of a minority, an earnest rather than representative sample of the working class. The chief chronicler of the working class in the later 1950s, Richard Hoggart, declared himself wary of the interpretations given by historians of the working-class movement' who tended to 'overrate the place of political activity in working-class life.' Caution was necessary, he argued, for it was 'easy for the reader to be led into at least a half-assumption that these are histories of the working classes rather than, primarily, histories of the activities – and the valuable consequences for almost every member of the working classes – of a minority.'[20]

The relationship between the people and party merits historicizing – especially in light of Labour's claim in 1956 to be 'The Voice of the People, their natural instrument.' The CPGB too claimed to be the party with a clear '.socialist programme that corresponds with the needs of the people'. The claim to represent was always political. In any stricter sense, it was highly partial – necessarily once an 'organisation seeks to speak for a wider constituency than its own membership.' Lawrence argues, representation 'always implies speaking in the name of others, constructing a politics based on an external .perception of other peoples' needs and interests.' Mediated by their own agenda, parties attempt (as outlined earlier) to assemble support by projecting interests with which a range of social groups can identify.[21]

The social history of working-class and popular culture might be brought to bear on the history of the political voices claiming to speak on their behalf, and in so doing a route out of the impasse of Labour history merges with the 'new' political history. This is Eley's case against Sassoon's *One Hundred Years of Socialism* – that the absence of social history' from its vision limits discussion of the interplay between socialism and its audience. As popular lifestyles were undergoing changes in the 1950s – commonly perceived to be undermining the left's sociological basis by eroding class differentials through working-class embourgeoisement, de-aligning class and politics and promoting political instrumentalism – it seems reasonable to propose that these changes and how socialists envisaged and spoke to these, had a bearing upon the left's fortunes.[22]

Work exploring this relationship, like Mike Savage's, has stressed how Labour developed in specific local contexts by successfully (or not) raising popular issues. Labour politics is presented in many studies (such as early work by Stedman-Jones and McKibbin) as a product of the defensive, conservative solidarity of turn-of-the-century working-class culture. Other work suggests a more limited relationship. Chris Waters' *British Socialists and the Politics of Popular Culture 1884–1914* discloses attitudes similar to those on the left in the 1950s. Ethical and puritan objections, it is argued, disabled the left in the face of the commercialization of popular culture and distanced it from many workers. Tiratsoo's discussion of 'Labour and the Electorate' suggests competition from the Conservatives and media and their financial resources, but also the limited appeal of Labour's own vision and its activists, limited its popularity.[23]

A notable probing of popular–political relations is undertaken in *England Arise!* Labour, it argues, even at the apogee of its success in the 1940s, was out of touch with the mass of voters. Popular attitudes proved resistant to the sorts of moral transformation Labour attempted and envisaged as a precondition of socialism. This leads the authors to question the reading of the popular political mood, notably in 1945, put forward by activists and historians alike, and to wonder why the view that the people's politics may have inhibited Labour's attempt to build socialism has never seriously been countenanced.'[24]

Activists and leaders, as early as 1951, considered the people to have fallen short of the standards required for socialism.[25] This sense became more pronounced in many quarters through the 1950s, as affluence was held to have further corrupted popular priorities. Socialists' distaste for 'affluence' (from its acquisitive ethic to American 'mass' culture), often toppled into contempt towards the newly affluent. In this vision, it seemed by the end of the 1950s that the people themselves, besides much in popular culture, were barriers to socialist progress.

Socialists, then, appeared as something of an elite, moral vanguard. Their disappointment at the condition of the people encouraged the very prescriptive attitudes, moralism and reliance on the state as an improving agent that were in large part at the root of their unpopularity. It is to these attitudes, the ways and lexicon in which socialism described and understood their audience, that socialism's difficulties are traced. What inhibited the left's progress, this study advances, was not so much the people as the ways socialists imagined them.

Those on the left were often also trade unionists, local councillors, Co-operators or active in groups like the Campaign for Nuclear Disarmament (CND), but it is to socialism that this book is attentive. Readers seeking a general account of the fortunes, events and people in the British Labour movement in this period might best be guided elsewhere. As affluence is the context in which socialist culture is placed, foreign and defence policy are also largely absent. CND might seem to suffer by this. Yet since CND spoke an ethical language – the link between morals and politics' was how Judith Hart saw it and urged British moral leadership through unilateralism – it hardly detracts from themes stressed elsewhere. Indeed the Labour left's interest in foreign affairs was attributable in part to its discontent at the course of domestic events. Tony Crosland will also provide company, for *The Future of Socialism*, the pivotal text of the period, is studiously national in scope.[26]

The 1950s were neither a period of progress nor crisis for the left. Labour lost elections under Attlee in 1951 and 1955 and Gaitskell in 1959. Wilson won a narrow victory in 1964, but with a smaller proportion of the vote than in 1951 and 1955 (and of the electorate than in 1959). Labour lost seats in four consecutive general elections during the 1950s such that Bogdanor could point out Labour's 13 years in opposition were the longest period spent in opposition by a major political party since the Reform Bill of 1832' (though Labour would soon surpass this between 1979 and 1997).[27] On the other hand, Labour's vote remained safely above the 40 per cent threshold first carried in 1945. And whilst party membership declined, it was falling from a peak of more than a million in 1952. The CPGB survived 1956 (Khrushchev's twentieth congress speech denouncing Stalin and the Soviet invasion of Hungary) depleted in numbers, but otherwise intact.

Indeed, it is since the resources of socialist culture, whilst challenged by affluence, were stable and well established through the 1950s, that this period can offer representative insights.

The ways affluence challenged many of the unwritten assumptions of the socialist constitution were not then always evident in conventional political registers. The instincts around which party feeling and political ethos formed, were not always or easily classified in conventional political language. More than votes, socialism lost confidence that history pointed towards its vision and, in part, its faith in the people – and in ways that Wilson's victory in 1964 could only partially restore.

Equally, socialist culture retained novel thinkers in its ranks. The revisionists, who figured large in Labour's search for new direction and the New Left that emerged on the Marxist left after 1956, vibrantly contested the tone and vocabulary of more traditional voices. The left's relationship to affluence was not predetermined – it unfolded between contested readings of social change. This was not a culture on the verge of extinction, but in a state of unease and flux.

Affluence animated the traditional ethical elements of socialism, but also created pressure to update. Modernization of party organization, policy and presentation, where it seemed to involve a complicity with affluence, thus met stern resistance (even where proposed in quite traditional terms). The picture of socialist culture that emerges in the period after 1951 was of a complacent, conservative, almost old-fashioned world. The Wilson Report of 1955 depicted a mass party, yet one that was also decrepit, amateurish, disorganized, and with an often dormant internal life. In the CPGB, 1956 demonstrated, above all, the remarkable durability of its party culture.

The tension between traditional socialist aspirations, modernization and a more populist approach dominated Gaitskell's leadership (1955–63) and culminated around the 1959 election. Wilson represented continuity, and electoral victory in 1964 only deferred resolution of this tension in Labour's project.

The book has three broad sections, each of two chapters. The opening section surveys the make-up and resources of socialist culture. Chapter 2 assesses socialist identity through internal party life, traditions and the values and lifestyles current on the 1950s left. Chapter 3 looks at branch life, appraising the condition of local organization and characteristic activities of local parties.

How the left understood and described social change associated with affluence is then addressed. Its attitudes are in themselves a commentary on its culture. Chapter 4 plots the left's encounters with youth, leisure, culture and 'Americanization'; Chapter 5 addresses television, advertising, suburbia and consumerism. Chapters 4 and 5 trace the ethical instincts provoked by affluence with which socialists interpreted modernity and how political culture fed into party image.

Finally, the left's political reactions to affluence are surveyed. Chapter 6 considers the efforts of the New Left and Labour revisionists, notably Crosland, to understand social change in modern Britain. The political meanings of affluence and debates around the 'affluent worker' and the 1959 election are appraised. Chapter 7 looks at how television, advertising and opinion-surveying impacted upon the nature and performance of politics and established socialist methods. In exploring the roles played by figures like John Harris, Mark Abrams and Anthony Wedgwood Benn, it also takes the story to 1964 and estimates the impact of Harold Wilson.

2
Identities

Socialist culture in the 1950s witnessed a revival of a moral emphasis and ethical language. This was encouraged by perceptions of its absence from the Attlee governments. As early as 1950 Richard Crossman wrote in *Socialist Values in a Changing Civilisation*, that the Labour government had finished.sometime in 1948 or 1949.the job which the Fabians had laid down.' Whilst the welfare state and nationalized industries had created the means for the good life', so far as Crossman was concerned, Britain's values were not as yet socialist. The Attlee governments' failing had been to be so Fabian: we were all such good organisers', he judged, but what the ordinary man meant by the socialism of the spirit, the pattern of values, did not occur.' It was on this, he ventured, Labour now needed to focus.[1]

From revisionist, New Left and Communist quarters, this was a clarion call through the 1950s. Philosopher and writer Iris Murdoch made the point as clearly as any in Norman Mackenzie's 1958 collection, *Conviction*. The welfare state', she argued, was the successful end of the first road along which the socialist movement in this country elected to travel.' It was now time to explore the other road, to go back to the point of divergence, the point not so very far back at which we retained as a living morality ideas which were common to Marx and to William Morris.'[2]

A second element in this shift, then, was a renewal of traditional ethical values from the forgotten sidelines of socialism. Look at our last two programmes and see how much is about this', Crossman suggested, very little at all'[3] – suppressed by the exigencies of war and disreputable by association with Ramsay MacDonald. In its mind's eye socialism always involved a moral transformation, a better society, a fellowship as much as simply a materially safer and wealthier society.

These values, ways of life and cultural preferences were evident in the ways socialists themselves lived. But this was not a simple excavation – divisions between socialism's respectable-puritan and more liberal strains were reopened. Affluence itself promoted a stress on questions of culture and values. Since material issues were now receding, parts of the left felt that socialism's focus (both theoretically and electorally) should now be on the quality of life as much as the standard of living. In so doing, Labour revisionists and the New Left, perceived themselves to be restoring emphases in socialist thinking that had been neglected. From this perspective, the key revisionist document on Labour's bookshelf in the 1950s was less *Industry and Society* than its cultural statement, *Leisure for Living*.[4]

What also animated socialism's inanimate ethical instincts were the contrary values it saw promoted in the affluent society'. In its acquisitiveness, cultural choices and lifestyles, affluence chafed with socialism. Socialists were hostile to hire-purchase, consumerism, commercial TV, advertising and American mass culture, since their values were far from those on which they anticipated socialism might be built. Politically, but also morally, socialism was ill-disposed towards affluence.

Equally, socialists were apt to take a dim view of those who indulged in activities constituting affluence. They were disappointed at the response of the people to the legislative lead given by the Attlee governments. Most in Labour hoped the citizenry would yield morally and spiritually towards socialism in everyday life' (as Crossman put it). Without this popular effort and involvement, Morrison argued in 1949, ideals and purposes which were enshrined in legislation' would be nothing more than another bit of bureaucratic routine.' Yet the prospects held out by the war did not materialize. Morrison, as Fielding has put it, then blamed the electorate for not living up to Labour's expectations.' Orwell shared this analysis. In the popular regard the Labour Party is the party that stands for shorter working hours, a free health service . free milk for school children' he noted in 1948, rather than the party that stands for socialism.' He hoped Labour might elicit a more socialist popular response, but should aim to do so, as Morrison argued, through a *Peaceful Revolution*. His fear was that the limits of popular support for Labour might tempt the party to impose socialism summarily, via the state.[5] Moralism was also, then, a response to the perceived failings of the people – as was the tendency to bureaucratism Orwell feared. And socialist suspicions of the people were only exacerbated by the affluent society'.

Piety and print

For the committed, socialism was more than a political belief, it was an all-encompassing way of living and thinking. The valediction commonly read at socialist funerals expressed this ideal of the meaning of a socialist life. Those assembled in July 1960 to mourn Communist (CPGB) leader Harry Pollitt heard that:

> Man .must live so as not to be seared with the shame of a cowardly and trivial past; so live as to have no torturing regrets for years without purpose; so live that dying he can say – all my life and all my strength were given to the finest cause in the world, the liberation of mankind.[6]

Although they were attributed to Lenin, Labour shared these sentiments. Francis Williams' epic *Fifty Years March: The Rise of the Labour Party* concluded in 1949 with the thought that ho service is too great for such a cause, for it is the cause of all mankind.'[7]

Socialism's belief structure had a strong affinity to religion – with a vision of the future that educed a moral code for everyday life and drew a firm sense of service from its followers. Roy Hattersley recalled socialism aimed not to reach the kingdom of heaven, but to build it on earth. In the title of Crossman's collection of recantations published in 1950, communism was *The God That Failed*. Palme Dutt's 'Notes of the Month' in *Labour Monthly* were received by CPGB activists as 'holy writ'.[8]

If the Anglican church was the Tory Party at Prayer', socialism was closer to non-conformity. In Edward Upward's novel of Communist party life in the late 1940s, *The Rotten Elements*, Alan Sebrill (its protagonist) saw party members as a Christian congregation from non-conformism's earlier, less respectable and more fervent days.' Frank Horrabin reminded Labour of its religious roots in 1958, arguing Methodism had provided apprenticeship for working men as speakers, organisers and leaders.' A 1962 survey in *New Society* found more than half of Labour MPs had a Methodist or Presbyterian background. There was a larger proportion with an Anglican background than in earlier surveys, but only a small number of Catholics. Almost two-thirds of respondents reported themselves active religiously.[9]

Labour's General Secretary Morgan Phillips was fond of stressing how the party's history owed more to Methodism than Marxism. Besides being an asset during the Cold War, this accounted for the puritan and ethical elements in socialism and these were a provenance of much of the unease socialists felt towards the affluent society'. A Lowestoft Labour member, invoking the Christian inspiration' of socialism to develop all that makes for gracious living', wondered: in our struggle to abolish the abject and debasing poverty of our people, have we forgotten that material things are not an end in themselves?' This was a vocabulary that socialists often issued against consumerism in the 1950s.[10]

The 1950s left did not approach the fervour of late Victorian Britain. By 1959 only 30 Socialist Schools remained.[11] None the less a proselytizing zeal was more prominent than for several decades. John Heardley-Walker, Labour agent in Merton and Morden, described how activists aimed to spread the gospel.' The express purpose of Socialist Union, founded in 1951, was to revive Labour's early ideals'. Socialism retained spiritual appeal. Sue Townsend has recalled the inspiration of Nye Bevan's oratory (itself derived from the non-conformist chapel). The passion for socialism that Nye projected suited my own longing for drama and for absolutes', she explained, Mr. Bevan filled the void left by God.'[12]

More often, the divine role in the socialist imagination was occupied by the idea that the destiny of history was socialism. Driven by economic and social forces – to Marxists the forces and relations of production; to Fabians the advance of Labour and collectivism – history pointed towards socialism. This notion was, according to Samuel, the basis of the socialist idea' until the early 1970s.[13] Socialists perceived themselves to be marching with history'. Even in defeat in 1951, Morgan Phillips was confident that the final victory of democratic socialism is assured.' Bevan told delegates at Labour's 1959 conference that history' was flowing in our direction .we represent the future.'　[14]

Yet the idea of history making a socialist future certain was harder to maintain by the late 1950s than it had been in the 1930s. There was a Fabian ethos to state planning and welfare, but the forces that socialists imagined determined the course of politics, no longer seemed to presage socialism. 'A significant change in the economic and social background of politics' had checked Labour's forward march, Gaitskell explained in 1959. The changing character of labour, full employment, the new way of living based on the telly, the frig', the car and glossy magazines', accounted for this. Labour had assumed that while there would be ups and downs in the long struggle for power, nevertheless over the years our advance would be inexorable', but, he concluded, this was no longer happening today.'　[15]

Socialist Commentary editor Rita Hinden noted in 1960 that the tide of history, which socialists were convinced was working in their favour, now seems to be turned against them.' In another sense, this faith remained evident in revisionism's attempt to re-synchronize socialism and history. Crosland accepted the social and economic changes of the 1950s and set out to consider how the Labour Party might put itself into a better *rapport* with them.'[16]

Communism believed, as Betty Matthews told the CPGB London district in 1959, that history' was on the side of the workers and socialism.' Mervyn Jones felt that whilst the CPGB might be wrong in particular decisions .the communist movement as a historic force must be fundamentally right and the errors would in time be corrected.' This offered recourse from an embattled status. After the party's annihilation in the 1950 election, Pollitt asserted – events are going to prove us right in the eyes of millions of workers.'[17]

'History' then was the key to socialist politics. Socialists looked back in anger. With slogans like Look Back .Think Forward' (1959) Labour indicted Conservatism by invoking memories of the 1930s. That decade was a leitmotiv in socialist thought. Novels penned by CPGB members penned imagined dickensian squalor' and 1930s unemployment to be true of Britain 1954.' Retrospection was a quality the New Left shared with the old. The first exhibition mounted at its Carlisle Street headquarters was a heaped conspectus of cuttings and souvenirs from the thirties.'[18]

The sense of the past within Labour, Drucker notes, was so central to its ethos that it play[ed] a crucial role in defining what the party [was] about to those in it.' The ghosts of the past were an everyday presence. A 1955 account by the *Manchester Guardian*'s labour correspondent argued Labour was haunted still by Mr. Ramsay MacDonald' and took its myths more seriously than the Tories.' [19] This was never more evident than during Gaitskell's attempts to annul Clause IV – enshrining Labour's belief in public ownership. He underestimated its power as the dominant idea within Labour's socialist myth'. Wiser to Labour culture, Harold Wilson knew revoking Clause IV was like telling the Labour party member that his political bible has been torn up' – sacrilegious', as a delegate at the 1959 conference put it.[20]

By temperament, the CPGB was a more strictly religious body, where Labour (in Wilson's phrase) was a broad church'. Procedure in the CPGB often took a religious method. Debate was frequently a form of exegesis, in which contemporary issues were serviced by instances from the past or reference to chapter and verse in authoritative (Soviet) texts. In 1957 Andrew Rothstein invoked the history of Bolshevism between 1907 and 1911 to condemn the spineless intellectuals' he found revolting in 1956. This belief structure was important in a party whose members, Harry McShane has recalled, kept shrines, Little Lenin corners' in their homes.[21]

This was what the 'Reasoners' – the rebels of 1956 – damned. That politics was more a test of memory than mind .encouraged attitudes of religious faith.' The party leadership acted as a fount of doctrinal purity' – more analogous with the holy church' than the critical temper, the constant return to reality of Marx and Engels.'[22]

Damning evidence of the Soviet system in Khrushchev's address to the twentieth congress of the Soviet Communist Party and the Soviet invasion of Hungary later in 1956, induced a crisis of faith in history. *Daily Worker* cartoonist Gabriel reported that Khrushchev's speech had left him in a rather schizophrenic state.' [23]

It was not only affluence that led to a diminution of Communist faith in 1950s Britain, but the revelations of 1956. The New Left that emerged from 1956, notably among junior members, was shorn of older faiths. For Stuart Hall, it marked, the end .of the belief that socialism would come about as a result of the inexorable laws of history.' On the other hand, faith was a resource for negotiating such traumas. Most communists, after all, did not leave the party. Dennis Pritt, a prominent communist barrister, wrote of 1956: I could not see why such shocks should so break one's belief.' Mervyn Jones's novel *Today the Struggle*, depicting left-wing life in the 1950s, characterized the mentality of long-standing Communist Alf: whatever the disappointments, the delays and detours of history, Alf never lost hope.'[24]

Socialists were instilled with great certainty by the idea that history was a comrade. One communist described how it meant you can always answer an argument of someone with, because you knew where you were going.' However, as another remarked in 1952, non-Party members felt us to be arrogant in our attitude'. [25] Labour socialists too, in this case Mary Saran, could feel that they had all the answers or, in our philosophical outlook, had the basis for discovering them.'

Such confidence diminished in the 1950s. As Saran continued: many problems became .more complex after the Second World War than they had .appeared to us, in the thirties.' In 1956 Llew Gardner confessed we do not have all the answers to all the questions' and urged communists to have a little more humility.' But old habits died hard. Ex-communists in the New Left were identifiable, Mervyn Jones noted, by a sharpness and intensity in argument, a seriousness about ideas .that differed from the tone of the dominant liberal.' [26]

Socialists were a rather intellectual species. Activists were well read, schooled in union rules and the art of argument'. Their skills made 1950s industrial activists a shopfloor intelligentsia.' Political life was filled with reading, debate and argument. Jennie Lee urged Foot, visiting Bevan in hospital in 1960, to have a good rough argument; make him feel that everything's normal.' They had only a mild altercation, but Foot took the patient some books – Mencken's *Treatise on the Gods* and J. B. Priestley's *Literature and Western Man*. A 1962 survey in *New Society* of Labour MPs' reading habits, replicating W. T. Stead's 1906 survey, found George Bernard Shaw, H. G. Wells, G. D. H. Cole and Marx to be the four most influential authors. In 1906 Marx had trailed the Bible and Ruskin, but was now ahead of them. Amongst contemporary writers, Crosland, Galbraith and Strachey lead the field. Few works of literature were mentioned and some MPs confessed their reading was confined to 'Alas only blue books and pamphlets!' [27]

For left activists in the 1950s, *Tribune* was more than a journal, it was almost a way of life.' When its price was cut to 4d. in August 1952, it declared Down Goes the Cost of Living!' Otherwise the left press was a cause for concern. Laurence Thompson wondered in 1952 whether this was due to the journalists or the readers?' Do we become, when we write in our own papers, so narrow and sectarian that we cannot hold the reader's interest?' But in a familiar 1950s refrain, he decided the readers were to blame: when I come to the readers I am speechless .eleven million people vote Labour .What did you say your circulation was again?' A survey of *Daily Worker* readers, desiring a brighter" .family"newspaper .comic"strips, sports features', suggested much of the left's constituency had rather different reading interests. Activists knew Cayton's importance as the *Worker's* tipster. A 1954 Midlands report lamented that Cayton's continued run of bad luck' was a powerful influence in factory sales.' [28]

Socialists were voracious readers even if their supporters were not. The CPGB, besides publishers Lawrence and Wishart, had a sales arm, Central Books (of 40 shops during the war) and ran factory sales. Elsewhere, progressive' bookshops – like Platt's in Morecambe – catered for socialist reading habits.[29] These tended towards non-fiction. What one historian terms Labour's Literary Dominance' over the Conservatives was in memoirs and diaries, though political novels by Lessing, Jones, Upward, Fienburgh and Maurice Edelman are valuable sources. Labour's Douglas Hawkins was an inveterate reader', but confessed he had not read a novel in 60 years. Mervyn Jones said of the New Left's historians, sociologists and theorists: 1 don't think they read my novels . .1 don't think they've got time for that sort of thing.'[30]

In the CPGB this was because, Gorman noted, communists did not read literature – they studied it.' The party introduced many to the habit of reading', but discouraged pleasure reading in favour of the Party's many publications. Once outside the CPGB many Communists read more widely – retaining a belief in the importance of books, but breaking from the Party's confined tastes.[31]

Socialists' intellectualism was balanced by an impatience and distrust of the intelligentsia' (as Heffer regarded the New Left). Activists, Heardley-Walker noted, were not mere talkers or armchair"politicians.' Communists were anxious meetings should not be talking shops' and should lead to, not substitute for, political activity.[32]

Anti-intellectualism had class dimensions. Intellectuals were vocal CPGB dissenters in 1956 – in the *New Statesman* and *The Reasoner*, the journal published by historians Thompson and Saville. The CPGB leadership portrayed these revisionists' as wobbly intellectuals', explaining, the introduction of petty-bourgeois ideas and practices into our party' would inevitably appear among those not closely linked with the working class struggle.' In short, the social origins of the rebels damned their criticisms. Intellectual was a euphemism for middle class.[33]

Labour was aware of this class aspect. Reporting on a learned disquisition' that Bevan delivered at a party meeting in Coventry in 1953, Crossman (MP for East Coventry) noted that during, many passages ... no one in the audience could understand what he was about.' If I talked in that way,' Crossman (an Oxford don) reflected on Bevan (a Welsh proletarian), 1 should be considered an intellectual, but somehow Nye gets away with it.'[34]

Political and party-mindedness

Socialists were nothing if not party-minded. Communists rejected the suggestion that Marxism was akin to a faith and the party was our church, but,' Jones admitted, it did have the same psychological power.' John Gollan told the CPGB's 1957 congress there was no such thing as Marxism without the Communist Party'. It was inimical to be a socialist on one's own, outside organization. Though its disciplines often chafed, party was seen as essential to political change and in giving form to discontent. 'You can do nothing with the Labour Party and nothing without the Labour Party' was Jennie Lee's maxim. As a communist in the early 1950s Jones felt: the party was achieving very little, but without the party it seemed impossible to achieve anything at all .it didn't appear that there was anywhere else to go.' [35]

This sense of a wilderness beyond party was common. Hobsbawm explained it as the old belief that, as Catholics used to say, 'outside the church there is no salvation', you have to be in the Communist Party or else there's nothing.' That many who harboured doubts in 1956, like Hobsbawm, chose to stay in the party indicated they 'no longer believed it in quite the same old way.' In Lessing's *The Golden Notebook*, a semi-autobiographical account of 1950s CPGB life, it was suggested that leaving the party would 'lead you straight into some morass of moral turpitude.' Labour too regarded those outside of the Party as 'lost', part of the barriers confronting socialism. One delegate told the 1959 Labour conference that 'women .are by and large, except those in the Labour Party, politically illiterate.' In the odd socialist this manifested itself in the idea, as a Trotskyist comrade said of Bob Shaw, that food, drink, sex, the 'night out', the ordinary pleasures of ordinary life are .distractions.' It was added that this 'holier-than-thou' attitude repels people.' [36]

Socialists of other denominations, as much as the non-political absorbed in the worldly pleasures of 1950s affluence, were represented as outposts in the wilderness. Morgan Phillips kept a file on Communists, Bevanite CLPs and others he deemed to have strayed politically, entitled 'Lost Sheep'. Socialism's true path had always been contested and the Cold War sharpened such claims. Communists denounced Labour as a party that 'preaches .class collaboration' and 'accepts capitalism'; Labour countered that communism was 'socialism perverted into capitalism writ large.' [37]

For the committed, there was little life outside of party. Dora Gaitskell (referring to barrister Frank Soskice and Crossman's work for the *Daily Mirror*) felt 'any sincere socialist should devote himself 100 per cent to the work of the party and should not combine it with other occupations.' 'Every waking moment and all my love of doing', George Hodgkinson, Labour leader in Coventry in the 1950s told, was 'given to the Labour Party and the movement.' Harry McShane, a Glaswegian Trade Unionist who left the CPGB in the early 1950s, described socialism in redemptive terms. 'The movement owes me nothing', he testified, 'on the contrary, I owe it much – life would have been empty without it.' This evoked the commitment Tressell depicted in Owen in his Edwardian novel, *The Ragged Trousered Philanthropists*, for whom socialism was .what drink was to some of the others – the thing that enabled them to forget and tolerate the conditions under which they were forced to exist.'[38] Commitment was a keyword. A description of a local Labour Party in 1954 noted the type of member of which most parties had a smattering – who spent all his waking hours .in political work of some kind.' [39] There was a heroic hint to this – the idea of entering a socialist valhalla', as one of Labour's regional organizers put it to Morgan Phillips. To reckon by Labour autobiographies, a socialist life might be *Uphill all the Way*, but they would *Never Give Up* and were *Fighting all the Way*. Communists typically chose titles such as *To Struggle is to Live* or *Born to Struggle*.[40]

For Richard Hoggart, socialists were a species who want to do something about things'. This marked them out, since this attribute was harder to find in the fifties.' CPGB vocabulary was replete with notions of obligations to the British people.' [41] This impulse was not entirely altruistic. In Bermondsey, Labour members were urged to join local organisations to improve Labour's image' and be seen as part of the community itself and not as a purely political party.' A 1955 CPGB country branches conference stressed the importance of work in the British Legion, Women's Institute and cricket clubs. Ross McKibbin famously observed that the *same kind* of people who founded pigeon-breeding societies also founded the Labour Party.' In some cases the *same* people – Labour's Douglas Hawkins was South Wales Pigeon Club secretary from 1962. The point was that this was not a strictly political impulse, but one that found realization in socialism. For Lessing, the CPGB was largely composed of people who aren't really political at all, but who have a powerful sense of service.'[42]

In other ways activity on the left prevailed against other activities. Trotskyist Harry Ratner held positions in Salford Labour Party, local unions, shop stewards committees, Trades Council and as factory paper editor. On top of this were paper sales, petitioning, visiting contacts. Even when Ratner and his wife managed to visit the cinema or go hiking they felt guilty at taking even this little time out.' [43]

That socialists were invariably in a rush attested to the scale of their aims and the limited numbers sustaining such activity. Time is short' was a recurring phrase of the nuclear age. Transport House, in a 1952 portrait, was frenetically busy, in a frenzy'. For Bob Darke, being active in the CPGB left little time for watching football or trips to the cinema. In any case, after a time he found he had lost a taste for them.' [44]

Socialists had what Mervyn Jones describes as the political temperament' for whom a political disaster was as painful to them as the loss
of a friendship or the break-up of a love affair [was] to the average individual.' This was evinced in British Communism by the trauma of
leaving the party. Gorman was in mental anguish .to resign would
be to walk into the wilderness.' The party,' he told, had been my life,
consuming me with a passion that shaped my work, reading, moral
attitudes and political action.' Darke, Les Cannon and Douglas Hyde
told the same story.[45]

Those who left the CPGB attracted media interest during the Cold
War. Labour politics in rural Tory strongholds and the professions were
tantamount to social isolation', but communists were perceived as
aliens' and suffered a pariah status'. Defectors were greeted (even by
historical accounts like Pelling's) as if they had returned from a foreign
adventure. McShane, who left to join Eric Heffer in the Socialist
Workers' Federation, rejected £500 from the *Daily Express*, but sold his
story to *Reynolds News*. Darke vented his rancour in the *News Chronicle*
and *Sunday Express*; Hyde in the *Daily Express* and *Catholic Herald*.[46]

To the party these were acts of defection. Flirtation with the non-
party press was punished as much as criticism of the party. Peter
Cadogan's letter to the *News Chronicle* criticizing the party's backing for
the Hungary invasion resulted in him being dubbed a traitor'. Cannon
rejected advances from ITV and newspapers for his recusant's tale, but
found the attitude of communists to ex-communists was that of some
harsh religious sect to an apostate.' Those outside the party were
addressed accordingly. In leadership documents dealing with *The
Reasoner*, those suspending the party membership of its editors used
the prefix Comrade' – those expelling them dropped this. The CPGB
was a tight-knit community, loyal to its own, but wary of others. A
Mass Observer visiting its Hendon HQ in 1950 reported a friendly
atmosphere between communists, but that they were considered an
intruder' and asked as much about M.O. as I asked about the C.P.' [47]

Language also differentiated socialists. One critic found the CPGB's
Marxism largely incomprehensible to outsiders'. Communist journal-
ist William Forest suggested sonorous terms like dialectical materialism' meant nothing' to British workers and propaganda couched in
language like that [was].a waste of time.' When Percy Clark took
charge of Labour publicity he argued its flowery language' was misplaced, unless it was imagined the average voter was thinking:
'Alderman Bloggs must be a very clever man, I don't understand a
word he's written about.' What was desired was the common touch,

like East Ham Labour MP Percy Daines, able to place himself on the audience's intellectual and financial level', with nothing superior 'in his attitude' and who thus went down very well.' [48] The left could be insulated by its own culture. Williams's criticism of Bevan's renowned oratory was that its beliefs [we]re presupposed from the start.' Christopher Hill told the CPGB in 1957 that it suffered from living in a snug little world of our own invention.'[49]

It was not only socialists that were to account for the mismatch with their audience. In the popular reflex of us' and them' Hoggart illustrated in *The Uses of Literacy*, politics and politicians fell into the latter. 'All talk and no do', how't to choose between 'em' or only out for their own ends' were typical popular attitudes. At a Bristol radio programme with 15- to 25-year-olds in 1954, Wedgwood Benn noted their cynicism about politicians', ignorance about Parliament' and dislike of party or intra-party squabbles except as entertainment', if also a healthy disregard of politicians' conceit.' [50]

This also denoted how politics more generically was a discrete part of everyday life. Even at general elections (and the 1950 election when turnout was 84 per cent), Mass Observers turned in reports that typically described how, for instance, in not one of seven Edgware café visited a week before polling, was the election being discussed.[51] When Attlee spoke at Sittingbourne Football Ground on polling day in 1955 (in Britain's most marginal constituency to boot), the local paper reported that his audience would have been low for a football match. For socialists, who as Dorothy Thompson describes, felt that when involved you think it really is the most important human activity', it was hard to realise that most people don't see it in that way.' She felt shock' at University when people .lumped me together with the Conservative secretary, because we were both interested in politics.' Thompson felt we were at the absolute opposite ends of world experience', but to the rest of the students, the politicos, Left and Right, were much of a muchness.'[52]

Activists of all parties might inhabit a similarly political world, but faith in socialism' a 1955 survey of Labour considered, was more fervent than the average Conservative Party member's faith in Conservatism.' Gyford's account of *Local Politics in Britain* also found Labour to be more single-minded in its devotion to politics.' [53] As such the 1950s were hard times for socialists. The decade witnessed, so one committed history tells, a decline in politics 'as a way of seeing the world.' Conservatism prospered in the 1950s, according to Sassoon, from a nonchalance towards ideology' that spared it the existential *angst'* socialists suffered. Crossman argued to Labour's NEC that in 1955 the Tories deliberately gave the impression that there were no great issues at stake' and that this proved shrewd election tactics'. 'A longish period of political apathy', felt Young Fabian Bill Rodgers, meant there would be no premium on belonging to the left.' [54]

Family ties

The insularity of socialism co-existed with a firm sense of togetherness. As much as a body of shared beliefs, it was to values like fellowship that socialists were loyal. Referring to the precept love thy brother', a Mass Observer noted in 1950, the active socialist worker is conscious of the Christian principle and strives to follow it.' Socialism imparted a sense of family to its adherents. Labour promised members fellowship .a spirit of good neighbourliness.' [55]

Political networks doubled as social networks. It is satisfying when you are right and your friend agrees' was how a Young Communist Leaguer (YCL) described the political basis of her friendships. For others, party was an extended family' – tied not by blood but belonging. Lessing noted how Communism attracted a contingent who are lonely and the party is their family.' Writer Jack Lindsay felt the most important relationship in his life' was with the CPGB. George Hodgkinson, dedicated his autobiography to My wife and Nye'. To judge by the final volume of Upward's trilogy of novels about the postwar left, there was *No Home but the Struggle.*[56]

As in other family units, socialism provided a home, but could confine. This was particularly true of the CPGB, whose politics were rebellious in content, but disciplined in form. Llew Gardner, who left it in 1956, explained, the rebellious nature which had brought us into the party also made us figures of suspicion.'[57]

It was the friendliness and trust that party members felt for one another' that *The Rotten Elements'* Alan Sebrill, feared he would miss should he leave the party. This was also useful when you came to a new town', as Mary Waters did post-war, as a way of getting to know people .my friends would nearly all be communists.' [58]

Through lifestyle and like-mindedness, socialists often lived together or married. Mervyn Jones could not imagine living with someone who wasn't a comrade.' Families were often at the core of local Labour organization – like the Woolets in North Ealing. There was concern in the 1950s that these could become private fiefdoms. Family ties in Southwark, it was found, froze-out newcomers'. [59]

Socialism was, in part, hereditary. Gould's 1954 survey of Riverside' Labour Party found a high proportion' of members whose parents were (or are) also members of the Labour Party.' To grow up in a 1950s communist household was to be, in the title of a recent collection, *The Children of the Revolution.* Activists' children were regarded as likely members' for the YCL or Labour League of Youth. As the Cold War froze other sources of membership, the CPGB turned in on itself. The CPGB organized holiday lectures, even events for those of a pre-YCL age', and parents were urged to promote friendships between children of progressive parents .and pen-friendships with children in socialist countries.'[60]

The family was a political stable where socialists were reared. A household which took the *Daily Herald* or *Worker,* where canvassing, demos and union meetings were everyday norms, and the book-shelves stocked with H. G. Wells, orange Left Book Club spines or exotic Marxist philosophy titles, could be as formative an influence as any. Versed in socialism by its rich culture in 1950s Tredegar and his mother, an early biographer of Neil Kinnock ventured the future Labour leader did not acquire his socialism – he was born into it.' Families aided the reproduction of left culture – CPGB traditions were handed down .like a family jewel'. As a 1958 survey of Labour in Manchester concluded, it was as difficult to disavow inherited politics as .inherited religion.' [61]

Socialism's family ties account for its reverence for the past. Self-proclaimed revisionists such as Crosland laid claim to the mantle of founding fathers' like Hardie or Tawney – anxious to portray their project in terms faithful to the party's ancestry.[62] The ferocity of 1956 in the CPGB owed much to its family-like qualities. Samuel has noted how schisms in British Communism were wont as in a family break-up .[to be] envenomed by old sores.' 1956 released many of the pent-up tensions suppressed in the skirmishes of 1947–8, the question of Soviet influence during the third period' (1928–33) and of opposition to war in 1939. Leaving the party, and not only in 1956, was tantamount to divorce – for Gorman, like the breaking of a solemn vow'. [63]

Clause IV provoked similar emotions in Labour. Stockport activist Jim Tucker explained, I was brought up on Clause Four.' Without approving, Crosland was aware of the traditionalism in Labour culture, the symbolic quality of Clause IV for the party faithful, and he reproached Gaitskellite efforts to annul it. This came not from a belief in public ownership, but from a comprehension that the party stal-wart, deprived of what had informed and symbolised his early years of struggle', would feel he was being asked to say that his whole political life, to which he sacrificed so much, was pointless.' Psychologically, Crosland argued, this feeling [was] wrong but natural.' To annul it was to discard the family heritage.[64]

The left itself fostered family values'. Long-lasting companionate marriages among CPGB leaders – the Pollitts and Gallachers – were showcased. Watch was kept on relationships felt to be in trouble or impeding political activity. In some cases Partners might even be referred by their district secretary to a party psychologist.[65] Goss described the social values of the Bermondsey Labour Party in 1961 as, traditionalist, patriarchal and a firm supporter of the family and moral values.'' In 1959 a ward of Grimsby Labour Party cautioned against the affluent society', that more television sets, more cars, more refrigerators do not bring happiness on their own' and that a good family life is essential for happiness and welfare.'[66]

According to Douglas Hawkins it was known amongst Labour activists that too much time spent canvassing could result in domestic disruption'. One disgruntled party wife' wrote to the *Daily Worker* in 1947 complaining she was left laying the oilcloth while he''is out shouting down with serfdom.'' Asking do reds make good husbands?', MacEwen admitted his political work placed a considerable domestic burden on his wife. However as a CPGB member, she agreed that work for the .party was important and .bore no resentment.' Though shared politics were no guarantee of domestic harmony – 1956 rent Marguerite Morgan's family asunder, with her young sons caught up in political arguments with her husband.[67]

Such strains were greater where a partner was not a party sympathizer. Darke tendered a hysterical account of the financial and psychological persecution his wife suffered. She complained: 'All you think of is the party, nothing else counts with you, Bob, not your family, not your home, not me.' It was suggested to Darke that if his wife would not join the Communist Party, he should leave her. Appearing as a surrogate family' was a problem to which the CPGB was sensitive. In July 1955 the West Middlesex party held a garden party for the kin of the 25 hardest working' comrades, those whose wives and families see little of them due to party work'.[68]

Socialism left its imprint on hearth and home in other ways. Homes were often campaign bases, quarters for meetings or citizens' advice bureaux. Liverpool Labour councillor Eddie Owen's house was renowned as the place to go for advice on council and housing problems, having, it was said, a door open all day'. [69]

Another feature of socialist homes, it seems, was their dishevelled state. Labour houses in West London in the 1950s seemed élegantly untidy' to Elizabeth Wilson – suggestive of a slightly bohemian intellectual life.' Tawney's home was total chaos' (and he notoriously shabby in dress'); the Thompsons' was a shambles, house and garden were rarely far from complete chaos.' In Wilfred Fienburgh's novel, *No Love for Johnnie*, Labour MP Johnnie Bryne was shocked to return to a tidy flat. Usually it was full of pamphlets, circulars, brochures, invitations .like a sub-district trade union office .paper, papers everywhere and never a thing to read.'[70]

Gardening symbolized socialism's indifference towards domestic matters. It was an activity they saw as trivial or suburban. Bevan's Chelsea home had its garden flagged, the *Daily Mirror* reported, so that he does not need to do any gardening.' *The Rotten Elements'* Alan Sebrill told how party activity left scant time for gardening and he rather liked the flowering weeds' in his. Others attested, in passing, to shambolic gardens. Gardening was a metaphor for political withdrawal into the wilderness. The Reasoners' reluctance to quit the CPGB in 1956, Saville explained, was because we had personal experiences of those who had left the party to cultivate their own gardens.'[71] For socialists, the garden was a wilderness in all senses.

This had political dimensions. During the 1959 election, Lady Lewisham suggested Labour homes could be identified by unwashed milk bottles; one Tory candidate that they had bedraggled gardens' where the roses needed pruning.' [72] Domestic disarray attested to a set of priorities that transcended everyday issues and subordinated the private to the public, political sphere. The domestic was regarded as a distraction – its own values placed personal and household matters secondary to qualities like fellowship and community. After all, the essence of socialist's indictment of the affluent society' was its privileging of individual acquisitiveness over public spending – the condition, in Galbraithian terms, of private affluence and public squalor'. Socialists were uneasy with the values of private living and acquisitiveness. They subscribed to a more altruistic notion of public service, giving their self to a higher cause. To sacrifice one's personal interests .is the highest manifestation of Communist ethics', a 1955 CPGB title explained.[73]

This was important in the 1950s, because such impulses informed socialists' objections to consumerism, centred as this was on domestic goods – TVs and washing-machines. Gaitskell equated private acquisitiveness, a declining sense of community and Labour's electoral problems. He and Bevan dismissed new domestic goods as 'gadgets'. The 1950s, Thompson ventured in *Universities and Left Review*, were characterized by 'the slavery of the human soul to material trivia.' One *Daily Herald* correspondent complained – 'my kitchen is full of things I don't want and never use.' As Galbraith put it: 'to furnish a barren room is one thing ...to continue to crowd in furniture until the foundation buckles is quite another.'[74]

Tied in here were socialism's affinities for the idea of the 'simple life' – that 'what was wrong with society was that there was too much luxury, too many goods, too much busy-ness'. It was a basic socialist tenet to master not be enslaved by material things. The 'simple life' retained appeal as life became more entangled in consumer capitalism. Socialists were enthusiasts for hiking and 'open-air' leisure. The popular 1950s Norfolk Forest School Camps, 'living with basic amenities' in a 'democratic community' were organized by Ronald Brand, a CPGB simple-lifer.[75]

Acquiring domestic comforts was thought 'petty-bourgeois', less because an ascetic lifestyle was more virtuous than because socialists were concerned with 'higher' matters and rejected ideas of material salvation. It was not only poverty that contrived the austere air of socialist domesticity. In Joe Kahn's home, 'money was never discussed but always political, social and musical ideas.' Gorman tells 'in many party homes, books took priority over new furniture.' MacEwen could 'well afford' to carpet his flat, but its floors remained bare. Dora Gaitskell told Benn in 1958 that 'a simplicity of living was an essential element of the leadership of the Labour Party.'[76]

Lifestyle was a sensitive issue in socialist culture. Suspicions of revisionists like Crosland, Jenkins and Douglas Jay centred as much on their urbanity (they were known as the 'Hampstead set') as their politics (the 'left', typically anti-American, dubbed them 'Jaywalkers'). Nor could family ties offset these suspicions – Jenkins' father had been a miner and Labour MP. Wilson, by contrast, profited from (and cultivated) the image of the 'common little man' many Gaitskellites thought him.[77]

These domestic characteristics were evident elsewhere – in ramshackle local premises or the New Left's atmosphere of 'creative chaos'. Collet's, the left's fusty central London bookshop, had 'well-thumbed and dog-eared' stock. It was not only by dint of its anarchist past that it was known as 'the bomb shop.' [78]

Sartorially, Labour could appear dishevelled. Bevan often wore a smart blue tie, but 'clumsily knotted, a real mess'. On his farm he 'would sooner buy a new cow than a new suit.' The well-dressed were not imagined to be Labour supporters. Hattersley's history teacher at Sheffield Grammar wore 'expensive suits and shiny shoes' which, his student recalled, 'made it hard to believe that he supported .Labour.' Vic Feather, TUC assistant general secretary in this period, complained that middle-class Labour members often adopted a 'proletarian look' of 'duffle coat and spats' and drove 'unwashed' cars, but were reluctant to mix with trade unionists.[79]

Feather demonstrated an instinctive sensitivity towards the middle class. An apocryphal (but indicative) story had it that Kenneth Younger, the Oxford-educated Labour MP for Grimsby to 1959, would drive from London to Louth, change clothes and board a train for the constituency. Socialists who contrived scruffiness, were as easily spotted as those who made no effort to disguise non-plebian credentials.[80]

There were ragged-trousered Communists – like Claud Cockburn – but most attired smartly.[81] *Punch* reported from the *Daily Worker*'s 23rd Birthday Rally that the 'crowd was well-dressed, respectable.' In the fashion of their politics, Communists were urged to be orderly. Darke's bright tie did not suit the sober image the CPGB wished to show Hackney voters – it was a 'bourgeois tie' and his election pictures were re-shot. Likewise, a *Labour Woman* grumbled in 1957 that 'husbands, even socialists, are very conservative and discourage their wives from dressing too glamourously.'[82]

In the most regimented of parties, communists followed a dress code – for women 'sensible shoes".slacks'. The early 1950s saw Gorman don the 'dress worn by earnest young comrades, baggy corduroy trousers and a red tie as wide as a red flag .enhanced by a dark coloured shirt.' On top was a Union official's 'drab, gaberdine, double-breasted raincoat.' This was all 'redolent of a cartoonist's picture of a 1930s subscriber to the Left Book Club.' From mid-decade, the required outer garb for young socialists became a hooded duffel coat.' Its place in the left's wardrobe was spurred by CND marches and the bright young things of the New Left. The CPGB was not, however, a dedicated follower of fashion – 'we stuck to our shabby raincoats and cloth caps', Gorman recalls.[83]

Equally, much of the left remained immune to new trends in dress brought about by affluence and associated with teenagers. They might be 'dressing in a way that distanced themselves from their parents', but the left remained in thrall to its past, 'moulded by the grey and grim thirties, oblivious of the revolution around.' Socialists disavowed concern with attire (which might account for a certain shabbiness), but were aware of the impression it left. The 'cloth cap' symbolized its identity crisis. Issues of appearance were generational. A delegate at the Labour Party Young Socialists 1961 conference, despairing at the apparel of many within the party, argued Labour would 'start attacking the Tories when we stop looking like them.'[84]

Moralism was really the left's favoured outfit. Bevan's repudiation of unilateralism in 1957, warning against sending a foreign secretary 'naked into the conference chamber', provoked a letter to *Tribune* from his Tredegar constituency which pointed out: 'We are naked without H-Bombs, but fully clothed in morality.'[85]

Prefiguring socialism

How socialists lived is of more than use in evoking how their values sat uneasily with those of affluent Britain, because socialists lived by values they held to be not only more worthy, but actually representa-tive of socialism. Socialism believed itself the germ of an alternative society and way of life. A 1952 Labour research paper explained that in their faith' were 'the principles upon which our society should be moulded.' Raymond Williams argued Labour, the unions and co-operatives were the right basis for 'the whole organisation of any good society in the future.' Thompson told *New Reasoner* readers in 1959, that socialism should not be 'merely a movement with a different *objective* from other political movements', but an altogether 'different *kind* of movement, made up of a different kind of *people*.' It had to be 'a movement in which .the objective itself, a society of equals, finds living embodiment; a society of equals as between leaders and rank-and-file .men and women and .British and African comrades.' [86]

It was this that Samuel lauded in the CPGB – the 'relative equality it allowed between young and old, men and women, immigrant and native, workers and intellectuals .in contrast to the elaborate defer-ence and rank of wider British society.' 'To be a communist was to have a complete social identity', he noted, and like the socialist vision, 'one which transcended the limits of class, gender and nationality.' [87]

Socialism's familial aspect was important in this respect. A Communist in Andrews' *Lifetimes of Commitment* described how 'you knew you had friends all over the world .I.went to America, I was in touch immediately with people who felt like I did.' Ultimately, com-munism promised an escape from class. In *The Golden Notebook*, it was 'a need for wholeness, for an end to the split, divided, unsatisfactory way we all live' that led Anna to join the party. Gorman has told how through the party I met professional people for the first time as equals.'[88]

The revolt of 1956 was a recognition that the idea of the CPGB as a unity of leaders and members' was mythical. The CPGB subscribed to a prefigurative ideal – it replicated the structure and vocabulary of the Soviet model. It was whether this was a socialist model that was at issue. Lawrence Daly, a leading Scottish party militant, argued the party was putting loyalty to the Soviet Union above loyalty to socialist principles.' 1956 was also a plea for democracy. Golders Green branch asked the leadership to make clear that .discussion and criticism is welcomed.' Often it seemed, the main thing is to get discussion over as quickly as possible.'[89]

The party's response was a Commission on Inner-Party Democracy. This showed the limits to democracy in the CPGB. The leadership appointed the majority on the Commission. Betty Reid, as secretary, dictated its course. For Bob Potter, who knew her as chief of a secret party security committee, Reid's appointment was a blatant insult to the membership'. He and comrades at Battersea Bus Garage resigned after permission to raise this at an area party meeting was refused.[90]

Knowledge that the CPGB was no microcosm of socialism (or that if it was, it was not an attractive model) was tied up with 1956's revelations about the nature of the Soviet regime. Cannon recorded how his attempts to amend a *Daily Worker* conference motion were met with shouts of shut him up'. Leaving the meeting he was aware that had he been in Hungary, there would have been two AVH men [security police] waiting at the door.' Imagining party leaders as authoritarian officials was a recurring nightmare in 1956. The prefigurative impulse was not easily purged, even when stifled by the CPGB. Behind Hobsbawm's decision to stay in the party was its continuing potential as an organisation and schooling for workers and .intellectuals.'   [91]

In common with the New Left and CPGB, Labour imagined itself a prototype socialist community. As Tam Dalyell, a new recruit to Labour in 1954, put it: Being Labour"does not only involve voting and supporting specific policies – Being Labour"is, to me, a way of thinking, and, one hopes, a way of living too.' According to a 1961 pamphlet, Labour was a party whose deeds [were] as impressive as its words.' *Labour Organiser*'s Quair reported most CLPs had a sprinkling of well-to-do"members who quite properly regard themselves as no whit superior to the fellow-member .who empties their trash-cans every Thursday.'[92]

That socialists should demonstrate their values at all times – that example is still better than precept' as Sheffield Park MP Fred Mulley declared – extended to everyday life. Shopping and holidays were subject to ethical judgements. Heardley-Walker was astonished by the number of socialists who take their holidays in Spain', given Franco's imprisonment of socialists. Whilst Labour campaigned in 1960 against South African goods, he asked, do we boycott Seville oranges or Spanish Sherry?'[93]

This prefigurative sense was as evident on Labour's right' as left'. Crosland called for a sustained offensive .by all socialists in their personal and political activities, and by example as well as precept, against the national vices of materialism, philistinism and social separatism.' Leaders and activists alike held to the notion of personifying socialist qualities. A Hackney North delegate told Labour Women's 1960 conference that rather than adjusting Clause IV, what was needed was for members to behave like democratic socialists .they must show their example .in constituency activities and in every way in which they appeared in public.' In the last analysis,' she contended, people would judge the Labour Party by the individuals they knew who were members of the party.' Attlee was of a similar mind, suggesting you cannot emphasise too much – that socialism demands a higher standard of conduct than capitalism .our movement is judged very largely by what our people are like.'[94]

Like Attlee, socialists believed theirs was a *better* way of life. As Golders Green branch saw it, Communists claim a higher morality than any other philosophy.' *Labour Organiser* urged all active members .leaders or rank-and-file .as workmates and neighbours .in the council chamber and trade union branch, [to] demonstrate that socialism as a way of life is superior to capitalism.'[95]

This could bring out a respectable side. Diligence at work was necessary to gain respect for socialist politics on the shopfloor and avoid the accusations of being trouble-makers or work-shy. Communist students were expected to excel – Saville was excused political activity in his final university year.[96]

Demonstrating socialism's superior values, combined with the impulse to serve, could lead away from strict political activity. A profile of a Labour constituency in 1954 admitted: We are what the Americans would call do-gooders''and in our actual work socialism, which was .our first objective, sometimes gets lost.' Lessing related the comments of a CPGB official's wife: I decided to do something useful for a change .So now I have a class of backward children ...

George says I'd be better occupied making Party members, but I wanted to do something really useful.'[97]
Peggy Crane told *Socialist Commentary* of a Labour member who ceased attending ward meetings through participating on a school care committee. Crane wondered if her friend 'was not a better socialist than many of us who spend two or three evenings a week on party business.' Crane was not suggesting that everyone should become a social worker or join a non-political voluntary organisation', but that 'if socialism is also a way of life and not merely or pre-eminently the programme of a political party, then its attainment depends as much on the individual's contribution as on Acts of Parliament and the efficiency of the political machine.' Mulley agreed. TV had curtailed the opportunity for the individual to make a positive contribution in the political field', he believed. Yet in the social field – running community centres in housing estates .old peoples' associations' – voluntary service by socialists' could bring the satisfaction of achievement' and pay handsome electoral dividends.' [98]

Moralism

Crossman argued the left – contrary to insisting that socialism was inevitable or economically superior – could at best prove .socialism is *more moral* than capitalism.' In arguing you *ought* to have socialism because it is morally better', they would have to rely on ethical principles' and the morality of our fellow citizens.' [99]
Labour's vision of socialism required not only popular support, but active participation. Labour's task' was to create the good society', but it was emphasized that the people have their responsibilities' – Labour's success depends upon their efforts .loyalty and willingness to make sacrifices in the common cause.' Socialism meant more than a vote, a job and freedom from want.' It required a quality of character consistent with socialist values and meant a society in which every citizen is seeking to play his full part .in which all give and serve as well as receive.' Progress towards socialism was contingent upon the moral condition of the people.[100]
Yet socialists felt exasperated with the people – that the popular mood had not lived up to its wartime promise or the Attlee administration. Through the 1950s they were critical of much in popular lifestyles. There was a strand of socialism that argued workers' own failings held them back – classically argued in *The Ragged Trousered Philanthropists*. As an estimation and criticism of the electorate's limita-

tions, this was manifest after the 1959 election. Michael Stewart deduced that if voters were 'feckless' then Labour had to 'remove the social causes that breed these defects.' As Michael Foot explained Labour's defeat: 'the Tories caught the mood of the public .but that mood was blind, smug, somnolent and, in some respects, evil.'[101] In short, the popular mood and values of affluence fell short of socialist requirements.

Crosland was concerned that morality could slide into moral*ism*. Socialism ought, he felt, be able to demonstrate its superiority without patronizing people. He deemed 'a puritan government of one's own life .admirable', but 'a pharisaical attitude to the lives of others ... revolting.' As with Victorian philanthropy, concern for the poor rarely came without an attendant attitude to their lifestyle. Whatever their good intentions, socialists often bore an 'improving' tone, where (as a respondent to a *Socialist Commentary* questionnaire put it), 'the deadly do-gooders prevail.'[102]

Socialists could appear as a moral vanguard – whose prescriptive attitudes and intervention, even at a personal level, were a response to their disappointment at the people. Labour councils were leading offenders. Young highlighted the 'petty bureaucrats' who 'think they know what is best for people', ordering houses painted, gardens tidied, 'as if tenants existed for them to 'do good to.'' Councils were blamed for Labour's poor result in 1959. Labour's Wellingborough agent reported criticisms of our .pigheaded''council members'; Morgan Phillips called for 'less petty restrictions on council house tenants.' Benn summarized Labour's problem: 'No amount of hymn-singing on May Day about human brotherhood can erase the irritation of being told you cannot keep a dog if you live in a council house.'[103]

However well-intentioned, busybody councils reinforced the image, as a respondent to a 1955 Mass Observation survey put it, that 'Labour is more for controlling you, what you should and shouldn't do.' An ex-Labour member told the survey, the Party contained 'too many Little Hitlers.' Lewisham South MP Carol Johnson complained at the 'little Caesars' within the party.[104]

Popular activities were subject to disapproval. Labour MPs moved to regulate pools betting in 1954. In the title of Ian Mikardo's pamphlet, gambling was *A Mug's Game*. The *Daily Worker* criticized the profits made by bookmakers (whilst celebrating the successes of its tipster, Cayton). Discussing hostility to greyhound racing, Baker has argued Labour was 'sympathetic towards its constituency but at times

despaired of the way of life of those they represented,' politically but
not socially.'[105]
  In the CPGB the notion of lumpen proletariat' denoted the tough'
parts of working-class life – swearing, gambling and drinking. It was
akin to the idea of the mob' and the contemporary notion of mass' in
(especially American) culture. Communists, in their representative role,
tended towards the respectable pole of this culture. Café were preferred to pubs for caucuses. London District organizer John Mahon was
a teetotaller. When the New Towns legislation passed through parliament, Communist MP Willie Gallacher attempted to ban pubs from
the New Towns.[106]
  A notable lumpen' was Lancashire and Cheshire CPGB secretary Syd
Abbott. His drinking and lax accounting (including taking loans from
party finances) were subject to party investigations. Relations in the
district, because he had several affairs, were fraught. In 1954 Cannon
complained at verbal abuse from Abbott. He expressed shock at a dis-
gusting demonstration from the one whose duty it is to be an outstanding example to .comrades in the district.' Cannon evidently
considered swearing to be the sign of a political philistine, a succumbing to emotion.[107]
  Physical fallibility was disparaged by socialists, a sign of being sus-
ceptible, rather than controlling circumstances. Emotions were evidence of weakness. Darke describes how at his mother's funeral: 1 did
not cry .it was selfish to give way to my emotions .a Bolshevik does
not give way to tears.'[108] In a more moral injunction, James Callaghan
was disturbed' at the philandering of the otherwise austere' Gaitskell.
Dutt reproached young CPGB members for voicing ideas of free love'
arguing they had not .related their communism to their private
lives.' One wonders what Dutt made of Marx's more high-spirited
behaviour.[109]
  The *Daily Worker* dismayed readers in 1956 with a mock budget
reducing arms spending to 1950 levels, enabling tax cuts on cigarettes
and beer. It was not only the prospect of cheaper alcohol that made
readers bitter, but pandering to smokers that choked. In the midst of
1956, E. P. Thompson asked, 'Why Make Smoking Cheaper?' – we do
not want to make it easier for young people to acquire the habit.'
Smoking was a burning issue for the CPGB in 1956 – even Pif', the
Daily Worker's cartoon pup, condemned it. Keep Britain Tidy' was
another initiative the left approved. For Mary Allen, litter represented
a sad failure in good manners and good citizenship.'[110]

Such instincts were under strain: not only through the diversification of popular choice and values involved in affluence, but through legislation such as that reducing controls on betting in 1960 or lengthening licensing hours in 1962. Traditional values were under pressure within the left too. Sinclair's 1955 *Notes on Joining the Labour Party*, noted how labour members complained that the policies of the Labour Party have a certain drabness .and seem to be aimed only at producing a tidy society.' Bevan had defended the Attlee government against accusations that, in its charge, Britain lacked colour' and that socialism itself was dull', but later in the decade criticized what he saw as Gaitskell's dry, clinical approach to politics. Crosland too, in *The Future of Socialism*'s ingenious closing, suggested it was not only dark satanic things and people that bar the road to the New Jerusalem, but also, if not mainly, hygienic, respectable, virtuous things and people, lacking only in grace and gaiety.'[111]

Crosland was as occupied with the left's moralism as questions like nationalization. He felt that socialists should keep a trace of the anarchist and the libertarian, and not too much of the prig and the prude.' This was not to license moral permissiveness – he regarded nonconformist Puritanism' as a healthy feature of the British radical tradition' – but to guard against erring into prescriptive attitudes towards others. To unduly inflict Labour's Puritanism on others was particularly nauseating today' he argued in *The Conservative Enemy*. With many on the left (notably *New Statesman* and *Tribune* contributors) in mind, he expressed detest' at the grudging reaction of those who have never themselves known poverty' to people who had at long last acquired the basic decencies of life never mind the luxuries.' It was not only the hypocrisy that perturbed Crosland, but that the left's moralism was a political liability, coalescing with Labour's officious image and fettering progress towards socialism. If affluence meant divorce-law reform will increase the sum of human welfare more than a rise in the food subsidies', it was inadequate for socialists professing to be concerned with human happiness and the removal of injustice' to act in a way more orthodox than the bench of bishops.'[112]

The New Left shared its elders' hang-ups. Clancy Sigal's proposal for the first *New Left Review* of a piece on sex, adolescence and marriage, provoked a furore at the first editorial board'. It was suggested a more sober piece .on women today' should follow this. Samuel has argued the early New Left was conspicuously silent' on questions like censorship, hanging and divorce law. There was warrant then for Young's comment that on almost any question affecting conventional moral-

ity" – homosexuality, opening hours – the left was just as conservative as its opponents.'[113]

Jenkins reminded the nationalization lobby that if socialism meant
more than relieving poverty or realizing equality, then it was also
more than the sum total of a more efficient gas industry [and] a more
efficient electricity industry'. Especially in the 1950s, Crosland argued,
when affluence obliged an emphasis on not only higher exports .but
more open-air café', longer licensing hours, more theatres, better food,
clothes and architecture. Yet the prim-lipped Puritanism' Potter saw as
a particular disfiguration of British socialism' and the Fabian ethic of
public service, bureaucratic diligence, hard work, self-discipline .and
abstinence', prevailed against this.[114]

A battle older than socialism, between radicalism's cavaliers and
roundheads, its Dantons and Robespierres, was rejoined in the 1950s.
In the nineteenth century, Robert Blatchford (like Crosland) felt socialism was lacking in colour and took itself too seriously' and would
more likely spread by cheerful entertainment'. Ramsay MacDonald,
however, felt the Labour movement must welcome puritanism', which
protects the movement against rascals.' For Hardie too, socialism
demanded serious work at the hands of its advocates.' Surveying the
battle in 1955, Alan Fox declared socialism today is nothing if not
serious.' Blatchford's and William Morris's visions had lost to dour
Puritanism'.[115] This was fortified by the Webbs' Fabianism, stressing
immunity from physical weakness', sobriety, an efficient filing system,
the sacrifice [of] private pleasure to public duty' and the expectation
others should do the same'.

Crosland revived the call for a popular' socialism, trying to put the
left in tune with the relaxation of traditional social values that accompanied affluence. Personal austerity, non-conformist or Fabian, was
unnecessary in affluent Britain. Personally, he saw no virtue in sitting
on a bed of nails when there was a comfortable armchair.' The Webbs'
public virtues', he argued, may not be as appropriate today.' It was
time for a reaction: for a greater emphasis on private life, on freedom
and dissent, on culture, beauty, leisure and even frivolity.' Total abstinence and a good filing system', Crosland asserted, are not now the
right sign-posts to the socialist utopia.'[116]

'Or at least if they are', Crosland continued, some of us will fall by
the way-side.' Jenkins and Crosland's comfortable lifestyle (though
both served on the Fabian Executive) would have perturbed the Webbs
as much as they provoked rank-and-file suspicions. There was other
evidence of a revisionist mood, such as Benn's tidings of a Fabian

school in 1957: a 'delightful crowd of young people ...interest in human beings is growing again ..the stick-in-the-mud bureaucrat is being cut-down to size.'[117]

The revisionists were reticent on the ethics of nuclear weapons, but elsewhere applied their libertarian nostrums. Bill Rodgers was among early contributors to *The Good Food Guide*, founded by socialist Raymond Postgate in 1951. Jenkins helped pilot the Obscene Publications Act through the Commons in 1959 (on which the *Lady Chatterley's Lover* case was won in 1960). If 1950s affluence began to breakdown and liberalize Victorian social norms, expanded popular choice and encouraged a degree of individualism, revisionism positively encouraged such trends in the later 1960s. The legislation passed during Jenkins' Home Ministry (1965–7) regarding capital punishment, abortion, homosexuality, theatre censorship and divorce, was arguably the Wilson government's 'greatest achievement'. [118]

Yet this was also a limited legacy. The revisionist moment of the later 1950s was lost, not so much to Fabian or Puritan impulses (though Jenkins was replaced as Home Secretary by the Baptist James Callaghan), as to Wilson's renewed emphasis on economic advance. Desiccated by the 'white heat' of technology, the momentum for a more cultural emphasis drifted back down the formal political agenda.

The left also had a vivid social life at the likes of Joan Littlewood's Theatre Workshop.[119] Bevan was as much of an epicure as any revisionist. There was something of Bevan in Crosland's call for a less prudent socialism. The 'affluent lifestyle' he and Jennie Lee lived – fine wines (including Spanish rioja), Marks and Spencer shares – meant, for Lee's biographer, that 'jibes about their champagne socialist lifestyle were not unmerited'. Hollis notes (and Crosland would have applauded) that they had 'not a scrap of puritan guilt about it all.' Bevan 'laid claim to 'aristocratic''tastes', hoping socialism would enable all to enjoy these.[120] He also had bureaucratic credentials, having guided the NHS into life. The animosity he attracted was partly because his background afforded him a lifestyle that brought disrepute to other Labour figures. Otherwise, and so long as the conversation stayed shy of politics (admittedly unlikely), it does not involve a leap of historical imagination to suppose that Bevan and Crosland would have got along famously over a lavish meal.

Bevan disliked the lifestyles associated with the new affluence. His conception of cultural worth centred on bringing 'high' culture to the people. Gorman similarly recalls a comrade who saw 'part of his mission as a communist to raise the standard of eating' and 'was scathing in his criticism of our fish and chips culture.' Wesker's Centre 42 promoted cultural activity for the average trade unionist. Labour and the Unions had raised living standards, he argued, but it remained necessary to convince the stultified worker that he was .entitled to his share of the nation's cultural life?' Wesker's concern was that the worker is only enjoying half of life; he may be an engaged body, but he's not an engaged soul.'[121]

In its cultural outlook, the left was also up against its own mind-set. As Hobsbawm later outlined, this tended to regard cultural revolt and cultural dissidence [as] symptoms, not revolutionary forces' and as politically ..not very important.' Historically, he added, the Robespierres always win out over the Dantons.'[122]

The left had its humourless types. A 1958 review noted Labour's jazz and skiffle sessions were peopled by rather earnest young men and women.' This might account for the distance it kept from youth culture – rock n roll, its dress and pleasure-seeking ethos. A survey of Glossop felt Labour lack[ed] the necessary social skills for the successful organization of whist drives, dances and similar functions.'[123]

'What kind of game of beer-and-skittles could you have with Palme Dutt, Frank Foulkes or the Dean of Canterbury?', the *Daily Mirror* asked in 1955, seeing as all the Communists Cassandra' had ever met had been worse than solemn'. Communist parties were poor social gatherings, Benn reported, as everybody splits up to talk politics.' A Labour gathering to which he was party, was rated quite fun as it was largely non-political.'[124] Socialists, in this sense, were not party animals. Legend has that CPGB members were reluctant dancers. Gorman found party socials an ordeal': neither his wife nor myself were dancers and there was no licensed bar to stimulate conviviality.' They were, he concluded, unsocial socialists.' The CPGB warned our party branches present a rather austere picture to the average worker.'[125]

It was indicative of the breakdown of political codes in 1956, that a satirical journal, the *Rhyming Reasoner*, emerged. It parodied party life in titles like Twentieth Congress Blues' and The Marxists-Leninists Song' from The Pirates of King Street' (sung to Gilbert and Sullivan's I am the very model of a modern Major-general' from *The Pirates of Penzance*):

> I am the very model of a modern Marxist-Leninist,
> I'm anti-war, and anti-God and very anti-feminist;
> My thinking's dialectical, my wisdom's undebateable,
> When I negate negations they're undoubtedly negateable,
> My policies and theories have an air of unreality,

> Because I am the victim of a cult of personality;
> But still as propagandist, agitator and polemicist,
> I am the very model of a modern Marxist-Leninist.[126]

The CPGB, Samuel notes, admired puritan virtues – hard work and punctuality.' What it termed revolutionary discipline' was a sibling of Fabianism. This tutelage was not easily shed. 'Too little formality, too much do-as-you- like," too few bourgeois virtues' was how Thompson chastized the anarchic office of the forthcoming *New Left Review* in 1959.[127]

If this chapter paints a rather unflattering, minority picture of socialists – downplaying their efforts to build a better society in favour of their external effects – it can claim sanction from Orwell. In a spirit of *advocatus diaboli*, arguing *for* not *against* socialism in *The Road to Wigan Pier* in 1937, Orwell had bemoaned the moral crankishness' of vegetarian, teetotal socialists, whose many minor prigishnesses' were alienating possible supporters in silly and quite irrelevant ways.' Orwell suggested the worst advertisement for socialism is its adherents'. The same point could be made in the 1950s – and not only about groups with an explicit moral agenda or vegetarian lifestyle like Socialist Union. Jay Blumler reflected in 1961 that, however unjust, the public image of socialists was often as '*spoilsports*, who cannot bear the sight of private affluence''; ' *bookworms*, whose vision rarely transcends the limits of a textbook on international trade'; and '*bureaucrats*, who want public officials to tell citizens how they should run their lives.' Orwell suggested the rudiments of this outlook seemed to have been taken over *en bloc* from the old Liberal Party', firmly non-conformist in the late nineteenth century. This would tally with the left's cultural thinking, outlined in Chapter 4. As an unconscious pre-socialist influence on 1950s left thinking, this might explain the left's difficulties in extirpating it.[128] The objection that these were myths, canards perpetuated by opponents can be dismissed – the myths the left lived by were not only its own and much of the evidence presented here comes from socialists themselves. These aspects of moralism and lifestyle are worth noting not because the left was wrong', but because they show how the left was distant from the popular' and disposed to be critical of affluence in the 1950s. This chapter has also stressed the common traits of different traditions within socialism. As Chapter 3 also details, this was in many ways an inveterate culture, with resources for reproducing itself, but resistant to and with limited resources for change.

3
Branch Life

The branch, more than the Trade Union, Trades Council, local council, Co-op, home or work, was at the root of being a socialist. Although it is relatively uncharted territory, branch life offers historians a guide to the texture of popular and local politics, activism, organization and, perforce, party culture.[1] The 1950s are an appropriate moment at which to step back into the characteristic features of branch life. A proliferation of local surveys reflected the burgeoning of electoral sociology in this period and interest in Labour's expanded membership.[2] For Labour not only achieved its highest poll at the 1951 election, but by 1952 its individual membership had topped one million and that of its Women's and Youth sections peaked in 1953. One historian has dubbed the period 1951–3, the climax of Labourism'. Labour proclaimed itself a 'mass organization' and envisaged a presence on every street in the form of 'street captains'. [3]

The reality, depicted in these surveys, was less glittering. There was arguably more a crisis of socialist organization in the mid-1950s. Labour's 'Interim Report of the Sub-Committee on Party Organisation' (eponymized as the 'Wilson Report') [4] and the CPGB's 'Commission on Inner-Party Democracy' embarked on detailed reviews of the local and internal condition of their respective organizations. Labour was investigating what it believed were the organizational causes of its defeat in the 1955 general election. The CPGB was responding to (and hoping to dissipate) dissent from democratic centralism aroused by its handling (besides the revelations themselves) of 1956.[5]

Organization was a point of departure too for the New Left, whose critique of Stalinism and Labourism was concerned with their organizational as much as ideological limitations. The New Left adhered to a more federal model. It held a conventional notion that organization was not for 'mere discussion', but for the purposes of education and propaganda'. But when Thompson informed readers of the *New Reasoner* that 'your town or locality .must decide what form of organization is appropriate – readers discussion or study group, Left club', this did provide an alternative conception, however short-lived.[6]

The value to historians of these self-examinations outweighs their contemporary significance. The enduring influence of the Wilson Report was the exposure its author received among local officials and activists.[7] The CPGB Commission, at least in its majority report, endorsed the status quo. This attested to the entrenched, conservative nature of party culture. The composition and workings of the Commission held out little prospect of change. Yet Communists were, on the whole, content to continue party life in the same mode. It was, after all, only a minority (if sizeable and vocal) that chose to leave the party in 1956 – most stayed.[8]

The Wilson Report hardly encouraged such complacency. It recommended a thorough rationalization and modernization of Labour's organization – from finance to agents and the use of cars to collection of dues. Despite Labour's mass membership of 843,000 it portrayed the organization presided over by Morgan Phillips (General Secretary) and Len Williams (National Agent) as thoroughly decrepit. By contrast with the Conservatives' wealth and recently refurbished organization, Labour appeared 'usty and deteriorating with age'. In its most striking and damning moment the Wilson Report considered that compared with our opponents, we are still at the penny-farthing stage in a jet-propelled era.'[9] Such criticism reverberated around the 1950s Labour movement as it struggled to come to terms with modernity. In 1958 an Independent Commission exposed a similarly decrepit state of affairs within the Co-operative movement. A year later, a more political cocktail, of Labour's 'old-fashioned' image and inability to win the youth vote, was blamed for electoral failure.[10]

Political conditions

A dilapidated atmosphere permeated branch-level socialism; it was not only socialist theory that was in need of renovation by the 1950s. Roy Hattersley has evoked the dusty ambience of 'dingy rooms over Co-Op groceries, rusty duplicating machines which vomited dirty ink .old ladies addressing envelopes with infinite care and obvious difficulty, piles of outdated leaflets that no-one delivered and loudspeaker equipment that dented car roofs but failed to amplify the spoken word'.[11]

Labour branches tended to 'muddle through', often in tottering premises, on a human shoestring' and fettered by the purse-strings. [12] The condition of Party premises was a constant anxiety. A survey of London constituencies in 1950 disclosed a depressing situation. East Ham North Labour headquarters had broken stairs, bare floors'; Kensington North's were shabby', its meeting room 'messy' and 'absolutely minus furniture'. Nor was the problem exclusive to war-damaged urban areas. Suburban Merton rented out part of its premises, but its agent considered the rent in excess of the accommodation provided' and the outside toilet unsuitable for the tenant's child. [13]

Labour Organiser, the Labour agent's journal, complained Party office windows were too often squalid rubbish dumps in which faded and fly-blown posters linger on in inarticulate life between elections'. Some offices were 'more like museums'. Apocryphally, Macdonald still adorned some and elsewhere was a picture of Keir Hardie hanging askew on a mildewed wall'. [14]

The picture was not utterly uniform. Considered more the order of the day were the efforts of the 'Riverside' Party whose bright and well lit' rooms were adorned with Labour and public service posters, or Fulham East whose rooms were 'exceptionally tidy' and 'artistically decorated'. [15] *Labour Organiser* found the Sevenoaks offices so 'orderly' in 1953 that it was possible to 'eat our dinner off the floor'. But these were the exceptions – Labour issued booklets on planning the requisite rooms, yet such environments remained few and far between. [16]

The situation had not appreciably improved by the turn of the decade. In June 1961 a 'Brighter Premises' competition was deemed necessary to relieve the 'year-long greyness' and to spruce up the party's appearance for 1962's Festival of Labour. [17] Despite advice on 'do's and don'ts' from designer Misha Black, the results were mixed. East Ham North now displayed photos of councillors with properties built by the Labour council. However, even where costly renovations were undertaken, problems remained. An Eastern region adjudicator criticized, 'designs which perpetuate the Village Hall atmosphere ... with its musty associations'; designs which were 'not modern and will repel ..young people' or 'so horrible that they ..discredit the Party.' [18]

Rather than headquarters worthy of our socialist cause' such displays were 'a rotten advertisement for the Party of hope and ideas.' That 'gloomy halls and unpainted premises' were 'anything but desirable advertisements for the cause' offended by erring from the ideal of socialism prefiguring in the here and now the new order it aimed to usher in. They also contravened the belief of socialists that 'well designed, attractive surroundings are the first priority for ordinary people'[19]

Party meetings were not an attractive prospect. 'People just will not come along these days to sit in a cold, ramshackle room' a 1955 Socialist Union survey concluded. Likewise Dulwich CLP reported in 1963 that 'it is not an easy task to compete with television and bingo'. This was socialist's key fear – that they could not hope to compete against or with modernity and particularly the television. Given the choice of a 'dull, business routine' in a strictly furnished Co-Op hall, 'of course people prefer to stay at home with the telly.'   [20]

This austere air was widespread in socialist culture: discernible in the appearance and homes of socialists, no less than party life and agitated by affluence, yet increasingly at odds with it. Ian Aitken has remembered the 'dingy offices' of *Tribune* in the 1950s. Based in a 'gloomy building', journalists worked amidst 'a thick blanket of dust.' Labour's HQ, Transport House, was 'strictly utilitarian from top to bottom.' [21]

The CPGB was as spartan. Branch meetings, John Gorman remembers, were 'held in a bare-boarded and cheerless room at a local school.' A similarly ascetic facade was advanced nationally by the 'iron-protected glass' of the King Street HQ and the bleakly 'Stalinist' *Daily Worker* office. Inside the latter was 'resolutely comfortless' – so too King Street, 'cold', 'dull' with linoleum flooring. [22]

Materially, there was a paucity of resources for CLPs. Wards often had a precarious existence. Morden ward – in an otherwise stable constituency – virtually ceased to function between 1957 and the 1959 election. Meetings were infrequent or abandoned due to low attendances (rarely more than five). 'The struggle to maintain a permanent organisation', as a study of Newcastle-under-Lyme confirmed, was omnipresent. Communist branches too, varied between frantic activity and the verge of extinction. A review of the Party's North East activities in 1955 found that only 14 of 30 branches could be said to 'regularly function.' In the legal provision for Labour premises, the possibility of 'the Party ceasing to exist' was felt to merit contemplation.[23]

Labour's condition was worst in large cities. Wilson found CLP organisation' to be 'almost non-existent' in Leicester. In Glasgow and Liverpool it was 'very poor'. Nottingham, similarly criticized, admitted that 'a major surgical operation' was needed in the Party organisation'. A specific criticism was that city parties centralized authority and finance and that this prevented effective constituency organization.

Both Preston seats would have been won in 1955, it was argued, if we had had an active CLP organization there instead of a costly and top-heavy Borough Party.' City parties were often reluctant to distribute trade union affiliations (the largest and most reliable source of income) to the constituencies. In Liverpool, Cardiff and Croydon the central party retained the whole trade union income. Elsewhere the situation was more equitable – Birmingham (which Wilson praised as a 'vigorous', model party) passed out 25 per cent of its union income; Newcastle 50 per cent.[24]

Another common difficulty was that over a period of a few years there [was] an almost complete change in the personnel of a constituency party.' A ward in Chippenham was 'a one man show" the agent recorded in 1956, and when he left the district it was impossible to replace him.' In Walsall the single Communist available to perform weekend rounds with the *Daily Worker* in 1960 requested a break from such rigours. In 1956 leading Scottish Communist Lawrence Daly estimated only 10–20 per cent of CPGB members were activists.[25]

Party membership was manifest in more ways than activism (such as payment of dues) and activism was apparent in social values and attitudes as much as canvassing or attending meetings. Yet measured in this conventional sense the exiguity of the activist layer features as an almost ubiquitous feature of branches – large or small, proletarian or suburban – even during Labour's heady days of 1951–3. A survey of Manchester Gorton ward in 1953 found only 19 per cent of members had attended a Party meeting in the previous year and that 'active members' were 'a fairly small minority'. This dovetailed with a 1951 Fabian analysis of Manchester Stretford which highlighted 'a small group of enthusiasts in each ward.' The very execution of these surveys was hampered by the indifference of the less active majority.[26]

This augmented concerns party leaders harboured about activists and their minority, vanguard character – they considered them unrepresentative, just as activists were prone to suspect their leaders of 'selling out' or 'careerism'. Douglas Jay, never Labour activists' favourite MP, remembered his Battersea party as populated by 'extremists, cranks and theorists'. Vic Feather, TUC assistant secretary, remarked in 1954, 'a Labour agent does not have to go out searching for the crackpot .the crackpot was searching for him before the agent took the office shutters down.' Rather than 'eccentric intellectuals', Feather felt it was the trade unionists that constituted the 'solid soul of the party'. Sidney Webb too had held the constituency parties are frequently unrepresentative groups of nonentities dominated by fanatics and cranks, and extremists' and thus it was 'impracticable' to permit party conference to decide policy.[27]

Through the 1950s Labour's leadership depended (and preferred to depend) upon the union block vote at conference, rather than upon rank-and-file support. This curtailed the extent to which constituencies could be seen as anything more than voter-gatherers and reforms like the Wilson Report's aim to vest increased authority in the constituencies. Proposals such as increasing individual 'subs' – often popular with members – were rejected for the increased importance it would accord them. The unions were also a bar to a more expansive role for local parties because they were rarely prepared to loosen their purse-strings outside of election campaigns.[28]

Apathy and agency

Contemporary surveys also concurred on the social aspect of membership, the monotony of meetings and their meagre attendance. The latter was an intractable problem. When Coventry Borough Party surveyed its wards after the Wilson Report, low attendance figured prominently in a catalogue of failings. At worst only the ward Chairman and Secretary or Executive Committee would be present. Attendance in most wards during the 1950s rarely touched double-figures, though it revived during moments of political fervour, such as elections or the Suez crisis.[29]

Even General Management Committees – the sovereign body within CLPs, composed of delegates from throughout the local Labour movement – could not rely upon a consistent turnout. Coventry found at most one-quarter of delegates turned out in its three constituencies (all of which returned a Labour MP). In Merton and Morden, the agent complained (in response to Feather's article claiming trade unionists as the 'soul of the party') that only 5 of 16 trade union delegates attended GMCs.[30]

An imminent election could be expected to raise numbers – but only briefly. In the wake of the 1959 election, John Heardley-Walker, agent for Merton and Morden, reflected that as the political temperature cooled:

> when the Party returns to its mundane and unglamorous affairs, we see who the real enthusiasts are. The 'meteorites' have burned out and returned to what they apparently feel to be more pleasurable (and profitable?) pursuits to occupy their spare time ..at the

General Election we were inundated with helpers, by May we had returned to the hard, loyal core of workers and even that had suffered some contraction.[31]

Apathy within Party ranks (and the wider public) was universally lamented. Labour's limited human resources constrained the range of activities that constituencies could expect to undertake. The more ideological and missionary temper of many members was frustrated by the limited time afforded for political education, discussions of policy, theory or political' resolutions. Local parties were often electoralist' (orientated to winning elections to the exclusion of other activities) more by default than intent.

'Electoralism' was deeply instilled in Labour reasoning. Its commitment to parliament was bound up with its belief in central, national planning and reinforced by the Attlee governments. Moreover, parliamentary politics were incompatible with extensive intra-party democracy', political scientist Robert Mckenzie argued in 1955, since government would become subject to the authority of the party conference. Ultimately, he alleged, the mass organization of any parliamentary party must be primarily a vote-getting machine.'[32] There were strict limits to the declared aim of the Wilson Report – to make the constituency party the centre of authority'.[33] Activists envisaging participatory local parties were bound to be frustrated.

If electoralism was to account for the problems of apathy that afflicted many Labour parties, then an organization less constrained by tension between its socialist mission and securing ballot box support, with a more regimented membership, committed to fusing the political and industrial spheres, might be expected to elude such difficulties. Yet a similar picture emerges from the CPGB, bearing out the idea that Labour's electoralism was as much a response to limited human resources and to the limits of the kind of commitment involved in actively propagating socialism as an innate part of its strategy.

CPGB branches worked frenetically. Petitions, visiting contacts, education and innumerable other meetings involved time and financial sacrifices' on the part of its cadres. The paper was the day-to-day axis of life, since the *Daily Worker* was the party's main campaigning force'. As Gorman tells it, selling the *Daily Worker* was a yardstick to measure commitment' and constituted an informal branch hierarchy – how many *Daily Worker's* did you sell today comrade?"was a rhetorical question that ended many a theoretical argument.'[34] The prospect of imminent success in the party's rhetoric maintained its pitch of activity. Yet, as a report to the Party's Political Committee in 1953 admitted, the painfully slow growth of the party is out of all proportion to the ceaseless activity carried out by our active membership.' It also confessed that the bulk of our work is carried out by about a third of our membership.'[35]

Socialists attempted to bridge apathy in their own ranks with pamphlets, speakers' guides, district schools and recruiting drives. Party education was very patchy' Labour's Research Department found in 1953. Only 27 per cent of CLPs had appointed a Political Education Officer and only 31 per cent sent members to regional or summer schools. More than two-thirds of CLPs failed to respond to the survey.[36]

Activists were also apt to despair of apathy and selfishness .the self-imposed barriers erected thoughtlessly by the workers themselves.'[37] Poplar's agent, H. E. Tate, struck a familiar (for the affluent 1950s) and revealing refrain in discussion of the 1955 general election. He reflected on the lack of active and voluntary workers now in the party'. Equally, he was anxious that voters between the ages of 21 and 40 were not coming out'. What troubled Tate were the attitudes canvassers had encountered from known Labour supporters': They [political parties] are all the same', Why trouble, we are alright.' Ultimately, he alleged, Labour's chief difficulty was that most people are satisfied' with what he saw as their false position of plenty.' [38]

This was then only apathy' as seen through the activist gaze: a moral, narrative device by which to self-justify and place those for whom politics was not paramount – a product of activists' ways of looking at the world. Apathy was no less real, however, for being in part a construct of activists' priorities. Raising the issue of nuclear war, but with a sideswipe at non-active party members and the sort of slighting allusion to affluence' that came readily to socialists in the 1950s, one activist argued it was only when everyone learns the same sense of impending danger which makes active members tramp the streets in all weathers [that] we shall all become more prosperous in the real sense.'[39] Activists rated their own work highly. Heardley-Walker told voters that they owed a great deal to Labour activists: on their efforts depend the future of your children .your own livelihood .the existence of peace itself,' and yet they performed these routine political jobs without thought of personal gain.'[40]

It was then troublesome for activists to confront the idea, as *Labour Organiser* columnist Quair considered with respect to Labour members whose commitment was limited to the payment of subs, that maybe

the fault lies more with us than them.' Only by recognizing that possibly we don't know enough about' voters and members, Quair told activists, might they come some distance to countering what you call .ápathy.' [41]
'Apathy', both within Labour and beyond, burdened local party agents. Full-time Labour organizers were a critical resource, but their numbers were dwindling. In 1951 there were 291 agents, 244 in 1955 and 210 by 1961. Agents claimed it was a 50 or even 80 hours a week job.[42] Such responsibilities tended to make agents demanding figures. As Jean Barnes depicted: 'An agent is never satisfied – he can drive you frantic with his everlasting demands on your leisure, your pocket, your ability and your friends.' In party agents can be observed a counter to the moralists and fanatics of local Labour parties – the Herbert Morrison-type bureaucrats with their efficient filing systems. Birch's account of Glossop reported the agent, who together with the geographical problems posed by a Pennine constituency, held down a full-time job, was a local councillor and National Union of Railwaymen branch secretary, to be (unsurprisingly) a lively and energetic man'. [43]

CPGB full-time organizers were expected to live above all on belief. The personal and financial problems of Syd Abbott, Lancashire and Cheshire district secretary, were traced to the low party wages, accentuated by not getting them regularly'.[44] Harry Ratner worked in 1957 as an organizer for a Trotskyist group 'The Club', on a weekly wage less than the then unemployment benefit.'[45]

Pay for Labour agents stood in 1955 at £450–550 per annum. By 1960 this had risen to £650–825. Compared with average industrial earnings (£560 per annum in 1955), as the Wilson Report chose to do, this was not uncompetitive. But by contrast with the pre-war it was now agency rather than industry that offered insecure job prospects. For a family man with young children there is real hardship and risk involved in taking an agency', Wilson concluded. Consequently, there was not the quality and nothing like the flow of new recruits that the movement enjoyed before the war.'[46]

The antinomies of this structure were evident. Poorer, backwater constituencies were the places in need of agency, while agents preferred the stability of Labour heartlands to a capricious marginal'. A history of Windsor Labour Party noted an agent could do many things for the Party .but the problem was that provision had to be made for his salary and, paradoxically, the agent could spend a disproportionate amount of his time promoting .money-raising schemes for that purpose.' Half of party expenditure in Swansea in 1957 went on pay.

Of the 91 key marginals the NEC identified after the 1959 election, 70 were without a permanent agent.[47]

Divisions of Labour: collecting and canvassing

The need for thrift placed great premium upon the collection of membership dues, but the dearth of activists to go 'on the knocker' for this and other labour-intensive rituals like canvassing, created a logistical besides a financial strain. Women were often assigned the tasks of fund-raising socials or 'subs' collection. Harry Underhill, West Midlands regional organizer, explained that in most constituencies women are the backbone of committee room work (writing, filling and on polling day) and for mass canvass.'[48] One of Labour's publicity experts, newly created in the early 1960s, considered it was the two kind middle aged ladies who .don't get up and make speeches ... make things for bazaars .offer you a cup of tea' who were ideal for removing overly political jargon from election statements.[49]

Mostly these were tasks dutifully undertaken. A *Manchester Guardian* correspondent sketched a local women's section, whose members were engaged chiefly with knitting and not terribly interested in politics.' They all hate the Tory Party' it was reported, although many of them have forgotten why.' It was also noted that without them the bazaars, socials and outings would flop miserably.'[50] Women's sections might be largely social, but served to congregate. Attendances at Poplar's tea parties in the 1950s, exceeded all but the most extraordinary events in other sections of the party.[51]

Without doubt there was discrimination against women in socialist circles. *Socialist Commentary's* satirical column 'Our Ward' told the story of one Prudence Mudd, who, much to the chagrin of the Women's Section, wooed a selection conference with her figure and blaze of red hair'. More common was Tessa Broome's memory of a selection meeting in suburban Manchester in the 1950s which interviewed a very able woman .[but] the attitude was well, she was very good, but she was a woman.'[52]

All in all, socialists were a traditional species that could not evade the divisions in British society. Labour and the CPGB were overwhelmingly male organizations in staff and membership. In Bethnal Green, CLP men outnumbered women by a factor of three. Nationally, women formed a (sizeable) minority of individual Labour members – in 1957, 385,200 out of a total of 912,987 (42 per cent). No less than 85 per cent of delegates to the 1957 CPGB congress were male.[53]

The ethos and language of the CPGB emitted a machismo. 'Members of the Communist Party go like one man into the struggle,' Pollitt was to be found arguing in 1956. Other (limited) evidence suggests women proved their credentials by adhering to party orthodoxy. For instance, Wood notes a disproportionate volume of pro-Stalin letters to the *Daily Worker* in 1956 were penned by women.[54] However unwittingly the prejudices of society were reproduced on the left, they cast a shadow across that aspiration to practise the ideals of a new society. Equally, this chapter emphasizes the importance of the social and 'mundane' aspects of everyday political activity – aspects often disparaged by policy-minded activists and (since they were often of the same mind) likewise neglected by historians.

In this division of labour on which Labour (and Samuel has hinted, the CPGB) functioned, women were considered ideal 'subs' collectors, since they were 'more methodical than men, more conscientious in keeping regularly to collecting dates.' Dues collection on the established model was atavistic, a remnant of Labour's poor working-class origins. It made little financial sense and was time consuming (given Labour's sizeable membership in the 1950s).[55] An option was to pay collectors. Leslie Hilliard, Secretary of the Agents' Union, cited the success of a scheme in South Lewisham. However, while payment was feasible and necessary and performance-related (one-third of that collected) in Lewisham (which was the largest local Labour Party through the 1950s, with 7,500 members) – its potential elsewhere was less certain. Heardley-Walker, who 'hated collecting', also argued that payments would increase income, release time for canvassing and acknowledge that collecting was an 'even harder task' given the rising cost of living in the early 1950s. However, the local party felt payment and the loss of the 'personal touch' was contrary to the ethics of collecting.[56]

Canvassing was an even more coded ritual. Abundant planning and value was invested in it. If the CPGB formed a 'shopfloor intelligentsia', as Samuel has argued, then Labour might be seen as the doorstep equivalent. This evinced a certain mistrust of the electorate. Quair worried about the archetypal voter, 'Jimmy Green', who 'decides the fate of nations and lays down the course of history .if nobody bothers about him personally, the odds are that he will not vote .we do the best we can with him.' Green was clearly a descendant of Henry Dubb, another imaginary voter socialists created in the 1920s, and like him male, good-natured, but simple-minded and apathetic. This also reflected activists' high opinion of their worth as the foot-soldiers of democracy. Political scientist Jean Blondel wondered what interest there would be in politics if Parties' militants did not devote themselves to their task so persistently.'[57]

Canvassing offers a useful canvas on which to lay socialists' attitudes alongside those of their audience. Evidently there was often a gulf – the result not only of popular apathy, but of activists' approach and outlook. John Horner has related his experience of canvassing in Oldbury and Halesowen, the West Midlands constituency in which he was Labour candidate in 1959. Horner's distaste for gardening (not uncommon amongst socialists) antagonized one constituent. He also chose, contrary to his agent's advice, to canvass while the local football team, West Bromwich Albion, were playing in a televised cup tie. The typical doorstep response was: It's Mr Horner, Mum' – Well tell him to come back next week, we're watching the Cup.' Horner's decision was the result of his professed dislike for professional sport (again not uncommon), but as evident was a dismissiveness of popular interests. Horner later reflected: I don't know how many votes I lost that day by knocking on doors in the middle of the television match.'[58]

Canvassing was partly an art. It was necessary to find common ground with the canvassed, such as healthy children .a well planned vegetable plot .a tidy, neat kitchen.' Timing was as critical; 6.30 to 8.00 in the evening judged best. This was after the husband is home and has had his evening meal', but before he settled into slippers and tele.' [59] As early as 1954 the TV was influencing the canvassing schedule. A Labour official told: I would certainly never send canvassers to call when *What's My Line* is on.' Disturbing televiewing or engaging a housewife who would only make a decision with her husband (an attitude canvassers deplored but often encountered), did not make for fecund canvassing. One canvasser was amazed at the apathy shown by some housewives .it would have grieved the suffragettes.'   [60]

Lamb further advised canvassers to speak gently and quietly in conversational tones' and not to draw attention to any oddities of your appearance or speech.' Apparel was significant. The emphasis was on a respectable, responsible image. To this extent Labour and the CPGB were rather similar. Labour canvassers were to dress simply and neatly.'[61] Communists, too, tended to garb soberly. In Doris Lessing's *The Golden Notebook*, communists canvassing an ugly area of uniform, small, poor houses' in North London refused to dress more akin to their audience, despite one arguing that to appear too posh' could put people on the defensive'. The resulting women canvassers were much better dressed than the women of the area'.[62]

Disclosed by these codes of canvassing were ways in which socialists imagined their audience and how such ideals interacted with the 1950s doorstep experience. The left preferred the respectable aspects of working-class culture, but concessions to the tele' habit or discourageable attitudes (the old idea of 'waiting for the old man to come home" [63]) seem not to have attenuated the wider narrative of socialism. Recourse was found in socialism as a faith and an immunized vision of the working class. Activists' rhetoric, conjuring up their own hopes and talking up the potential of events, was designed to survive as much as break through those values and attitudes which they mistrusted in their audience. Pessimism (at the failures of others to conform to their own touchstones of political and moral worth) went hand in hand with a rhetoric of optimism.[64] This vision of the working class was ultimately, Lessing suggested, 'a platonic image, a grail, a quintessence, and by definition, unattainable.' Where is this proletariat?' Quair similarly wondered about the way activists conceived of their audience, 'I've looked around and I'm damned if I can find it.' Canvassing was often unrewarding in the 1950s, a sacrifice, testing of one's faith. As Lamb saw it, canvassers had to learn to suffer fools gladly or they would go crackers.'[65]

There was a tension to canvassing – was it to 'make' socialists or to win votes for them? This was a tension also found in Dennis Potter's Labour Party play, *Vote, Vote, Vote for Nigel Barton*. It was a tension at the heart of CLPs between functioning as a socialist propaganda body and as an electoral machine'. Yet this was also an imagined dichotomy of organizational efficiency counterpoised to political principles and ethics that sprang from fear of change.[66] This related to debates within socialism about whether the working class harboured an innate socialism in need of awakening, or whether a more limited assessment of working-class consciousness occasioned more paternalistic nurturing.[67] In the 1950s opinion swung towards the latter.

In vogue from 1951 was the 'Reading System' – patented in Bevanite Ian Mikardo's Reading South constituency. This was a more scientific method of canvassing. Its premise was that in marginal constituencies the aim should not be to convert anyone to our views, but, instead, to identify our own voters and then get them all to the poll'. We do our arguing and our converting,' Mikardo continued, '*between* elections.' Canvass routes were meticulously plotted and a polling register and coloured voter index (Labour voters on white card for purity!') were used to trace returns and 'removals' (the re-housed, a major problem of the 1950s).[68]

With an emphasis on postal votes, this became the approved model. In part this was expediency – there were more volunteers around at elections – but it also tallied with the belief that Labour had the support to triumph electorally, if only it could channel it to the ballot.[69] The problem, in short, was not politics, but efficiency of organization.

The 'Reading System' was not without critics, specifically of its indifference towards 'making' socialists. Richard Wevell, a regular contributor to *Labour Organiser*, argued that 'unless people are converted to socialist ideas all the time .there won't   *be* any agents .or any Labour Governments.' '*Better organisation* was not enough', he contended; an emphasis on '*making more socialists*' was also required, and to this end Wevell proposed paying 'Missioners' to preach socialism. [70]

Meetings

If canvassing was a laborious and inefficient means of communication, also at odds with modernity were Party meetings. In an electric age, the allure of the mass meeting was dimming – except amongst believers who attached great authority to such assemblies, perhaps all the more so in light of their fading lustre. This was especially so for the CPGB, for which public meetings and demonstrations, allowed an imagined influence that compensated for the absence of a real popular following.'[71] Communists were compulsive organizers of public meetings – in 1952 they held over 7,000 – 'mainly the Sunday Night Pitches"... established in the past by the pioneers of the socialist movement.'[72]

The stirring tones of Bevan, Bessie Braddock or Pollitt or national demonstrations – against Suez in Trafalgar Square and the Aldermaston Marches from 1958 are part of left lore – still seemed moments charged with historic potential and the ability to shake the political languor. It was smaller meetings, formerly a mainstay of Party diaries, whose drama was being outmoded by alternative theatres, notably the nefarious television. Not only did TV diminish meeting audiences, but increasingly politics looked to it and to new 'advertising' strategies. On the whole socialists were pessimistic about this trend away from local initiative. For Jones it meant the 'decline of democracy'. Some constituencies held 'teleparties' – using a TV or radio broadcast as a focus for debate. But TV's communicative range was replacing the 'educating"and 'agitating"functions' of CLPs, which were increasingly (a trend already evident in the 'Reading System') 'left with the humdrum task of 'getting the vote out". [73]

Attempts to revise public meetings met with mixed fortunes. The Brains Trusts' – borrowing the title of a popular radio show – a panel of speakers staffed by Bevanites, toured constituencies to great success in the early 1950s. This showed the thirst for, yet absence of, discussion in the typical party meeting. But their popularity, Jenkins explains, was also because the early 1950s was not yet the era of television as far as millions of workers were concerned'. Others held that to sugar the pill of education' with entertainment' as the trusts did, was not a substitute for more substantial methods of political education.'[74]

The overwhelmingly procedural and administrative content of Labour meetings did not enhance their appeal and was widely reproved. This was not an arena for theoretical display or socialist imagination, but for fetishists of protocol and points of order. Procedure was the life' of some members. In Wilfred Fienburgh's 1959 novel *No Love For Johnnie*, one local member, Miss Welsh, is introduced as a formidable expert in procedure' who expressed herself and made everyone aware of her by launching innumerable points of order.'[75]

CPGB meetings differed in this respect, being more explicitly political' in content and formality. Branch meetings were worthy of the most thorough preparation' and should be devoted to discussion of some political question.' Time discipline was critical – a component of political reliability. Pollitt believed meetings should not wait for latecomers, since they would then remain unaware of their tardiness.[76] The chair was to see that each item starts and finishes on time'. This did not always ensure meetings were brief – district committees could last the best part of a weekend. Samuel relates this mania for organization to the craving for order, planning and regimentation that characterized the Communist mind. A different symbolism was evident in the vocabulary of a 1961 edition of the CPGB handbook, *Forging the Weapon*. In an otherwise unlikely phrase (except for its allusions to hard-working discipline and the shift towards more modern communication methods on the left after 1959) it stressed the importance of developing businesslike methods of conducting meetings'.[77]

Organization had a definite symbolic aspect. Sound democratic principles', it was alleged, were involved in the preparation of an agenda for a Labour meeting. Links between organization and politics were pervasive. The titles of local party newspapers were voted on and expressed Labour thinking. Lowestoft CLP's paper, *Contact*, was named on the basis that we cannot live in isolation and call it living .there must be association to form a society.' The bureaucracy of meetings was, arguably, also linked to Labour's image in the 1950s as the party of controls and regulation.[78]

'The high proportion of their time devoted to procedure' (nearly a third, a survey of Manchester calculated) made Labour meetings 'dreary' and 'dull' meetings in the eyes of many. [79] Political discussion was a luxury that concentrated on local concerns (predominantly housing in the 1950s) and often slipped into parochialism. Orpington CLP spent several years arguing over the fate of its youth football team jerseys. One member in Camberwell recalled how the Party 'could talk solid about paving stones for two hours', but political discussion was 'non-existent'. [80] Conversely, where 'political' resolutions were introduced, notably by Bevanite and other left-wing groups, these tended to centre on issues of foreign policy. The *Manchester Guardian* painted a typical picture of party meetings in 1954:

> interminable discussions on the football competition, the party social, the outing, the best way of getting the crockery back from the public hall. Most of the political resolutions come from the Trotskyites and are about Malaya, Indo-China, Korea or are just plain anti-American. Mention of the *New Statesman and Nation* brings screams of rage from the right and howls of derision from the left of the left.[81]

Calls for brightening up .meetings and making them more purposeful' were loud in the 1950s, yet beyond employing visual aids – like films – old habits persisted.[82]

Finance and geography

More modern techniques were more costly – beyond the shallow pockets of all but the national organization. Survival on the financial brink – symbolized in the persistence of aged labour-intensive routines, at a time when the politics was increasingly capital-intensive – constrained branch activity. So much more could be done in the way of propaganda if the funds were available' Bethnal Green's agent reported in 1962. Changes were introduced in 1957 to the Hastings Agreement, by which the trade unions and Co-operative Party sponsored parliamentary candidates, increasing allowances. Yet even such a traditional stronghold as Nelson and Colne in Lancashire was forced to raise its affiliation fees by 50 per cent in 1958, protesting that it had 'struggled along trying to maintain a post-war organization and expense schedule on less than pre-war income'.[83]

Buying cars, loudspeakers, tape or record players, not to mention premises, could take branches to the verge of insolvency. On election day 1955, 79 per cent of CLPs had fewer than half their quota of cars available. The Tories had an advantage here – with larger budgets and full-time agents in most constituencies.[84] Fund-raising methods tended to be irrational, ineffective', Reg Wallis, North West Labour regional organizer ventured. He believed Labour might take note of the example of churches: very often a single church, with a small congregation, is maintaining a full-time minister and is raising in excess of that of many CLPs .the Parson does it, why not the agent?' [85]

Operating margins were narrow even for larger parties; Birmingham Borough Party, with an income of £9,608, in 1955 was working on a surplus of £338. Premises (the purchase of which was popular in part as indemnification against financial instability) made voracious demands on funds. Chichester CLP, which bought and opened William Morris House in 1955, had a £3,500 mortgage, leaving an annual surplus of £30 and the party living hand to mouth'. Yet the party agent confidently predicted the purchase would soon yield profit.[86]

But ideas of profit and hire-purchase chafed with Labour's values. Profit was all very well for a business, but we're a political party,' one activist argued in 1956. Anyhow, Labour had managed quite well ... on a shoestring' for most of its life.[87] This poor ancestry as much as anti-capitalist frame of mind was evident in Labour's financial ethos. The custom of regular subs' collection evinced that for many members this (rather than larger, less regular instalments) was the only way of keeping up payments or a clean' party card. Equally, socialists had a puritan streak. This was as true nationally as locally. Labour's general election fund grew at every election between 1945 and 1966, yet CLPs – such as Dulwich, which in 1955 took an overdraft from the Co-op bank – were often forced into debt at election time.[88]

As anachronistic was the model by which constituencies affiliated to the national Party at a rate of 6d. per member. This system did not discriminate between Labour strongholds and more marginal seats with a more active, larger membership. Thus Barnsley (with a Labour majority of 24,000, but a membership of only 357) affiliated at £9 per year, where Chislehurst in Kent (with a small Tory majority, but a membership of over 5,000) paid £133. Wilson attended to this by adding a rate of £2 per thousand votes (if this was greater), to penalize indolence not dynamism.[89]

Relations between such different constituencies could be sensitive. Marginals often felt it was useless to appeal for volunteers to what one described as sluggardly parties', where an I'm allright Jack, I weigh my votes' attitude prevailed. In response, Ron Evans of Ebbw Vale CLP argued that to imagine that these seats descended like manna from heaven without raising a finger to win them over to our point of view' was wrong, and complained of the martyrs in marginal or safe Tory seats'.[90]

All told, both CPGB and Labour branches tended to live separate, iso-lated lives. For Labour this was a consequence of the dearth of activists even in strongholds and their preference, as the Wilson Report saw it, to bask in large majorities at the expense of winning more seats. During the 1955 election, such exchanges were limited compared with the Conservatives. Only one CLP (Southwark) had loaned canvassers to a neighbouring marginal (Dulwich) before the election. There was also evidence that far too little was done to ensure they were properly used, or, in some cases, even civilly received, in the marginal constituency.'[91]

By the peculiarities of democratic centralism, association between branches in the CPGB was viewed as turning democracy on its head.' [92] Authority in the CPGB was strictly vertical, a means for the leadership to segregate dissent. 1948's minor revolt, headed by Eric Heffer's Welwyn and Hertford branch, was isolated from others who shared their thinking, like the Upwards in South London.[93] Such discipline – while also causing dissension – was maintained in 1956. It was ruled that for Malcolm MacEwen (who was invited to Uxbridge Borough Aggregate as a critic of CPGB support for Soviet action in Hungary) to speak outside his own branch would be contrary to party practice and would conflict with the principle of democratic centralism.'[94]

British socialism's geography was complex. CLPs, dominated by Unions in the industrial heartlands, were apt to scorn, as Samuel has put it, the extremist resolutions emanating from such tranquil places as the Merton and Morden CLP.' CLPs with fewer prospects of electoral success did often have the time and inclination to devote to radical posturing.[95] Although this was not always so. The outstanding instances of local party radicalism in the 1950s were the refusal by Labour councils in Coventry and St Pancras in 1954 to carry out their civil defence responsibilities in protest against nuclear arms.[96]

Local peculiarity played a part. Only the presence of their old foe Herbert Morrison explains the resources – £582 for 578 votes – the CPGB poured into Lewisham South during the 1951 election. Equally, West Fife (Willie Gallacher's seat to 1950) was politically sophisti-cated by tradition as much as its social make-up, Thompson insisted. Even in the late 1950s,' he remembered, the miners' club saw political discussion raging as furiously as football debate in another district.'[97]

Critical variables in this geography were electoral marginality and the local presence of labour culture. The Royal Arsenal Co-Operative Society, for instance, affiliated to all CLPs in its trading area. It was no coincidence that Woolwich West was the largest CLP, with a membership around 10,000. Faversham in North Kent, also profited from the strong local Co-op. That it was also the most marginal seat throughout the 1950s (held by Labour in 1955 by 59 votes) contributed to it being the best organised constituency in Britain.' It also sustained a vibrant Labour culture. At its acme in the early 1960s, the party maintained 8 Labour Halls and its Tote (with 150 local collectors), generated up to £25,000. Its annual fête was a notable event, to which *Reynolds News* dedicated a page of photos. In 1957 over 16,000 people attended.[98]

Social and associational life

These Social' components of the socialist community were important. Dances, jumble sales, gift days, rallies and May Day made the movement', quite as weighty as the cause'. Lottery or football tote competitions were vital to most Labour branches – often *the* main source of income. In the first half of 1955 North Paddington collected £201 in members' subs and £241 from such competitions.[99] Accordingly, much consideration was put into these schemes. Football results were taken from *Reynolds News* (to avoid the advertising of any capitalist newspaper in our weekly competitions', Bethnal Green explained) and weekly bulletins issued.[100] This was the most regular form of contact between the party and the majority of its members.

There were concerns at this. Gambling, even expediently, offended socialism's puritan strain. The *Manchester Guardian*'s labour correspondent reported that many Labour members felt there was a contradiction between football pools and a party that owes so much to Nonconformity.' Darlington's strong Quaker and Methodist traditions meant such schemes were unsuccessful, although in North Norfolk such schemes were organized despite the Methodism of the local agent and MP.[101] A tone of moral disdain, yet resignation, was redolent in Eastleigh CLP's justification of its decision to venture into the bingo craze'. Nobody could claim that bingo is an intellectual pastime, but then neither is watching *Coronation Street*', it argued. But as large numbers of people like both' and Eastleigh believed it was the business of a political party to find out what people like and to get with it," it felt it had done the right thing in boarding the bingo bandwagon.' [102]

Gambling was considered deleterious to the quality and quantity of political content within party life. That constituencies depended for financial stability on the success of football and other competitions', interfered with political work. Sara Barker (National Agent from 1962) preferred social activities which (casting a nod to Morris and the Clarion Club) demanded an individual creative and imaginative effort' and raise[d] lively members as well as money.' 'A largely lottery membership' one activist felt would not attract the kind of members … likely to become enthusiastic workers for socialism'. Some CLPs negotiated this by introducing politics into the weekly bulletin. But to judge from the ink spilt dissecting the 1958 Small Lotteries and Gaming Act, it was this more than political vicissitudes that threatened the well-being of branches.[103]

In response to an earlier clampdown on small lotteries in 1954, the National Union of Labour Organisers and Election Agents had founded Clarion Services Ltd to put the party's football pools on a legal basis. Leslie Hilliard, its director, rejected the charge that this was helping to found the Labour Party on the gambling instincts of the British Public', arguing that it was efficiently coordinating the efforts previously made by small parties, freeing up time for agents and generating revenue for CLPs. Profits were returned to the CLPs, and by 1954, 301 local parties had joined up.[104] A similar scheme from 1960 to secure CLP finances via a national Tote system was Robert Maxwell's National Fund Raising Foundation. While it was popular locally, the NEC and Transport House, prudent as ever, were reluctant to give official backing.[105]

Ostensibly, the social life of parties appeared to have little political content. The Social Secretary of the CLP brought to life by the *Manchester Guardian* in 1954 was the financial backbone of the party and keeps us solvent with football and racing sweepstakes .nobody can recall his ever mentioning politics, but nevertheless we are all grateful for his efforts.' In other ways social activities were more in keeping with socialist politics. For example, the surplus made by Faversham's tote enabled donations to the Spanish Democrats Defence Fund and South African Defence and Aid Fund.[106]

The social aspect of the socialist community also helped maintain organization when fortunes in the political provinces ebbed. In Orpington in the later 1950s it was as social clubs that wards avoided extinction. Labour clubs were places to meet and associate with the like-minded. In Glossop scant distinction was drawn between Club and

Party membership. Subs were paid at the club, obviating the need for a doorstep dues collection. A town-centre terrace, with a bar, domino tables and a dart board in the back parlour and upstairs for meetings, the club was overwhelmingly social in its interests.' [107] Lessing remembers London CPGB weekend marches as rather 'like picnics, family occasions' with 'people ringing each other up to meet, or go to a pub before or after'. In a sense they were a 'continuation of Church picnics', though also in the Cold War years, 'affirmations of togetherness.' 'For many people,' Lessing deduces, 'demos''were their social life.'[108]

The extension to Bradford Labour Club in Manchester was to accommodate demand for popular Sunday lunchtime concerts. *Labour's Northern Voice*, reporting its inauguration by Will Griffiths (Manchester Exchange MP) in October 1958, noted the presence of Labour pioneers, the club's (rather biblical) rise from origins as a stable, and its floor 'constructed from maple', which was 'excellent for dancing'. An earlier survey of Manchester indicated 'many of the ward parties activities are social''rather than political' and concluded that between elections, members attended meetings 'rather as they would go to a club; to meet their friends and discuss the business of running a club.' If this was the case, the party ought to try and improve the whist drives, the dances, the children's parties' to at least 'make it a good club'. There was unease that social activities might attenuate political organization – minus a Labour club, Buxton CLP, was better organized and had thrice the membership of its neighbour, Glossop.[109]

A Party premises was advantageous socially, especially for youth sections, whose social capacity was vital to their appeal and few other options within financial reach. When the Young Socialists (YS) were (re)born in 1960, they were anxious to manage their own rooms, if party elders would allow. In Darlington, the YS restored a derelict house, owned but neglected by the party for 25 years. A reading-discussion room, jazz basement and coffee bar replaced dilapidation. In four Manchester constituencies, by contrast, the YS had no control over its own rooms.[110]

Generational differences accounted for friction here. Coffee and jazz pointed to the 1960s and were more consonant with the brief flowering of the counter-cultural left clubs. Senior members could take a dim view of this or often adopted a 'condescending' attitude towards younger members. According to Paul Rose, a Labour activist close to the New Left and secretary of the Manchester Left Club, patronizing enquiries – 'Are you enjoying yourselves?' – were unwelcome but commonplace.[111] *Labour Organiser* advised shortly after the YS was reformed in 1960, that there was an 'appropriate stage to interrupt their fun and games [to] tell them about the Labour Party and the real objects of the club.' Another correspondent told how members of 'advanced middle age' had 'an unfortunate habit of prefacing their speeches with 'for forty years now I've been a member of this party', a statement which renders the younger members speechless with rage.'[112]

Aging presented real problems. Quair compared a 1930's CLP, 'small but bold and challenging', with its 1950's descendant, six times larger in membership, but with 'no posters on the hoardings' and 'seldom any public meetings.' Bethnal Green's report for the first half of 1959 in Bethnal Green explained, ''younger''element do not really come forward in the active work entailed, and therefore the 'older''members who do this work get discouraged.' 'Resentment' at the seeming irreverence of youth towards the memories and relevance of past struggles, compounded the contrary state of 'nervous anxiety' that officials had about a lively YS.[113]

The YS could run, at times gauchely, on rails to the left of the mainline, but for the most part there was a narrow cultural gulf. Youth sections and their social activities were in the main bridges to the parent party. Peter Pike, the left-wing leader of Morden YS, for instance, left to become Party agent and later MP for Burnley.[114] The Young Communist League's (YCL) sports and cultural activities were judged by their volume of recruits and ability to bring young people closer to and into the YCL'.[115]

The YS still undertook traditional socialist youth activities, familiar to its League of Youth predecessor; speakers' contests, camps and rambles – the Aldermaston marches were not such a novel departure. As with its parent the emphasis in leisure and music was very much 'active'. The YS bemoaned 'watchers rather than players of games' and 'inarticulate audiences'. Even the modernity of coffee bars was of orthodox intent: that 'young socialists have a centre where they can meet like-minded people' where 'numerous contacts are made with those not yet interested in politics.'[116]

Socialist rhetoric appealed in terms of companionship with the like-minded. The Labour League of Youth offered 'good fun with good companions.'[117] This sense of association was most acute in the CPGB. For Communists, a 1955 guide to branch organization explained, 'the essence of Branch life is that action, discussion, study are carried out collectively members feel that they are not living and working in isolation, that they help one another with their problems whether political or individual.'[118]

The dusty realms of branch life disclose not coherent ideologies, but informal ways of thinking, moral imperatives and established mores of political activity. Something of the diversity of political activity is scrutinized – how the associational often prevailed over the more explicitly political'; how àpathy', while real enough in the 1950s, was also a consequence of activists' imagination; how organization could shield socialists from as much as connect them to their audience. In this broader context, politics appears a rather discrete activity. It was often performed on an improvised, *ad hoc* basis, partly by dint of meagre resources and interest, partly by force of the conceptions that informed it. And these were generic qualities of varieties of socialism, shared by right' and left', by Communist and Labour. Aspects like apathy were generic qualities of popular politics *per se* – in other periods and for other parties like the Conservatives.

The anatomy of branch life (like socialism) was a mesh of influences – ancient and modern, moral and political. This was not an unchanging world, although today it appears a world away – almost a lost world' to judge from the sense of loss apparent in an emerging corpus lamenting new' Labour values through celebration of the old'. [119] But it exhibited distinctly conservative qualities – a reluctance to countenance change that, while often presented as concern about the unsocialist' principles of more modern techniques, was often simply organizational entrenchment and cultural intransigence. Socialism itself was something of a fixed, unchanging vision, to be realized in set ways and by established methods. Branches operated within strict financial limits and perceived the erosion of their role in newer techniques, but many were also content to carry on in time-honoured fashion. Neither the CPGB nor Labour was much altered by their mid-1950s organizational assessments.

And yet the need for renovation exposed by the Wilson Report was clear. The sort of efficiency Herbert Morrison tried to instil in Labour's organization in the inter-war London Labour Party was found to be sparse, if not mythic. This chapter argues that the contradiction in Labour's status as a mass party, yet one whose local organization was palpably decrepit, was to be explained less by a centralized power structure or by trade union influence, than by the prevailing party culture.

After all, its strong sense of tradition and passion for orthodoxy and togetherness meant that in left culture amongst the strongest terms of abuse was 'revisionist'.

The Wilson Report was confronted by financial, political and cultural barriers. It was itself a product of this culture, arguing for a better organized reliance on voluntary workers and that 'even if sufficient money were available, we are convinced that an attempt to build up a streamlined professional machine would be offensive alike to our traditions and our principles.' Despite the indictment on Labour's condition passed by Wilson, Morgan Phillips, General Secretary since 1944 and resistant to the emerging techniques of the later 1950s (especially opinion polling), remained *in situ* at Transport House and was only succeeded on his death in 1962 – and then by his deputy, Len Williams. Reformers were frustrated. Crosland told Gaitskell in 1960 that Labour's flawed efforts to update its organization made 'a sad contrast with the systematic efforts of Butler – Woolton – Maxwell-Fyfe after 1945.'[120] In 1965 a 'Plan for an Efficient Party', endorsed by *Tribune*, the *New Statesman*, *Socialist Commentary* and *Plebs*, attested to the endurance of old problems – 'Labour lost ten to fifteen seats through sheer inefficiency' at the 1964 election it held. Criticizing aspects of local organization, finance and Transport House, it argued the penny-farthing bicycle of the Wilson Report of 1955 'is barely holding together ten years later.'[121]

An apt conclusion can be found in a pamphlet entitled *The Failure and Salvation of the Labour Party* written by a Labour member in Manchester under the psuedonym O'Dee. The author exhorted Labour to end:

> the inefficiency, the anarchy, the unplanned 'which characterises the great majority of local Labour Parties 'and which 'more than any question of policy, of 'left-wing' or 'right-wing' or of the times we live in' is responsible for the present stagnation 'of the Party'   [122]

That the pamphlet was written in 1938 is suggestive of the timeless qualities of this culture – also evident in Samuel's reconstruction of the 'Lost World' of British Communism. What the Wilson Report diagnosed in 1955 as a Labour organization losing touch with modernity was a cultural sign. And therein lay the failure of Wilson's organizational prescription.

4
Socialism and Social Change I: Youth, Culture and America

Old Labour

The archaism of branch life was apparent elsewhere in 1950s socialist culture. Opponents portrayed Labour as an old, backward-looking party', and Morgan Phillips confessed in 1960, there was enough evidence to make such charges stick'. Labour's leadership to 1955 when Attlee (leader since 1935) stood down aged 72, were veterans and sickly – living proof that for the past few years the Party has been living unashamedly on its past.'[1] Crosland felt it a depressing fact, for a party of change, that the average Labour candidate in 1959 was several years older than his Conservative counterpart.' In 1960 Labour had 18 MPs aged under 40 (the Conservatives had four times more) and 80 aged over 60 (the Conservatives had 37).[2] Similarly, the Communist Party (CPGB) was staffed by a generation whose political experience was predominantly inter-war. Harry Pollitt was ill – his eyes (like his Soviet vision) rapidly failing. The new guard of George Matthews and John Gollan took the reins after 1956.[3]

Socialists' concern was that in a period when the pace of change has never been so rapid, the formative ideas and experience of the older generation are very different from those of today's young people.'[4] In the *Daily Worker* series, A Young Man Looks at Britain', Llew Gardner asserted what was good enough for our grandfathers is not necessarily good enough for us.' Veterans struggled against this. After all, Communists hoped not to wither away, but, as Edward Thompson adapted the words of Tom Mann in the final *New Reasoner*, to grow *more* dangerous as we grow more old.'[5]

Norman Mackenzie reported that to a University Labour Club he addressed, the names Jarrow, Guernica and Munich were no more than yellowing newspaper clips, a Picasso print, a scrap of newsreel film.' As early as 1953 Labour's research department warned of 'conflict between the younger and older members', as with a raised school leaving age, 'young people coming in to the party will have had a much better education than many already in the party' and exhibit a 'more forward-looking outlook'. [6]

A related anxiety was that Labour had 'adapted neither the premises nor the procedures of [the] party to the standards expected in the 1960s.' It was feared that for young people and new white-collar professionals, the appearance of the party' must be 'unattractive and even repellent.' And it was precisely these voices, of the young and salaried, that were 'only faintly heard in the councils of the party.' Phillips despaired, in a telling phrase, that Labour was ceasing to be 'a mirror of the nation at work.' Labour was then clearly less *The Voice of the People* than it liked to imagine.[7] Socialism itself – during what Labour described as an 'epoch of revolutionary change' – appeared dated, out of touch.[8]

The turn of the 1950s saw a general debate around Britain's 'stagnation', concern at its limited economic modernization, complacency and penchant for its imperial past or rural 'merrie England'. [9] Crosland, in his spell as secretary to the Co-operative Independent Commission (1955–8) was impressed by its conservatism and noted also how 'Labour suffers from the national vice of conservatism.' Wilson's trademark was to pillory the amateurism of gentry-led Conservatism, with a rhetoric of national progress through scientific, planned industrial modernization.[10]

Socialism was not anti-modern. Post-war reconstruction in cities such as Nottingham and Coventry was undertaken by Labour councils. The New Left, as its title implied, was consciously modernist – whether favouring the modernization of Britain's housing stock and road network or defending avant-garde art.[11] The new *Daily Worker* office, designed by Erno Goldfinger, or the TUC's new Congress House (into which it moved in 1956), were unmistakably modernist. Embellished by Jacob Epstein's sculpture, the latter thought itself 'one of London's most notable examples of modern architecture', and Labour was proud that it was 'uncompromisingly of the modern age.' [12]

None the less, traditionalism was difficult to elude in an encounter with socialism. The 1962 Festival of Labour, attended by 100,000 in Battersea Park, was ostensibly a determinedly modern affair, with jazz, films and a town planning exhibition. Congress House hosted a modern art exhibition that promised 'not a parade of the established, but a glimpse of the future' in works by Peter Blake, David Hockney and Henry Moore. Yet alongside was more traditional fare. The Young Socialists held a public speaking contest; a Colliery Band provided music; the National Labour Women's Advisory Committee organized an exhibition of embroidery, knitting and home-made preserves. There was even country dancing courtesy of the Woodcraft Folk – a simple life' group, long associated with the labour movement. Good thing too, as it was reported for many' festival-goers the paintings and sculptures on view were too advanced.'[13]

Nor was the New Left quite the original its title suggested. It was apt to cast itself more as socialism *redivivus*, recovered from Stalinism and Fabianism. The editorial of the first *New Left Review* opened and closed with citations from William Morris. Raphael Samuel, a founder of *Universities and Left Review*, has recalled the rupture with the old 'left' was much less decisive' than it had seemed at the time' and was more like born-again socialism'. The Partisan, the Soho conventicle which doubled as a coffee bar, linked the New Left with the new youth culture, but preferred to avoid the look of the newer espresso bars in favour of the character of older coffee-houses.' For design historian Reyner Banham, it typified the janus-faced quality of the New Left – the overt historicism' which it instilled in a purportedly new, modern project.[14]

CLPs were urged to keep an eye open for Party Archives', the hidden treasure in that pile of old agendas, posters for the last-but-one election .tucked away at the back of the secretary's cupboard.' The idea of a socialist museum was mooted in 1957. Peter Eaton (a friend of Michael Foot) proposed a National Museum of Socialism"in the South Kensington area near our other national museums.' He hoped it would feature Hardie's clothes, photos of the pioneers and the shoes of a Jarrow marcher. When the Society for the Study of Labour History was formed in 1960, Frank Horrabin, erstwhile editor of *Plebs*, the Labour College monthly, reflected: a cynic might remark that the present was an appropriate time to found a Society for the Study of Labour History, since the Labour Party seems determined to become a thing of the past.'[15]

Youth

This was all troublesome, for socialism was fond of invoking its own youthful, forward-looking properties. Youth frequently served as a metaphor for socialism. It was, as Attlee put it, the impatience of youth which gives thrust and impetus to the socialist movement.'[16] Socialism shared with young people an irreverence towards respectable convention and instinct to look forward with hope.' 'Youth,' the CPGB's 1956 congress averred, was naturally rebellious, adventurous, militant and revolutionary.'[17]

If, as Norman Mackenzie outlined, memory and hope [were] the two qualities which blend into a socialist conviction', then the 1950s left seemed prone to dwell on the past rather than look forward.[18] It stood accused, by friend and foe, of relinquishing its youthful élan. Labour was too occupied with the stubborn perplexities' of office. After the Attlee governments, it seemed apparent to many in the party' (Sinclair reported in 1954) that the original emotional drive of the Labour Party is to some extent exhausted.'[19] Indicatively, Labour had no national youth organization between 1955 and 1960 – the period in which the teenager and a distinctive youth culture came of age.[20]

The healthy iconoclasm' of younger socialists who would not be polite and respectful, but will pass resolutions of no confidence in everybody on the platform .and inform us how we can have the socialist revolution in 24 hours', as Richard Marsh told the 1959 Labour conference, was less welcome where it challenged party leaders. When a national structure was rebuilt in 1960 in the form of the Young Socialists (YS), it soon fractured. At the first YS conference (1961), Roger Protz, the editor of its journal *New Advance*, resigned, protesting: the NEC is the editor of *New Advance*, not me .they have produced a journal *for* YS, not *of* YS.' Radicalism was the least of Labour's problems with regard to its youth organization. The predecessor to the YS, the Labour League of Youth (LLOY), had been dissolved into constituency youth sections in 1955, less because of its insubordination than a rapidly depleting membership. By 1953 one-third of LLOY branches had already shut down.[21] The Young Communist League (YCL) was (perversely, given its politics) notoriously pliant.[22]

By contrast, the Young Conservatives (YC) flourished in the 1950s. It was a more social organization – appearing to socialist eyes little more than a marriage bureau, messenger service and job promotion agency'. Holroyd-Doveton's account of Young Conservatism admits as much, attesting to the vibrancy of its political and social life, if also a 50 per cent fall in membership between 1950 and 1959. This points to a wider decline in party political association (as suffered by the left). Nevertheless, the YCs still claimed to be the largest political association of young people in the free world", with a membership in 1959 approaching 150,000.[23]

With greater resources and a less prescriptive code, the YCs were less prone to the division of political and social spheres. One woman, shunned by the YS, reported to Young Fabian Ray Gosling in 1961, that she would have to join the Young Conservatives if she was to continue her sailing without being victimised.' The YC's success, so Gosling saw it, was that it was run by the young people for the young people' and was in contact with the idiom of the 1960s'. Twickenham YS and the YCL admitted the YC benefited from being seen to enjoy themselves.[24]

Young Socialists, where they had rooms in party premises, often had little control over them. The YS Model Branch Programme', featuring lectures on politics, a hike, a dance and classical music, modern jazz and coffee evenings, also drew Gosling's ire. In trying to appeal to everybody, it failed to cater for anybody, Leicester City Youth Venture's secretary felt. He suggested that in youth organization, there was a need for the professional and specialist, rather than the general, all-embracing and amateur' to which socialists inclined.[25]

The left's difficulties in recruiting and relating to young people were widely recognized. Dennis Potter told *The Times* in 1959 that Labour was a timid, excessively cautious association for the middle-aged'. A Labour Youth pamphlet for the 1959 election acknowledged as much. The party chairman, it confessed, was often the dullest man in the district' whose dullness stems from old age', and it ventured there were not enough young people in politics.' A 1959 *Manchester Guardian* series anticipated Labour's distance from the younger generation might prove electorally deleterious. And so it seemed when a post-election Gallup survey revealed that Labour's heaviest loss of support was from the under-30 voters. In 1955 Labour's advantage over the Conservatives amongst such voters had been 9 per cent, in 1959 just 1 per cent.[26]

The CPGB shared Labour's concerns. Like the rest of the Labour movement' its Political Committee heard in May 1959, we make little effort to appeal to and attract young people.' The attitude that youth questions are the concern of the YCL and not of the Party is widespread in our ranks', it noted. Even on peace, the issue around which young people have been active', the Party and Youth' report was disheartened that students and other professional and middle-class youth have tended to dominate.'[27]

More often it was the apathy and disinterest of youth that furrowed socialist brows. Thus, the emblematic teenage hero of *Absolute Beginners*' was constructed by Labour-sympathizing author Colin

MacInnes as entirely non-political', the type who instinctively con-
tracts out of the whole Labour–Tory struggle.' The Fabian General
Secretary found a generation of undergraduates in 1959 not angry',
but sceptical, detached and busy with their own pursuits.' If anything,
Bill Rodgers thought their eventual political destination may be right
of centre'. Mark Abrams uncovered among young people .a complex
of barely conscious Conservative sympathies' and found that most
know very little about the Labour Party's programme' in his 1960
survey for *Socialist Commentary*. All told, then, socialists' difficulties
were not entirely of their own making. It was more, as a 1954 analysis
of the Hammersmith Labour Party concluded, that the hesitancy of
the [party] machine to recruit young people [was] equalled by the hesitancy of the young people to be recruited.'[28]

The left did contribute to its own difficulties. Efforts like Coventry's
annual Welcome to Citizenship' ceremony, to engage the year's new
voters, had limited effect, Tiratsoo argues, because elsewhere (in
council policy and informally) Labour maintained a rather sniffy attitude. Teddy boys and girls were viewed as enjoying the rights of citizenship without taking any of the responsibilities or exhibiting the
civic spirit upon which progress towards socialism and Labour's reconstruction of Coventry depended. Labour, in short, was not a party that
was much interested in youth, unless of a very wholesome and sani-
tised variety.' Richard Crossman, MP for Coventry East, put Labour's
disappointing 1955 showing down to a loss of support among young
voters.[29]

In response to perceptions of the party's weaknesses Labour's NEC
appointed a working party in April 1959 to look at its youth organization. After election defeat, Morgan Phillips felt, recruitment of young
people must now become the main organizational task of the party.'[30]
He admitted that rather than Ask Your Dad', the phrase he coined
during the late 1940s, that today dad [is] often regarded as square' and
should now consult junior.' The YS, it was hoped, would give a
younger appearance to our annual conference.' Yet the YS was at best a
partial acknowledgement of Labour's shortcomings. Like its fore-
runners, the YS had neither representation on the NEC, at Party conference, at Transport House, nor the right to produce its own
publications.[31]

April 1959 also saw the creation of a Labour Party Youth
Commission. Its remit was the problems of young people and the contribution which the government and local authorities and other public
or voluntary agencies can make to their solution.'[32] Its chair was

Gerald Gardiner QC – member of the Society of Labour Lawyers and Lord Chancellor in the Wilson governments. Other members included Jimmy Hill of the Professional Football Players Union; jazz trumpeter Humphrey Lyttelton; Elizabeth Pakenham, a close friend of Gaitskell; Bea Serota, LCC councillor for Brixton; film and TV writer and ex-Communist Ted Willis; and actress Sylvia Syms, star of *Expresso Bongo* and Willis's kitchen-sink drama, *Woman in a Dressing Gown*.[33]

Their report was published two days after the election date for the 1959 election was announced. *The Younger Generation*'s principal proposals were to raise the school leaving age, abolish the means test on students' parents, lower the voting age to 18 and institute a day-release scheme for further education and an adventure scholarship for young people who did not go to university.[34]

Excepting the last, this was little different from existing Labour pronouncements on education, *Learning to Live*, or cultural provision, *Leisure for Living*. Gosling detected an 'affinity' between the Commission report and the 1960 report of the government Albemarle Committee on the Youth Service. Both called for more money for the existing Youth Service' and assumed the jazzing up' of the existing service would attract the required number of late teens.' Gosling considered the juke box c/o the Ministry of Education is no answer' and that it was 'a pity that the Labour Party's thinking was only a few months in advance of the government's.'[35]

Similar concerns were raised by young Labour members asking why the report was not formally endorsed by the party. The party stressed the report was 'not an official statement of the Labour Party.' The report's reception from the leadership was lukewarm. Its coincidence with the election meant it was only 'discussed briefly' by the NEC. Gaitskell offered Gardiner only the tepid promise that 'a Labour government would examine your proposals sympathetically.' Despite the efforts of the Commission secretary, Peter Shore, it was not possible to lure an NEC member (except Phillips) to attend the report's press launch. This left MacInnes to conclude that the 'last-minute Plan for Youth"at the election .impressed nobody' and was perceived by most young people as 'a quite transparent afterthought'. [36]

Labour's remoteness from changes in young lifestyles was not the cause of its electoral debility. Teenagers did not have the vote and this was why the Youth Commission was eclipsed by the impending election. But how Labour described and understood these social changes was important, if only because, MacInnes pointed out, 'at the next election, these teenagers will vote.' The misfortune of Labour's utter failure to interest, let alone inspire the several million teenagers' was for MacInnes that they *are*, potentially Labour supporters much more than Tory ones.'[37]

Yet socialists were uncertain how to make good this potential. For Gosling, Labour was talking in a language that does not make contact with .the new conditions and the new code of behaviour and living of this younger generation.' When MacInnes read Labour propaganda addressed to youth' and thought of the teenagers I've met in coffee bars, jazz clubs, at the Palais, buying separates or Italian shoes or holidaying together on Lambrettas' he had the feeling of a total failure of communication.'[38]

Socialists were increasingly conscious that there was, as Paul Rose put it in *New Left Review*, no place for socialist squares'in the age of Humphrey Lyttelton, Aldermaston and Manchester United.' Phillips told Labour women to learn how to jive and rock'n'roll as well as they could do the Charleston or ballroom dance.[39] MacInnes suggested Labour leaders should .get to know young people   *outside* the range of the Partisan-Aldermaston type.' Others were wary that coffee bars and rock'n'roll must not be an end in themselves' and urged recruits should not just come from those imbibing coffee around the juke box, for fear that Labour's idealism, might become ground-down by pandering to self-interest.[40]

The New Left clubs that flourished between 1959 and 1961 – at their peak there were 33, from Tunbridge Wells to Tyneside – achieved that blend of social and political activities. They were places, as Mervyn Jones wrote in *Tribune*, to find Comrades among the Coffee Cups'. Enthusing over the Manchester Left Club and coffee house, newly opened in a warehouse basement, and how it had become home to CLPs, trade unions, the Fabian Society and Unity Theatre, *Socialist Commentary* wondered if the coffee house movement might be to socialists of the sixties .what the Left Book Club was to socialists of the thirties.' Like jazz, coffee was an unofficial component of a certain left style in the 1950s: its cosmopolitan, convivial and intellectual aroma was well-suited to the New Left, since, Lessing mordantly notes, talking is what one does most of in a new dawn.' [41]

The CPGB might have deemed this mere froth and scoffed at the atmosphere of the petty-bourgeois left', but the Left Clubs were perceived as cultural resources for socialism. The Partisan's founder had a vision of a café-based broad left culture which spanned from intellectuals to a transformed working class on the Parisian or Viennese model, with old proletarians sitting around talking theory and playing chess.'

And Martin Mitchell has recalled, alongside those who lingered over a single coffee or came to þlay chess all day', were patrons who would ġo downstairs into the cave – the alcoves – and sit with their typewriters on their knees and type their novels.'[42]

Despite Jones's distaste for the drugs he witnessed at the Partisan, the New Left was more favourably disposed towards youth cultures than most on the left. It imbued new music and dress with proto-socialist meaning – as gestures of dissent and alienation from capitalist mores. Samuel has reflected that for the New Left the young took the place of the absent – or sleeping – proletariat as a force for protest.' Its submission to Labour's Youth Commission, posited that the new ẏouth culture' was ñot merely an out-growth of individual problems of individual adolescents', but that it was ŝociety, not merely one's parents, which [was] being rejected.'[43]

The Commission agreed that Italian and Edwardian style clothes, skiffle and rock-and-roll, coffee bars patronized wholly by the young' were convincing signs that youth increasingly feels that it belongs in a community of its own.' It was ŝignificant', the Commission decided, that this self-awareness should coincide with decreased interest by young people in adult organisations', though it added that many political and social organizations, had ḿade surprisingly little effort to recruit the young'.[44]

Others on the left concurred. In an early anatomy of the teddy-boy, Peter Wilmott discussed how the welfare state had vitiated traditional socialist policies: talk of the evils of capitalism' held scant appeal to a generation brought up on state orange juice, cod liver oil, free school milk, social security and full employment'. But, through its paternalism and pedantic local councils, Labour was associated with this bureaucracy towards which young people were hostile. It was ñot so much that the younger worker has deserted politics', Wilmott concluded, às that he feels politics have deserted him', or that politics ño longer appears to deal with live questions'.[45]

Mervyn Jones also decided the charge of youthful disaffection was misplaced. It was not that ẏoung people don't care about politics', but that in 1958 they ďon't care about political organisation or .party controversy', he declared. More worryingly, Potter observed in *The Glittering Coffi* : to the young worker, the Labour Party is as remote and as puzzling as any other British institution.' More positively, Stuart Hall imagined socialist potential in youthful alienation. Instinctively, young working-class people are radical', he contended in *Universities and Left Review*; they hate the stuffiness of the class system, though they cannot give it a political name; they hate the frustrations of petty conservative officialdom, though they cannot spell bureaucracy.' [46]

Others were less impressed that youthful indifference only required a vocabulary to bear its latent radical political consciousness. MacInnes, for all his anxiety at the left's approach to young people, felt teenage 'irreverence towards respectable convention', existed 'merely as a state of mind, which wastes itself on frivolous 'revolts' 'and doesn't yet constitute a positive political attitude.' Edward Thompson similarly mocked the 'Angry Young Men'. They 'feel themselves to be rebels against 'the establishment'', but 'since they can see no social force capable of making headway against this .their 'revolt' 'consists in imagining themselves to be 'outside' 'this'. Thompson argued they were 'outside nothing but the humanist tradition.' [47]

Many socialists empathized with the anti-authority 'anger' of writers like John Osborne. Osborne's play, *Look Back in Anger*, was declared 'a more important political document than anything the Labour Party has said since 1951.' [48] *Tribune*, though shared Jimmy Porter's frustration at the absence of 'good, brave causes', but was anxious at these rebels without causes. It pointedly despaired of those who filled the void 'merely with an outlet .found in the new rock 'n roll music, the teddy-boy craze and idle violence' and linked this lifestyle and outlook to the outbreaks of racial violence in Notting Hill and Nottingham in the summer of 1958. [49]

Socialists were apt to dismiss the energy of youth culture as misplaced; its 'withdrawal into private worlds', 'dreamworlds', as an escape from reality; and its worst behaviour, 'anti-social'. Bednarik's 1955 study cast young workers as 'cynical, irresponsible, amoral, pleasure-seeking .submerged in the make-believe world of the cinema.' For Tosco Fyvel, *Tribune*'s literary editor, the 'teddy-boy' was 'the distorted reflection of a materialist society without purpose.' [50]

Much that socialists articulated about young people related to their wider concerns about social change. A primary objection to 'youth culture' regarded its emphasis on consumption. *The Younger Generation* noted, for the first time in British history, teenage likes and dislike are expressed through purchasing power.' It valued the teenage market at £500 million per annum. The most ostentatious display of this affluence, the teddy-boy, might be 'in the main working class', but were far from 'proletarians'- spending £25–30 for the complete outfit of clothes and 15s .for fancy haircuts.' Fyvel opined: 'everything about the 'teds' 'proclaims that they have plenty of money to spend on their pleasures and are single-mindedly determined to do so.' [51]

This triggered socialist reflexes about consumerism's deleterious influence. As the Commission saw it, the major message that the adult society transmits to youth is the necessity to consume.' Not only was personal consumption presented as in itself the most important goal of human endeavour, but as the outward and visible sign of personal success.' Vast resources of cash and persuasive talent are today mobilized to educate the young as *consumers*,' but, the Commission regretted, virtually nothing is done to awaken them to the tasks ... of a democratic society.' When Gosling declared for a club for the ordinary consumer' and to create a society by the young consumer for the young consumer', *New Left Review*'s Bernard Davies rebuked him for accepting the unflattering commercial image of young people and what they are capable of.'[52]

As MacInnes saw it, Labour needed to establish itself as the party that *likes* the present and the future, as most young people do', but it rarely managed this.[53] More often they joined the chorus dismissing rock'n'roll, campaigning against horror comics or deploring how the activities of the teenage lunatic fringe provide material for the moralist.' Even those well disposed towards the young, like Hall, thought in terms of the aimless frenzy of their leisure life.' [54] A characteristic flavour of such thinking can be tasted in a 1956 Labour youth pamphlet, *Take it From Here*:

> The familiar round of pin-tables and café, the hours spent reading comics and half listening to the radio .the hypnotic glamour of the American movies: these are not life, they are a feeble substitute for it. This doesn't mean that socialists don't have their fun, don't go to movies and dances .But they keep these things in proportion. They enjoy life at deeper levels and they enjoy it .more intensely because enjoyment' is not their main object.

Nobody,' it continued, outlining an idea of alienation, was more chronically frustrated than the self-centred seeker of enjoyment.' Labour's alternative was not an appeal to selfishness', but an invitation to service and friendship'. Those who accept it whole-heartedly' would find self-fulfilment in this service and friendship.' Len Williams, Labour's National Agent, underlined the point. Our aim must be to attract a far greater range of recruits from the ranks of youth' he argued in 1958, and to provide a properly balanced programme of activities which will create for them the happiness that comes with fellowship.' Here was the idea that socialism's spiritual values provided a means to real happiness and that Labour was more than a political machine', but also an attitude to life and a way of living.' [55]

Leisure and culture

Socialists had definite ideas about the appropriate uses of leisure and culture. Their thinking was rather akin to the nineteenth-century notion of tational recreation' – that leisure should be morally improving, but that invariably working-class pursuits were not. Like their nineteenth-century forebears, 1950s socialists held forth against mass entertainment, the commercial, vulgar and trivial, and newer contagions – television, consumerism and America. As far as matters of culture and leisure were concerned, Labour's Youth Commission urged that the young should be educated in how to distinguish between what is genuine and good and what is phoney and bad.'[56]

Literature dealing with sport commonly stressed its affinities to socialism – a 1959 youth leaflet was entitled *Teamwork's the Answer*. Interest in more individual' sports – tennis and golf – was regarded with unease, as was professionalization.[57] Professionals' conditions thanks to union action, have improved greatly in recent years', but they were still .exploited', Labour argued, by those whose primary interest in sport is commercial.' Sporting opportunity, it was noted, had a class dimension, where the playing fields of Eton' were a modern luxury as well as ancient history.' That Britain had only 61 public athletics tracks in 1956, compared with 800 in Sweden, was an unpleasant fact' for those who liked to think of Britain as a great sporting country.'

Socialists' objections to Britain's national passion' for sport were that it was an interest quickened by the extra thrill of gambling' and all-consuming to the extent that when there was an international football match on television, seeing it takes precedence over most other engagements (including, of course, voting in a local election).' Above all, socialists remonstrated that this was a passive rather than active engagement and that Britain was too much a nation of watchers rather than players of games.'[58] Hugh Jenkins, Arts Minister in the 1970s Wilson government, was troubled that millions' were content with the indirect excitement of gambling on dogs and pools', whereas only a minority' were satisfied by direct personal participation in a brass band, operatic or dramatic society, choir or sports club.' Pollitt too argued that socialism meant more recreation where the working class are not merely spectators, but join in to the full.'[59]

A related verdict was reached on skiffle – the music linking folk and blues to rock'n'roll in mid-1950s Britain. Socialists were pleased at its presence on .the hit parade', but concerned that the original conception of enthusiastic amateurs gathering together to amuse themselves with cheap and easily made instruments seems to be conforming to the modern trend of professional entertainers and their inarticulate audiences.'[60] The distinction between genuine and phoney socialists applied to popular music, was the difference between folk' and live' music and more commercial productions. Rock'n'roll was understood as the latter. Bruce Turner in the *Daily Worker*, regarded it as a depraved offshoot' of the authentic folk music treated by working people as a cultural form', produced by professional song-writers who think of culture only rarely.' The New Left held there was Something Rotten in Denmark Street', London's pop music publishing district. Rock'n'roll was hot something generated spontaneously' Alf Coram argued in *Music and Life*, the CPGB's music group journal, but sold ... by commercial interests in the same way .as toothpaste or canned goods.'[61]

Real popular music, to the socialist ear, was folk art'. As Labour's main cultural statement *Leisure for Living* put it – a spontaneous, non-commercial, popular art, springing from the people and expressing their emotions' It was also necessarily live. The Musicians Union urged Keep Music Live': don't tolerate records and recorded music in substitution for live music' and argued this led to unemployment for musicians and that there may eventually be insufficient musicians even to make records.' No bands anywhere,' it continued, make a living from making gramophone records alone.' Francis Newton (a.k.a. Eric Hobsbawm) argued similarly in 1959's *The Jazz Scene*. Yet with jukeboxes, radio, TV and 45 rpm discs replacing sheet music (and easily breakable' 78s), such thinking was decreasingly tenable.[62]

Opposition to mass entertainment – increased in the CPGB's case by the strong American connections' of much rock'n'roll – left many socialists supporting a folksong revival against the commercial advances of (what Newton called) a peculiarly unappealing Texan lad called Elvis Presley' or occasional Conservative rhetoric of ruling this country in the spirit of adventure and rock h' roll'. [63]

The revival of interest in traditional folk' was strongest, *Leisure for Living* found, away from cities the strongholds of commercial entertainment' at the Celtic fringe where non-standardised popular art' was rooted in local culture.[64] Communists Ewan MacColl and A. L. Lloyd were prominent revivalists, supporting composers like Vaughan

Williams in recovering traditional folk songs. In *The Shuttle and Cage*, published by the Workers Music Association in 1954, MacColl introduced worksongs that had rarely 'appeared in print before, for they were not made with an eye to quick sales – or to catch the song-pluggers ear, but to relieve the intolerable daily grind.'[65]

Rock'n'roll mystified socialists as much as they declaimed it. Asked to change the record at a teenagers party, fictional Labour MP Johnnie Byrne found himself looking 'desperately through the handful of discs, conscious that the labels meant nothing to him.' *Socialist Commentary* mused in 1956 'why *Rock Around the Clock* has given rise to the fuss it has is not easy to explain.' Comparing it to 'the teddy boy brouhaha', it wondered 'can nothing be done to produce creative outlets for the ... high spirits of the nation's youth?' In the *New Statesman* Hobsbawm was similarly unmoved by Bill Haley – 'why the fashion has grown up is anybody's guess'.[66]

Hobsbawm later suggested that 'young people who flocked to rock found in it, in a simplified and perhaps coarsened version, much, if not everything that had attracted their elders to jazz: rhythm, an immediately identifiable ..'sound,'' real (or faked) spontaneity .and a way of directly transferring human emotions into music.' In the 1950s Communists were more apt to question the constitution of pop fans. Reviewing a performance by Frankie Vaughan (more crooner than rocker), Alison Macleod confessed: 'I feel sorry for the young girls who shriek in a frenzy of frustration at these young men.' Rock'n'roll's appeal, another *Daily Worker* correspondent posited, was to those 'easily affected by elementary rhythmic effects.' *Commentary* too admitted the music was 'strongly rhythmic, and, to those who like that sort of thing, exciting.'[67]

In this separation of living and processed music, which broadly equated with what socialists saw as worthy or not, jazz was harder to categorize. The CPGB formally regarded it as 'decadent' – in its vernacular a euphemism for American. It was unacceptable enough to make Hobsbawm, in jazz critic persona, adopt a psuedonym (Francis Newton). According to Labour, jazz was 'closely related, in its nature and personnel, to the lucrative commerce of tin-pan-alley.'[68] Yet in other ways jazz was more compatible with socialist criteria. Where folk music' had been 'crushed out' by 'commercialisation' into 'a thing played by lifelong professionals and for the masses to listen to' Labour Young Chartists saw 'in jazz .a return to earth and the people.' *Leisure for Living*, recognizing the music's struggle against racial prejudice in America and how it was 'a perceptible influence in the works of

Stravinsky, Walton and other serious composers', conceded jazz was of great interest to many young socialists.'[69]

Indeed it was – the New Left's Paddy Whannel and Alan Lovell produced *Living Jazz* in 1961, a film about the Bruce Turner Band, interviewing their subject in *New Left Review*. Collets opened a jazz and blues shop on New Oxford Street in 1953. Monty Johnstone has recalled jazz was popular at YCL socials – clarinettist Sandy Brown entertained the 1956 YCL congress. Labour supporter Humphrey Lyttelton explained that the *Daily Worker* gave the impression' that jazz customers were solid dependable proletarian types ..whose coloured shirts and erratic dancing were simply an expression of revolt .against capitalist hell.' [70]

Not least in jazz's appeal was its legion of styles. Divisions between trad' and modern be-bop, or in the early 1950s, revivalist and mainstream, were analogous to divisions in socialism. The respective talents of Coleman Hawkins and Lester Young could evoke sectarian passions.[71] Sociologically, jazz was something of a cult of a minority', whose enthusiasts' were above the national average in education.' Jazz had its own language.[72] American Jazz fan Tony Crosland saw in the post-war revival of traditional and progressive jazz, as against the standardised large-band swing" evidence of successful popular revolts against commercial standardisation.'[73]

Socialists deplored what they saw as the gap between the most brilliant artists of our day and the mass of the working people'; that there were the se rious"arts enjoyed by an educated minority and ... mass culture concerned mainly with commercial entertainment.' Labour's Youth Commission saw this divide in almost every .aspect of our social life: Third and Light programmes; BBC versus ITA; quality"papers versus the popular"press.' *Leisure for Living* traced it to the disintegrated society .ours has been for the last two centuries.' This made it difficult for a child to grow into a whole man', yet it required a whole man to enjoy the art of Henry Matisse as well as the art of Stanley Matthews.' Before industrial capitalism it was supposed divisions between the aesthetic and athletic or elite and mass culture were absent. Labour, then, declared it would help bridge these gaps', but only as part of the more purposeful replanning of the economic and social structure of society.'[74]

Though if *Leisure for Living* is any guide it was clear on which side of the bridge Labour's sympathies stood. It looked forward to when more people' would consider the purchase of a picture as natural as the purchase of a chair' or of an oil painting of real merit for half the price of a television set.' It applauded BBC policy of 'giving the public not what it wants, but something a little better than it thinks it wants", which had enabled millions to enjoy music of a quality previously heard only in concert halls and opera-houses.' It approved the efforts of theatres such as London's Mermaid and Coventry's Belgrade in bringing drama to a largely apathetic public.' At its most high-minded *Leisure for Living* expressed concern at shortening British Museum opening hours and the threatened closure of the Covent Garden Opera House. Even the CPGB was minded to call a conference, whose opening speaker was Communist composer Alan Bush, on what it described as The Crisis in Opera.' [75]

Of a piece with such thinking was how Bevan believed that only the best was good enough for the workers and was determined to smash open the great houses, their libraries and wine cellars, to their assault.' His rallying speech to Labour's 1959 conference made clear his distaste for the pop culture and lifestyles of the so-called affluent society.' More the concern of *In Place of Fear* was that as a characteristic of competitive society .aesthetic values attend upon the caprice of the financially successful.' The Titian and the Renoir' Bevan argued were bought more for their prospective appreciation in capital value than for their intrinsic merit.' Wealthy collectors displayed them for a few choice friends, whose eyes glisten with avarice rather than with appreciation of the .craftsmanship contained in them.' It was insufficient for such treasures to sit immured in museums and art galleries, where they look reproachfully down on the long procession of sightseers, who can catch, in such a context, only a glimpse of their beauty.' Rather, Bevan imagined that with collective action, we shall enfranchise the artists, by giving them our public buildings to work upon; .our housing estates, our offices.our factories.' The state then might serve as a patron to the arts, restoring artists to their proper relationship with civic life.'[76]

Nor was this, as Campbell suggests, a highly convenient rationalisation' for Bevan's Bollinger-Bolshevik' lifestyle. It was more, as Hollis has noted, that in Nye's New Jerusalem' it was envisaged that everyone would display aristocratic tastes.' As Labour housing minister to 1947, it was the *type* as much as the *number* of houses that occupied Bevan. If we have to wait a little longer, that will be far better,' he argued, than doing ugly things now and regretting them for the rest of our lives.'[77]

Bevan's thinking was akin to what Bevin termed working people's poverty of de sire' – that their sights were set too low and needed raising by socialists. This could slip into hostility towards popular culture. In *Tribune* in 1952 socialist artist John Berger described the type of socialist who despaired of the pampered worker who cares for nothing but football pools and fish and chips' and felt such indifference to the finer things in life' kept artists starving in garrets and corrupting in advertising agencies.'[78]

Bevan was responsible for section 132 of the 1948 Local Government Act, allowing councils to levy a 6d. rate to provide municipal entertainments. As *Leisure for Living* saw it, this was evidence of Labour's enlightened policy' for the arts, which Tory governments had treated with doctrinaire niggardliness'; although it admitted the response of local authorities had been meagre'. Less than 3 per cent of the funds available under this provision had been raised and Labour ascribed this to the human nature of ratepayers being what it is.' [79]

Others were chary of state patronage. Priestley warned of central committee art' and insisted the state must leave the artist alone with his work after creating reasonable conditions for them.' Labour clearly beheld the improvement of the nation's cultural life via a generous approach by the state'. The tone of rational recreation and moral uplift was persistent. Labour considered it the duty of the state to provide something of the best in the arts as an example or inspiration to the whole of the country.'[80]

In this gaze, culture was not ordinary', as Raymond Williams proposed, but understood in a conventional sense of a body of elite and European arts, music and literature. Williams's *Culture and Society* traced how this meaning of culture was established from the mid-nineteenth century. A key assumption of rational recreation' was that passing down this package of arts, music and literature could make good the shortcomings of the people. Socialist thinking was of this tradition in the 1950s – discussing less the development of a common culture' as Williams urged and more how to improve the uses of leisure by acquainting Britons with the fortifying pleasures of high' culture. In breaking down its elitism, its qualities were none the less assumed to outclass the values of popular pastimes. No less than Labour, when the CPGB turned its eye to culture, it was to sing the praises of Mozart, Robert Burns or the queues in the Soviet Union for pianos.[81]

Priestley's hope for post-war cultural life was that people freed from .desperate worries .free too from the pressure exerted upon them by big commercial enterprises to entangle them in trivialities (an aspect of capitalism .frequently overlooked) and people living in reasonably civilised conditions' would have far more mental energy to spare than they have had in the past.' Their minds,' he anticipated, will look for things on which to fasten and among the arts they will find some of the most exciting of those things.'[82]

Socialists claimed true happiness' came not .from material prosperity', but from leisure richly filled with the good things of civilisation.' Yet generally, they were also apt to think of culture' in the traditional sense of high' culture or in a secondary, subordinate sense, rather (as Hugh Jenkins put it) as though TV, cinema and the theatre were a sort of fluff on the surface of existence'. [83]

And this was all the more limiting an outlook in the affluent 1950s, where as *Leisure for Living* recognized, with full employment and increased automation, the focus for socialists should not be on jobs for all, but on leisure for all.' As Dennis Potter argued, questions of leisure were integral to those of work, yet too often our politicians refuse to make this simple equation.' The difficulty in making this equation related to non-conformist impulses in socialist culture. It makes for an interesting analogy with the ways socialism conceived of culture' as separate and secondary to work, to note the lingering puritanism evident in Crosland's habit of total seperation of work and play.' Crosland's revision of socialism re-emphasized leisure and culture at the expense of Fabianism and Puritanism, but while *The Future of Socialism* was being written, the puritan's self-discipline predominated in his life: he preferred to work at home and until he finished the task he set himself, playtime could not begin.'[84]

For Raymond Williams the integration of work and life and the inclusion of the activities we call cultural in the ordinary' were the basic terms of an alternative form of society.' If socialism,' *The Long Revolution* argued, accepts the distinction of work"from life," which has then to be written off as leisure"and personal interests," if it sees politics as government".and art as grace after meals', then it was nothing more than a late form of capitalist politics.' Williams reasoned it was the gravest error of socialism .to limit itself, so often, to the terms of its opponents: to propose a political and economic order, rather than a human order.'[85]

The New Left took up such thinking. A cultural approach would enable socialism to engage the changes involved in affluence – consumerism, the mass media and youth culture – which confounded the left's customary analysis and to transcend social democracy and Communism. A cultural language would consider the diversity of life and social activities rather than just work and wages. Setting out the New Left's stall in *Out of Apathy*, Norman Birnbaum declared it had enlarged the usual scope of political discussion to consider (with Richard Hoggart and Raymond Williams) the possibility of a common culture in industrial Britain.' The problem of the quality of daily life in industrial society ought to be at the centre of socialist thought' Birnbaum averred, and not, where it is usually found, at the periphery.'[86]

The CPGB was an easy target for Williams's critique. It assigned culture to the superstructure' of society, determined by the economic base'. The socialist realist', Communist novelist, Jack Lindsay held, ought to be directly *linking his artform with the productive process.*' The role of Communist cultural workers' as they were designated, was to pay homage to Soviet achievements and rescue indigenous cultural heritage from American invasion.[87] The Communist writer's lot, in Lessing's account of Lawrence and Wishart, was not a happy one – their vocation and individualism questioned.[88]

Communist priorities were disclosed in a 1956 document by James Klugmann, head of Party Education, on the *Daily Worker*'s contents. This stated the paper: must deal with questions of 1.Wages, 2.Jobs, 3.Automation, 4.Rent and Housing, 5.Arms and Peace, 6.The Colonial Liberation movement, 7.A selection of Parliamentary news, 8.Essential Foreign Affairs, 9.Developments inside the Socialist World.' Only then should it attend to social events of a relatively non-political character, cultural developments – the cinema, radio, television and theatre – and give the best possible summary of the sports news.'[89]

Others were unhappy at this relegation of leisure and culture. At the 1954 CPGB conference a Birmingham delegate called for cultural motions to be taken more seriously. With reference to English football's humiliation at the feet of Hungary in 1953, she complained of how when the Hungarians came to play football here, some of the leading Party members suddenly started going to football matches.'[90]

Such divisions were evident across the left. Crosland's *The Future of Socialism* made a case against the earnest, Fabian tradition that put blue books before culture' in favour of an emphasis on private life .on culture, beauty, leisure and even frivolity.' Yet in Crosland's cultural turn' economic achievement necessarily preceded this concentration on social' policies. [91]

Even in the New Left, for which culture' was the keyword to unlocking the impasse of socialism, the same fissures were present. Hall contends that its cultural activities which ranged from the Royal Court to Whitechapel Gallery, were considered as important as the *more* political"ones.' But Mervyn Jones has suggested the New Left didn't succeed in escaping from .a cultural split.' There was little meeting of minds between the artists and the .sociologists and economists.' Jones felt his novels went unread and that New Left conversation was of politics more than film, theatre or novels. This denoted that it had not really overcome a certain attitude which regards the arts as peripheral rather than central to politics, or – something much more important than being central to politics – central to life.'[92]

The *Review* admitted as much when in a 1960 review of pop music it wondered is it true that when you scratch a New Leftist you reveal an old puritan?' Lessing's *The Golden Notebook* – a milestone in British Feminism' and penned by a former *New Left Review* editor – drew no comment in the 1962 *Review*. Thompson bemoaned how in 1962 the un-economic and socio-cultural sidings of the New Left ..were abruptly closed down'. Yet before 1962 (when Perry Anderson became *New Left Review* editor), Samuel admits the New Left was little concerned with individual rights – censorship, hanging, divorce law – consigning them to some apolitical limbo'. [93] Disregard for personal issues was characteristic of the socialist condition.

Leisure and culture were rarely foremost in socialism's thoughts. Historians ambling along *The British Road to Socialism* in search of culture', might happen upon a couple of paragraphs (telling little most Tories would dissent from). Those requiring detail would have to scour the back roads or head off-road. And such exploration was diversionary if, as Williams saw it, socialism in the 1950s mostly thought that when you have said politics and economics you have said society; the rest is personal and incidental.'[94]

Williams drew on the moral, humanist critique of industrialism and utilitarianism (Burke, Cobbett, Ruskin) and from the approach of Leavis and Arnold (while opposing their elitism). Aware that the problem of capitalism was no longer its economic failure (as in the 1930s), Williams provided an explanation for the left's difficulty in adapting to social change in post-war Britain. In challenging the ranking of high' and popular' culture, the left's reflex unease at mass entertainments, its tendency to sideline and reduce culture to its material base' or political use-value – Williams rendered what for Perry Anderson amounted to the most original body of thought to have been produced on the left since the war.'[95]

But Williams's account was not typical. More characteristic of the anxieties that haunted the left was the wrath poured down from the pages of the *New Statesman* by Priestley on admass' – mass culture, advertising and consumerism. Richard Hoggart's *The Uses of Literacy* was just as critical. Its full flavour can be tasted in the author's sojourn amongst the juke box boys'. Their café and milk-bars, he beheld to indicate .in the nastiness of their modernistic knick-knacks, their glaring showiness, an aesthetic breakdown so complete that, in comparison with them, the layout of the living-rooms in some of the poor homes from which the customers come seems to speak of a tradition as balanced and civilised as an eighteenth-century town house.' Nor was he enamoured of the denizens themselves – young men with an American slouch', who put copper after copper into the mechanical record player' to select tunes doctored for presentation so that they have the kind of beat which is currently popular' and blare out so that the noise would be sufficient to fill a good-sized ballroom.' Their clothes, their hair-styles, their facial expressions' indicated that they were living to a large extent in a myth-world compounded of a few simple elements which they take to be those of American life.' Hoggart concluded with the double-edged comment that compared even with the pub around the corner' this was a world of a peculiarly thin and pallid form of dissipation, a sort of spiritual dry-rot amid the odour of boiled milk.'[96]

The gist of *The Uses of Literacy* is disclosed by its working title, *The Abuses of Literacy*. Hoggart's approach owed much to the Arnold–Leavis cultural tradition. For Mulhern, Hoggart's vision was Labour Leavisism' and in him the post-war British Labour movement found its own Matthew Arnold.' Arnold was esteemed on the 1950s left. Crosland was amongst his followers. Francis Hope, writing in 1966, noted how many on the left expressed their admiration for Matthew Arnold and pointed out that a great many of his points are still applicable today.'[97]

Hoggart, a Labour member and WEA tutor, saw in socialists, co-operators and WEA tutors, something of Arnold's earnest minority'. Hoggart was wary of this type and of those with a nostalgia for those best of all'kinds of art, rural folk art or genuinely popular urban art, and a special enthusiasm for such scraps of them as .he can detect today.' But his own vision, with its sense of lost innocence' and nostalgia' for traditional working-class life was widely shared on the left.[98] Sociologist Hannah Gavron related the left's deification of Hoggartsville', to a tendency to sentimentalise working-class life' and a dislike of middle-class mores. The Lowry cover of *The Uses of Literacy's* was familiar by the turn of the decade, thrice reprinted before Penguin issued *Culture and Society*.[99]

It was to Hoggart that Labour turned for ammunition in its assault on 'mass' society and culture. Williams argued 'masses was a new word for mob' and agreed the 'gullibility, fickleness, herd-prejudice, lowness of taste and habit' of any mass, together with the forces of 'mass suggestion' threatened cultural standards. But he rejected the category – arguing in *Culture and Society* that 'there are in fact no masses; there are only ways of seeing people as masses'.[100] Labour was more assured of the uses of 'mass'. *Leisure for Living* cited *The Uses of Literacy*, arguing that in modern Britain 'the older, the more narrow but also more genuine class culture is being eroded in favour of the mass opinion, the mass recreational product and the generalised emotional response.' ' Mass entertainments,' it continued, were 'what D. H. Lawrence described as 'anti-life''.'full of a corrupt brightness, of improper appeals and moral evasions' and had 'a view of the world in which progress is conceived as a seeking of material possessions, equality as a moral levelling and freedom as the ground for endless irresponsible pleasure.' Mass productions offered 'nothing which can really grip the brain or heart', but assisted the 'drying-up of the more positive, the fuller, the more co-operative kinds of enjoyment.'[101]

While it was recognized that affluence brought issues of leisure to the fore, 'culture' remained low in socialists' priorities. The New Left and revisionist's efforts to break free from a framework where culture was of a secondary order had limited effect upon mainstream socialist thinking. What appealed to socialists in Hoggart was his critique of modern, commercial culture. This coalesced more with their fears of the break-up of traditional working-class, industrial communities than a lament at the demise of a specific working-class 'culture', of which they were often critical. 'Culture' to most socialists meant 'high' culture and it was here, not in 'popular' culture that their own preferences lay.

What united the high-minded, those who looked to 'real', folk culture and those taken with Williams's call for a 'common culture', was hostility towards the encroaching presence of commercial, 'mass' culture. Thwarting it and promoting more appropriate recreational activities seemed to most socialists to be a task most viably pursued through the agency of the state. Implicit (and often explicit) in this was a definite notion of cultural worth and rather circumspect, or Reithian, assessment of popular cultural expectations and choices. Yet the expansion in popular choice involved in affluence was eroding the authority and legitimacy of the state to administer in such matters and questioning traditional cultural hierarchies. Even the parts of the left that were less sceptical towards popular' activities (notably the more libertarian revisionsists) or uneasy with state influence (like Priestley), still hoped that by choice people would graduate up the cultural ladder as affluence permitted a contemplation of higher matters. Criticisms of new cultural activities and forms often doubled as criticisms of the popular tastes and preferences they seemed to reveal.

The New Left theoretically recognized that in these new cultural conditions, the struggle between what is good .and what is debased is not a struggle *against* the modern forms of communication, but a conflict *within* these media' (that is, to take an example from the next chapter, that there was the potential for worthwhile or shoddy television, but the medium itself was not intrinsically corrupting). But as Hewison highlights, it could not break free from older assumptions: the tendency still to couple good' and high culture' or, in a more puritan vein, to see new pop, mass culture as corrupting. In practice then modern forms of communication or expression were too often and easily criticized *en bloc* (as if they themselves were the enemy) rather than in a more differentiated way. So too were participants – young Britons were criticized in tandem with youth culture and televiewers were seen as a reflection of TV program quality.[102]

America

As socialists saw it, the USA was the provenance, the 'American way of life' the form, of an encroaching mass' culture. Many socialists perceived that American lifestyles, no less than American foreign policy, were gaining a hold over Britain. Britain then threatened to become a footless, acquisitive, shoddy and processed version of capitalist America.' Verdicts as to its pervasiveness varied, but its presence was universally detected. The growing ownership of cars, TVs, washing-machines, was termed by Gaitskell in 1955 a growing Americanization of outlook'. In 1959 Bevan scorned these affluent' parts of the population as thoroughly Americanised'. [103]

Anti-Americanism was shorthand for criticism of capitalism and the general tenor of post-war social change. 'Admass' was Priestley's neologism for the system and its shoddy cheapjack set of values', though it was not, he insisted, synonymous with American. The name had been coined in order to stop calling it American.' True,' he conceded, 'America is at the head of it .but the notion that this society only flourishes in America and is merely fleetingly reflected .elsewhere' was no longer acceptable.' [104]

'Most Americans (though not all; they have some fine rebels) have been *Admassians* for the last thirty years,' he asserted in 1955 – the English only since the war.' Since then, Britain had become one of the most progressive *Admass* colonies.' It was more easily enticed by mass communications, showmanship, ballyhoo', for where Americans had grown used to and developed a resistance to Admass, British minds were still wide open as well as being empty.' [105] The susceptibility of the mass-mind, a variant on socialist's mistrust of the people, was an essential component of Admass.

A thinly veiled contempt for America, concern about commercialized leisure and a nostalgic vision of traditional working-class values had been salient in Priestley's writing *ab initio*. His persona since the 1930s he told *New Statesman* readers, had been as, the man who does not like America.' He saw in Gaitskell's perception of 'Americanization' what some of us were publicly noting .ten years ago.' Priestley feared, Britain was *en route* to the world of Southern California, that advance post of our civilisation .with its automobile way of life (you can eat and drink, watch films, make love without getting out of your car) ... its lack of anything old and well-tried, rooted in tradition.' Though he saw resistance to this cultural standardisation in Britons' lingering respect for private life .the wealth of our odd hobbies and pastimes, in the wide network .of our voluntary associations.' [106]

The war was thought a key moment in mass culture's advance. Before, there had been no elaborately organised and publicised mass culture' and, Priestley argued, ordinary people were supposed to tag along somewhere on the fringes of real culture.' After, they were kept by sinister magic in a closed circle of false mass culture.' The circle was completed at a time when large numbers of people suddenly found themselves with more money to spend and more leisure'. This explained the failure of the promise of the war years.' [107] Others blamed the Attlee administration's elitism for the demise of wartime initiatives like the Council for the Encouragement of Music and Art (CEMA) – notably the appointment of Lord Keynes as chair of the Arts Council (CEMA's successor).[108] By 1960 Samuel concluded that Britain was afflicted by both the traditional divisions of the English class system' and by status anxieties on the American model .giving to society a tone more blatantly snobbish and vulgarly commercial than would have seemed possible in 1945.' Priestley argued the left had been too optimistic' about its prospects in 1945 and failed to realize how easily mass culture, with its immense resources of publicity, could defeat us.' He described how today there were thousands of extremely clever men and women now engaged not (to use the old-fashioned phrase) in the task of élevating the masses," but in the business of catering to all their whims, prejudices and idiocies.'[109]

The CPGB struck a very British note of anti-Americanism, in tune with its march along *The British Road to Socialism* and sharpened by its affinities in the Cold War. The Party craved, as during the Second World War, to pose as radical and pro-British. Its National Cultural Committee convened conferences through 1951 and 1952 on The American Threat to British Culture' and Britain's Cultural Heritage'. Anti-Americanism gave full vent to its polemical talents, providing relief from its isolated status. Communists opposed what Sam Aaronovitch called the toca-colonisation .swamping Britain with American cultural products of the most degraded and reactionary kind.' Jack Lindsay warned of torrupting dope mass-produced to condition our people to war, brutality, violence – films and comics from America.' This was the cultural side to the idea of a USA-dominated world state overriding national sovereignties.'[110]

Others were less reticent. Audiences at Unity Theatre, John Gorman remembers, foared approval at the anti-American songs of the review, *Here Goes*.' Derek Kartun, later a *New Reasoner* editor, wrote of the cheap, hysterical wilderness of American life today' in a 1951 pamphlet, *America -Go Home!* . America, he declared, was the most dangerous, grasping, brutal and degrading capitalist power the world has ever seen.' Kartun felt Britain could get along in our quiet way without coca-cola, American admirals .we want Britain for the British.' A 3d. *Daily Worker* pamphlet poured scorn not only upon southern racism, but on levels of crime, alcoholism and mental illness. These were the fruit' it argued, of the outlook generated by the movies, the radio and the comics, financed by big business, which glorify brutality and war.'[111]

Against this the CPGB proposed a popular front of Britain's cultural heritage. Henry Purcell, Adam Smith and (less surprisingly) William Morris, were amongst those recruited as true patriots', fighting for the interests of the people which are the true interests of the nation.' American Independence Day 1954 saw a Pageant of British Freedom' in Trafalgar Square with crowds invited to Stand up for Britain' and Break the Yankee Grip'. Efforts to revive morris-dancing, square dancing, or Kent YCL's pageant using forgotten episodes of that county's history', were organized.[112]

Soviet culture was promoted – films at the Scala Theatre or by the Society for Cultural Relations with the USSR – but was discordant with the pro-British refrain. The cumulative effect of this 'Hate America' campaign, as *Punch* soberly reviewed the *Daily Worker* 23rd Birthday Rally, was 'negative' and showed up the sterility of the contemporary Communist appeal.' Indeed by encouraging historical excavations of indigenous thinkers and traditions as resources for the left, Communist leaders laid fractures in the Party's ideological make-up that would crack in 1956.[113]

It was neither coca-cola, which some European socialists sought to ban or tax,[114] nor Hollywood, but comics that brought concerted opposition from the British left to cultural imperialism. American horror and crime comics like *Vault of Horror*, it was argued, were in cahoots with the American military and involved in the creation of the war mentality'. They dwelt on 'violence', presented 'power and personal riches' as the most desirable things in the world' and human nature as 'ruthless and aggressive' to the exclusion of any sign that human beings could be co-operative, social or loving.'[115]

The *New Statesman* considered the readers of such material to be 'sub-normal'. Like the typical American film,' Communists argued, the comic strip drugs the mind.' They were dangerous to any minds, but particularly to young, impressionable minds.'[116] Compared to the 'innocent amusement' of the *Beano*, the likes of *Manhunt* and *Ghostly Weird*, *Socialist Commentary* reported, were 'sordid strip sheets'. CLPs, MPs and councillors, the BBC, church leaders and the Council for Children's Welfare, condemned their anti-social values, portrayal of women and of sex.[117] In 1954 the main American publisher and three English counterparts were forced to close. The campaign then divided over whether the obscenity laws should be extended to cover such material. As *Commentary* observed (portentously of Penguin's 1960 prosecution over *Lady Chatterley's Lover*), there was the 'difficulty of discriminating in law between genuine literature of horror and sex and the trashy comics.'[118]

Anti-Americanism took many guises. An American Trade Unionist in Britain in 1952 reported he felt like a negro in the American South.' 'Even with some Labour Party members', Bill Shore found himself 'apparently suspect .so far as I know because I'm American.' It was in American foreign policy that he located the near-hatred of some Labour people for things American.' The CPGB found itself defending the monarchy at the time of the coronation. Given the way the idea of monarchy was cultivated, it argued it was 'small wonder if many have fallen for it', but the CPGB also suggested part of its popular appeal was that 'it's British not Yankee'. [119]

Anti-Americanism extended to language. Pollitt criticized Page Arnot: in these days when we are fighting for our national identity, why use the Yankee expression 'gotten?' Socialists dressed to avoid American associations. John Gorman tells how as the Cold War set in he discarded his 'Manhattan coat, an American symbol of Western decadent capitalism', but retained 'English' items – a country cap and brolly.[120] Hollywood was a longstanding bogey of the socialist imagination. By the 1950s British cinemas were unable to sustain the 30 per cent quota for home-made films and the industry, Hugh Jenkins complained, was too anxious to cast US stars, 'with an eye on American distribution.' The 'native product', *Leisure for Living* adjudged was often crypto-American'.[121]

It might have seemed socialists' fondness for jazz would have defied their dislike for America. The CPGB partly called the tune in the Musicians Union – Communist Ted Anstey was Assistant General Secretary. He vetoed tours by American jazz bands in the early 1950s, on the grounds of protecting British musician's jobs.[122] Humphrey Lyttelton's home piano bore a 'Yanks Go Home' sticker. Bruce Turner grumbled to *New Left Review* about modernists, whose 'whole mentality is American'. 'Absolutely pathetic' he thought – they even use American haircuts, dress and everything.' To Turner, jazz was music of social protest against the American way of life'. Indeed it was 'a most un-American music!'[123]

While the Cold War provided 'an emotional rather than an intellectual basis' for formulating attitudes towards America and the Soviet Union, political factors like McCarthyism also spurred the British left's anti-Americanism. The CPGB campaigned vocally on behalf of actor, singer and Communist Paul Robeson, whose US passport was withdrawn in 1950. It celebrated the return to the USA of folk-singer Pete Seeger, who had been barred from TV and radio. There were, Communist literature stressed, two Americas: capitalist and its opponents, Robeson or writers like Howard Fast.[124]

Others, notably revisionists around the journal *Encounter* and Congress for Cultural Freedom, saw the USA as a bulwark against Soviet totalitarianism. Revisionists enjoyed close links with its liberal-democratic elite, saw egalitarian qualities to US society, but in the context of the Cold War, anti-communism was their guiding principle. The democratic left could at least operate in capitalist liberal democracy. As even Priestley put it, whatever contempt he felt for 'Admass', he 'would prefer writing TV advertisements for Cornflakes to lumbering on thin cabbage soup in Siberia.'[125]

Moreover there was an emerging critical corpus within America. Galbraith's *The Affluent Society* was influential across the left. Its allure, Hattersley explained, was dual. Its analysis of the 'imbalance" between private affluence and public squalor' – appealed to Labour's vestigal Marxist belief .[in] the contradictions of capitalism' and affirmed its belief that whatever the buoyancy of Western capitalism, it remained flawed. Galbraith also attracted left moralists because he condemned the glossy, meretricious society they so hated.' *The Affluent Society* , then, conformed to traditional socialist thinking, but carried the fight to the enemy' on the battlefield of affluence. [126]

Also influential was David Riesman's *The Lonely Crowd*, charting the shift from work-production to leisure-consumption in post-war America and how conformity was the main social issue. Buhle argues Riesman's thesis was a variant of the Frankfurt school view of an advancing totality crushing the individual mind and collective conscience.' C. Wright Mills contributed to debates on the managerial revolution' and was admired by the New Left. In Clancy Sigal, the British New Left had its own American accent. Vance Packard's 1957 critique of advertising, *The Hidden Persuaders*, expressed disparate concerns of the British left. In a later work, *The Waste-Makers*, that considered the 'planned obsolescence' and throw-away spirit' of ever-mounting consumption', Packard, in socialist mood, dedicated the book to his parents – who have never confused the possession of goods with the good life.'[127]

Such analyses intrigued socialists who believed Britain was following in America's wake. For Crosland this was a positive course. In America, he argued, class distinctions were less pervasive .social attitudes less class conscious .the social ladder as a whole much shorter .in sum, social equality .greater.' Nor was he persuaded of 'American cultural conformism and low mass standards.' Magazine, clothing, cooking and design standards were significantly higher than in less egalitarian Britain'; more dollars were spent on classical concerts than on baseball.' Crosland even found the output of Hollywood .less standardised than many non-film-going intellectuals suppose.'

Crosland's point was twofold. Firstly, cultural standards and quality of life were not threatened by greater social equality. Sweden was another example here, with a world famous ..level of popular culture' achieved largely by state patronage'. Secondly, equality on its own was insufficient as a socialist aim. It ought to be accompanied by values that aimed to beautify our country and civilise our way of life.' Here he was hopeful. For given the cultural values presently being disseminated by commercial television and the Beaverbrook press' and the oppressive ugliness of our older industrial towns', he argued, no one can say British capitalism has set a very high standard for British socialism to improve on.'[128]

5
Socialism and Social Change II – TV, Advertising, Consumerism and Lifestyle

Television and mass media[1]

Socialists were not implacably opposed to the main agent of mass culture – television. Labour heartily approved of the BBC's long exercise in educating public taste', but commercial television, broadcasting from 1955, was a different matter. From May 1952, when a government white paper proposed ending the BBC's monopoly, socialist hackles were raised: not least because it was felt this was being foisted on the nation in the absence of popular support, and contrary to the report of the Beveridge Committee on Broadcasting (1949–51), by a commercial lobby and Tory MPs exploiting the government's slender majority.[2]

The advent, structures and output of commercial TV were sharply contested in 1950s British politics. US coverage of the coronation with car advertising slogans like Queen of the Road' and featuring TV chimp J. Fred Muggs', gave warrant to socialist scruples. Attlee cited this as evidence of the 'vulgar' content of commercial TV and warned that if the government permitted it in Britain, Labour would 'alter this when we get back into power.'[3]

In chorus with the left, the majority of elite opinion in the churches, TUC, universities and Tory ranks, was outraged. Lord Reith, architect of the BBC's public service ethos, compared commercial TV to the arrival of the Black Death. Business expressed unease – ABC cinemas worried about rivalry from TV, and some British advertisers felt American expertise might dominate the new market.[4]

Christopher Mayhew, Labour MP for Woolwich East, was ITV's foremost critic. He was the founding force behind the cross-party lobby group, the National Television Council. Countering this was the Popular Television Association, backed by the Conservatives and leading advertisers. Mayhew's pamphlet *Dear Viewer* .sold 40,000, but the respective campaigns sparked little popular interest in 1953. The unpopularity of party political broadcasts suggested a dislike of politics interfering with television.[5]

Mayhew was not shy of TV. A BBC documentary-maker, he presented Labour's first telecast in 1951 and featured in its 1959 election series. *Dear Viewer* ... outlined Labour's objections. It concluded on the Reithian note that if TV was 'going to be a dominant force in our national life' then it was necessary to 'make sure it has ideals and integrity, or it will ruin us.' Commercialism would ruin standards viewers were told, because the wishes and interests of the advertisers would be paramount' and broadcasters 'would have neither the motive nor the means to resist the advertisers 'demands.' As John Heardley-Walker viewed it in Morden, commercial TV had to be made to 'serve values and purposes which the nation approves – not those which ad agencies force upon us.'[6]

Mayhew rebutted the counter-argument that advertisers needed popular programmes and that the audience's interests and taste would thus predominate, suggesting that for advertisers it was not the enjoyability of a programme, but .the universality of its appeal' that mattered. This distinction – that programmes with a mass audience were not enjoyed as keenly (or register as highly on the BBC 'appreciation index') as those with more discriminating viewers – was the essence of socialists' case against mass culture. 'To get a maximum audience,' he argued, 'a TV programme must appeal to everyone at once, even if this means appealing keenly to no-one.' It must 'appeal simultaneously to the 15 year-old and 50 year-old .the highbrows and lowbrows; Scots, English and Welsh; Swing fans and Beethoven fans; male and female.' In short, 'it must play down to the lowest common factor in us all.'

Mayhew turned to the USA for evidence. 'American TV', he argued was 'horrible .not because it [was] run by Americans, but because it [was] dominated by commercial motives.' He saw US imports as a danger 'not only to our TV standards, but to our whole national culture and way of life' and considered 'it would be an excellent thing if we British asserted ourselves a bit against the colossal cultural impact of America.' Ultimately, Mayhew rejected commercial TV on the ethical grounds that 'a great weakness of our whole Western Civilisation is the way we put things on a commercial basis which might be done for their own sake.'[7]

Cultural elitism here merged with a belief in public ownership – aimed not at economic democracy and accountability, but at cultural control and to promote non-commercial values. In Labour's mind, the state could (and should) act as a source for cultural good. Also apparent was Labour's defence of the BBC's gentlemanly, British ethos of public service. With the BBC, Patrick Gordon Walker told the House of Commons in 1954, 'we are dealing with a public service', but with ITV 'we are dealing with people broadcasting for profit.' Commercial broadcasters, he continued, were 'people who cannot be trusted in any way' and he identified a 'special danger of domination by American interests'. In the socialist outlook the opposition between cultural quality and commercialism was clear.[8]

Communist thinking was of a kind. Harry Pollitt refused an interview on the question of commercial television on Ed Murrow's CBS show *See it Now*, but informed them that 'commercial television would not hesitate to indulge in the vilest forms of pornography and the portrayal of crime, murder and sadism if the advertisers thought this would achieve their aim'. He continued, this was 'what happened in the United States'.[9]

Labour's campaign was based on the premises that 'all responsible ... opinion condemns commercial television', that 'the standard of programmes will slump when the commercialisers get busy on the TV screen' and that 'the public is opposed to sponsored television; it revolts against the very idea.'[10] But the veracity of (particularly the last of) these assumptions was not entirely clear. It was clear soon after ITV started broadcasting that its programmes were not unpopular. By the summer of 1957 it was drawing 73 per cent of the TV audience. There was then, Crossman noted, a cultural irony and a political flaw to Labour's espousal of 'high' culture contra-ITV, for 'there were far more Conservative voters who object to commercial television than Labour voters'.[11]

Labour's campaign asked, 'what have *you* done to save us from commercial television'. Mary Allen confessed to *Labour Woman* readers that she was 'chilled .by the prospect .that in ten years' time there will be eight million TV sets in this country, with half the adult population 'looking-in''on the average night – the thought appals me!' Doris Lessing later commented on how 'many socialists refused to get one' and television became a sort of litmus test whereby 'one could more or less work out someone's political bias by the attitude he took towards television.'[12]

Socialists were doubtless amongst the group Harrisson identified in a 1960 survey of Bolton, who 'ostentatiously do not have television ...

explain that ..they only look at it occasionally' or refer to it by derogatory remarks'. Socialists were apt to disparage TV as an idiot's lantern'. Harrisson related this to a non-conformist wariness of sinful activities. At present' he felt TV fills this bill better than anything else.' Socialists imagined Hollywood, gambling, milk bars and TV, to involve some such downfall. In this vein *Leisure for Living* vowed to not allow television to be used – as Karl Marx and Charles Kingsley said that religion had been used – as the opium of the people.'[13] Hugh Jenkins warned of television that drugs most of us nightly'; Priestley of being half-hypnotized' peering into a magic mirror.' Left-wing voices resounded with the one-sixth of Britons a 1957 *Sunday Times* survey classified as abstainers', in regarding TV as a byword of all that was wrong with the new society.[14]

Though applauding it for keeping the family together, socialists were mostly contemptuous of televiewing. It was too passive a lifestyle for their taste. The lifeless time-wasting of so many older people who find in TV almost their only pleasure, but are apt to be numbed rather than stimulated by much of its present output' Labour twinned to teenagers hanging around aimlessly in pin-table saloons.'[15] Mary Allen told how she would rather read a book, go occasionally to a theatre.' John Heardley-Walker, saw TV as a distraction. After a low council election turnout in May 1959, he wondered: was Diana Dors or Bob Monkhouse, more important than exercising the long-fought-for right to vote?' In the Trotskyist paper *Revolt*, Lindsay Mountford disapproved that if you go into any working-class home today and you will find in place of a bookcase, a TV set, usually bought on the never-never system." Frank Horrabin, discussing a sketch of a Rhondda skyline strewn with aerials, supposed its title, Sheep may Safely Gaze', referred to the two-legged animals gazing absorbed at their TV screens.' [16]

The left press scorned TV standards. Reviewing performers on *Saturday Night is Variety Night* for the *Daily Worker*, Alison Macleod was reluctant to mention those who sent' her over to the commercial channel.' Another double-edged 1956 review declared, all this American entertainment has made me think more favourably of Wilfred Pickles.' Yet early in 1957 Macleod urged all left-wingers' to save up for a television'. This was not because of improved schedules, but through recognizing that without viewing what people were watching, socialists were not able to talk to them on equal terms.' [17]

Pickles' was begrudged his popular appeal by commentators like Macleod and Hoggart. Based around his northern warmth and common touch with audience and participants, Hoggart (himself from

Leeds) found his TV show *Ask Pickles* condescending. The sentimental (or trivial), whatever its popular appeal, was given short shrift by socialists. *Dixon of Dock Green* was savaged in *New Left Review* as 'a piece of jetsam salvaged from *The Blue Lamp*'. Even *That Was The Week That Was*, the toast of most anti-Conservatives in 1963, received a tetchy review from the *New Statesman*.[18]

Dennis Potter was the *Daily Herald*'s TV critic from 1962 to 1964. Though given less copy than the theatre reviews and open to TV's creative potential, Potter still found space to damn 'the little grey-faced monster squatting in our living rooms.' His predecessors had taken a similar tone. Phil Diack regarded the plays on BBC and ITV on a Sunday in April 1960 as 'junk'. A week later he considered that had you wanted 'something with a minimum of thought and a maximum of mental stagnation, then last night was your night.'[19]

Political scientist and Labour's broadcasting adviser, William (not to be confused with Wilfred) Pickles, contended that in partaking of the 'daily drug' of TV there was 'a connection between social conservatism and political Conservatism.' Pickles' particular target was the BBC. He lambasted *Woman's Hour* for assuming 'women's interests are almost entirely limited to housework, clothes, marriage and children.' He railed that in *Mrs Dale's Diary* 'everybody in the Dale family does and thinks what is traditionally done and thought by his class'. Such programmes attracted 'vast, faithful and partly moronic audiences', whose 'low IQ', Pickles vouched, was 'well known.' [20]

It was not only the commercial imperatives of the programme makers that were to blame for disappointing TV standards then, but the audience itself. Even the culturally tuned-in New Left argued in its submission to the Pilkington Committee (1960–2) that 'in the end, the quality of the service provided will depend upon the critical awareness of the audience.' The committee had an opportunity to make providers more responsible and accountable, but also 'to help raise the quality of response and critical appreciation of the audiences themselves; to help them become more discriminating over the whole field of television output.'[21] Visiting Hollywood in 1956 Alma Birk reached similar conclusions. A report of Hollywood's discrimination during the McCarthy era and its synthetic atmosphere, ended with the thought that the place and its product was 'ghastly' and in need of reform. But, she concluded, 'the film-going public will have to become even more discriminating before this happens.'[22]

TV's impact on children was high in socialist concerns. The thrillers and westerns in ITV's children's output were, Mayhew argued in 1959, financially shrewd, but otherwise execrable.' Commercial drives made ITV's output all the worse. Advertising which played on children's 'suggestibility' Mayhew deemed the lowest form of activity open to a British citizen, short of actual crime.' The Council for Children's Welfare that campaigned against horror comics (and which Birk vice-chaired) turned its attention from 1957 towards the social attitudes portrayed in children's TV.[23]

The link between TV and wider social attitudes was unquestionable to socialists. New Left reviewers could see 'in almost every programme ... *some* view of life, some implicit or explicit social or moral attitudes.' ITV quiz shows like *Dotto* and *Double Your Money* were held to 'encourage an attitude of total passivity, relieved only by positive appeals to mercenary greed.' The materialist message crept onto the BBC too. The purpose of *Juke Box Jury* was 'not to criticise the music, but rather to determine whether the records are likely to be a hit or not.' Worse were the values of advertising. There was 'something fraudulent about the way in which the genial bonhomie of Wilfred Pickles' was 'used', the New Left's Pilkington deposition felt. It did not believe that 'direct appeals to status – the invitation to compete with one's neighbour for social prestige' were 'a sound way to sell goods', involving as they did the idea that emotional problems may be resolved by the acquisition of material goods.' These were precisely the values socialists were averse to in the affluent society.[24]

After 1955, when ITV started broadcasting, the left's suspicion was unabated. Commercial television was not averted, but the 1954 Television Act introduced restraints on advertising and in the form of the regulatory Independent Television Authority (ITA). TV was recognized as an influential social change: ownership of sets grew from one to 13 million between 1951 and 1964 and expenditure on TV advertising from £13 million in 1956 to £48 million by 1958, meanwhile the average radio audience fell by more than half between 1954 and 1957 and around 800 cinemas closed in five years after 1954 and admissions halved.[25]

As a research department memo by Wedgwood Benn early in 1955 made clear, the popularity of TV (and particularly ITV) made it a more problematic issue. Labour's 'long campaign with its warnings and threats against the commercial lobby may', he predicted, put it 'at a tactical disadvantage.' He thus urged a policy that 'would reassure viewers about their new programmes', but also 'scare the advertisers about their new investment .divide the Tory party into two and precipitate the collapse of commercial television from lack of confidence.'

Benn reaffirmed Labour's belief that all sound and television programmes must be .controlled, produced and broadcast by a public
service system.' Benn carried this principle forward in proposals for a
National Broadcasting Corporation and took it into battle with pirate"
radio later in the 1960s.[26]

Mayhew renewed his attack in 1959 in *Commercial Television –What
is to be Done?* This accused ITV companies of contravening the 1954 TV
Act by concentrating adverts in prime-time slots and inserting unnat-
ural breaks into programmes. The ITA was accused of having never
really challenged the power of the programme companies.' As Mayhew
anticipated, standards were low: a 1958 BBC survey found that one
third of its own peak-time output was serious' programming, compared to a mere tenth of ITV's.[27]

Entering the debate on a third TV channel, Mayhew was hopeful.
Surveys found 81 per cent of the public were annoyed by adverts in,
rather than between programmes and a majority supported Mayhew's
bill to prohibit these. Popular support was for BBC to run the new
channel. This was despite the fact that ITV attracted more viewers than
the BBC and confirmed Mayhew's belief in a negative correlation
between size of audience' and appreciation index'. Thus, he contended, there was no possible argument – political, technical or ethical
– for letting admass'loose on new TV channels.'   [28]

Labour, then, advocated the formation of an Independent Public
Corporation (along BBC lines) and a strengthening of the ITA's powers
over the regional companies.[29] As the CPGB observed, the struggle to
give this channel to the BBC' was a rather negative way of fighting
against' commercial influence, but the only way out at present.'
Funding was to come from the licence fee and either a tax on ITV's
fabulously profitable advertising monopoly' or by increasing the rates
the ITA charged programme contractors for the use of transmitters.[30]

Whether this involved a retreat from outright opposition – Raymond
Williams considered it a shameful decision to compromise with commercial television' – Labour's *dirigisme* still provoked the sort of scare-
mongering associated with its nationalization proposals. Two days
before the 1959 election the *Daily Sketch* reported that a Labour victory
would mean the end of ITV. Morgan Phillips described this as a fantas-
tic lie'; meanwhile the Tories took 100,000 copies of the *Sketch* to distribute in London marginals.[31]

The 1962 report of the Pilkington Committee on Broadcasting
ratified the left's concerns. It tendered that ITV had fallen short of the
terms of the 1954 Act, criticized its programmes as trivial' and called

for a strengthened ITA to sell advertising time distinctly from pro-
gramme-makers. As it stood ITV should not provide any additional
services of television.'[32] Critics vilified Richard Hoggart as the killjoy
behind a socialistic and unrealistic report'. The pro-ITV *Daily Mirror*
complained Pilkington had effectively told viewers: you can't have the
television programmes which .two-thirds .of you prefer. You must
have .an Uncle'ITA, just like 'Auntie'BBC.' [33]

Mayhew saw Pilkington as an opportunity to renew the attack on
ITV, but his attempts to get Labour to back the report were thwarted.
Whatever evidence Mayhew could muster and however forceful
Pilkington's case, the two thirds of constituents who preferred watching ITV to the BBC were a pressing electoral calculation. Mayhew felt
let down, but Gaitskell pointed out, Pilkington did not please all socialists.[34]

Crosland notably, felt the report had come to broadly the right conclusions, but for largely the wrong reasons.' He made a case for state
intervention to introduce more educational choice.' This was not just
to cater for minority tastes or erase the inane, banal' product that it
seemed most of the public currently wants' by imposing (àla Reith) a
particular view or level of taste.' Rather to demand à wider range of
serious programmes than would be chosen by immediate majority
vote; in the hope that over the years the public, having been offered
this range will more and more freely choose it.' Crosland conceded his
thinking was premised on the BBC theory behind the light, home and
third programmes .that over time, with increasing education and discrimination, listeners would graduate from the first through the second
to the third.' It was also redolent of Matthew Arnold and suggestive of
the extent to which Labour was heir to nineteenth-century liberal traditions of cultural improvement and rational recreation'. [35]

For all the libertarianism of the closing pages of *The Future of
Socialism*, Crosland still saw a deep dividing line .in the field of cultural values' and Labour on the side of determined government planning.' A Labour memo during the Beveridge Committee stated ending
the BBC monopoly would mean the audience, who prefer to be entertained rather than educated, would no longer receive .features, discussions, news'. Labour's desire to improve the people, but fear that
they were falling short of their potential and could not be trusted to
improve voluntarily, was accentuated by affluence in the 1950s. The
state – already seen as a force for cultural improvement – also offered
recourse from what the left regarded as the people's limitations. This
raised the question – which Conservatives posed – of whether suspect-

ing the people would make the 'wrong' viewing choices was a valid reason for denying them the choice? There was a Cold War dimension to this. In a free', affluent society, should cultural standards be the responsibility of the state or of popular choice. Affluence diversified lifestyles, values and choice. The state was no longer the sole source of authority, arbiter or provider in such matters. The left's cultural *dirigisme* was increasingly at odds with popular attitudes and culture. As Corner comments, the vocabulary of 'moral' and trivial', that Labour deployed, was, in the post-war cultural climate, too easily reducible .to the sort of explicit paternalism that could no longer find support or deference quite so available as .a. decade earlier'.   [36]

Labour's opposition to TV diminished through the early 1960s – as fears of 'Americanization' faded, it accepted its popularity, dodged Tory charges of threatening ITV or sneering at affluence and the 1963 Television Act enacted some of Pilkington's criticisms of ITV. But it remained a presence. Jim Northcott's 1964 Penguin election special thought TV adverts might be dispensed with altogether' to improve the programmes' and that funding could be found in taxing TV sets or doubling the licence fee.[37] Labour remained of the opinion that an organic change was required in the structure of commercial television', because Pilkington confirmed its suspicion at the concentration of economic power in ITV companies. So did the fortunes and influence of its owners – Roy Thomson, Canadian proprietor of the *Sunday Times* and *Scotsman* and the major shareholder in Scottish TV (a licence to print money'), or Val Parnell of ATV, for Mayhew an 'admirably clear exponent of the ideals and standards of 'Admass".   [38]

These new tycoons', as Sampson comments, defied the managerial revolution'. Rather than the diffusion of power and control, they were a throwback to the days of the early press barons.' This seemed to weigh against the left. The *Daily Worker* (with undertakers, marriage bureaux and moneylenders) was barred from advertising on ITV. The ITA rejected a bid from a consortium of *Reynolds News* and 15 East Anglian Co-operative societies. This had claimed to involve for the first time local finance, control and popular participation in the running of a commercial television station.'[39]

The newspaper industry took a sizable stake in the new TV stations – around a quarter of the issued share capital. The *Daily Mirror* had a large holding in Associated Television, amongst the most profitable companies. Pilkington had proposed that unless Thomson's interest in Scottish Television was reduced, its contract should not be renewed.[40] Socialists mistrusted monopoly and the 1950s saw a spate of mergers in the mass media. No less than 17 daily titles and 88 weeklies closed between 1949 and 1962. Notably, the liberal *News Chronicle* was sold to the *Daily Mail* in 1960.[41]

This partly resulted from competition for advertising from TV. The *Daily Herald*, linked to Labour through the TUC's 49 per cent shareholding, saw its circulation fall from 2,071,000 (1950) to 1,407,000 (1960). As Waller pointed out, the *Herald* had predominantly working-class support', but a newspaper directed simply at these readers' with shallower pockets, would not be attractive to the advertiser.' In 1964 the TUC sold it to the Mirror Group and the *Herald* rose as *The Sun* during the 1964 election – blazing support for Labour, but with radical accents like James Cameron, dimmed. This left the *Sunday Citizen*, as the Co-op's *Reynolds News* had been re-badged in tabloid form in September 1962, as the lone independent voice of the labour trinity.[42]

Socialists were disturbed by the standardization of taste in popular publications (and by what those tastes were). The uniformity of commercial mass culture seemed to socialists' to strangle alternative (and as they saw them more edifying) leisure activities and values. The left's own resources, like the Workers' Travel Association (WTA) were hard-pressed in the 1950s. Founded in 1921, *Socialist Commentary* recalled how the WTA had fought for paid holidays and become the third largest travel organisation in the country.' Its holidays were still organised on a simple non-commercial basis' and offered open-air adventure', but the WTA found people now went abroad not for fellowship" or international understanding, but to taste the sweets of fashionable resorts' and with motor-cars .began to prefer individual travel to group travel'. Its 1958 Annual Report reported a two million pound turnover, but diminishing interest in its traditional holidays. *Commentary* was uncertain what could be done, but was certain something ought to be. Otherwise, while individuals who no longer like to think of themselves as workers".crowd the Costa Brava café or display their bikinis on riviera beaches .something will have been lost from our movement.' The sense of impending extinction was heightened by the demise of the Workers Sports Association in 1960. The same fear was found amongst Clarion cycling clubhouses, whose membership had dwindled to below 3,000 by 1957. Car ownership was held to blame. But there was also fear that fellowship, blending recreation and politics, was dwindling.[43]

Instead it was feared workers were increasingly in thrall to the mass media. We are surrounded by a press, radio and television and cinema', the CPGB warned in 1961, which were feeding us a continuous diet of false values and phoney moral standards.' Day after day a false picture of the world', Priestley argued, was flashed onto millions of innocent minds.' Its political prejudices notwithstanding, it seemed to many socialists that it was the proprietors of the *Daily Scream* .the advertising gang, the haters of the arts' who were winning.' For E. P. Thompson, commercial journalism (like British film stars)' was beginning to affect an American accent' and eulogising the 'American way of life". It was impossible to combine sensational commercial methods with really free and independent working class politics' and he deplored the popular press, where headlines and short news flashes'replaced argument and factual presentation.'   [44]

The *Daily Worker* was not spared such criticism. A Harrow CPGB member wrote in 1958 demanding less of the frivolous imitation of the bourgeois press and if not less space devoted to sport, some of it reserved for exposure of its money grabbing and corruption.' Crossman had similar concerns about the *Daily Herald*'s new Editorial Director, enlisted from *The People* in 1955. If it were felt necessary for business reasons to permit the standard of the *Daily Herald* to fall as low as that of *The People*' he told the NEC, the result would be positively harmful to the good name of the Labour Party.'[45]

It was one of the chief refrains of *The Uses of Literacy* that contemporary popular publications had limited worth. As nothing was demanded of the reader, nothing can be given by the reader.' Hoggart found middle-class papers as trivial and trivialising as those for the working classes.' Deploying sex and sensationalism, the mass-art' of the popular papers was to hold down the level of taste.' If capitalism was inhibited now from ensuring the degradation'of the masses economically', the papers were ensuring that working-people [were] culturally robbed'.[46]

Yet, as is one of the chief refrains of this chapter, socialists thought there a good deal of working class complicity in this. This made them question the fitness of workers for public life or for building socialism. In *Revolt* Mountford despaired that workers reading today rarely go past the sports page of the daily newspaper' and were too tired to read a serious book due to working anything up to 20 hours a week overtime.' Priestley advanced, If our papers are trivial' it was because our people are trivial'.[47]

Advertising

Advertising was another bugbear of the socialist imagination; purportedly an agent of uniformity, manipulation and acquisitive values.

Advertising seemed a pervasive presence in affluent Britain, using a new medium in TV and increasingly a political device too. Expenditure grew from £134 million in 1953 (1. 6 per cent of national income) to £323 million by 1959 (2. 2 per cent).[48] Socialists regularly indicted the priorities of the affluent society, by explaining these sums exceeded spending on education or research, or that more was spent advertising the washing detergents, *Tide* and *Omo*, than by the Arts Council.[49]

Ethically, advertising chafed with socialism. Most on the left instinctively agreed with Orwell that advertising was little other than the rattling of a stick inside a swill bucket', with all this implied about the herd-like response of the swine. In a 1953 speech Bevan told how advertising [w]as one of the most evil consequences of modern society.' Advertising was nothing new of course – Labour MP Maurice Edelman even thought it was probably the world's second oldest profession'. For designer Ken Garland, advertising was about appealing to people's greed, whereas we are trying to appeal to their ideals.' To this end, socialists felt advertisers employed dubious methods. Psychologist Leslie Corina wrote in *Socialist Commentary* of the obnoxious' use of sexual symbols'; notably of a current cigarette advertisement' that suggested the cigarette will complete a successful seduction.' Those who made such associations need not have a suspicious or dirty mind', he remarked, but it seems to help.' For Stuart Hall, advertising was simply a debased art of persuasion'. [50]

Misgivings were widespread, in a Cold War idiom, about advertising. For Labour Peer Francis Williams, advertising was part and parcel of *The American Invasion* of Britain. American Vance Packard's critique of *The Hidden Persuaders* – which Offer notes reverberated strongly across the Atlantic' – placed advertising in the chilling world of George Orwell and his big brother.' He warned that 'Americans have become the most manipulated people outside the Iron Curtain', but that Britons had little ground for complacency', since manipulation by playing upon the public's subconscious is .spreading.' For Packard, this meant regress rather than progress for man in his long struggle to become a rational and self-guiding being.'[51]

Specifically concerning to socialists about advertising, sales and public relations, was that it was engaged in fostering and bolstering the values of consumerism amongst the newly affluent. Its activities were specially important at the present time' Corina considered since some sections of society have money to spend, but no ready-made social habits for spending it.' In women's magazines, the CPGB saw close ties between editorial and advertising matter.' Ideologically' magazines like *Woman's Realm* concentrated on consumer goods as women's only interest', on household goods, fashion and beauty aids.' Their effect on women's minds' the CPGB feared was 'inestimable.' In stressing household and consumer goods, advertising was held to boost private at the expense of public spending and thus to be 'anti-social'. [52]

In socialist eyes advertising exploited the powerlessness of the individual consumer. 'Advertisers', the CPGB proposed, often 'claim[ed] extraordinary qualities for quite ordinary and in some cases quite useless commodities.' Potter found the sovereignty of the consumer a phrase that reeks of dishonesty.' If 'not actually a dupe' in the hands of advertisers and big business, the consumer was at best 'an innocent abroad', Socialist Union reasoned in 1956. In 1961, Labour's George Darling erred towards indicting consumers for why this might be so, arguing 'advertising also exploits ignorance'. *The Battle of the Consumer*, an earlier Labour foray into consumer issues, argued: 'people can be deceived – and the deception is often deliberate – by advertising blurbs which make entirely false claims about the quality and performance of goods.'[53]

So while the unscrupulous methods of advertisers and salesman were condemned, socialists also pointed to the gullibility of consumers. Having heard speakers at the 1960 Labour Women's Conference denounce 'the super salesman with their slick American talk', Northumberland County Councillor Mrs M. Barras was left 'wondering what kind of fools and mugs housewives were.' 'It was not possible to protect everyone from all her weaknesses and foolishness all the time' she argued and anyhow, 'there were worse things than door-to-door salesman, such as housey-housey.'[54]

The left also thought of advertising as creating demand for brands and products which were 'not genuine''or spontaneous wants, such as the need for food or clothing or shelter, but purely artificial .wants which would not exist were they not created, contrived or stimulated by advertising or sales promotion.' As Priestley put it, the Admass populace did 'not know what they want until they are told'; its 'interests and tastes [had] to be created rather than reflected or catered for.' Consumers, in other words, were regarded as puppets of advertisers and big business. For Francis Noel-Baker, amongst the attractions of a planned economy' was that it can liberate society from high-pressure salesmanship and the need to 'create demand.'' [55]

Crosland's objection to such thinking was that socialists could no longer afford to dismiss – as artificially created or of secondary importance – demands that fell outside core needs of health, food and shelter. Affluence had made quality and choice central issues. The demand for greater variety and higher standards of food, clothing and housing' were not innate needs, but were they therefore to be considered as not worth satisfying?' Crosland felt not. This was not a question merely of yet more elaborate tail-fins on even longer cars or frippery gadgets', because, almost all wants above the basic minimum .are in some way artificially stimulated.' Education or immunization campaigns relied on state backing, rather than spontaneous demand. Crosland's liking for opera was no less real' and brought no less contentment because it was recently acquired rather than something he was born with. And while demand for ..refrigerators, washing-machines and the like was artificially contrived by advertising', such goods also served to reduce drudgery and increase domestic leisure.' Crosland considered the distinction between innate and created wants', that socialists were apt to apply to advertising, at best, uncertain'. [56]

Raymond Williams argued advertising (in collusion with the media) deflected attention from all the long-run structural problems of the society' by offering up a lively series of short-term definitions and interests': the celebration of the affluent 'society and of happy consumption.' This ability to conceal or displace real' problems hinged on the trickery of commercial advertising' – the magic system' – the organized deflection of need and reason, by the organized propagation of false images of need and satisfaction.' Williams's reasoning (like the miscreant advertisers he portrayed) stood or fell on the assumption that a large portion of the populace was thus deceived.[57]

Socialists saw in advertising (especially of brands) an ersatz quality and wastefulness. They associated this with the triumph of the trivial' that gave not cheap houses or enough to eat in Asia, but striped toothpaste and coloured toilet rolls.' Even when its standards are high', Christopher Mayhew still found, the underlying message and philosophy of advertising .often unedifying.'   [58]

There was not a consensus on the left about the effects of advertising. Crosland felt it tended to exaggerate the power of advertising.' He highlighted campaigns that had failed and post-war tastes that had spread without the invisible helping hand of the advertiser – coffee bars, skiffle, Scrabble, Marks and Spencer clothes. Others pointed to how salesmanship .developed in the consumer its own antibodies.' Hall suggested growing consumer awareness of the pressures to which they were subject was a widely developed critical technique.' It signalled a pulling away from a social culture shot through with .new appeals, bright sales clatter, phoney debates, bland interviewers, neutral panel game quiz-masters, meretricious demands of one sort or another.'[59]

Still, the left was set against advertising, which explains its reticence towards its political uses. Crosland accepted 'advertising as the price we pay for a high and varied standard of consumption', but also favoured 'a heavy tax' on it. This 'would discriminate against the most obtrusive and least informative advertisements' and 'encourage price reductions as an alternative to promotional competition.' The CPGB favoured state regulation. Its submission to the 1961 Royal Press Commission proposed papers should derive no more than 20 per cent of their income from ads, relieving pressure on them to indulge advertisers – such as the pretence of the tobacco interests that excessive smoking has nothing to do with lung cancer.' Max Corden's Fabian pamphlet, *A Tax on Advertising?* also supported prohibition of tobacco advertising. Corden argued an advertising tax might help fund a Consumer advisory service. There was a precedent in the Attlee government. In 1947 Chancellor Hugh Dalton allowed only half of advertising expenditure to be written off against tax. As with the voluntary scheme introduced by Cripps in 1948, the aim was to reduce inflationary demand for goods in short supply and boost exports rather than domestic demand for household goods. The advertising industry was wary of Labour's hostility and threatened by its talk of taxation.[60]

Particularly vocal amongst critics was Francis Noel-Baker. In 1958 Noel-Baker introduced a Private Member's Motion for a Royal Commission into advertising. It was 'talked out', but its impetus led to the formation of the Advertising Inquiry Council (AIC) in March 1959. Though cross-Party, the council had a strong left aspect. Noel-Baker served on its executive; Labour MPs Christopher Mayhew and Arthur Skeffington were among its founder members, as was Richard Hoggart, and among its 'observers' were trade unions, the London Co-operative Society, the Consumers' Association (see below) and the Council for Children's Welfare. Criticism of advertising was not confined to Labour quarters, and as Tunstall's showed, it was as widespread and old as advertising itself. Pressing for an independent enquiry, the council scrutinized the advertising world through its amenity, ethical, medical (looking at cigarettes and alcohol consumption among young drinkers) and television panels.[61]

The AIC was part of a general trend towards regulating the industry, like the Advertising Standards Authority (ASA) created in 1962. Its call for a national enquiry, widely supported by Labour MPs, was partially realized in 1962 when Gaitskell invited Lord Reith to chair a party

Commission on advertising. The choice of Reith, an austere rational recreator, showed Labour's disposition. Mark Abrams and Elaine Burton (Labour's leading voice on consumer affairs) were amongst those on the Commission. It reported to Prime Minister Harold Wilson in January 1966.[62]

Its recommendations were moderate. It supported the ITA's ban on cigarette advertising on TV introduced in 1965 (though a minority favoured a general ban) and noted the US system of issuing health warnings on packets. It felt there was 'a strong case' for 'a public advertising service' that 'using the same techniques of mass appeal, would provide the consumer with effective guidance both on existing commodities and on new products'. Its recommendation for a National Consumers Board, incorporating the activities of the ASA and Consumers' Council, was deemed to 'warrant substantial support from public funds', but from a levy on advertising rather than new taxation.[63]

Responses to the report were muted. A sub-committee was appointed to suggest action. Reading the report, Wilson may have been struck by *déjà vu*. In 1952 he had discussed the potential of a Consumer Advisory Service to counteract false claims made for goods and publicise the findings, but concluded that the cost of communicating advice, requiring a public subsidy, was likely to outweigh the value of that advice.[64]

Consumerism

Advertising was part and parcel of a consumer society. Between 1957 and 1960, ownership of household goods like refrigerators, washing machines, vacuum cleaners and televisions expanded rapidly. Over the 1950s the number of cars on the road trebled and the proportion of owner-occupied housing almost doubled. There was doubtless something to socialists' scorn for this as a virtual affluence – material atonement for the loss of Empire, limited to the upper echelons of the working class, lacking a firm base in economic growth or oiled by hire-purchase – but there was little denying the qualitative change. The 'washing-machines and hi-fis Harrisson saw in 'Worktown' were 'cheap and commonplace now where before they were for the few and well-off.' That to many people things *seemed* better, explained why Macmillan's claim in 1957, that most Britons had 'never had it so good', came to be the decade's epithet.[65]

Consumerism entailed values and attitudes as much as the acquisition of specific commodities. As Norman Mackenzie put it in

Universities and Left Review, it was as if capitalism was inculcating a new 'psychology of wants', different to those socialists wished to satisfy. Socialism was thus destabilized by affluence. Crosland announced the passing of capitalism. Others reached no less contentious conclusions. Hall (borrowing from Marx's idea of commodity fetishism) argued the 'working class and lower middle class people can *realise* themselves through the possession (on hire purchase perhaps) of 'alien things" and that Britain was now a 'people's capitalism' that 'as a social system [was] .based upon consumption.' Similarly, Michael Young saw the significance of the post-war in the switch of people's interests from production to consumption.'[66]

Consumerism questioned the longstanding focus in socialist politics on the workplace. That labour was the source of all value was part of socialists' intuitive knowledge. It tended to be trade union organiza-tion, rather than savings or spending power, that socialists used as an index of working-class strength. European reformist parties might be mostly social democratic in title, but Britain's went by the very name, Labour. Most accounts portray Labour as being consumed in the 1950s with debates about production and nationalization. Phillips' chief worry about *Labour in the Sixties* was that its members were ceasing to be 'a mirror of the nation at work.' [67]

Socialists' neglect of domestic matters and notions of a 'simple life' might be held to account for its ambivalence to consumerism, as many of the new consumer goods were home based. Whether as gadgets or for eroding traditional working-class values, 'the washing-machine took on a symbolic significance' for socialists in the 1950s, as Mervyn Jones tells 'and was deplored as a nefarious agent of corruption.' [68]

Disregard for the everyday subordinated the private to the public, political arena. Socialists were uneasy with the values of privatism, the enclosure of the home-centred world, competitiveness of 'keeping up with the Joneses' or passivity of televiewing. Personal or household acquisitiveness came second to qualities like public service, fellowship and community. 'The moral basis of the new society', Labour's 1950 manifesto vowed, would 'rely on friendship .not on greed.' Gaitskell attributed his sense that 'people nowadays are more family and less community conscious than they used to be' to the standard of living having 'risen in ways that especially affect people's homes – television, kitchen gadgets'. This 'reduction in community consciousness' came from 'people wondering all the time whether they can do better for themselves alone' and had he felt 'created problems for the Labour Party.'[69]

Other commentators equated consumerism and socialism's hard times. The sound of class war', Tory Charles Curran noted, was being drowned by the hum of the spin-dryer.' Roy Hattersley concurred, arguing the television set and washing machine, the continental holiday all helped to blur the boundaries of the class struggle.' A later account related this orgy of acquisitiveness' to what it saw as a rather quiet age politically.'[70] Yet quite as much the problem for the left was its mind-set, which disqualified these domestic and personal consuming desires. As Baxendale argues, socialism was apt to regard the displacement of struggles to change the world, on to struggles over dress lengths and soft furnishings' as more like a defeat', than a commentary on its failure to address these desires.[71]

Largely this was because socialists rejected the idea of material salvation. *Labour Woman*'s editor deplored the Tory's crude materialistic appeal to the purely self-regarding interests of the electors – How many more refrigerators, washing-machines, TV sets, vacuum cleaners and motor cars under the Tories!"For those on the left, never having had so much did not necessarily mean never having had it so good. Another concern was that advertising which whets the appetite for higher personal consumption', worked at the expense of public services and meant children are given an admirable choice of breakfast foods, but little choice of playing fields.' Morally worse was that it promoted the notion that life was nothing more than a race for prizes and to consume.' Priestley's concern was that the British were a people who would cheerfully exchange their last glimpse of freedom for a new car, a refrigerator and a 14-inch TV screen.'[72]

It was not only socialists who disparaged materialism. Richard Rose has recalled many in the elite thought Macmillan obscene in wanting people to have more money to spend.' Macmillan himself, while responsible for the introduction of Premium Bonds (government securities paying no interest but cash prizes) as Chancellor in his 1956 budget, a measure which caused some furore in non-conformist circles' and standing by the mantra of never had it so good', was hardly a hedonist. He did not own a TV and disliked .affluent suburbia.' He too wondered of popular consumerism, what is it all for?' But it was a call mostly sounded by the left against affluence and sprang from expressly socialist reasoning – that the hope of a new heaven and a new earth in return for pennies is doomed'. Socialism abhorred poverty, but we must reach out to spiritual as well as material needs' as Jim Griffiths, Labour's deputy leader from 1955 to 1958, put it.[73]

For many this ethical emphasis was also politically necessary. Tosco Fyvel concluded in 1955 that so far as the standard of living was concerned Unilever, Ford Motors, Marks and Spencers .and the   *Daily Mirror* [were] not doing too badly'. For Labour, promises of mere material progress may no longer be enough.' This was Socialist Union's preference too – that the quality of life was now central. The goal of material equality' it held in 1956 was ho longer sufficient to inspire a generation which has all the jobs it wants and more money in its pockets to spend on pleasure than its parents had to live on for weeks.'[74]

It seemed to most socialists that the Conservatives were drawing political credit from consumerism. Restrictions on hire-purchase were relaxed in August 1954 and October 1958 just prior to general elections, and tightened, for instance on domestic electrical appliances in April 1960, shortly after. Hire-purchase was not new, but widely used for acquiring new commodities. A third of vacuum cleaners and half of television sets were bought on hire-purchase, a 1956 survey showed. Hire-purchase debt doubled between 1958 and 1960.[75] Labour subs-collectors were aware of it as on their Friday rounds were met by anxious enquiries: which instalment is it?' [76]

Both Labour and the CPGB acknowledged that hire-purchase put a wider range of goods within reach of most pockets, but were suspicious of it – partly because it blurred socialism's work-orientation, by divorcing spending power from income.[77] J. C. Binns, a Labour subs-collector, wondered if people would be happier if hire-purchase was illegal and they had no Friday night phobia and fewer material possessions, but some pocket-money to go out with.' Worry and mental breakdown' he considered concomitant with getting it good the Tory way.' [78]

When Labour women debated consumer protection in 1960, the complexity of hire-purchase systems were condemned. H-P was also seen to involve popular complicity with capitalism. A Birmingham delegate complained at how women were being hoodwinked when they bought things on hire-purchase' and that they were playing the Tory game when they did so.' Colin MacInnes asserted Labour could never prosper by trimming its sails to the winds from the never-never land of hever had it so good.' Darling vowed under Labour there would be ho return to the 1959 free-for-all'. According to another Labour Party Research paper, hire-purchase was nothing less than a method by which disreputable retailers sell shoddy goods to ignorant customers.'[79]

The consumer was a figure that troubled socialists. Hall saw, a bland half-thing of a man .the folk-hero of corporate capitalism'. In a competitive society,' Bevan held, the consumer is passive, besieged .and robbed.' The consumer was generally seen as 'widely exploited', the victim of deception, false advertising, misleading claims for products', if also gullible'. For the 1955 election the family was proffered as a less atomized alternative to the categories of the individual and consumer to target with Labour propaganda. The Family', one research paper argued, was a more convenient and realistic unit to aim at than the consumer'; another favoured the family because it contrasts strongly with the Tory emphasis on the individual.'[80]

Sassoon argues the left-wing battles of the 1950s against the consumer society were as hopeless as those of the Luddites of yesteryear against machines'. There was a Luddite air to Lessing's description of Harry Pollitt demonstrating in the early 1950s outside Ponting's, an emporium in Kensington High Street.' The CPGB leader raised his clenched fist .then lowered it to point an accusing finger: 'When we take power, we're going to pull all these places down."Lessing saw this as evidence of the puritan, pleasure-hating' strand in British socialism, where the masses, who, clothes rationing having just ended, dreamed of nothing but a little fashion, a little glamour.'[81]

In other ways socialists were more aware of consumerism's political dimensions. In March 1960 Labour supported a boycott of South African Goods. In the same month as the Sharpeville Massacre, this demonstrated a potential for an ethical consumerism. Labour's agent in Merton urged: 'maybe, like me, you will keep it permanent.' [82]

The Consumers' Association (CA) was a response to the challenge and growth of consumerism. It was formed in 1956 by Labour's former Research Director, Michael Young and initially supported by a loan from the American Consumers Union. Its rapid growth – 165,000 members by 1960 – showed popular interest in consumer issues.[83]

If not technically *on* the left, CA's founding figures and thinking were *of* the left. The Association imagined itself informer and protector, in what, like Labour, it saw as a 'world of bewildering variety, controlled to an increasing degree by large companies and powerful trade associations, the consumer stands almost alone.' In short, the CA defended the *individual* against commercial exploitation.[84] It also fulfilled the desire in Labour circles for some consumer advisory service. Young had proposed such a scheme in Labour's 1950 manifesto and it was periodically revived, such as in a 1953 Fabian pamphlet by Jim Northcott. The CA claimed some credit for bringing about the Molony Committee on Consumer Protection (1959–62) and the ensuing creation of the Consumers' Council in 1963.[85]

Many on the left welcomed the CA. Labour women's sections were advised that they could do a great deal towards consumer protection by subscribing to *Which?*', CA's magazine. Crosland thought it one of the most exciting developments of recent years' and praised its efforts to combat misleading advertising' and raise our low national standards of quality'. A member of its governing council, he argued CA should have access to ITV (besides the BBC that broadcast *Choice* based on *Which?* research) to allow it to reach a mass' rather than mainly middle-class audience.' Crosland added, a left-wing party should always be in the van of consumer radicalism.'[86]

Young took this point a stage further in his 1960 manifesto *The Chipped White Cups of Dover*. By its affinity to the Trade Unions, Labour was linked to a producer interest even more openly than the Conservatives' at a time when class based on production' was slowly giving way to status based on consumption', he advanced. Labour needed to adopt the mantle of a reforming, consumerist party.' Mayhew, like Young later to leave Labour, also favoured a consumers' party.[87]

The labour movement always had a consumer's eye. It evinces the preoccupation with work, production and struggle in labour historiography that its co-operative wing has been paid less regard. In 1961 the Co-op supplied a third of the milk and ran a third of all supermarkets in Britain. Its annual turnover was a billion pounds. It also wielded political weight – sponsoring 38 Labour candidates in 1955, the largest number ever. Yet by the end of the 1950s the Co-op was stricken. It had long been losing ground to private multiples and in 1955 its share of the retail market began to fall. Although even those on the left (Gorman relates) shopped at the Co-op for the divi'rather than from socialist conviction', the acquisitive ethic of affluence seemed at odds with Co-op values. As Hoggart intimated, a Co-operative outlook was less typical' of most 1950s shoppers. What are we to do,' Richard Crossman was asked by a Coventry Co-operator in 1955, when our members draw the divi'to spend at M and S round the corner?'   [88]

For Hattersley, the Co-op had long been the home of drab uniformity .and shapeless clothes.' And as the Gaitskell Commission, appointed in 1955 to investigate the movement's crisis, reported (and thought positive), the consumer rejected inter-war austerity more and more.' Edited by Crosland, the report found from a tour of Co-operative shops that .the word co-operative"was associated with a drab, colourless, old-fashioned mentality.' This, it declared, was not good enough for the consumer in 1958' and showed a patronising and insulting attitude to the wants and expectations of the ordinary Co-operative member.' Like Labour, the Co-op needed renovating. Rehearsing an argument revisionists would apply to Labour, the Commission criticized the Co-op's inefficiency and un-professionalism. Specifically it felt its part-time, lay, elected, management was, however democratic, a dangerous anachronism.' [89]

The Report was rejected by the 1958 Co-op congress. Critics – traditionalists like the Co-operative Women's Guild and the left-wing – felt the comfortably uncommercial style' of the Co-ops should not and could not compete with the glittering supermarkets, neon lights' designed to please and dazzle the customers.' 'Why,' *Tribune* asked, should Co-ops ape the capitalists?' Modernization was stalled. The London Co-operative Society had been the first to introduce self-service to Britain, but by 1962 less than half of its grocery stores were thus arranged. [90]

New shopping habits met a mixed reception from socialists. Some enjoyed perusing and comparing goods, rather than being served from the counter; others lamented the lack of product knowledge and attention from shop assistants. One of the main thrusts of Labour consumer policy, its demand for quality marks and an Institute of Labelling to increase reliable information about products, was a response not only to the often ludicrous claims made for goods or the dim view they took of consumers, but to a new style of shopping where information was not so readily available at the counter. [91]

Historical opinion has concluded that Labour's inability to tackle consumer issues and gain the support of women voters, helps explain its electoral deficit during the 1950s. [92] Some contemporary opinion agreed. According to a survey of advertising, Labour was at best pessimistic towards consumer affairs – offering in *Fair Deal for the Shopper*, a mournful review of the perils that beset the buyer or shopper.' In 1956 Elaine Burton urged Gaitskell to take up the consumers' angle or it will be lifted from us entirely.' The Labour and Co-op candidate for South Battersea in 1959, admitted to being disturbed by the fact that the image which had been created of the Labour movement in this country, so far as the great majority of women were concerned, was that of a party which pays far too little attention to the problems of the consumer.'[93]

The left certainly approached the housewife in the 1950s, but was not as well received as the Conservatives. The Women's Co-operative Guild campaigned against the higher prices that accompanied the Conservative decontrol of food and the ending of rationing through the early 1950s. Labour too attacked *The High Price of Toryism*. However, this was not always a consumer-friendly strategy. *Labour Woman*'s editor for instance, felt little sympathy for those innocent electors' who voted Tory in 1951 in anticipation of being set free' and now, as prices rose, must be feeling a little dazed.' [94]

Still, the interpretation of consumer issues plied by the left struggled to make political profit out of the rising cost of living. In 1955 the *New Statesman* suggested three reasons why. Price rises fell most heavily upon the poor, old and unskilled, who tend to vote Labour anyway.' Secondly, price rises were concurrent with wage increases – boom conditions enabling less wage restraint than in 1945–51. Finally, when the Tories agitated on consumer issues before 1951, they had tapped into popular disaffection with rationing, controls and queues (queuetopia', as Dr Charles Hill put it during the 1951 election) and proposed an alternative policy. The middle classes in particular, the *Statesman* argued, were prepared to brook higher prices as the cost of marketplace freedom'. [95]

Labour was strongly associated with an interventionist, paternalist policy. It was more than a product of the war, nationalization or a language of fair shares'. As with attitudes towards culture and leisure, it also aimed to compensate for the shortcomings, as Labour saw them, of the electorate. Burton's 1955 pamphlet, *The Battle of the Consumer* did little to dispel this impression, declaring it, the duty of the government to give the shopper some protection and guidance'.[96]

Labour anticipated being portrayed as the party of controls at the 1955 election. The Conservatives issued fake ration-books, in which Labour's putative fondness for controls was likened to Soviet totalitarianism. Wilson damned their accusations as a deliberate Tory lie!' Labour's candidate in Hitchin unsuccessfully applied for an injunction to stop a grocery shop manager distributing them. But Phillips reported that the ration-book scare had affected support in middle income housewife groups.' Earlier responses to Phillips' slogan, 'Ask Your Dad!', point in the same direction. The *Daily Mail* located a (fortuitously) named Mr Hubbard, who felt electors might 'Ask Mum Too,' about queues and rationing.'[97]

This conjured up an infamous maxim of Labour's philanthropic statism. Douglas Jay's *The Socialist Case* (reprinted in 1947) had argued: housewives as a whole cannot be trusted to buy the right things .in the case of nutrition and health, just as in the case of education, the gentleman in Whitehall really does know better what is good for the people than the people themselves.' Exploiting anxieties over a nanny state, Jay was regularly cited in Conservative literature aimed at women voters.[98]

Labour's paternalism, however beneficent or educative its aims, could be experienced by others as interfering. A 1955 *Manchester Guardian* report argued the public resented the remote official' controlling council housing or the price of coal and were associated in many people's minds with the start towards socialism that Labour made in 1945.' However fair or necessary such systems were, the public would always be on Mr. Pilgrim's side.' In short, it was not free enterprise or capitalism that irked, but the imperfections of the kind of system that Labour is supposed to want.'[99]

Crossman was amongst those increasingly aware of the deleterious influence this had on the Party's relationship with voters. Criticizing a draft of *Signposts for the Sixties* in 1961 he warned it was, written too much from the point of view of the bureaucrat organizing things, too little from the point of view of the people at the receiving end.' Labour's NEC heard at the inquest into its 1959 defeat, that bureaucratism had contributed, to a generally unfavourable image of our party.' Too many of the electorate', the report reckoned, saw us as .a. party of restrictions and controls.'[100]

'Ask your Dad' also prompted the question of gender. Labour's limited support amongst women voters was noted in 1959, but most analyses of defeat centred on class, image and generation. When Phillips disowned 'Ask your Dad' in 1960, it was criticized on the grounds that it was square' – just as the Co-op's mid-1950s audit remonstrated above all with its old-fashioned and middle-aged air.' [101]

Despite growing numbers of (especially married) women working, Black and Brooke note, the limited number of Labour Party pamphlets actually addressing women specifically identified them as housewives and mothers.' Children's games and Favourite Recipes' were regular features in *Labour Woman*. The CPGB too left whole areas of women's lives .unquestioned.'   [102] There was a conservative streak in socialism here, attesting to the masculinity of Labour culture, but also conforming with the post-war emphasis on family and domesticity.

This was partly a recognition, as Michael Young put it, that affluence has not benefited the pub but the home' – the private and domestic more than the public. It was an attempt to offset the disruption of customary relationships in the atomized lifestyles of affluence and cleave to a sense of community, but there was also a maternalist aspect to it. A family union, Young noted, was stronger than any trade union could ever be.' Socialist Union urged family allowances be given priority over day nurseries so that mothers no longer feel the pull of the labour market trying to pull them out of their houses.'[103] The left saw women to have benefited in the form of labour-saving devices' coming into the working woman's home.' Yet automation, via the vacuum and washing-machine, no more ended the division of labour at home than it did in industry.[104]

Socialism's gender traditionalism, puritanism and *dirigiste* sympathies and language, combined to cede the field of consumerism. The Conservatives, posing as liberators of the consumer in the early 1950s and not describing the consumer goods of the later 1950s in such ruinous terms, could more easily appear as champions of the affluent – actively associating themselves with affluence and its ample political value.

Suburbia[105]

As much as anything the new lifestyles of the affluent society troubled socialists. They felt unease at their individualism, encapsulated in the car. Socialists were not enthusiastic motorists and there were political connotations to this. Car ownership seemed linked to Conservatism. Gordon-Walker reported a 1958 Gallup poll, had showed that 60 per cent of car owners were Conservative.' Gorman recalled that the one inhabitant of his East-end street who voted Conservative' was the only man in the street who owned a car.' Gaitskell had been unpopular with the motoring press since his 1951 budget.[106]

Other evidence blurred this picture. Abrams' investigation of the car's political qualities in *Must Labour Lose?*, found equal numbers of Labour and Conservative voters amongst working-class drivers. Where there was a significant difference was that car ownership amongst the middle class was more than double that of workers. And it was this that the left, whose instincts were to equate middle-class symbols with the enemies of the labour movement, socialism and the working class', had picked up on.[107]

Yet this equation was dubious. As Crossman reported from Britain's motor-city, ownership of a car ceased to be a middle-class characteristic in Coventry at least a decade before anywhere else.' Willmott and Young's study of the post-war LCC housing estate at Greenleigh' in Essex, noted that residents acquired cars and phones to attempt to hold onto the community ties they had enjoyed in inner London. One of the weaknesses in the planning of such estates was that a garage was as rare in Twentieth-Century Greenleigh as an indoor lavatory was in nineteenth-century Bethnal Green.'[108]

Labour was neither *a* party of car-owners (79 per cent of Labour candidates used less than half the number of permissible cars on election day in 1955);[109] nor *the* party of car owners, to judge by the scant regard drivers received in the party policy. This indifference towards modern lifestyles, produced by socialist culture, fed into policy and party image. A special NEC meeting in 1960 admitted 'many issues of immediate relevance to the lives of our fellow citizens were omitted' from Party literature. The problems of the younger generation, the uses of leisure were tardily recognised', but 'most striking was our failure to deal with the whole nexus of problems connected with urban development – location of offices, inadequate roads, suburban commuting.'[110]

Amongst causes of the left's hostility towards suburbia was as Young reported in 1954, that Labour councillors in London and elsewhere are worried .that they are, by building more houses in the countryside weakening their own Party.' Labour agents on the borders of cities,' he told, knew of dozens and dozens of people who were sound Labour voters before they moved and have changed over to Conservative since.'[111]

More familiar patterns emerged from a 1960 survey – of close community .extended family, informal and collective organisation', but still did not allay the left's unease. While some suburban residents were setting out to become middle-class themselves, in attitude, house and furniture and in politics', Willmott and Young thought a vital difference remained that the working class do not know how to spend all their extra money .they have got a middle-class income without the ingrained middle-class sense of how to spend it.'[112] It was its failure to address this that lost the left ground.

Suburbia was thought less communal, more self-centred and, *ergo*, unwelcoming to socialism. Among comments from estate residents were those of Mr Tonks, who was surprised at the way people vote Conservative at Greenleigh when the LCC built these houses for them.' One has a little car or something and so he thinks himself superior,' he continued – people seem to think of themselves when they get here.'[113] Circumspect conclusions were licensed further by Labour's performance at the 1959 election. Epping and Hitchin, containing Harlow and Stevenage new towns respectively, and peopled by re-housed Londoners, saw increases in their Tory majorities. After the election Stephen Swingler, Labour MP for Newcastle-under-Lyme talked of the spiritual vacuum that exists on so many new housing estates and in New Towns.'[114]

The suburban and affluent condition was correlated with political apathy, or worse, Conservatism.[115] Potter explained socialists were apt to think it 'not the most natural thing in the world to be a radical when surrounded by suburban hedgerows and new supermarkets.' Merlyn Rees, like Potter a miner's son and defeated Labour candidate at Harrow in 1959, recalled how in his 'home the singing of the red flag, the Co-op, the trade union are things that get an answer in the tingling of my blood.' Yet they received 'no answer in tingling blood in the suburbs of London.' Quite simply, Jones has recalled, 'Labour canvassers reckoned that house-owners were bound to be Tories.'[116]

Suburban living seemed to threaten the Labour movement's sociological footing. In Swansea, Tanner tells, Labour saw post-war estate-dwellers as 'a new generation, devoid of morals and of social respect, pampered and materialistic.' 'All political parties had to face such changes', he argues, but in West Swansea in particular, it was the Labour party's 'core''vote which was contracting, and the party's ideals which were increasingly challenged.' Millar's history of Labour Colleges tells how suburban housing estates meant large numbers of trade unionists left the city centres.' 'Attempts to organise classes in the suburbs were not often successful', Millar lamented – 'many of the men preferred to tend their gardens .or .watch the television.' Gordon-Walker was concerned that as more people commuted to work, the bond between unions, Labour and the local community would dissolve.[117]

Others were more optimistic. Communists Ted Rodgers and David Grove, found the social structure in Crawley, the second New Town, conducive to their politics. In 1952–3 they campaigned against rent increases, organizing marches and a rent strike. As all New Town residents worked in the town, it was easier to develop 'tenant–worker unity'. In this sense (demonstrating socialists' propensity to view modern Britain through older paradigms), Rodgers compared Crawley to a Welsh mining village.[118]

Architect Jane Drew, a contributor to the *Daily Herald's* 'Dateline: 1984' series also took a more positive view of modern living. She lived near Crawley, which she judged 'successful' and, like revisionism, had turned her eye to questions of 'street furniture', social amenities and design. She thought favourably of domestic gadgets and that homes could 'lose a lot of our Puritanism.' The one aspect of new lifestyles she could not countenance was the prospect that 'the TV set will take the place of the fireplace as the centre of the family circle.'[119]

Other evidence queries the assumptions about the social and political meaning of the new lifestyles socialists reached. In Stevenage many residents did not initially own the durables that supposedly promoted private living. Thus, shops and launderettes remained social centres. Far from encouraging individualism, the washing machine became a cause of communal action. Neighbours clubbed together to hire a machine, carrying it from house to house, although they never knew if the laundry man [from whom they hired it] ever found out.'[120] It was not only its political effects that worried socialists, but the suburban condition itself. In a section cut from *In Place of Fear*, Bevan described the suburbia which is emptied and filled each morning and night with the ebb and flow of the city, having no deep waters of its own.' It was an aesthetic monstrosity, an ethical crime'. As housing minister Bevan loathed the fretful fronts stretching along great roads out of London.' Socialists were at ease in the country and the city, but not a suburban mix. Bevan himself left his Belgravia town house in 1954 for a Buckinghamshire farm.[121]

The *Architectural Review* issued a broadside against what it termed subtopia' in 1955. Its author, Ian Nairn, argued subtopia was a mean and middle state, neither town nor country, an even spread of .fake rusticity .gratuitous noticeboards, car-parks .which spreads both ways from suburbia.' Nairn's assault struck a chord with socialists. Not least, in its opposition to mass culture and call for the defence of the individuality of places' against the doom of an England reduced to universal subtopia.'[122]

Leisure for Living joined the attack in 1959, claiming public indifference, private avarice and, in some places, municipal ignorance' were responsible for the growth of what has been nicknamed subtopia." Labour's attack was less indiscriminate though – it saw the principal offender' as private industry.' The *New Statesman* regarded St Helens as a classic example of the way unrestricted capitalism created so many of our ugliest industrial cities.' Ugliness besides poverty motivated socialists. Pollitt told the 1955 CPGB Congress, we want to tear down the slums and rebuild the city beautiful.'[123]

'Public authorities', Jenkins argued offend much less against the rules of planning and good design than do private concerns', though like Nairn he criticized the Atomic Energy and Electricity authorities. Jenkins and Labour praised the Festival Hall, LCC estate at Roehampton and TUC's Congress House and the efforts of the Anti-Ugly Association and Councils for Industrial Design and the Preservation of Rural England.[124]

There was a long left-wing ruralist and preservationist tradition. As an escape from urban conditions, the simple life' of hiking, climbing and cycling were an informal part of socialist leisure. The Green Belt, National Parks and protection for the Pennine Way were all recent Labour initiatives. *Leisure for Living* closed with an incantation on the fortifying virtues of the open air' and found cause in contemporary concerns like litter, the need for removing unsightly advertisements from the countryside' (a concern too of the AIC's amenity panel) and for the use of local stone on new buildings.' [125]

Socialist summer schools were invariably held at rural retreats like Beatrice Webb House in Surrey or Buscot Park in Oxfordshire. In tune with Labour's cultural priorities, country house visiting was a trait they applauded. Jenkins took the Tory housing expansion of the 1950s to task, arguing that strangely for such a self conscious representative of English traditional values' Macmillan's government was responsible for urban sprawl.' [126]

Chapters 4 and 5 have documented how the ambivalence and hostility of socialism towards the affluent condition merged with its moralizing, interventionist tendencies and an estimation of the limitations of the electorate. Labour, as Barbara Castle told the 1959 conference, felt its ethical reach was beyond the mental grasp of the average person.' [127]

Socialists' prescriptiveness and willingness to intervene, drew from their own ethics and notions of moral worth and lifestyle. These were animated by the values and activities involved in affluence'. But they were also a response to disappointment at the moral and mental fibre of the people – falling short of socialist hopes and requirements. Socialists found the people wanting – and wanting the wrong' things. It was the people then, who were to blame for Labour's malaise. Gaitskell characterized this attitude as expressed by the likes of Bevan and Castle, in the words of Oscar Wilde: The play was a great success, but the audience was a failure.'[128]

Socialists brought about much of their alienation from popular affluence. In his 1962 account of Britain, Labour-supporting youth commentator Ray Gosling admitted: the people didn't seem to want a revolution .I.hadn't then come across the idea that when you spend twenty years working for a semi-detached and you get it, you just hold on tight', and that to them Labour .seemed a bore .do-gooders …
out of contact with the world outside.' It was a mark of this that socialism appealed as an escape from the affluent society'. For Elizabeth Wilson, pained by the commercialised vulgarity of advertising and pop .vulgar advertising .suburban sprawl and the stupidities of

television' (that, besides the stupidities of the nuclear bomb, had led her to read the *New Statesman*), socialism offered salvation. It was this cultural snobbery and moral revulsion' she explained, that began to be transformed into an abstract socialism.'[129]

Much of social change in the 1950s were cast by socialists in an unfavourable light. Their criticisms could be argued to have contributed to the regulatory moment of 1962–3: the post-Molony Consumers' Council, the CA, ASA and post-Pilkington TV act. Certainly part of Conservative reasoning behind the first and last of these was to rein in affluence – guiding the consumer or controlling ITV profits. Where the left's criticisms of the affluent society' were more widely shared, they struggled to articulate these in terms that did not simultaneously indict televiewers and consumers too – casting them too unfavourably to reap political rewards. The success of the likes of the CA was to accept consumers and consumerism and take up their grievances in those terms. Without this more discerning view and with the sort of state paternalism that was at odds with the expansion of popular choice and values, the left's outlook was disabling.

By the close of the 1950s, socialism faced profound questions. Crudely, the issue was whether they or the people' had read affluence wrong. As socialists saw it, affluence had made its ethicalism more necessary (to provide values and cultural guidance), but also more problematic (interfering and out-of-date). Other than a critical distance from affluence or a final push for electoral victory, could the left develop an effective response? Could its intuitive objections be built into a systematic approach towards affluence?

6
Must Labour Lose?: Revisionism and the 'Affluent Worker'

Socialists' understanding of affluence was not predetermined. Its extent, meaning and implications for socialism were hotly contested. Most viewed it from an ethical perspective and were hostile on the grounds that affluence was morally and culturally corrupt. Enmity also centred on the perception that affluence was undermining the left's sociological base in working-class communities and consciousness. Believing affluence to have been bought on credit and transitory, based on a short-term boom, the CPGB and Labour left' saw little reality or economic achievement to it. Labour revisionists and the New Left used an ethical framework to propose ways of building upon affluence rather than opposing it. Revisionism believed it a condition with unrealized socialist potential. As Fabians and social democrats had long done, they believed socialism would evolve from capitalism. And affluence – since it stood as evidence of economic dynamism and it was hoped the relief of material need might attune people to ethical and cultural goals – affirmed this perspective. Revisionism, then, and the figure of the 'affluent worker', can be recognized as a quite traditional socialist mode of thought. What was novel about Crosland, as Inglis suggests, was that he saw, as few in the labour movement could, the candid delight with which people, the people, enjoyed their new leisure, their new comforts and domestic toys.'[1]

This chapter questions the idea familiar to contemporaries and commentators since that affluence necessarily and naturally benefited the political right – that social change explained and underpinned Conservative success in the 1950s.[2] It suggests there was nothing inevitable to Conservative success and little sense in which Labour was bound to suffer because of affluence. Political fortunes were less clearly related to social change than to how it was conceived by the parties.

Popular Conservatism predated affluence and was more culturally substantial than simply a measure of Labour's failure.

Affluence confused socialists. Their predicament was deeper than that Labour had faced in 1931. For while their electoral support diminished only by a slight (if vital) amount, socialists encountered a Britain that defied their expectations – a Britain that seemed a good way short of socialism, but without any of the worst side-effects of capitalism. This confounded their belief that capitalism was economically inefficient and unjust (which 1931 had confirmed). Rather, capitalism produced the goods – full employment and a range of new consumer wares. Affluent Britain was also a disappointing sequel to the Attlee governments. Many socialists shared the surprise of a social history of the period, as from the austere but substantial foundations of Socialist Egalitarianism the gleaming structure of the People's Capitalism now rose bizarrely.'[3]

The change from the social, economic and ideological characteristics of Great Britain from the 1830s to the 1930s', convinced Crosland that Britain could no longer usefully be understood as capitalist.[4] The New Left felt that a society in which choice not need (consumerism not poverty) predominated, meant capitalism was more pervasive than ever. But socialists were united in their aversion to the commercialization of culture and everyday life. Affluence brought into question the relationship between social and material progress. For Communists this was also germane to the revelations of 1956. Khrushchev's secret speech made it clear that economic progress in the Soviet Union had come not with, but at the expense of, social, cultural and ethical advance.

Coming to terms with affluence?

Socialists of all brands were anxious at the course of social change in the 1950s. The *New Statesman* considered, few tears will be shed for the fifties'. It had been a cynical, meretricious, selfish' decade in which the Tories had made Britain into a .national casino with loaded dice.' Nye Bevan spoke in no uncertain terms at Labour's 1959 conference: this so-called affluent society is an ugly society still. It is a vulgar society. It is a meretricious society. It is a society in which priorities have gone all wrong.' For those of this ilk, faith in socialism was a means of surviving in a vulgar society of which no decent person could be proud.' Mervyn Jones, in the first number of *New Left Review* in 1960, envisaged socialism as a total rejection of the practice and values of the existing society.' Bevan's 1959 conference speech closed by invoking socialism as history's destiny. His audience applauded his assurance that once voters had 'got over the delirium of television ... when they realise that all the tides of history are flowing in our direction .then we shall lead our people to where they deserve to be led.'   [5]

No decent person, then, would be proud of British society in the 1950s. Labour and the left seemed in opposition in the 1950s – not only to the government, but society more generally. Malcolm Muggeridge struck up a familiar *New Statesman* tune, describing the Thirteen Years Soft's between 1951 and 1964 as years of 'political, economic and moral free-wheeling, with the encouragement of every sort of soft indulgence from betting and bingo to The Beatles .the records set up have been in road accidents, hire purchase, juvenile delinquency and telly-viewing.'[6]

Yet socialist fears about social change and the condition of society easily translated into doubts about its citizens. Electoral defeat in 1959 occasioned a questioning of the moral condition of the people. *Tribune* feared 'millions of our people have been subtly acclimatised to the ... casino society, the I'm Allright Jack"society .nobody has taught them to do otherwise than pant after the scramble for personal prizes, scream their applause and envy at the catchword 'double your money".' Edward Thompson felt the electorate's choice had 'confirmed our more pessimistic estimates of the direction of social drift within the opportunity state.'[7]

Nor were fears that the popular mood and its politics were some way adrift of socialism, confined to the 'left'. The 'right-wing' Labour MP Woodrow Wyatt was dismayed that 'all .most electors care about is what will happen to them personally' and that 'the general sense of responsibility is so low.'[8] Keeping faith in workers as agents of socialism, when they were seen as so ethically corrupt, was problematic.

Elsewhere, workers' 'interest' in Labour, more than its moral condition was exercising socialists. Defeat in 1959 led to profound questions about Labour's future. Variously, it was asked: *Must Labour Lose?*, *Can Labour Win?*, 'Must Tories Always Triumph?'. With contributions from psephologist Mark Abrams, political scientist Richard Rose, and Rita Hinden, *Must Labour Lose?* was a sociological obsequy of Labour. It answered its title affirmatively – 'Yes it must – at least in the near future.' Labour's class appeal and 'ethos of class solidarity', Hinden maintained, were crumbling 'in the face of the new fluidity of our society, the new opportunities for advancement through individual effort.' Labour's appeal to overcome poverty and the instability of capitalism through planning and public ownership 'mean[t] little now that the terrible economic depressions of the past appear to have been left behind.' This argument was not confined to revisionism. Perry Anderson, the New Left's theoretician-in-chief, was also persuaded that full employment and rising incomes rendered the classical socialist solutions – in particular social ownership of the means of production – redundant.'[9]

For revisionism, economic being largely determined class-consciousness. Crosland argued in 1956 that 'a majority of the population is gradually attaining a middle-class standard of life and distinct symptoms even of a middle-class psychology.' If capitalism was extinct – the working class was also a threatened species. As Douglas Jay put it in the aftermath of 1959, Labour was in danger of fighting under the label of a class that no longer exists.'[10]

Working-class prosperity was convicted at inquests into Labour's electoral setbacks. In 1955 Morgan Phillips ventured that the main factor was probably the comparative prosperity"which has lulled many of our supporters into inactivity.' By 1959 the charge could be levelled with certainty. Labour's election sub-committee concluded: 'We were defeated by prosperity: This was without doubt the prominent factor'. This analysis was shared locally. A defeated Labour candidate in Nottingham reflected: Beeston and Stapleford is an extremely prosperous centre. The workers in Ericssons, Boots, Beeston Boilers ... are completely 'deproletarianised"and many have succumbed to Tory propaganda of recent years.'[11]

Encapsulated in the figure of the 'deproletarianized' or 'affluent worker' were assumptions disclosing much about socialist attitudes towards the social changes of the 1950s. The 'affluent worker' was less sociological entity than political construction. Warde argues, 'embourgeoisement theory was primarily an invention of the social reformists'. The 'affluent worker' emerged from deep within the socialist imagination.[12]

Recent sightings include the 1980s 'Essex' man and woman, but the 'affluent worker' also resembled the nineteenth-century 'Labour aristocrat'. Certainly the presence of the 'affluent worker' can be recognized in Hobsbawm's description of the Labour aristocracy in a 1954 article. They were, he argued, a 'distinctive upper strata of the working class, better paid, better treated and generally regarded as more 'respectable" and politically moderate than the mass of the proletariat'. Socially speaking' the Communist historian continued, the best paid stratum of the working class merged with what may be loosely called the 'lower middle class". Hobsbawm concluded in terms proximate to

Crosland's revisionism. Looking at the twentieth century he saw a new labour aristocracy of salaried, white collar, technical and similar workers which considers itself so different 'from the working class as to remain largely conservative in politics' and wondered about the prophetic implications of Engels' remark that the English proletariat is becoming more and more bourgeois.'[13]

Crosland, citing the same passage from Engels in *The Future of Socialism*, was certain of its prophetic qualities, and that if its author was disapproving in 1858, then he would have been even more horrified could he have gone canvassing round new housing estates in 1955, or read the Gallup surveys of what class people think they belong to.'[14]

There were differences of course. Where the aristocrat' was bribed' with the crumbs from the super profits' of British imperialism, the affluent worker' was seduced' by the merchandise of a consumer-oriented capitalism. Yet the process was the same: the corruption of capitalism, whether in imperialist or consumerist garb, combined with the corruptibility of the working class.[15]

Tied in here was the strand of socialism that held the working class accountable, in part, for its own situation and for the limitations of British socialism. In this regard, Perry Anderson's 1964 piece, Origins of the Present Crisis', was very much of a piece with contemporary socialist thinking. In England', it proposed (like Engels), a supine bourgeoisie produced a supine proletariat', with an immovable corporate class consciousness' but almost no hegemonic ideology.' This defensiveness and paucity of theory were embodied in Labour. Yet in this sense, Anderson held, Labour's limitations were only an expression of a deeper failure' of the working class to evolve a political will'. In short, the density and specificity of English working-class culture ... limited its political range and checked the emergence of a more ambitious socialism.'[16]

From a sharper pen such reasoning could be little less than disparaging of the populace. J. B. Priestley denounced the mass communications – advertising – salesmanship complex of the 'Admass' society, but was as censorious of its citizens. His *New Statesman* columns in the 1950s typically contemplated the idle-minded mob' who do not really want anything until they are told they want it.'[17]

Such poverty of desire', as Ernest Bevin once put it, was a long-held concern of socialists – and never more so than in the 1950s.[18] Hobsbawm expressed exasperation with the damned modesty of the British worker's demands' in 1961. Hattersley explained socialists felt the British worker [was] too willing to accept crumbs from the capitalist table and too reluctant to insist on his fair share.' Socialists saw the new affluence as the latest palliative.'[19] This was aggravated in the 1950s by what they conceived of as the limited cultural and spiritual horizons opened up by affluence and people's preparedness to settle for these. In the 1950s socialists, while not believing in it themselves, feared that many people had developed an interest in popular capitalism'.

The very designation, affluent worker', was anomalous to socialist reasoning – ironic in the manner of the labour aristocrat'. To the socialist mind, workers' consciousness was formed by poverty and exploitation. In this era of Tory prosperity' Richard Crossman argued, each year which takes us further, not only from the hungry thirties, but from the austere forties, weakens class consciousness ..more socialist voters turn first into don't knows and then into active Tories.'[20] The spectre of embourgeoisement haunted socialist politics based solely on the drive to reduce poverty.

Revisionism, by contrast, embraced embourgeoisement and the affluent worker' as an ideal-type around which Labour politics could convene. Yet it did so in a recognisable manner. Class remained its main analytical category. Crosland's *Can Labour Win?*, the most systematic account of the revisionist project, asserted the symmetry of party and class. The Labour vote will probably decline .by about 2 per cent at each successive election', Crosland predicted, as this was approximately the rate at which the newly emerging white-collar class is replacing the manual working class.'

'People normally vote for the party which is associated with the social class to which they assign themselves' he declared. Working-class Toryism was to be explained as either deferential''voters who cast a consciously *inverted* class vote for their social superiors' or by the newly prosperous skilled workers who have acquired an almost middle-class standard of income.' The latter, by virtue of their new prosperity, may assign themselves to the middle class', and thus were likely to affirm this by supporting the Conservatives.[21] Prosperity, then, was equated with middle-class and, in a sense, the affluent worker' was not a worker at all! Revisionists, like other socialists, saw in affluence an embougeoisement of values, evinced in support for the Conservatives.

Revisionism attempted to alter socialism's profile to take account of new times. It accepted post-war social change and ratified its political case with opinion surveys, to check and assert it was in tune with these changes. *The Future of Socialism* was central to left-wing debate in the

1950s and after. As Drucker would have it, Crosland's was the sole British socialist text since the second world war to achieve an international audience.' While other parts of the left, Ellison contends, sought 'withdrawal from the gathering pace of modernity' or could only thrive by 'narrowing .their egalitarian vision to more manageable social policy issues', revisionism prospered.[22]

After the 1959 election there was broad agreement – Labour's defeat was ascribed to the perceived threat it posed to affluence. Crosland argued 'many voters undoubtedly felt, vaguely but strongly, that in the event of a Labour victory the current prosperity would be threatened.' Bevan agreed that 'young men and women in the course of the last five or ten years have had their material conditions improved .and their discontents have been reduced, so that temporarily their personalities are satisfied with the framework in which they live.'[23] Communist George Matthews subscribed to the consensus. Discussing the desire to have a TV set and a washing-machine', he berated Labour: 'if young workers are blamed for wanting these things, the implication is that they wouldn't get them under Labour.' Such analyses endorsed the 1959 Tory election slogan, 'Don't Let Labour Ruin it' and the suggestion that Britons had 'never had it so good.' Few socialists dissented from *The Economist* cartoon showing a victorious Macmillan seated in a comfy front room and thanking a fridge, car, television and washing-machine – 'Well, gentlemen, I think we all fought a good fight.' [24]

Yet beneath this unanimity lay a tangle of opinions on the meaning of affluence. Its very existence was contested by British Communists. Where it was discussed in CPGB literature, prosperity was invariably accompanied by adjectives such as 'so-called' or 'apparent' or by speech-marks, denoting its merely discursive, not material status. 'Who's Having it Good?' CPGB public meetings asked early in 1960. They were told that 'apparent 'prosperity''was based on hire purchase' where the average debt by 1959 exceeded the average weekly wage or involved both husband and wife working.

Communists did not suggest the impoverishment of workers, but pointed out that 1959 had been 'a year in which profits went up by 13 per cent .but wage rates .by less than 1 per cent.' As John Gollan, the CPGB's General Secretary put it, 'the worker today is being robbed of more surplus value than ever before.' The 'real picture of Britain' remained one of a 'tiny class of rich capitalists' parasitic on 'millions of low paid workers .pensioners and sick.' The 'so-called prosperity' Gollan argued, left 'millions in near starvation'. Such gains as workers had made were only achieved through trade union struggle and were insecure. Capitalism remained crisis-prone – there had been three partial crises since 1945' and automation threatened permanent unemployment for a section of the working class.'[25]

Tribune was as apt in the early 1950s to predict impending doom. Our economic situation is much more perilous than most of our people recognise', a 1952 editorial estimated, our very livelihood may be at stake.' The transience of affluence was central to the affluent worker' recognized by the Labour Left in the later 1950s. Their politically unadventurous' conservatism, Bevan told *News of the World* readers, was a product of contentment and apprehension.' Contentment', Bevan's dialectic suggested, because their material horizons have expanded and apprehension because they know their new found improvement is perilous and fragile.' Labour, then, was only afflicted by a temporary unpopularity' in what was a temporarily affluent society'.[26]

For the left', affluence was rendered illusory by credit. This was virtual affluence – based not on economic achievement but on the never-never", on homes mortgaged to the hilt', and buying domestic equipment and gadgets of all sorts on the hire-purchase system.' For Bevan such commitments accorded with a venal political psychology, a brash materialism shot through with fear.' [27]

Others shared Bevan's aversion. George Hodgkinson considered it a spurious affluent society'. [28] In *Labour in the Affluent Society* , Crossman argued that Labour should be refusing in any way to come to terms with the affluent society.' It could then warn the electorate of the troubles that lie ahead', with the prospect of gaining the confidence of the electorate when its harsh predictions come true.'

Common to Crossman and Bevan's accounts was the idea that the coming crisis' was not the collapse of capitalism, but the challenge of Communism. In this, the left' aimed to associate itself with historical trends, an affinity it was less able or willing to strike up at home. Crossman anticipated that when the trend of world development becomes clear and the Communist victories are undeniable ... our people will be shaken out of their comfortable affluence.' Likewise, the left's interest in foreign and defence policy in the 1950s has been attributed to frustration at the course of domestic matters.[29]

In others ways Bevan was wary of attributing Labour's unpopularity simply to affluence. His 1959 speech recalled how during the hardships of the inter-war years, when by such reasoning there ought to been some spontaneous generation of socialist conviction .still the Tories got a majority.' But the conviction that economic stagnation and unemployment were imminent and would bring support to Labour, was widespread,[30] not least in Labour's 1953 programme, *Challenge to Britain*. Crossman warned in 1954 that neither of the chief premises of *Challenge to Britain* – that Labour was likely to inherit an economic crisis on resuming office (a traditional fear) and that it was this that would have turned voters against the Conservatives – were necessarily tenable.[31]

Other studies belied the assumption that politics reflected economic being or that the social basis of Labour's support was fixed. A New Left survey of the deference voter', found them to be more pervasive and deep-seated' in attitudes and less the isolated deviant', or myth', than many supposed. Once rid of the myth that before 1939 almost all wage-earners and their wives voted Labour as a matter of course', Raymond Williams found it difficult to see any radically new pattern' in 1950s voting behaviour. Indeed Williams pointed out that Labour's vote was healthier, in the period of washing-machines and televisions than in the period of high unemployment'.[32]

In this respect Bevan conceived socialists' task in familiar terms. Just as pre-war workers had been too easily satisfied' and not sufficiently conscious of frustration and of limitation', so affluence required socialists to enlarge .those personalities so that they can become again conscious of frustration and of limitation.' This formulation was very much in the mode of William Morris' education of desire'.[33]

Bevanism craved old struggles. Crosland found Bevan's *In Place of Fear* like a browse amongst socialist first principles"without any new policies or fresh .justification for old ones.' Its belief that the old dogmas are as good as ever' as Michael Foot asserted in 1958 was evident to sympathizers besides opponents. The traditional left", Dennis Potter complained in 1959, spoke a language remote from almost everything except the memories of the thirties, meaningless as these must be to the post-war generations.' Mervyn Jones, a sometime Bevanite, has recalled how Bevan was not at home', with the new working class – the car-driving, home-owners of the Midlands. Crossman (an occasional ally) was similarly perturbed. From the forefront of social change in Coventry, where mass unemployment was unknown and unfeared by the younger generation' and poverty .had become a minority problem', Crossman reported the collapse' of the way of life' on which the Labour Party had been based.[34]

Revisionism

The revisionists (new realists or modernizers, in modern parlance) also had quarrels with modernity. Crosland took issue with the distribution of affluence and neglect of social spending, the vulgar commercialisation of culture.' *The Conservative Enemy* railed against the imbalance of private affluence and public squalor'. [35] Revisionism (and the New Left for that matter) was, in its mind's eye, a return to older socialist values quite as much as a modernizing impulse. Crosland urged in 1956 that as the pre-war reasons for a largely economic orientation are .steadily losing their relevance', socialists could divert .energies into more fruitful and idealistic channels and to fulfilling earlier and more fundamental socialist aspirations.' Roy Jenkins closed *The Labour Case* by calling for socialists to be on the side of those who want people to be free to live their own lives .of experiment and brightness, of better buildings and better food, of better music (jazz as well as Bach) and better books.' In the long run,' Jenkins concluded, these things will be more important than even the most perfect of economic policies.' Rita Hinden summed up *Must Labour Lose?* by detecting hopeful lines of development, the paths forward from a higher standard of life to an improved *way of life* – one in keeping with the idealism of the socialist vision.'[36]

In seeking to revert' socialism to underlying moral values', from a preoccupation with the economic, revisionism claimed to be quite traditionally socialist. Like the New Left's interest in the ethical issues raised by Morris, revisionism was part of what in the later 1950s was not so much a cultural turn in socialism, as a return or renewal. Crosland invoked Morris as sanction and guide for rearranging socialism along more liberal, social and less prescriptive or Fabian lines.[37]

Perforce, any revisionism' must refer to an original corpus, however wide the departure from it. Revisionism affirmed the notion in all guises of socialism that rated the spiritual over the material aspect of life. Bevan castigated capitalism on these grounds. Its values were awry because economic prevailed over human values: efficiency was its final arbiter – as though loving, laughing, worshipping, eating .a happy home, the warmth of friends, .revelation of new beauty.will ever yield to such a test.' Crosland held the same values dear. As economic and welfare matters were resolved he conceived attention would turn towards more important spheres – of personal freedom, happiness and cultural endeavour: the cultivation of leisure, beauty, grace, gaiety and excitement .a full private and family life.' [38]

For Bevan, socialism meant 'moral considerations' would take 'precedence over economic motives.' Crossman and the Socialist Union held that to argue for socialism in terms of its economic worth was erroneous – the language betrayed the reasoning. We should take to socialism' the Union argued, citing Robert Blatchford, because it is ethically right, otherwise we shall stop short at collectivism'. As early as 1950 Crossman suggested the left needed to revive its 'ethical principles' since they were far more important .than any economic betterment we have achieved', he reflected.[39]

This ethical ingredient was part of the left's daily diet in the 1950s and from it a reflex suspicion of affluence grew. CPGB meetings regaled the audience with the idea that socialism meant 'more than 'prosperity"and would involve 'a full, rich, life of opportunity of all kinds for people; greater leisure; wonderful facilities with which to enjoy it.'[40] Labour's widely distributed policy primer of 1958, *The Future Labour Offers You*, closed with an exposition of the full life':

> True happiness does not come from material prosperity (but poverty causes an immense amount of human unhappiness). Happiness comes from a full, free, satisfying life – a decent home, a secure job that you like doing, leisure richly filled with the good things of civilisation.[41]

Revisionism then had much in common with the shared culture of British socialism. As Francis shows, Crossman thought *The Future of Socialism* 'cunningly left-wing', and felt, Nye [Bevan] should have been clever enough to think ..up' its main proposals. [42] This common ground was further disclosed by the framework in which this return to a concern with values, lifestyle and culture was envisaged – for ironically, it was understood to be derived from economic achievement.

For Crosland, that 'sociological and cultural issues ..will come increasingly to the forefront as the traditional economic problems recede' would 'require a mental adjustment in many quarters on the left' because 'socialist thought has been dominated by the economic problems posed by capitalism: poverty, mass unemployment, squalor, instability and the possibility of the imminent collapse of the whole system.' Yet it was uncertain if revisionism had dislodged the primacy of the economic in its own mind. There was a familiar order to Crosland's case for the possibility of an emphasis on more 'social policies' now (but only now) Britain was 'on the threshold of mass abundance.'[43]

There was also a Fabian air to the idea of socialism evolving from capitalism. The abiding concern of *The Future of Socialism*, that Britons should not enter the age of abundance, only to find we have lost the values which might teach us how to enjoy it' was reminiscent of Marx's leap into freedom evoked in *Capital'* which only becomes possible with the advent of generalised abundance.' Perry Anderson thought collaterally to Crosland. Reviewing 'The Left in the Fifties' in 1965, he noted that as material deprivation to a certain degree receded, cultural loss and devastation became .more evident and important.'[44] From different tacks, revisionism and the New Left attempted to focus socialist politics upon culture' and social issues in the knowledge that immediate material needs were in recession. Both attempted to engage socialism with modernity, but made their case with due respect to tradition.

Crosland had a firm sense of Labour tradition, distinguishing him from other revisionists. Unlike Gaitskell, he recognized, without particularly approving of, the symbolic charge of clause four. So did the New Left. For Anderson clause four did not involve any attachment to the living values of an ideology – only to the dead sediment of a tradition.' And consonant with the New Left, Crosland entertained doubts about Gaitskell and whether he was a sufficiently radical leader for a left-wing party.'[45]

The shared territory between the New Left and Revisionism was extensive. Both New Left and revisionists were anxious that clause IV and socialism, had become associated with the bureaucratic, Morrisonian' model of state-owned industry. Revisionists held that as control of industry, in the hands of managers, was separate from ownership (shareholders), public ownership was no longer necessary to control the economy and Keynesian planning would suffice. This diffusion of power in the managerial revolution' was recognized (if not always welcomed) across revisionism. They also emphasized that nationalization was only a means towards socialism and not an end in itself. Nationalisation', Labour's *Industry and Society* noted, was designed to make a real contribution to the broader aims of socialism – to social justice, economic security and a new spirit in industry.' Crosland added that while the Soviet economy was publicly-owned just as much as in the United States, the employer and the labourer confront each other .control ... is separated from the workers; and the possibility of exploitation, and of all the other features of capitalism," is present.'   [46]

This was pertinent to British nationalized industries; but just as critical for the revisionists was, as *Must Labour Lose?* discovered, that

Labour voters, who had been in favour of extending public ownership in 1949, were by 1960 firmly opposed. Affluence undermined national-ization, but so during the Cold War did the menace of Soviet totalitar-ianism. The Conservatives tried to build and exploit this association. There was little new in this – the fear and taint of Communism had been used against Labour since the 1920s, but the Cold War gave it new impetus. A 1958 Conservative pamphlet, *They've Got a Little List*, listing 500 British companies supposedly threatened with nationaliza-tion by Labour, depicted Gaitskell on its cover as Chinese.[47]

The New Left disagreed with revisionists' reappraisal of power rela-tions and the 'managerial revolution', but concurred that public own-ership was not making the hoped-for contribution to socialist aims. Clive Jenkins' *Power at the Top* argued that since the composition of the boards of the nationalized industries remained dominated by company directors and professional managers, there had been only a nominal change. This explained the disaffection many workers felt towards public ownership.[48]

Crossman merged the revisionist case on the managerial revolution and New Left case. Just as .the person who owns shares, has no control of the company' he argued in 1950, when we nationalise the companies, equally the people have no control.' The reason is the same,' Crossman contended, because the mangers control the economy whether it is privately or publicly owned.' The shortcoming of Labour's nationalization, he adduced, lay in its Fabian values. The rationale behind Morrison's model was economic efficiency, aiding struggling and vital industries and if public accountability, not more workplace democracy. We were concerned with getting things ship-shape and efficient,' Crossman felt, and not with getting them humanised.'[49]

Another typically socialist characteristic of revisionism was its claim to the radical high ground. Crosland insisted nationalization ought no longer be the sole register of radicalism. It was social, consumerist, lib-ertarian and educational policies which a radical, progressive, revision-ist Labour Party would stand for'. The terms left and right should be transposed in their application to the two wings of the Labour Party,' Crosland argued, if left is taken to imply intellectually radical and right intellectually traditional.' *The Conservative Enemy* targeted the conservatism not only of the Conservatives, but also of the old and new 'left in the Labour Party.'   [50]

Even in its desire to modify Labour, revisionism wrapped itself in tra-dition. The authority socialism placed in the past remained a firm presence in its mind. Crosland invoked Tawney for sanction to treat sanctified formulae with judicious irreverence' and comforted die-hards that hothing is more traditional in the history of socialist thought than the violent rejection of past doctrines.' Keir Hardie would be a poor guide to the reality of the mid-twentieth-century world', Crosland genuflected, as indeed he would have been the first to realise.' Once British socialism succeed[ed] in adapting itself and its doctrines to the mid-Twentieth Century' Crosland was assured, it will find plenty of genuine battles left to fight.'[51]

This revivalist tone was struck too by the New Left. As editor of the suggestively titled *Out of Apathy*, Edward Thompson refuted claims that how that extreme want and mass unemployment [were] things of the past', socialism had lost its original dynamic'. Ending poverty, he held, was not a uniquely socialist aim anyhow. Rather, socialism looked to a society's relations of production .ordering of social priorities and .whole way of life.' And from this point of view, contemporary British society gives as much reason for outrage as the society of the 1880s or 1930s.'[52]

Where revisionism diverged from mainstream socialist thinking was in its optimistic prognosis of capitalism. Most shared revisionism's view of the values and ways of life that socialists would like to see, but not its belief that material conditions now allowed and obliged these to head the socialist agenda. Affluence, for revisionism, was not temporary but permanent and would become more widespread. Its confidence that capitalism could be put to socialist ends was in a long tradition of reformist socialism, from Eduard Bernstein to Evan Durbin. For Rita Hinden, all pervading economic crises' were things of the past.'[53] Crosland was confident that the present rate of growth will continue' and that even with occasional minor recessions, something approaching full employment will be maintained.'[54]

Most socialists noted a change in capitalism. Crossman labelled it welfare capitalism' or declining capitalism'. The New Left characterized it as consumer capitalism', last-stage capitalism' (like Strachey) or (by allusion to feudalism) bastard capitalism'. [55] For revisionism the change was qualitative – based upon a quantitative breakthrough. Crosland heralded crossing the economic threshold where for the first time in history, entire populations and not just privileged minorities have escaped from the hormal condition of mankind"– squalor, hunger, deprivation and despair' as the most beneficial social development in world history'. Revisionism perceived itself grappling with a transition from the material(ist) to the post-material epoch. Like

Galbraith – who closed *The Affluent Society* by arguing, 'To have failed to solve the problem of producing goods would have been to continue man in his oldest and most grievous misfortune, but to fail to see that we have solved it and to fail to proceed to the next task would be fully as tragic' – Crosland deemed the problem of production solved, but those of distribution, consumption and culture, very much alive.[56]

What was also familiar in revisionism was the belief that capitalism (or whatever it now was) was fixed in character. Galbraith speculated if British socialists in the 1930s assumed that capitalism was not only immoral but unworkable .a. system which must destroy itself because of its own inherent weaknesses', then if that assumption is not true, would that not mean the snapping of the mainspring of .Labour?'   [57] Not necessarily, for revisionism had replaced this faith in imminent collapse with a vision in which all was benign, growth was assured and licensed a little faith in the future.

Just as the 1950s disorientated socialists anticipating the scenarios of the 1930s, so the assumptions of 1950s revisionism were debilitated by economic crisis in the 1970s. Ironically, discussing the 1930s in *The Future of Socialism*, Crosland had reflected how it was easy to forget today, not merely how unanimous socialist writers were in anticipating the collapse of capitalism, but how completely their analytical systems, their prophecies and their recommendations, all hinged on this central belief.'[58]

Yet Crosland's prescription for what Labour ought to do to buttress its declining position' similarly hinged on the conviction that this was causally related to underlying social and economic changes' which were not merely .irreversible, but .not yet even complete.' The affluent worker' as the embodiment of a certain lifestyle, and associated social attitudes and voting behaviour, was the figure and voter of the future.

Yet revisionism also contended that Labour need not be fatally injured by the social and economic changes' of the 1950s, so long as it was prepared to adapt itself, for there was nothing innately counter-socialist to them. Crosland reassured a patient with a weighty sense of tradition, that adapting did not involve basic party principles' and had little to do even with detailed party policy'. Rather it concerned the way in which the party presents itself and its policies to the public ... the tone and content of its propaganda and generally the impression which it makes on the voters.' [59]

Many commentators felt Labour needed to attend to its image. For Michael Young, Labour gave an impression of surly opposition to consumer prosperity.' Crosland suggested it suffered from an image of being pro-austerity and anti-prosperity', when, surprisingly enough, ordinary people like to be materially well-off.' This was partly a hangover from the post-1945 period of rationing and controls.' Conversely, they felt their own success had germinated the seeds of electoral defeat. Crossman argued the Attlee government's main achievement had been to make the working class in this country forget what it felt like to be afraid of unemployment and so become full of the grievances which were previously the monopoly of a prosperous upper class.' Crossman's point was reinforced by the experience of his Coventry constituency. One account relates the cruel irony' of the Labour Council's success in rebuilding Coventry's shopping precinct, while the party's vote in the city waned from 1955 and argues Coventrians found connections between the availability of consumer goods in bright new shops and the ideals of municipal socialism .difficult to make.' [60]

Roy Jenkins, too, argued in *Pursuit of Progress* in 1953 that Labour had suffered electorally from making the mass of the population aware of their unsatisfied demand for many things to which they previously laid no claim'[61] – demands or aspirations which Labour was neither able nor willing, in many cases, to articulate. Carolyn Steedman's mother, for example, grew to political Conservatism out of a Labour background' as the only political form that allowed her to reveal the politics of envy' and aspiration for glamour', for a New Look skirt, a timbered country cottage.'[62]

Labour's associations – production, public services, collectivism – did not seem to hold out such prospects – of luxury or even prosperity'. Nor were full employment, housing and the welfare state identified exclusively with Labour, but with the Conservatives too by the 1950s. As Crosland reflected, political parties often pay a harsh penalty for their own success.' Why should we be Labour just because we live in council houses?' tenants in South London asked a Mass Observer and proceeded to assert their independence by voting Conservative.' If this all seemed to threaten Labour's working class support, Stedman Jones has suggested affluence also dislodged its middle class support. As workers were seen to acquire goods and lifestyles previously the preserve of the middle class, so the middle class sense of difference from the working class and of helping the Labour movement .from an unassailed privileged position', from which Labour had benefited in 1945, was eroded.[63]

Yet Labour's anti-prosperity image, as Crosland despaired, had other sources – the moralists in the Party who repeatedly condemn the

whole affluent society as .evil' and those who decry prosperity as
bogus"and anticipate its collapse under the excessive weight of hire-
purchase debt or .in an inevitable slump.' For Crosland, the former
view failed to distinguish between the fact of affluence and certain
avoidable attributes' of it. The latter, besides its economic naivety',
implied Labour would win power on the shoulders of the unemployed,
which Crosland found hideously immoral.' Both, by giving the
impression of disliking and resenting' affluence, allowed the Tories to
appropriate the sole kudos of being the party of prosperity.'[64]

Like Crosland, Richard Hoggart suggested the left had allowed
Conservatism to define the image and terms of affluence. It had not
answered the questions raised when new opportunities, new choices,
new options open before people .who have previously lived in com-
paratively static and unendowed groups.' Hoggart urged the left to rec-
ognize most people are glad to have the new goods' having gone
short' for so long, but that there remained the question of how social
change was represented, the values and image promoted by the new
society. The question many (and notably newly affluent workers)
wanted answering was, How does one live in the new conditions?' The
left had neglected to address this in anything other than partial and
negative terms. The right's advantage, Hoggart argued, was that it had
given some sort of answer.' It had depicted social change in what was
at bottom an unworthy image: parochial, bourgeois in bad senses ...
individualistic' and undervalue[d] many in-built decencies' in
working-class life. These qualities generally found their political
expression in the radical, communal, nonconformist, charitable
aspects of the Left', but the left feared they had been lost to affluence.
Moreover, the picture of affluence painted by the right was not entirely
ugly to Hoggart's eye. It was also bright .cheerful .and open' with
a sort of positiveness before the new opportunities' that gave it
popular appeal, since, (unlike the left), it d[id]n't assume that to
accept many of them [wa]s in essence wicked.'[65]

Equally, the welcome revisionism extended to affluence was not
unconditional. In *The Labour Case* Jenkins highlighted the paradox
whereby our standard of living is amongst the highest in Western
Europe, but our towns are the most dismal and least well provided
with amenities.' Crosland denounced as vulgar' the bias towards
unregulated private interest ..of our prosperous society.' Young
lamented Britain's low standards of design, service, quality and cleanli-
ness and related this to national decline in *The Chipped White Cups of
Dover.*[66]

Nor was revisionism's welcome merely gestural, designed to curry electoral favour. Affluence involved advances deemed compatible with socialism. It expanded personal freedom, by enabling families to acquire tastes and develop expectations which would previously have seemed impossible.' As this was entirely desirable', Jenkins thought it unjust of those who themselves enjoy living standards which are above average' to be pointing out to others the corrupting effects of ... motor cars or .refrigerators.' For Crosland, since rising consumption increase[d] both the fact and consciousness of social equality', socialists might celebrate it as egalitarian. He declared higher personal consumption' a socialist goal'. As conspicuous consumption of cars, holidays, TV – became widespread, Crosland argued, so became stronger the subjective feeling of equal living standards.' It was a trait of the modern mass distribution economy' that it brought new products quickly to a mass audience, making it almost impossible to preserve large disparities in socially conspicuous consumption.'[67]

The trend towards the new era of abundance' extended to poorer workers .peering across the threshold .thinking of the day when they too will acquire these goods.'[68] Former luxuries and emblems of rank were recast as classless. For historian Sidney Pollard, the car, once a middle-class symbol, now became a leveller.' Credit and instalment buying promoted affluence, by enabling the working class to buy more goods than their financial assets unaided would permit' and contributed to a sense of classlessness by dissociating spending and lifestyle from a work-derived income.[69]

That affluence felt' more equal was arguably Crosland's critical insight. However much it could be shown not to be, that Britain remained *The Split Society*, suffered from low growth rates or tracts of deprivation exposed – was less important than what appeared to have happened.[70] Affluence seemed fairer, an economic miracle' even, thrown into relief by wartime devastation and post-war austerity. Crossman's 1950 discussion of egalitarianism was resonant for the encounter with affluence. It meant, he argued, that people are feeling .that they are getting what they deserve', which may be very remote from strict, statistical equalitarianism.'[71]

The point was noted elsewhere. Stuart Hall agreed consumer capitalism did genuinely – about the middle of the roaring fifties – break through some kind of sound barrier in public consciousness', though in the sense that prosperity'had become much more a question of how people could be made to see themselves .and much less a solid affair of genuine wealth and well-being.' Hall was then doubtful of dealing with actual prosperity, but convinced of a powerful 'mythology of prosperity.'[72]

Revisionism presented affluence in a socialist light – as 'fair shares' or an escape from the confines of class. History then was still progressing towards socialism, if in unexpected ways. The 'new thinking' restored the notion that socialists were history's tribunes (as the revisionists would not have put it). Revisionism also hitched itself to affluence. Its thinking and project were contingent upon the persistence of affluence.

Not coming to terms with affluence

All this gave revisionism its characteristically optimistic tone, discordant with the more wary note struck by most socialists with regard to affluence. In a sense, revisionism clung to a vision of 'progress' that was in doubt elsewhere. The notion that economic progress would deliver social and cultural progress – as Sassoon puts it that 'things will get better" – was present in most socialisms. But the 1950s gave cause to reflect on Crossman's note that the 'delusion of progress' was deep in all of us.'[73]

Some clung to old faiths. Willie Thompson joined the CPGB in the early 1960s because it appeared, on the demonstration of Soviet space technology and Khrushchev's report to the CPSU 22nd Congress, to be materially outstripping a brutal and imperialist West. and probably before long would be doing so morally and culturally as well.'[74] But for many British Communists 1956 had been a revelation that economic advance did not necessarily yield social advance. 'Economic progress has been made' Lilla Fox, observed of the Soviet model, 'but what of ethical and intellectual progress?' Was there after all some substance in the criticism that materialists neglect the things of the spirit,' she wondered.[75]

Heavily populated by disenchanted Communists, the New Left was largely the upshot of Fox's point. Thompson and Williams revived critiques of industrialism that were as much romantic as rational in their register and as much ethical as economic in their notion of progress. The New Left's involvement with CND further disposed it against identifying socialism with scientific or technological advances into space or nuclear energy. Equally, since affluence rendered capitalism a more awkward target economically, the New Left increasingly focused on issues of culture and the quality of life. And it detected in affluence (just as 1956 had revealed in the Soviet Union) a cultural and moral loss as the price of material progress.[76]

New Lefters without a Communist background were even less bound by old orthodoxies. Stuart Hall contested the traditional ordering of economic base and superstructure of ideas. Rather than in economic relationships, Hall suggested that the sense of classlessness – the ideological representation of how people lived and worked – might be the primary location of ensuing class conflict and ideological struggle.'[77]

In 1958 the part-Communist-founded history journal, *Past and Present* dropped its subtitle, *A Journal of Scientifi History* . In view of 1956, history no longer seemed to proceed according to a causal structure where economic, industrial and scientific advance would yield commensurate social and cultural progress. Vere Gordon Childe, a prominent Marxist pre-historian and advocate of the primacy of technological change in social progress, died in 1957. The Sputnik launch in 1957 produced none of that wonder and admiration that the British left of the 1930s had accorded such relatively more humble technological feats as the .building of the Dnieper dam.' The CPGB issued a tepid *Satellite Special*, which asked How could they do it?' and lamely answered, because Russia is a socialist country.' [78]

At a more down-to-earth level, progress' involved the question of automation. *The British Road to Socialism* asserted automation can further increase our power to produce', but mostly led to redundancy and frustration for large numbers of workers.' TGWU Assistant Secretary Harry Nicholas saw ho real grounds for this fear.' Nicholas argued automation had helped .to obtain full employment' and painted a vision of more, better jobs and a hew aristocracy of workers.' Whether it was the influence of the 1958 boom or of revisionism, he confidently predicted: 1 do not think we will have any unemployment in the next 25 years.' Communism and the New Left's wariness about the consequences of economic advance were explicable as part of the doubts induced by 1956, by affluence and by the limits they saw to the welfare statism introduced under Attlee. It would no longer suffice, Llew Gardner wrote in the *Daily Worker* in 1956, for communists and socialists [to] still conduct ourselves as if socialism was nothing more than an improvement in the material well-being of the people.' Not least, of course, this would leave them open to the same charge they were levelling at affluence and the Conservatives – of materialistic, self-centred politics.[79]

Most on the left judged affluence socially, culturally, even politically, regressive. Hoggart concluded *The Uses of Literacy* glad that most working-people are .better-off, have better living conditions, better health, a larger share of consumer goods, fuller educational opportunities', but anxious that the accompanying cultural changes are not always an improvement but in some of the more important instances are a worsening.'[80] Socialists desired a classless society, but not classlessness, as Hoggart saw it, defined by Conservative propaganda and ITV commercials.' For Morgan Phillips the problems of affluence were closely related to the defects in the order of values which the nation has been taught to accept during the 1950s.' 'We cannot build a sane society,' he held, 'so long as the values of private acquisitiveness, strongly excited by the techniques of mass persuasion are permitted to dominate the values of service and mutual aid.'[81]

As early as 1951 Edward Thompson despaired that 'in place of the great proletarian values ..class-solidarity and militancy, we now have, even among sections of our working-class movement, the values of private-living growing up .the self-interest and timid individualism fostered by pulp magazines and Hollywood films.' Stuart Hall argued, 'if it is true that the skilled worker is becoming part of what Mark Abrams recently called 'the home-centred society," the loss is not the loss of a good man 'to the other side," but a loss in the quality of the new working-class community itself.' In short, the values of commercialism, individualism, privatism and a home-centred lifestyle were feared to be displacing the qualities associated with traditional' working-class culture – solidarity, community and co-operation.[82]

Contempt for commercial leisure and nostalgia for a traditional' way of life were hallmarks of Priestley's writing. In the 1950s his pen bent against 'Admass – a consumer race with donkeys chasing an electric carrot.' Admass was the result of thinking in terms of statistics .and not in terms of human beings' and turned people into money-chasers, with lower and lower standards of personal integrity.' It was better to live in *admass*' Priestley begrudged, than to have no job, no prospect of one and see your wife and children getting hungrier', but that was all that can be said in favour of it.' [83] For Wiener, Priestley gave pungent, uninhibited expression to sentiments observable in leading Labour politicians.' Gaitskell, for instance, felt modern society deliberately encouraged .a materialistic outlook and the idea of getting on better for yourself never mind what is happening to other people' and that 'touch your cap"snobbery' had given way to 'keeping up with the Joneses"snobbery'. [84]

It was not only leading figures that exhibited this mood. Labour's agent in Wellingborough reported, 'we came across the view 'I'm all-right why should I alter it"many times' in 1959. The shift was registered by Labour's ally the *Daily Mirror*, which dropped its long-standing masthead 'forward with the People' after the 1959 election. Henry Fairlie commented: 'forward with the People"hardly rings true in a day when 1'm allright Jack"more accurately expresses the mood of the nation.'[85]

This contravened the idea of the 'responsible society', where, as Labour put it in 1956 the citizens' sense of responsibility must keep pace with the increase in his rights and powers if society is to renew itself spiritually and materially.' For Phillips, conjuring up memories of the popular mood of the 1940s, this meant the need to call on the British people once more to show themselves prepared to subordinate private interest to the needs of the community and postpone the increase of some personal satisfactions.' Attlee reflected in 1954 that wartime Britain had a strong socialist flavour' because the public good [had taken] precedence over private interests.' Instead, with full employment socialists were witnessing the demise of the old idea that one doesn't rise out of one's class, one rises with it"and the diffusion of the typically Conservative notion that rising standards depend on individual choice and effort rather than on collective bargaining or state provision.'[86]

Yet the Conservatives were less than certain of the changes in political psychology stemming from affluence. As Turner and Green have shown, they were concerned with the persistence of traditional attitudes where the working class tend to think of progress more as a collective process.' The Conservative Research Department feared in 1958 that the new working class' were apt to attribute that they have never had it so good' to socialism, because so many of the tangible benefits come to them through the hands of socialist local authorities or trade unions' or the welfare state.[87]

Socialists often made the point that the improved standing of workers resulted from trade unions and the welfare state as much as individual getting on'. The Labour left' and CPGB, keen to evince the relevance of a strategy of workplace and class militancy, emphasized it was through struggle in spite of the Tories', that some workers had been able to lift up their living standards.' [88]

Full employment did enable workers to boost wages through (invariably) brief, unofficial shopfloor action. Some on the left were uneasy at this. After the 1959 election Bevan warned of the dangers of syndicalism. With Parliament seemingly beyond Labour's reach, he feared workers might turn to industrial action, if the burden of the weekly [HP] payments becomes too grinding and excessive.' The shop steward, more than the Labour MP appeared the guarantor of working-class economic well-being.[89]

Bevan prefigured historical interest in the economism of late twentieth-century trade unionism. His concern was the affliction of trade unionism with the acquisitiveness of Toryism – where what is good for the City they will accept as good for the organised worker.' Doubtless Bevan also had in mind TGWU General Secretary Frank Cousins' comments at the 1956 TUC, that in a period of freedom for all, we are part of the all.' Delivered in defence of free collective bargaining against government overtures for wage restraint, this echoed, in a period of full employment and economic growth, the self-interested ethos of Conservatism.[90]

Others sensed affluent values within the Labour movement. The film *I'm Allright Jack*, an industrial relations satire starring Peter Sellers, was released in 1959. Williams considered by 1961 that the widespread extension of the selling"ethic' had effected the visible moral decline of the Labour movement.' While demonstrating the I'm allright Jack"ideology' was not new, he argued it was more potent in a context where sections of the Labour movement [had] gone over .to ways of thinking which they still formally oppose.' Williams was unsurprised that many people now see in the Labour Party merely an alternative power-group' and in the unions merely a set of men playing the market in very much the terms of the employers they oppose.'[91]

The New Left iterated the point. William Norman criticized Labour's *Signposts for the Sixties* – he found the phraseology .bastard to the thinking' in language such as children are the nation's most valuable asset.' Has the Labour movement come through the fire and brimstone of the last fifty years', Hall asked in 1960 to lie down and die before the glossy magazines .to fade away in front of the telly and the frig'?' Ralph Miliband's inculpation of *Parliamentary Socialism* took up the point. If politics seemed a decreasingly meaningful activity' and apathy was rife in 1950s – this was as much Labour's responsibility as problem. The cause, Miliband argued, was not only the the hidden and overt persuaders' (advertisers), but Labour leaders' who felt the affluent society"required more urgently than ever that their party should appear classless" and who failed to propound an alternative vision. Labour's anxiousness to attune itself with the affluent society was likely to prove its nemesis. For Miliband, this showed a mistrust-cum-fear of the electorate. Never', he argued, had Labour leaders been so haunted by a composite image of the potential labour voter as quintessentially *petit-bourgeois* and therefore liable to be frightened off by a radical alternative.'[92]

Labour's 'left' concurred. Foot tendered that rather than a full-blooded appeal, Labour's moderate attempt to entice the floating voter' was an approach that played into the hands of Macmillan and his publicity agents.' Stephen Swingler argued Labour had offered only a 'half-hearted' alternative to the commercial salesmanship of the every-man-for-himself .I'.m allright Jack variety', and in the absence of a vision of a society with more sensible values than commercialism offers' most voters preferred to opt for what is, for fear of something worse.'[93]

The New Left stressed that capitalism, far from the domesticated beast of revisionist legend, was through consumerism, advertising and TV, stealthily sinking its claws ever deeper into everyday life. Williams argued the patterns of thinking and behaviour it promotes have never been more strong.' Samuel thought business had been tamed in important directions ..but in others its power has rather been extended, shaping the character of the country's future and .increasingly, its quality of life.'[94]

For Hall the categories of consumer' and prosperity' were complicit with capitalism. Society had come to think of prosperity almost entirely in terms of the things which it could purchase, possess and enjoy as private individuals' and thus entered as separate consumers, directly into the mythology of prosperity.' Affluence was a trick of the zeitgeist whereby the consumer goods industry did not to any significant extent give us the goods: instead it gave us a definition of the good life.' It was an imaginary state entered into in anticipation of the things we *might* – or others might – conceivably possess, although we did not seem to have very many of them *yet*.' A subsidiary myth', was that poverty and neglected public services would soon be resolved – we had only to let prosperity to take it course.'[95]

Socialists felt that through consumer goods, ideology was not imposed, it was purchased.' A stake in society generated consent for the prevailing order. Blackwell and Seabrook saw the 1950s as the moment when capitalism succeeded in imposing through its version of prosperity, what it had been unable to impose through its version of poverty.' The question to be asked about the washing-machine' was how a growing dependency on the necessarily rising income, without which such fragile gains are snatched away, involves us all in a deepening acceptance of capitalism.' Even those who saw consumer goods more positively recognized this process. Crosland felt a consequence of enjoying a previously un-dreamed of level of con-sumption' was that the working class no longer feels to the same extent outside''society.'   [96]

The instincts of the market also troubled socialists. The more things that we are able to enjoy without their having to pass through the price system,' Bevan argued the more civilised and less acquisitive a society becomes.' This ethos underpinned any number of salvoes dis-charged at Party conference or in local party literature against advertis-ing or commercial television. Bevan was reaffirming what Tawney had demonstrated as *The Sickness of an Acquisitive Society*, some thirty years earlier.[97]

The issues raised by the affluent society', so far as socialists were concerned, were of the values at large in society. Foot argued Labour must never apologise for the moral inspiration of socialism', as with the commercialization of daily life, it was the only basis on which it could provide an alternative to a Toryism' that still worships at the shrine of the Great God Grab.' Debates on Labour's *Signposts for the Sixties*, showed an ethical hostility to the emphasis on private con-sumption and the imbalance between private and public spending. The notion that things provided privately are good and to be indulged in without limit, while things provided publicly are a burden", Crossman argued, spreads right through our economy' and led to an illogical use of our resources: we can afford'fancy packages; but not fancy pensions .there's prestige'in new office blocks .but we have to exercise economy'in .new hospitals'. Head of his concerns was that consumption was promoted, forcibly through advertising, as though this was the only source of satisfaction in life.'[98]

The political meaning of affluence

So far as affluence had a bearing upon political behaviour, revisionism was in harmony with prevailing socialist thinking – it detected an embourgeoisement of values, registered in support for the Conservatives. It differed in thinking affluence a condition whose political effects were not fixed but contestable. In this last respect, it chafed most of all with socialist sensibilities by extending a cordial hand to affluence.

This meant it was accused of accepting a Tory, or capitalist or mate-rialist, or ..worse still an American, philosophy of life ..that is somehow unethical and unsocialist.' Crosland refuted that the goal of higher material standards' would encourage an accent on material

gain, extreme individualism and aggressive competition', producing an acquisitive and antagonistic society' at odds with a socialist emphasis on fellowship. If socialism was about more than eliminating poverty, he goaded critics, how were high consumption and brotherly love .incompatible' – why should not the brothers be affluent and the love be conducted under conditions of reasonable comfort?'[99]
Revisionists did not regard the meaning of affluence as predetermined and viewed its potential, optimistically. Jenkins denied affluence promoted materialistic values, arguing it would have to be shown that, as one moved down the income scale, there was a steady improvement in spiritual values.' The acquisition of a washing-machine' he held was not in itself going to make a woman .more happy.' Yet, and this was the nub of his case, the satisfaction of material wants [was] at least as likely to free people's thoughts from material things as to concentrate them there.'[100]
Assuring socialists that revisionism was not pandering to acquisitive values and retained a higher' vision, Crosland cited Matthew Arnold: In spite of all that is said about the brutalizing influence of our passionate material progress .man, after he has made himself perfectly comfortable and has now to determine what to do with himself next, may begin to remember that he has a mind and that the mind may be the source of great pleasure.' Following suit, Crosland anticipated that as spending on drink, tobacco and domestic goods was approaching satiation point', higher incomes might thence be taken out in leisure, and may even be spent on culture.' He added: as material pressures ease and the problem of subsistence fades away, people become more sensitive to moral and intellectual issues'. In that case an ethical, idealistic appeal, such as a true socialist should always make' would be more in tune with the temper of the country.'[101]
Hoggart (another Arnoldian) shared this projection. He did not believe, unlike many on the left, that affluence had altered Britons. Rather that some of the new opportunities will let light into dark places', that there remained an enormous reservoir of decent intention' in people, and that the left should aim to speak for that side.' He wagered that if it does it will be surprised by the response it will *gradually* elicit.' In other words affluence held potential as much as danger for the left. And, underscoring the proximity of the New Left and Revisionist thought highlighted by this chapter, the same point was made by Miliband. At pains to show how the attribution to affluence"of a soporific social effect' was doubtful', Miliband felt affluence was, if anything, a prerequisite for socialism since experience

strongly suggests that it is only *after* elementary needs have ceased to be an incessant, gnawing preoccupation, that the socialist critique of capitalism may carry conviction.'[102]

Hinden had concluded *Must Labour Lose?* similarly, arguing the stage is being reached .when people may become less intent on acquiring more personal possessions, and more anxious to improve the quality of their lives and environment in ways that can only be met by social expenditure. She adduced Abrams' hopeful evidence of changing atti-tudes towards the young and old, underdeveloped countries and public spending. In seeking to change society so that these impulses might find greater expression', Hinden hoped to realign socialism from working-class interests' in quantitative progress, to a more qualitative footing. Labour's renewal was contingent upon it championing an ethical agenda, because now that the majority of people are moving towards easier circumstances' they would be more able than ever before, to respond to it.'[103]

An ethical rather than class appeal dovetailed with the idea of politics as the product of underlying social forces. Labour then ought to shed its proletarian and one-class' image (since the affluent society was class-less') to become a broadly-based, national people's party.' Crosland also welcomed that instead of voting instinctively in accordance with class-identification' voters might now make a more reasoned and pragmatic judgement of issues, programmes and the abilities of various parties.' Instrumentalism, the political correlate of a more self-interested society, he surmised would make voting behaviour more fluid' and open to rational persuasion.' Instrumental voting should benefit Labour, Crosland believed, because as status factors superseded economic con-cerns, the new rising classes' would come to feel their social status was out of kilter with their new economic status and may resent, more than in the old days of material poverty, the contrasts in educational oppor-tunity' and other social and cultural provisions. In such inequalities Labour's appeal would receive a good hearing.[104]

Revisionists supported causes to improve the quality of life: the Consumers' Association, Advertising Inquiry Council, Good Food Guide and Keep Britain Tidy. Affluence, *pace* Stedman Jones, not only eroded, but gave cause to middle class desires to help those less well off. If less centred on the labour movement, it still centred on the working class as parvenu, passive, lacking moral fibre and cultural taste.[105]

There was little strikingly original in revisionist thought. Readers of MacDonald, Tawney or Morris would find familiar bearings. The language was modern, Keynesian, managerial and sociological, but the belief remained that progress, a Fabian 'Forward March', to a better society would come from economic advance. What lent this force was the 1950s boom. Revisionism's politics were justified by social and economic change, yet also contingent upon the continuance of affluence. And its optimistic reading of the effects on attitudes and politics were highly conjectural.

As Williams pointed out in 1961, Labour's vote was stronger than ever: to 1939, Labour never got more than 38 per cent of the total votes .since 1945 it has never got less than 43 per cent.' This reduced the usual analysis to nonsense'. The revisionists' own evidence was uncertain. Abrams' research into prosperity and politics confounded one of his working assumptions – namely, given ownership of consumer goods (except TV) was higher in the middle class than in the working class, and since the middle class vote is almost entirely Conservative one would expect that in the working class, higher rates of ownership of these goods would be associated with Conservative voting.' But *Must Labour Lose?* found little difference between Conservative- and Labour-voting workers in ownership of washing-machines, fridges or cars. Indeed TV seemed to aid Labour – 81 per cent of Labour voting workers owned sets, 76 per cent of Conservatives. Nor was the idea of young people rejecting the left convincing. Abrams asserted today's young people are more likely to be Conservative than Labour', but found in the working class 35 per cent of young people support the Conservatives, and *only* 50 per cent are Labour.' Telephone and home ownership differentiated in Conservatism's favour, but the gap was slight: 30 per cent of working-class Conservatives were homeowners and 20 per cent of Labour supporters.[106]

The political qualities ascribed to such goods were doubtful. Samuel reminded psephologists and revisionists who used their research, that it was not fridges or vacuum cleaners, but people who had the vote. There was also cause to reflect on Crossman's counsel, that what used to be one of the basic socialist assumptions (that one should treat man as an economic creature) may be one of the causes of our present troubles and our present uncertainties.'[107] Despite the revisionist mind to move to post-material thinking, this assumption remained salient in its scrutiny.

Nor was the extent of affluence in the revisionist case overwhelming. Abrams found fridges, cars and phones were owned by less than 20 per cent of workers. Even ownership amongst the most prosperous half of workers was below 50 per cent in 1960 – 16 per cent owned fridges, 32 per cent cars. Ownership doubled between 1956 and 1959 and would, as Crosland willed, be much higher by 1964', but this was only half the story. The other half of the working class constituted one-third of the electorate.[108]

Poverty, assumed lost in the past, was 'rediscovered' in the mid-1960s. Peter Townsend and Brian Abel-Smith's work demonstrated that for the elderly, children and many working-class women, judged on levels of National Assistance, more people were in poverty. Yet the pervasive rhetoric of affluence meant that by the end of the 1950s, as Ellison puts it, the traditional 'submerged fifth 'in poverty had diminished in the public mind to a 'submerged tenth'." Befitting a theory subscribing to and promoting affluence, revisionism talked up the disappearance of poverty. Discussing 'inequalities of Wealth' in *The Conservative Enemy* Crosland was at pains to make reference to the submerged tenth', and there was no more evident absence in his writing than that of Townsend.[109] Yet Abel-Smith and Townsend had worked with Richard Titmuss on Labour's Superannuation pension plan. Both contributed to *Conviction* in 1958, a mainstay of left bookshelves. Unless it was Crosland's dislike for the Fabian traditions of the LSE, where Townsend and Abel-Smith worked, it would seem to be that revisionism marginalized evidence that contested its vista on the affluent society.[110]

Affluence had an uneven influence on ways of life and in some regions little immediate impact was apparent. The backdrop to the 1961 film of Shelagh Delaney's *A Taste of Honey* was Salford – looking more *The Classic Slum* than portending affluence. A Mass Observer, who observed Bolton in 1937, returned in 1960 to find the areas of unchange in [Bolton] life ..astonishing.' Elsewhere (notably the Midlands and south-east) change was apparent, 'when you had to search for a parking space in Dagenham or Llanelli.' But that working-class communality persisted in New Towns around symbols of private affluence like the washing-machine, suggests more continuity than change in workers' lifestyles. So too Tiratsoo's history of post-war Coventry, which argues new life-styles and identities did not mean embourgeoisement, but that there were an increasing number of different ways of being working class.'[111]

Affluence, then, was contested, uneven and specific. The ways social-ism described and engaged it were informed as much by its intuitive political culture as by any formal ideological approach. In the figure of the 'affluent worker' were syncretized a range of responses. The 'affluent worker' embodied: the uncertainty of socialism in the 1950s, its attempts to understand unexpected social changes within existing ways of thinking and how it was out of touch. For the 'affluent worker' was neither as pervasive as the revisionists believed and other socialists feared or as venal as all suspected.

The left struggled to orientate itself on a new social landscape. Its existing terms and ways of thinking were undermined by change. This was illustrated by a special Labour NEC meeting, convened in July 1960 to discuss 'The State of the Party'. It heard how 'issues which have served for decades as political landmarks, for example, mass poverty and mass unemployment, are slipping below the political horizon.' The new landmarks by which people can recognise their society and define their attitudes to it have not been clearly identified', it was argued, and 'consequently, there is within the nation as a whole and within the party too, a considerable uncertainty.'[112]

The left articulated change in 'halting and confused' terms, Hoggart argued in 1959. He diagnosed a left 'afflicted by its own fears, bred from its own blurred image of people.' This suspect vision divided socialists into two kinds, he suggested:

First are the shocked Puritans, whose knowledge of people is by now so generalised and distanced that they are convinced that masses of us have been ruined beyond recognition in a decade .glued to the telly every week-night and roaring down new Tory roads in H.P. cars every week-end. Second are the cheerleaders .uncritically in love with the gloss of the new society and only want more of it – but with the left in the lead. They would suburbanise a great tradition.[113]

Such was the vision of the populace in the 1950s assembled by the left's conventional language and frames of reference. For a tradition that saw itself as *The Voice of the People* or workers as the agency of socialism, this was problematic.

This chapter, then, endorses Tiratsoo's conclusion that, as in Coventry, Labour's problem 'was not mass desertion by newly affluent workers', but rather its 'inability to communicate with groups at the centre of social change'. It concurs with James Cronin that the left 'struggled to countenance or articulate the compatibility of dramatic material improvement and persistent class identity'.[114] There was nothing innately anti-socialist to social change in the 1950s, rather it was in how the left viewed and invested change with political meaning that its faltering fortunes in the 1950s are to be explained.

Socialists operated with assumptions that struggled to conceive the working class or capitalism in terms other than those transcribed during the inter-war period. Critical was what sociologist Hannah Gavron described in 1962 as a tendency to regard middle-class symbols as enemies and to 'always describe the prosperous in terms which reveal their prosperity to be an illusion, which show the economic victories of capitalism to involve such great cultural losses as to render them useless.'[115] Labour and the left were, in short, their own worst enemy in contriving social change as middle class. This was a cast of mind as much as a formal political approach and while both revisionism and the New Left made creative shifts within it, they also remained recognisably part of it.

This chapter reinforces Hodge's case that Labour's difficulties in the 1950s 'could not be attributed to altered circumstances alone', but were due in no small part to the nature of the social democratic tradition itself.' The 'affluent worker', whether the projection of social changes the revisionists imagined or a more inimical character, was squarely a product of this tradition. And a political culture that, as Widgery puts it, either thought the working class was bribed by corrupting fridges and reactionary motor-mowers into voting Tory' or had been somehow bamboozled into thinking .that capitalism had mysteriously vanished', discloses much about why those who thought we'd never had it so good were rather more convincing than the socialist stalwarts.'[116]

7
Political Communication

Socialists' misgivings about the 'affluent society' and suspicions of TV and advertising were also manifest in a dubiety towards newer methods of political communication. Changing styles of political activity, and Labour's own attempts to modernize its image and approach, offer critical insights into the political culture of socialism in the 1950s. Not least, assumptions, values and instincts are disclosed that seem quite unrecognizable through the dimness of the New Labour project.

It is now commonplace to see politics in terms of marketing and advertising. New Labour's mastery of public relations (PR) is acknowledged even by opponents, who decry the submerging of policy in presentation and image. Recent works have told *How the Left Learned to Love Advertising* and Labour's polling guru Philip Gould has explained *How the Modernisers Saved the Labour Party*, mainly from itself.[1] Labour's 1998 conference had ID cards sponsored by Somerfield supermarket (the GMB union issued alternatives) and stairs at the Blackpool venue (mooted to be dropped for its 'old' Labour associations) bore advertising. Certainly the political culture this chapter explores appears 'old' by comparison with contemporary practice, yet also apparent are the sorts of debates about communication more readily associated with New Labour.

The left was instinctively suspicious of the incursions made into politics by TV, advertising, professionalism and opinion pollsters, and its own methods were amateurish. During the 1950 election, Attlee toured Britain in a family car driven by his wife. Nicholas relates how they would stop by the roadside if ahead of schedule. The Prime Minister would attend to a crossword puzzle and Mrs Attlee to her knitting.[2] As late as the 1970s, when Percy Clark headed Labour's publicity, planning was still fairly slipshod.[3] By contrast the Conservatives use of advertising and communications techniques for publicity', Cockett has concluded, has seen extraordinary innovation – certainly compared to that of other British political parties.'[4] The Conservatives certainly shared some of Labour's anxieties. But their use in this period of the advertising agency Colman, Prentis and Varley (CPV), who they had employed since 1948, was not simply due to their wealth – the difference between the parties was cultural.

It was, Pearson and Turner noted in their 1965 anatomy of *The Persuasion Industry*, an interesting side-light on the different psychology of our two main political parties, that the uneasy conscience which some Labour supporters [had] over the introduction of Public Relations techniques to Transport House, never seems to have troubled the Conservatives at all.' The difference was partly because in the 1950s, since Conservatives accepted advertising as an integral part of the economy, they did not question the propriety of using it for political ends.'[5] Socialists were wary on both counts. Bevan indicted Conservatism hand in hand with advertising and salesmanship in his 1948 'Vermin' speech. Noting Lord Woolton's modernization of Tory propaganda, Bevan ventured: what is Toryism but organised spivvery? .I.warn young men and women: don't listen to the seduction of Lord Woolton. He is a very good salesman. If you are selling shoddy stuff you have to have a good salesman.'[6]

Work like that of Dominic Wring signals interest in New Labour's PR skills, but also provides historical context. It shows Labour's long-standing concern with marketing, image and publicity, since its reorganization and the advent of a mass electorate in 1918, through Sidney Webb's stratified vision of the electorate in the 1920s, Herbert Morrison at the London County Council and the efforts of his descendants. In this respect New Labour is not as new as it likes to imagine. Wring has explored a number of narratives for the history of Labour's communication – Americanization, modernization, centralization (of power within the party) and the refinement of techniques from mass propaganda to modern marketing.[7]

Exploring relations between party and people focuses attention on political communication. How effectively a political message is conveyed is as important as its content to its reception. Persuasive communication is vital to politics and advertising alike. Conflict over communication strategy and how Labour could modernize, was not simply the upshot of faction struggles, but resulted from different ideas about how best to communicate a message and with voters. As in other chapters of this volume, these debates did not cleave easily along 1eft' and tight' within Labour and socialism.

How a party communicates with voters also discloses much about how it defines and imagines them. The new techniques provided more and new rather than necessarily better information about voters and ways of communicating with them. They were far from foolproof, and used to fashion and assert as much as to reflect political claims and opinions. Public opinion' was not made more transparent by opinion polling, rather it became a more sharply contested category. New methods were themselves subject to political contestation. As early as 1951 Morgan Phillips was warning of the Tory's hew technique of propaganda .the publication of polls.' This remained a charge – that the medium itself and not only its message were politically loaded – through the decade and was also evident in Labour ranks during debates about Mark Abrams' *Must Labour Lose?* survey.[8]

This chapter argues reform was forthcoming in this period, but distinctly partial. Plans for Labour's 1959 election broadcasts were withheld from most in the party, because, Rowland explained, many would have dismissed the radical proposals using a professional team of broadcasters', as somehow wrong"or frivolous, dangerous, too entertaining, new.' Much as defeat (as in the 1980s) empowered the reformers, there was also a sense that Labour's own experiments with new approaches had failed and its 1959 conference in Blackpool duly made a solemn vow: better death than the dishonour of Colman, Prentis and Varley.'[9] The limits to reform stemming directly from defeat in 1959 were evinced by Crosland's lament to Gaitskell late in 1961 that, the Labour Party uses polls and surveys less than any other major party in the world.'[10] It was in 1962, well after the election but prior to Wilson becoming leader, that Labour appointed its first Director of Publicity, John Harris, with Percy Clark as deputy. That such reform as was undertaken was presided over by the ancien regime at Transport House and by former opponents of the newer techniques denotes the spirit in which it was embraced. Besides the evident shortcomings of traditional techniques, the modernization of Labour's communication methods proceeded as its circumspect opinion of its audience and fear that it might be led astray by Tory propaganda, lessened resistance to newer techniques.

Traditionalism and local politics

It was not as though image was not of radical concern. John Armstrong's famous 1945 poster – 'And Now– Win the <u>Peace</u> – Vote Labour' – earned a prime place in socialist folklore. So did Gerald Holton's CND logo, designed in 1958 and reworked (sliced') by Ken Garland for the 1962 Aldermaston march.[11] But many socialists were possessed, according to Wedgwood Benn, of the absurd idea that all publicity is unimportant and that all you need is the right policy.' Propaganda adviser Richard Wevell suggested in 1956 that there was, a lack of understanding of modern publicity methods from top to bottom of the party.'[12] Nor was resistance and disregard towards modern publicity methods the preserve of the 1950s. In 1984, Neil Kinnock declared, our strength cannot be bought from a huge PR budget, it will not be bestowed by a generously biased reporting media; it has to be worked for'.[13]

It was mainly traditional local activities, even local politics *per se*, that seemed threatened by newer approaches. Mervyn Jones has recalled how Communist street corner meetings at regular pitches were a tradition that died out in the 1950s.' In Labour the days when public meetings were useful are over' or 'TV has made the ordinary election meeting something of the past' were fast becoming hackneyed phrases.[14] The focus of politics seemed to be shifting towards the national level – from the doorstep and local meeting to the TV and advertising hoarding. Political scientists now see a thoroughgoing professionalisation of political advocacy' in the 1950s. That politics was becoming more capital and less labour intensive disabled socialists, who could compete with activists, but not Conservative financial resources. Anyhow, as Rowland's evocative account described, many socialists felt that if the street corner and blotchy handbill have had their day, then they would rather have none of it.'[15]

Edward Thompson registered disquiet in 1960. Until the highly bureaucratised post-1945 era', the labour movement had been responsive to the local social and industrial context .ground-swells of opinion at the rank-and-file level.' In a 1961 talk (symbolically) rejected by the BBC, delivered from the standpoint of .the underworld of British political life', those who had done their share of door-knocking .and of organising thinly attended meetings on behalf of minority causes', Thompson argued, this kind of dissent' was being isolated by changes in the means of communication.' Crosland, less uneasily, noted the same change. With the growing penetration of the mass media', he argued, political campaigning has become increasingly centralised; and the traditional local activists and door to door canvassers and the rest, are now largely a ritual.' The fan of the rank-and-file', he held, were now less essential to winning elections.' [16]

Activists resisted televised politics, national advertising or professional opinion research, supplanting established methods. Llew Gardner was roundly denounced in 1956 for arguing that the CPGB spent time and energy on propaganda that no longer rings a bell in this age of television' and that selling .socialism' from street corners and small meetings rather than advertising hoardings was to fight a twentieth century battle with nineteenth century ideas'. Wally Davis from Chesterfield saw the ease of the television studio' as a short cut' and would not agree with the abolishing of many forms of our activity, which though old are not antiquated.'[17]

In Labour ranks too, the cry that we should get back to the street corners' was often heard. Clem Jones, South West regional organizer, lamented that TV had superseded meetings. Local agent John Heardley-Walker reflected in 1961 that he remained old fashioned enough to believe that even in these days of armchair politics via the TV screen, the personal approach still counts for a lot.' Hugh Jenkins argued at the founding of Victory For Socialism (the post-Bevanite Labour Left'), that Labour lost the 1955 election because too many people stopped knocking on doors.'[18]

Local publicists faced more parochial problems. It was generally accepted that late evening loudspeaker work [did] more harm than good.' The 1960 Noise Abatement Act limited such activity. It particularly grated with local parties who did early morning loudspeaker work .at factory gates', by prohibiting their use before eight o'clock. [19] Propaganda during the holiday season was problematic. Yarmouth activist Arthur Clare told how a CND campaign in the resort in the summer of 1960 failed to have any impact upon the holidaymakers who had come to enjoy themselves and to get away from it." A CLP secretary called everyday for the first week of his holiday' at Labour's office, he recalled, until being dragged away by an irate wife who muttered that they had come to Yarmouth to get away from politics.' Labour Clubs might provide social amenities, whist drives, dances and so on' Clare thought, but discussion groups or public meetings while on holiday? Brrrr!'[20]

CLP's attitudes towards publicity inclined towards the haphazard. In 1955 more than half canvassed less than 60 per cent of their constituents. Pamphlets for the election of 1959 had virtually the same layout and the same typeface as the leaflets pushed through doors in 1945', Hattersley recalled. Faded slogans on one side .closely packed, carefully reasoned copy on the other were more appropriate for an appeal for a new church hall', he felt, than a reforming political party.' The story of the *South East Derbyshire Clarion* spoke volumes for Labour's amateurism. Published for free by a local press, the party agent revealingly reported: Does the party make a profit from the advertisers and who gets it? .I.don't know. We don't find the advertisers – we wouldn't know where to look.'[21]

Newer techniques, where engaged, tended to be incorporated into older paradigms. Labour's *Party Organisation* manual suggested party broadcasts made political personalities, who were hence a draw for public meetings. Benn, a proponent of the political uses of TV, urged socialists to make it serve us as surely as the pioneers made the leaflet and soapbox carry their message to the people of Britain.'[22]

It pays to advertise' [23]

TV broadcasts or advertising campaigns involved a more centralized, national politics. The cost and specialist expertise needed for such productions put them beyond the reach of all but the national party. Even at the national level, however, Labour was at a disadvantage financially, if more through prudence than poverty. The Party's general election fund was a healthy £196,408 in 1954.[24]

Butler and Rose calculated in *The British General Election of 1959* that Labour spent barely a fifth of what the Conservatives did on advertising and public relations in the two years before the election.' As Morgan Phillips noted, Labour Party income is still geared to a different and far less expensive era.' Conservative spending – £468,000 from mid-1957 – Butler and Rose judged, an unprecedented sum by British political standards.' This excluded the amounts, enormous by political standards', spent by business and organizations like the Economic League and Aims of Industry, on anti-nationalization publicity. Butler and Rose estimated expenditure by this lobby at £1,435,000 between June 1958 and September 1959.

That this was fourteen times the Labour Party's outlay on public relations' and £400,000 more than the total expenses of all the candidates in the general election' sanctioned Labour's claim that this expenditure was subverting democracy'. Phillips accused the Tories of using unprecedented sums of money to bewilder and bamboozle the electorate and destroy the democratic process.' There had never been an election in this country,' he inveighed, in which so much has been spent by so few.' 'Even by commercial standards,' Butler and Rose noted, the efforts of Mr. Colin Hurry, the Iron and Steel Federation ... were on a large scale, although not matching the amounts spent in advertising some beers and detergents.'[25]

The left could not compete with such resources. Yet it is difficult to imagine that had the left enjoyed greater wealth it would have chosen to expend it on more advertising, PR or opinion research. Socialists felt that such media and their methods had an in-built prejudice against their cause. Ken Garland, despite being a professional photographer and designer, typified Labour thinking. In 1963 he explained how just about all the communication skills in this country – copywriting, photography, illustration, layout, media distribution .are in the hands of the ad men; and most of the ad men are no more interested in the Labour Party than they are in my Aunt Fanny.' What they were interested in was the highest bidder, and as far as politics is concerned we all know who that is – *them* and their Institute of Directors.' Even if Labour had free access to the best advertising copywriters .photographers and .layout men', he was not so sure they could do anything for us.' So far as Garland was concerned, 'we ruddy well don't need them.'[26]

Socialists had a long-held mistrust of the press and broadcast media, stemming from the idea of its nexus with business and ruling interests, but also rooted in the daily misrepresentation socialists felt they suffered. Labour lore was rich with instances where it was allegedly manoeuvred out of office by media sophistry working at the behest of commerce – the Zinoviev letter of 1924 (from whence the *Daily Mail* was known as the 'Forger's Gazette' in Labour circles), but more recently Tate and Lyle's anti-nationalization Mr Cube campaign from 1949. Bias was encountered more surreptitiously. Lowestoft CLP complained of warped reporting of political speeches in the *Daily Sketch*'s accounts of handling hecklers – how Macmillan brushed their qualms aside', while Bevan insolently .obstinately refused to listen.'   [27]

Whatever the veracity of its concerns, Labour developed a neurosis about political bias, notably on television and radio. Morgan Phillips investigated a host of allegations, though reassured Lewisham South MP, Carol Johnson, that inquiries into the allocation of tickets, make-up of speakers and question-master Freddie Grisewood, on the BBC's *Any Questions?*, had revealed no evidence of significant political bias. From May 1958 Labour ran a monitoring service staffed by 300 party volunteers who submitted reports on all commercial television and

BBC television and sound programmes likely to be of political interest.' *Panorama, Tonight, Any Questions?, Free Speech* and the main news broadcasts were amongst those monitored. An interim report found 'very little direct party political bias in the programmes', if à tendency towards bias in favour of the establishment when considering foreign affairs.'[28]

Indeed àllegiance to NATO' seemed to Thompson part of .the Establishment which one may not question.' Despite CND and the New Left's efforts, dissenting thought was sidelined. Thompson mused this was not only due to the control of the major media of communication, but the hegemony of its values – the manipulation of opinion by the techniques of the salesman – the brand-image .the play upon status anxieties .Get on, get ahead, get up!''say the advertisers.' More than the conspiracy Labour imagined, Communists saw political influence in the media as part of a systematic ideological apparatus. The CPGB was 'squarely against the private ownership of newspapers .commercial TV and a BBC controlled by representatives of the ruling class', all of which were 'selling ideas which will hide the ugly reality of .society.'   [29]

Common to Labour and Communist thinking was that the media's power was relatively unquestioned and understood to wield considerable influence over its audience. In this equation, it wasn't only the press, but (as was often the case for the 1950's left) the people that were to blame. As a Stroud delegate told the 1959 Labour conference debate on the election:

> the biggest single reason why we lost .is right in front of our noses. We only have to look there (to the press). The biggest reason was that 90 per cent of these people have for five years literally brainwashed part of the population of Britain and made them into immoral people who have put self-interest first.[30]

Labour's Wellingborough agent reminded the Party in 1959 to 'always bear in mind the majority of the press is against us.' Such thinking was recognized as integral to Labour's 'lamentable failure to understand the need to communicate with the public' during the election. Whatever 'the reactionary nature of many local papers', Phillips contended, Labour's frame of mind encouraged à morbid dislike of publicity and an unreasoned fear of the press.' It was also a useful line of argument for party leaders. 'For the more the official leadership loses the support of the general public,' Crossman noted in 1954, 'the more they lay the blame on wicked journalists.'[31]

Socialists were wary of association with the meretricious world of the press and advertising. Like Garland, they viewed the advertising world as divided between 'us' and 'them'. This explains the impact of the Khrushchev revelations within the CPGB. Until evidence came from the horse's mouth, communists tended to dismiss criticism of the Soviet bloc with the reasoning, 'Why should I believe the bourgeois press and not my political comrades?' When Bob Edwards left his post as *Tribune* editor in 1955 for Beaverbrook's *Evening Standard*, it was seen as a betrayal. In Morden, where Edwards was prospective parliamentary candidate, 'indignation' was expressed at his careerism. Edwards later admitted that his choice of new job was a little difficult for my friends to understand.'[32]

Opposition to professional advertising and PR also sprang from egalitarian impulses in socialist culture – the idea that specialists were unnecessary since, as Crosland put it, all jobs can be done by laymen.' It led Labour to spurn a proposal from sympathetic advertisers in 1959 to spend £22,000 on a professional billboard and press campaign. Instead it designed its own, described by Rosenbaum as 'drab'. [33] This anti-professional ethos was widespread. It guarded against publicity-seekers, social climbers or those who George Hodgkinson reckoned, saw in socialism a profession, a way of earning a living, a commercial proposition.' It was on these same grounds that socialists were opposed to the professionalization of sport and music.[34]

'Most of the people at the top of the Labour Party', Thompson snorted in 1959, were professional politicians' and a very bad and untrustworthy sort of people'. The New Left's rejection of this explains something of its amateurishness. 'By the end of 1961', Kenny notes, several of its commercial projects lay in ruins.' The number of *New Left Review* designed to avert financial collapse became a lengthy double issue, appearing months late and over-budget. Saville proposed *New Left Review* should accept adverts incompatible with its politics – in order to revenge those that were false and hostile by rebutting, say an advert opposing steel nationalization, on the facing page. The Partisan, its Soho coffee bar-cum-meeting house, was run more along lines of idealism than financial responsibility and was sold. 'In the 1950s it was difficult to lose money with a coffee house', Jones has reflected, but the New Left managed it.'[35]

Communists had what Kartun felt was 'a philistine mistrust of professional standards of work.' Crosland sensed Labour was apt to confuse egalitarianism with anti-professionalism.' Percy Clark, charged with modernizing Labour's publicity after 1962, told how he was never allowed to have anything to do with press relations before 1959 .because that's what I knew about.' The *ancien regime* at Transport House Clark found to be terrified of anybody who knew anything about the job.'[36]

This belief of politicians in their own inspired amateurism' was reinforced by advertising being notoriously a field in which the layman believes himself to be as good as his master.' Rowland argued the Labour politician was prone to think his rise in the party show[s] that he knows intuitively what goes and what doesn't'. But this was flawed, he held, for knowing what is acceptable or popular to the party rank-and-file does not necessarily mean knowing what the public as a whole will respond to.'[37]

Labour's efforts contrasted with the Conservatives ready embrace of modern PR methods. While the Tories embarked on the Roll Call for Victory' in 1958, a campaign Labour acknowledged was impressive not only for the size of the operation, but the professional skill with which it is being conducted', Labour was planning a caravan propaganda tour of East Anglia.[38] The Conservatives accepted, while Labour rebuffed, the BBC's proposal to televise party conferences from 1954. Labour's reluctance came from experience with newsreels, which it felt had been biased and showed .conference from unfavourable angles.' It was also loath to expose its ardent internal divisions (and bloc voting procedures) to public scrutiny, though some argued the presence of TV cameras might moderate exaggerated reporting of these. When TV was admitted to conference, Labour's dilettantism meant little thought was put into accommodating its gaze. At the 1958 conference the rostrum posters appeared blurred on TV screens. Due to some trick of colouring or lighting, the posters were not readable', *Socialist Commentary* reported, and a real opportunity was missed for good party advertising.'[39]

Speakers donned sunglasses, not to curry favour with the new youth culture, but in defiance of TV lighting. Edith Summerskill's, a Co-op reporter noted in 1956, protected her from the discomfort of sleepless arc-lamps.' Gaitskell wore a pair in 1960. His fight and fight and fight again' speech was delivered against unilateralists and the gaze of TV, for he wanted to start by trying, despite the television lights, to lower the temperature a little.' Socialist morality was responsible for some wariness. That they thought being photographed was rather petit bourgeois and self-indulgent' (as Lessing put it) might explain why Barbara Castle tells it was only in the later 1950s that Labour began to cultivate the (for us) neglected art of the photo-call.'[40]

Another reason Labour considered public relations à dirty word and a field in which the party's conscience-keepers preferred to remain studiously amateur', was that it devalued political life. For one *Labour Organiser* contributor, the advent of TV meant à further deterioration in our political standards.' In 1960 MP Alice Bacon, chair of Labour's publicity committee, declaimed the Tories relationship with CPV: 'The Conservative Party places itself in the hands of an advertising agency which produces a so-called image of the Tory Party by advertising methods. I believe that in doing this it introduces something into our political life which is alien to British democracy.' This, Hattersley noted, captured exactly the mood of Labour.' [41]

Thompson saw 1959 as the most discreditable general election since George III bought the House of Commons out of treasury funds.' Two major parties competed like soap manufacturers to sell the îmage''of their branded product'; and, he added, the thing about this kind of advertiser's îmage''is that, more often than not, it is put across to sell a shoddy or indifferent product.' Hopkins agreed the changes associated with affluence had permeated into politics. His impression of the election was òf two large rival commercial concerns, manufacturers of detergents or breakfast cereals, competing for the same carefully researched market.' When seen on TV', he found, the echoes of the familiar rivalry of Daz and Omo were irresistible.'[42]

For many socialists political advertising, TV and PR threatened to import the values and methods they deplored in the àffluent society' into politics. As Heardley-Walker saw it, Tory canvassers were now operating like salesman .but not selling brushes or vacuum cleaners, these doorstep smoothies will be selling you a fairy-story.' Politics was becoming a variant of consumer choice or incorporated into the tinsel and glitter civilisation' (as Foot described it). The 1964 election was the first on which commercial bookmakers (very successfully) took bets.[43]

The process was not simply one of marketing invading politics – the number of MPs acting as advisers to advertising or PR firms doubled in the two years before 1963 – Labour saw it as such and implicated the Conservatives in the change. Cartoonist Vicky branded the PM, Supermac'. Just as Patrick Gordon Walker had raised the spectre of the coronation being broadcast between adverts for beer and deodorant as part of Labour's case against commercial TV, so he saw a debasement of British political standards in the Conservatives use of PR and the way Macmillan was promoted as a brand like Chocolate penguins ... Payne's Poppets and Amplex'. Gordon-Walker also charged the Conservatives as responsible for the worst sort of Americanisation' of

British politics. Unease with America, which was the provenance of organizations like Gallup and leading psephologists like Robert McKenzie, was an element in the left's wariness. Priestley regularly warned that TV politics was 'around the corner' and had already arrived in his *bête noire* , the USA. According to Pearson and Turner, even Labour's new PR professionals, appointed in 1962, 'were anxious not to 'Americanise the campaign'' of 1964.   [44]

Socialists were suspicious of any such dabbling in their own quarters. Communists sought to expose the reality hidden beneath the welter of glossy publicity which seeks to give an acceptable 'brand image''to capitalism.' The New Left's William Norman scanned and detected in Labour's *Signposts for the Sixties* signs of what he labelled 'the iron law of glossiness''applied to content.' Some in the New Left were disappointed that *New Left Review* 'was on glossy paper', which to Sandy Hobbs signified 'a selling out to the consumer society that we were all against.' In this vein, Samuel's criticism of Mark Abrams' post-election survey of popular attitudes was that its methodology was bogus in seeing 'people as *consumers* of politics, behaving in politics much as they would – in the motivational research imagination – when confronted with mass-marketed commodities: they 'buy''political labels and allegiances as they would any brand image.'[45]

Harris and Clark, Labour's first PR professionals, wished to render it more marketable. Clark, as Regional Publicity Officer, recommended a 'vote only for those candidates who will be 'sellable''to the public' and not for those who were 'a public relations liability.' None the less, Clark trod carefully through Labour culture. He made a case for this by putting it to activists that 'every adverse piece of publicity .every neglect of socialist duty which overtakes us locally, leaves the party ... worse off.'[46]

The quandary Labour and other socialists faced was how to improve publicity without using 'the weapons of the enemy' – how to modernize without endorsing the methods current in the 'affluent society' or being used by the Tories. Labour opponents of modern methods struggled to differentiate medium and message. The fear was not only using the weapons of the enemy, but that the weapons of PR *were* the enemy. ''Public relations'' was anathema to many Labour supporters,' Hattersley considered, because it seemed to them that the process would inevitably corrupt the party.' Rowland recounted a typical exchange on publicity: 'reference is usually made to 'sticking to principles,''then somebody counters with 'why should the devil have all the best tunes,''and in no time morality and efficiency seem to be opposed rather than complementary.' This was some way from Herbert Morrison's ideal of Labour as an efficient machine for a high moral purpose.'[47]

Socialist publicity (and its assumptions)

Crosland argued in 1960 that Labour's publicity efforts were hopelessly amateur and old-fashioned compared with those of the Tories'. Labour conceded that alongside its own efforts, Conservative pamphlets appeared 'well-produced' and 'extremely attractive'. Brierley Hill CLP felt that 'compared with the Tory posters ours were very poor' and should have used the luminous paint which is so effective on those used by the Tories.' Too often Labour's publicity tended towards the 'crummy and verbose.' [48]

The Future Labour Offers You, a summation of Labour's mid-1950s policy review, was an exception. A bright, glossy guide, filled with photographs, it featured a tapering policy index along its right edge. Conservatives commented that Labour, for all that it decried PR superficiality, had a 'glossier than thou' streak. Gaitskell hailed it, after 1959, as the best propaganda pamphlet ever produced by a political party.'[49]

Not all were so certain. Hoggart felt it presented Labour as the party 'offering you a future''– like a premium bond win.' Benn, for similar reasons, petitioned to get the title .changed .to *The Britain We Want*.' Hopkins felt *The Future Labour Offers You* 'enveloped its very few specific details in multi-colour layouts and euphoric photogravure', but was at least 'a far cry from the poky, crowded, serious manifestoes of earlier years.' Lowestoft CLP damned it as succeeding only in 'showing up the 'shabby and un-enterprising appearance of earlier pamphlets.' Reading CLP felt that 'in the attempt to give the leaflets a popular appeal, the designers have given the front covers the appearance of holiday camp and travel brochures, having no discernible connection with our political cause.'[50]

Labour's 1959 conference was resistant to PR techniques. Hattersley recalled how 'delegate after delegate included in his speech (often irrelevantly and gratuitously) a denunciation of the techniques of Madison Avenue.' Anything less was tantamount to 'an admission that Tory PR techniques were needed to convert people to socialism.' A twin fear was that rather than converting people to Labour, the use of PR, advertising or opinion research might convert Labour to the popular mood. The prospect of Labour dancing to the tune of public opinion was one few socialists relished and amongst the chief reasons for their ambivalence towards opinion polling. Labour's Ormskirk candidate was 'appalled .to find .so many people at this conference .concerned with satisfying .public opinion', and asked delegates: since the Tory press' helped to make public opinion, was Labour but to placate the Tory press?'[51] Socialist assessments of the popular mood in the 1950s tended towards the conservative. They were wary of succumbing to the standards of the affluent society. This was some commentary on Labour's distrust of the electorate in the 1950s and remoteness from the popular'.

In any case, socialists disliked blending entertainment and politics. Politics was imagined too important to be affected by everyday activities. Explaining a poor attendance at a public meeting by its coincidence with a football match, Coventry party secretary R. B. Ritchie, was answered with the pointed view that it was not the .cup tie match which kept people away, but that .they were not satisfied with our policy for the next Labour government.' Activists were grudgingly aware of growing competition from TV and of elector's irritation at being dragged away from his favourite "western" by evening canvassers.[52]

Labour was annoyed by ITV's evening schedule for the evening of election day 1959. It featured *Rawhide* and *Dotto*, programmes they disliked, but which also attracted large audiences and the ITV audience was known to be predominantly Labour.' *Rawhide* particularly excited concern, for it occupied a time slot (eight o' clock) when working people normally voted. Labour argued that to leave it in the schedule .was to be responsible for a situation that was likely to interfere with the democratic process and damage the Labour Party's chances.' *Socialist Commentary* suggested both BBC and ITV should shut down from six o'clock on polling day.[53]

Politics had always contained a theatrical element. But it was clear from Harold Campbell's description of how the new mass media of public information and entertainment (the area which separates the two is marginal)' had managed to invade the conference hall', that the left were uneasy about this. Priestley despaired that for many Britons, politics, to exist for them at all, must be a show.' The left were amenable to the argument advanced in one of the new works of electoral sociology, *How People Vote*, that electoral legislation, rather than reducing bribery, had in some respects .increased its possibilities'. Graham Wallas, a Fabian political scientist, had noted in *Human Nature in Politics* in 1910 that if groups wished to pour money into politics, no

Corrupt Practices Act yet invented would prevent them from spending it.' The art of using skill for the production of emotion and opinion has so advanced,' he argued, 'that the whole condition of political contests would be changed for the future.'[54]

As socialists saw it, financially able and willing to professionalize electoral campaigning, the Tories found new means with which to misrepresent opponents and deceive voters. As Morgan Phillips declared after the 1959 defeat, intimating that the result was a tribute to Tory dishonesty: 'If the voter's decision had been determined only by a choice of programmes, the result would have been very different.'[55]

Gaitskell was another brake on Labour conforming to a more gaudy politics. His 'high-mindedness and moral honesty and his genuine belief that the electorate respond mainly to reasoned argument,' Rowland explained, 'made him temperamentally unsympathetic to showmanship.' And this was at a moment when doorstep canvassers might be struggling to gain attention, but party leaders could now address the electorate from an intimate corner of their own home. Yet Gaitskell was not the most telegenic figure. His awkward acclimatization to the TV studio was documented by Benn, his tutor in such matters.[56]

Gaitskell's notion of politics disposed him to be publicity shy. 'I am a rationalist', he told the *Daily Mail*; and felt that 'in a mature democracy people reach their conclusions mostly on the basis of actual evidence and argument' rather than because something appeals to their unconscious.' Like Bevan he believed publicity came second to policy and was proud that Labour had an intellectual centrepiece to its 1959 campaign, National Superannuation pensions, to sway informed voters.[57]

'The belief that the voter will calmly weigh up the pros and cons of arguments' went hand in hand with another assumption, 'to which left-wing politicians [were] particularly prone', that 'the man in the street [was] as interested in politics as they [were].' This underscored that publicity was of secondary importance. But, Rowland insisted, it was mistaken to imagine that all but a minority of people were preoccupied with political debate. Socialists were reluctant to accept there were 'headline readers, strip cartoon fans, television watchers' amongst voters. Its contempt for the comic-style, *Form*, that the Tories produced for the election and scruples at issuing anything comparable, 'showed a high-minded unawareness of what has popular appeal.'[58]

Priestley saw the gap between the popular and political in Gaitskell. Labour's leader saw himself as a serious man who must restrict his attention to serious matters, the sort of stuff that finds its way into the city columns of *The Times*.' It would never occur to him to take a look at *Mabel's Weekly* or *Filmfan's Pictorial'*, Priestley argued. Yet it was in this popular reading, frivolities and trivialities, far below the level of a public man's attention', that showed which way the wind is blowing.' [59]

This apartness cut both ways. Politics and politicians were treated warily in the popular inflections evoked by Hoggart – they're all talk', all politics are crooked.' Political rhetoric and propaganda, like advertising, was apt to make bold, claims and project fanciful images (and Labour no less than the Tories). Orwell was not alone in finding that as one came to compare commercial advertising with political propaganda, one thing that strikes you is its relative intellectual honesty.'[60]

The exclusivity of politics, of which vocabulary was perhaps the clearest expression, was evident in socialist publicity in the 1950s. Labour was staffed by men and women with an omnivorous capacity for paper and speech', for whom words [were] their lifeblood, small print their delight.' The CPGB too, Gorman remembers, produced more printed matter than any other political movement in the world.' This impressed itself on socialist publicity, which as Rowland concisely argued, tended to be too long' and too wordy.' Under CPV's tutelage the Conservatives were simpler in their use of illustration and language.' The Labour Party Research Department's *Twelve Wasted Years* ran to 471 pages – evidence of the detail of its critique of the Tory years, but of this prolix quality too.[61]

Reflecting on Labour's post-1955 policy review, Benn noted that twelve policy statements have been published since spring 1956' which together ran into over 600 pages and nearly a quarter of a million words.' Except for some of the really active party workers,' he contended, most people have not and will not read them.' In a 1953 report to the NEC on 'The Labour Party and Broadcasting', Benn argued it was pointless issuing four pages of closely reasoned argument in small type against a coloured and illustrated glossy pamphlet.'[62] Others took up the point. The NEC heard in July 1960 how the opinion that the bulk of the electorate forms of the party ha[d] very little to do with its detailed policy.' Rowland shared Benn's recognition that whatever socialists themselves preferred, one photograph of Mr. Macmillan pruning his rose garden .[was] worth half a dozen solid speeches by Mr. Gaitskell.'[63]

Related to this was socialists' use of language. They were apt to talk in their own tongue, among themselves and to those uninitiated in such terms. Chief amongst Percy Clark's aims as Regional Publicity Officer, was to ban local election jargon"– the secret code' to which

Labour was prone. The agent in one East Midlands marginal complained of the intellectual language' of Labour's 1959 programme. The New Left was similarly afflicted. After 1962 the *Review* became more like a group of marxist swots' (as Widgery wittily put it), who poured wrath down upon Labourism's failings. Ex-editors like Malcolm MacEwen found the new *Review* unreadable, even with a dictionary'. Mervyn Jones suffered its articles as esoteric and baffling'. [64]

Left-wing journals were as absorbed in griping at the Labour leadership or other socialists, as with communicating beyond. *Tribune*, the *New Statesman* and *Socialist Commentary*, thrived on the factional discord of the 1950s. Only the *New Statesman* had a significant readership beyond. A 1955 survey revealed only 40 per cent of its readers considered themselves left of centre' and fully a quarter of its circulation went overseas. With a circulation around 80,000 during the 1950s, it was the only journal to attract a good level of advertising. *New Left Review* and *Socialist Commentary*, struggled on circulations of around eight thousand, the *Evening Standard* reported in 1960. Both operated on a surplus of barely £1,000, adverts were few and far between, and contributors mostly went unpaid.[65] Journals shared the qualities of the movement. Photographs were rare. In a '*Socialist Commentary* Questionnaire' readers submitted that its articles needed simpler language' and gave the impression of [the] enthusiastic but lazy amateur rather than expert.' Journals shared readers of differing socialist persuasions. The *New Statesman*'s letter page was a CPGB battlefield in 1956 and the New Left took Mark Abrams' surveys to task in correspondence with *Socialist Commentary*.[66]

The left's tendency to talk to itself was marked in the 1950s. Attempts to break out were limited. Fronted by *The Future Labour Offers You*, of which one and a half million copies were printed, 1958's into Action' campaign was launched by a TV broadcast featuring Wilson, Bevan and Gaitskell and followed by regional rallies. Yet too much effort', Butler and Rose submitted, was spent preaching to the converted and not enough communicating with the general public.' Rowland, too, felt that as internal propaganda' *The Future Labour Offers You* was undoubtedly effective', but doubted if it got into the hands of the public to any significant extent.' It was not available at ten different W. H. Smith's bookstalls,' he reported, for several days after the television broadcast.' Symptomatic was Labour's pledge to increase pensions by 10s. per week. Activists had known of this since 1957, but it came as a surprise to many voters in 1959 and was portrayed by Tory papers as an election bribe.[67]

The *Wilson Report* had reinforced this introspective sense. Its diagnosis of Labour's defeat in 1955 freighted poor organization and apathy amongst party workers for the failure to get its vote out and recommended enthusing activists with policy documents, such that they would tramp the streets. This reflected Labour's estimation of electoral apathy, but that its essential bond with the mass of the people was intact. The *Wilson Report* assumed Labour's predominantly working-class support was a permanent and natural sociological feature. The only issue was to ensure that voters obliged this sociological model of politics by turning out in sufficient numbers.

Yet this – not only the assumption of Labour's affinity with the people' or of Labour voting as some sociological norm' for workers, but also that Labour had suffered only from apathy in 1955, from a poor turnout amongst workers rather than from their desertion – was far from certain. Crossman told David Butler of a different process in Coventry. He described his feeling that the votes were slipping out of our hands, not merely as a Labour abstention, but in a new working-class Toryism.' Crossman related this to the general prosperity of the country' that was likely to repeat itself more violently in the future.' [68]

Opinion polling

The assumption that Labour was intimately in tune with its electorate made it dismissive of the fashion for assessing public opinion. If Labour perceived itself to naturally represent popular social aspirations – what need had it of researching these? To do so was to question the intuitive bond it had with the people.

Bevan felt opinion polling took the poetry out of politics.' Politics', *In Place of Fear* asserted in defiance of psephology and political sociology, was an art, not a science.' Sociology, psychology .political economy' could help to work out correct principles to guide' socialists, Bevan explained, but the application of those principles to a given situation' remained an art.' It was then the skill and instincts of socialists that were critical to their ability to represent their audience. This was evident in how activists had to learn the canvassing art' (and in Priestley's claim to an intuitive insight into what English people in general are thinking').[69]

A socialist poetics did not involve, for Bevan, having a desiccated calculating machine' as Labour leader. Applied to Gaitskell this was harsh, as he too intuitively felt of political PR that the whole thing is somehow false' – Bevan and Gaitskell were never quite the romantic-rationalist foes they and subsequent commentators have assumed.[70] A socialist poetics rather involved, as Thompson approvingly quoted Harry Pollitt, 'painting the vision splendid .showing glimpses of the promised land.' Thompson was deeply sceptical of the new statistical approaches. *New Reasoner* researchers, he revealed, had calculated a half per cent per annum drift from Chartism since 1848' and would publish their conclusions in the *American Journal of Communicational Guphology*.' He derided both psephologists employed by the mass media to research into what people think the mass media has told them to think' and the ephologist', employed by the *Observer* or BBC to interpret the results of psephology and who makes an ephing good thing out of it.' The ironic tone pointed to a wariness (in the post-CPGB Thompson) of scientific methods and language.[71]

Surveyors of popular attitudes challenged traditional sources of socialist knowledge. As reader of the political mood and policy-maker, the pollster threatened to displace the local activist or socialist theorist.[72] The new techniques also chafed by seeming to place socialist principle in thrall to the popular mood – and it was a mark of the gap between socialism and the popular' in the 1950s that this so offended.

Exchanges over Mark Abrams' post-election survey well illustrate this. The first of four instalments by the director of Research Services and President of the World Association for Public Opinion Research, of what became *Must Labour Lose?*, appeared in May 1960's *Socialist Commentary*. It related Labour's electoral malaise to attitudes it discovered amongst workers and young people. The *Daily Telegraph* reported that according to Dr. Abrams, the party hierarchy seemed horrified" at any suggestion that the cause of this decline should be discovered by any such rational method as systematic interrogation of the voters.' Phillips rejoined that Labour was not .hostile to the study of public opinion and to the use of social surveys', but that surveys were costly and Labour never had money to fling around.' He saw dangers in poll-lead politics, where the major means of persuasion in this country are .anti-socialist.' And in cases like Suez or corporal punishment, where he was convinced that my view is right', there could be no pandering to the popular mood.[73]

Their high profile use by Labour's opponents was another reason why socialists used opinion surveys little and regarded them as politically dubious. Notable was Colin Hurry's 1959 survey. Hurry, a business consultant, was funded by (mostly steel) companies to survey attitudes towards nationalization. Almost two million Britons were polled by the British Market Research Bureau (BMRB), a subsidiary of

American advertisers, J. Walter Thompson. The results – 63.4 per cent favouring no more nationalisation', 18.5 per cent favouring more – were publicised in the press and a poster campaign in September 1959, just weeks before the election. Labour became aware of the survey in November 1958 when the wife of its Kirkdale (Liverpool) candidate contacted Harold Wilson explaining she had taken a job with the survey and spotted its bias. The questions are framed', she wrote, in such a way that they suggest certain answers (and so act as a very strong form of propaganda) which certainly do not help the Labour Party.'[74]

Labour countered in early 1959 that the survey's concentration on the 129 most marginal constituencies betrayed political intent. Among residents who received a call in Gourock was Jean Mann, Labour MP for Airdrie. Elsewhere interviewers avoided known Labour supporters. This made Bertha Elliot, Darlington CLP secretary, wonder if the Tories were supplying the quiz firm with marked registers.' Elliot also reported that now the survey was public knowledge, Labour supporters were telling questioners they were Conservative voters in favour of more nationalisation.'[75] Phillips demanded to know the financing of the survey and why, if it was aiming to survey public opinion, it was confined to marginal constituencies. He estimated its cost at £750,000. The charges stuck and the BMRB, concerned for its professional reputation, returned the responsibility for the survey to Hurry. What also stuck, by dint of Labour's protest, was its association with nationalization.[76] Above all, the survey confirmed socialist scepticism about the ethics of such surveys.

As much as their methods jarred, the findings of these surveys perturbed the left. Socialists took an unfavourable view of affluence, seeing in it popular attitudes that they could not, or would not, represent and Conservative political attitudes. Research threatened to reveal the difference between popular and socialist attitudes and to dispel the myth of Labour as the voice of the people.

A £500 survey by Research Services for Labour in 1957 found that abolishing private schools and the 11-plus exam were not (as Labour's current policy believed) the chief popular educational concerns.[77] It was also symptomatic that criticism of Abrams' *Must Labour Lose?*, where changing popular aspirations were correlated to Labour's difficulties, centred less on these findings than the methodology that had excavated them. Its importance lies,' Samuel wrote, in the underlying approach to man and politics.' Notwithstanding this criticism, as Samuel later suggested, it was arguable that many on the left feared during the postwar boom that historical research might prove the right correct.'[78]

Samuel's main charge against Abrams' research was that it over-looked how the left had built up its support and overdrew a picture of politics where electors were seen as instrumental clients of parties. This married more with revisionist thinking, as did Abrams' conclusions, showing popular unease with nationalization and Labour's 'cloth-cap' image to be outdated. Samuel suspected the survey to be a premeditated exercise to ratify the revisionist position. Abrams and the survey funders, Rita Hinden and Michael Young, were revisionists. Samuel complained that Abrams' framework was set forth as a self evident truth' and, echoing Labour criticism of the Hurry survey, that 'many of the 'answers''to the questionnaire were plainly determined by the questions themselves.' Abrams' 'dexterity in handling statistics' he argued, meant that whatever the results, his conclusions would hardly have altered.' Abrams countered that Samuel's critique was similarly premeditated. In July 1960, before the final instalment in *Commentary*, he claimed to have been told by a *New Left Review* editor, that Mr. Samuel had already done 'a beautiful hatchet job on the survey.' [79]

Surveys the left did undertake contested existing assumptions. Samuel's survey of popular Toryism, questioned the 'assumption ... that the social composition of Labour's support [was] a fixed, immutable fact' and the only barrier to an electoral victory was the 'reluctance''of the working class to cast a vote.' It saw politics as less a matter of compliance with sociological criteria and more culturally manifold. *Must Labour Lose?* queried 'modern inhibitions about the value of the survey.' Its aim was 'establishing facts' contrary to the 'mystique' of those socialists who claimed a 'special insight into 'what the people want'' or imagined 'some intuitive bond between them-selves and the whole of the working class.' This was a species of social-ist of which 'within the Labour Party there [were] too many.' Fear that surveys would scale socialism down to 'what the people want' was also misplaced. 'The point of the survey', *Must Labour Lose?* held, was to indicate where the obstacles' to socialism lay and 'provide a realistic basis to the strategy of change.' 'Political sociology', it warned, 'may give the facts', but 'so much else is required .leadership, organisation and most important, the enthusiasm and idealism of .supporters.' [80]

Opinion surveying introduced an unfamiliar vocabulary to the left. With David Ginsburg (previously at the government's social survey unit) as head of its research department head from 1955, Labour com-missioned two surveys before 1960. Research Services undertook both and outlined their approach in a 1956 memo. 'In putting over ideas,' it argued, the Labour Party faces problems similar to those of a commer-

cial organisation.' It needed to know about our market, i.e. our supporters and opponents' and about the reactions of consumers to our
product'; though it added the Party was not bound to change our policies to take account of public opinion.'[81]

Revisionists warmed to the new techniques. The study of voting
behaviour and political attitudes – that is political sociology – is a
proper study for the politician,' Crosland informed those who would
morally condemn such studies.' [82] Its appeal lay not only in
confirmation for the revisionist project, but also in the viability of sociological accounts of voting behaviour in the 1950s. As Lawrence and
Taylor note post-war Britain seemed to provide ample evidence of a
close fit between the two-party system and the basic realities of a
divided, but none the less mobile, class society.'[83]

Electoral sociology and psephology burgeoned in the 1950s then on
the back of these voting patterns. Samuel remembers early 1950s politics as two great parties' that confronted each other in two class
blocs.' Crosland too asserted the symmetry of party and class. Socialism
shared with electoral sociology the notion that underlying politics
were economic and social forces, that politically people's choice was
not based on a rational assessment, but on unseen social forces.'[84]
Mapping electoral behaviour according to social trends had then a
persuasive logic.

Yet in Crosland (as Gaitskell) there also remained a hope that voters
would make rational, self-informed choices. He anticipated that the
classlessness of affluence would enable voters to make a more reasoned
and pragmatic judgement of issues, programmes and the abilities of
various parties .instead of voting instinctively in accordance with
class identification.' Nor were activists persuaded of the magic of
psephology. It seemed to surrender their role in elections – knowledge
of local contacts and tradition – to political behaviour predestined by
intangible social forces.[85]

None the less a significant minority in socialist ranks were using
public-opinion research. Benn was receiving Gallup material from the
British Institute of Public Opinion and under Ginsburg the research
department acquired political sociology works: Milne and Mackenzie's
Straight Fight, Bonham's *The Middle Class Vote*, the Greenwich survey
How People Vote and the Nuffield election series.[86]

The main fillip to incorporating this into Labour strategy was the
1959 election. Defeat prompted the thought, as in Herbert Morrison,
that Labour needs to study what sort of people these British people
really are.' But it was only in 1962 that detailed polling was commis-

sioned from Abrams. This targeted floating voters' in marginals and the Party's advertising in 1964 drew on its findings. Yet by 1966, *The Economist* reported, Labour had abandoned the exercise for no very obvious reason.' Instead it reverted to type and banked on Wilson's instincts', signalling the enduring traditionalism in Labour culture and the extent to which Wilson shared in this.[87]

Television

Advocates of using television for socialist purposes faced similar problems. Even a believer in modern technology, like Benn, who felt TV was the greatest .and most important thing that has happened to British politics', confessed reservations: however much one believes in it', televised politics was still a frightening prospect'. There was a degree of wonder' in the left's attitude towards the modern magic box' – that Labour must learn to master its tricks.' With its dislike of much programming and disdain for televiewing, this gave rise to the situation Benn highlighted in May 1958, where, none of [the] Party leaders have television sets.' Labour, he feared, was unaware of how TV was influencing the minds and thought of the voters.' How can one lead a great party,' he wondered, unless one keeps in touch with the people?'[88]

Labour leaders had an uneasy relationship with the TV camera. Attlee's first experience with a medium for which hitherto he had displayed little enthusiasm' was in 1954. *Attlee at Walthamstow*, presented by William Pickles, suffered a broken camera. Benn found Bevan frightened' of TV and completely anti-professional in his outlook.' Gaitskell was no less cranky. Before a TV interview in 1958, Benn described: Gaitskell was as quarrelsome as hell, just as Nye Bevan had been.'[89]

Television altered the temper of politics. For Pickles, Labour's broadcasting adviser in the mid-1950s, it meant a fall in political temperature.' The traditional skills of the socialist orator in public meetings – inveighing against opponents, enthusing the audience – did not always suit TV. Party broadcasts were a more relaxed, detached medium. They enabled more intimate communication, yet gave parties a potential audience of millions. Benn relished that TV brought the party leaders right into millions of homes to make their case quietly and un-heckled, to those who might otherwise never have heard it.' It seemed to Pickles, the audience received a much higher proportion of political education and a much lower proportion of political propaganda.'[90]

The new electronic hustings' that interposed the whole mid-century world of specialisms, of producers, camera-experts, make-up artists ... market-researchers between the politicians and the public' were disabling for the CPGB. It relied heavily upon emotional fervour and conjuring up the gleam' of socialism. In Upward's account, Communist orators affected mannerisms, lending background rhythm' to speeches.[91] Labour was more conscious that full-blooded polemics issued by the likes of Michael Foot on ITV's *Free Speech* (where he and CND-supporting historian A. J. P. Taylor locked horns with Tories like Bob Boothby), were not to the taste of all viewers. One of the biggest assets the Tories had to help them in the last election,' one disgruntled viewer wrote to Morgan Phillips in 1959, were Michael Foot and Alan Taylor.' A 1955 report to the NEC by Pickles, suggested party broadcasts might even toy for deliberate contrast with the tub-thumper.'[92]

But traditional styles were not extinct. If Sue Townsend is any guide, despite his wariness of the medium, Bevan's oratory was powerfully conveyed by TV:

> The lumbering black-and-white television in the corner was turned on, but I paid it no attention. Then onto the screen came ... Mr.Bevan, who was making a speech .I. was immediately mesmerised .I. put my book down and watched .His body dipped and swooped as he started to make a point .His voice wheedled seductively, dropped until it was only a whisper and then whooshed back up the register, ending in a shouted joke.[93]

In its post-war electoralist mood, the CPGB was anxious to claim broadcasting rights.[94] It encountered an array of problems. In 1950 it protested that its radio broadcasts were not to be aired (like those of other parties) after 9.00 p.m. and that most factory workers' would be unable to hear Pollitt in his 6.15 p.m. slot. In 1959 it made efforts to ensure it was permitted a TV broadcast. Its exclusion, at the behest of the BBC and main parties (the CPGB felt), it described as a gross violation of democratic rights.' With Dutt's dialectical skill, such prejudice was easily intelligible. Communists ensured that the real issues are faced', but other parties evaded these, which explained why they were so panicky-afraid of the Communists appearing on television' and why their own broadcasts were so confusing.'[95]

Certainly Labour was prepared to experiment with presentation. Perceptions of its audience were a cause. A 1951 research paper proposed radio broadcasts should be briefer than 20 minutes as for the ordinary listener, the optimum period is much shorter.' This paper, Pickles' and Michael Young's reflections on the 1951 election, also noted that TV would be of greater importance at the next election, how Labour needed to experiment with programme styles other than straight talks and how professional expertise would improve its performance.[96]

Progress in this respect was slow. The cost of professional producers was prohibitive. By 1958 (six years after the Conservatives) a TV studio had been built in Transport House. A broadcasting officer, Ken Peay, was responsible for this and training petulant politicians. Yet Labour remained largely reliant on the goodwill of BBC figures like Cliff Michelmore, to provide advice.[97]

Resistance and reluctance was broken down as Party leaders gained experience on TV. Labour was involved with 26 of its own TV broadcasts between 1953 and 1959. Things did not always go to plan. Rosenbaum relates how during 1955's *Your Money's Worth*, hosted by Wilson and Edith Summerskill, the butter and cheese used to demonstrate rising prices melted under the heat of the television lighting. A BBC Audience Research Report on 1960's *Question Time for Youth*, found opinion critical. One respondent felt it sounded like a commercial on ITV – artificial and lacking in spontaneity.' But Labour broadcasts were also admired. After a 1955 broadcast the *Observer* commented that Morrison always spoke and looked and bore himself like a man chatting things over in the living room, not booming them out on a public platform.' Elaine Burton's *Value for Money*, produced by David Attenborough, was applauded by the *Daily Telegraph* for achieving entertainment mixed with homilies'. Only the *New Statesman* found it deplorably lacking in personality.' [98]

Labour's 1959 election broadcasts, masterminded by Benn, modelled on the magazine format of the BBC's current affairs series *Tonight* and produced by *Tonight's* assistant producer, Alasdair Milne, were a breakthrough in political viewing. Rosenbaum estimated the five broadcasts 'achieved a higher level of professionalism and inventiveness .than anything done before.'[99]

Benn was regarded as an iconoclast and modernizer in his approach to Labour's communication. Crosland favoured consulting him on the whole question of public relations, propaganda' for his enlightened views.' He proselytized for newer techniques in terms that would have his latter-day persona (more conscious of socialist tradition) wincing. In *Forward*, the social democratic journal which John Harris deputy edited, Benn wrote in 1958 that just as one hydrogen bomb packs more power than the total load dropped in World War Two, so one television broadcast more than equals a lifetime of mass rallies and street-corner oratory.'[100]

Woodrow Wyatt and Chris Mayhew (a firm opponent of commercial TV) also aimed to acquaint Labour with the BBC studios. But Benn, like both a one-time BBC producer, was most insistent.[101] This was not so at odds with the later Benn as Samuel, a contemporary adversary of his desire to apply the media to politics, has suggested. Benn remained a critic of both ITV profits and BBC conservatism. His proposal to Labour's election committee in 1958 argued the artefacts surrounding Gaitskell on camera might include a bust of Keir Hardie'. [102] His thinking on the uses of political TV was also of a piece with that formally espoused by Labour by 1959. *Leisure for Living* explained that to be prejudiced against television as such – as some .snobbish people are' was to confuse the medium with the uses to which it is sometimes put.' While far too many of the programmes at present broadcast [were] of poor quality or unduly preoccupied with getting-rich-quick or violence', television remained potentially an invaluable instrument for enlarging .people's awareness of the world.'   [103]

Presented by a suave Benn, *Britain Belongs to You* featured interviews with party leaders and testimonials from public figures like playwright John Osborne, scientist Ritchie Calder, actress Jill Balcon and trumpeter Humphrey Lyttelton.[104] Friend and foe were impressed. The *Daily Worker*'s Peggy Lucas felt the introduction of well-known personalities .was a piece of telling TV propaganda'. The format held the attention [by] not dwelling too long on separate issues'. The *Daily Sketch* reported that, if there is any ground to the belief that this is a TV election, then the Tories are in real danger of losing it.' *The Spectator* conceded Labour had produced a piece of expert, shrewd propaganda.' [105]

There were more circumspect evaluations. Trenaman and MacQuail's survey of *Television and the Political Image* found a small majority of the opinion that Labour's broadcasts had been too slick"compared to the Conservatives'. A poll of 300 Labour candidates similarly found the most common doubt expressed was that the programmes were possibly too slick.' Worse, though related, was that 10 per cent more of those quizzed by Trenaman and MacQuail considered Conservative rather than Labour broadcasts to have accurately portrayed an impression of present-day Britain.' There was substance then to the jealous charge of Tory papers like the *Yorkshire Post* that Benn's wizardry was no more than an artful, artificial barrage.' [106]

Nor was 1959 the 'TV Election' Benn's strategy imagined. Only 22 per cent of Britons watched a party broadcast. With the advent of outside broadcast technology, 1964 was more deserving of the title. Like opinion polling, party political broadcasts were hardly foolproof. They were unpopular viewing. Black reports 80 per cent of viewers turned channels when a Party political was broadcast. This led in 1956 to the parties making both channels show party broadcasts simultaneously.[107] 1959 helped persuade Labour of the virtues of modern broadcasting. Comparing himself to Peter Mandleson in 1992, Benn reflected that in 1959 he fought a brilliant campaign and lost.' Defeat raised the importance of television in the minds of Labour leaders, not least through this perception of the greater success of the Tory party in the use of election television.' Political broadcasting was felt too important to be left to broadcasters. Even Wilson, better disposed towards advertising and opinion polling from 1963, had a distinctly conservative' attitude. Precisely because of its perceived importance, Rosenbaum advances, he and his cohort refused to leave it to those with professional skills.' [108]

After 1959

Defeat in 1959 induced Labour to confront modern methods. Amongst explanations of Labour's defeat, *Reynolds News* felt the Tories had considerable success in imposing their 'image"of Labour on many electors'. Labour did not succeed in imposing [its] own image' as the party of adventure, gaiety, respect for the individual and healthy social values.' Lillian Allaun agreed the Tories .painted an image in the public mind of the Labour Party' and that this was a largely gloomy picture' of austerity, controls, nationalisation, levelling down instead of up.'[109]

Conservative publicity played up perceptions of Labour's paternalism. A 1957 advert asked whether a young child would, be fenced in when she grows up?' and concluded, despite the socialists, we are human beings, not figures on adding machines.' Labour was prone to accusations of busybody councils and more general *dirigisme*. It was an image its publicity did not always dispel. Amongst Labour's main posters was one of Gaitskell with the caption The Man with a Plan' and, as Butler and Rose observed, looking very much the man from Whitehall.'[110]

The Tories attempted to identify themselves with consumer affluence in the later 1950s. CPV's two-year campaign from 1957 targeted women, the young and the better-off workers' and was directed towards enabling these groups to identify the Conservative Party with prosperity and opportunity.' With the slogan Life's Better with the Conservatives, Don't Let Labour Ruin It' were shown a family with a television set in the corner of the room and, in another shot, washing their new car. The election result, Gordon-Walker conceded, suggested the Tories identified themselves with the new working-class rather better than we did.'[111] The duration of Conservative publicity also weighed against Labour. CPV's advertising campaign ran from June 1957 to election day. Labour's efforts were more short-term, improvised and impoverished. Allaun reflected: three weeks isn't long enough to wipe out five years of lies and misrepresentation.'[112]

Business campaigns stressed the same values. Free Enterprise has given you Prosperity' the National Union of Manufacturers warned in September 1959, but nationalisation can ruin it.' Conservative and business aspersions were abetted by Labour's divisions over nationalization. Its confusion, Crosland maintained, meant it was almost impossible to counter the widespread and damaging rumours that every large firm .was on the list for nationalisation.' [113]

After 1959 some revisionists felt Labour might reinvent its image by disassociating itself from the working class, nationalization and trade unions. Even its name should be altered, Douglas Jay contended in *Forward*. Most gave this emotional spasm short shrift. Prior to Jay's article, Gaitskell was discussing the disadvantages of the name Labour, especially on new housing estates.' This gut reaction to defeat was calmed by Benn's assurance that Labour need not change name, but work on promoting it more positively. In a revealing analogy, Benn reminded his leader, the prune had been resuscitated without a change of name by clever selling.'[114]

The New Left too, scorned Labour's name. Its disquiet was Labour's ideological deficit not surfeit. For Anderson, Labour's very name' underscored the point. It was called neither a social democratic nor a socialist nor a communist party', but the *Labour* Party – a name', he argued, designating not an ideal society, as [with] the others, but an existent interest.'[115]

Image' occupied socialists because it was a venerable issue not one newly invented by the PR business. Crosland deployed Wallas's earlier argument in *Human Nature in Politics* that a party was primarily a name, which, like other names, calls up when it is heard or seen an Image". The business of the party managers' was to secure that these automatic associations shall be as clear as possible [and] .shared by as large a number as possible.' In this vein, a 1960 Labour research document accepted that the majority of the electorate is unlikely to have a very clear knowledge of .policies', but would hold a more general idea of party image.'[116]

The 1960 American presidential election focused attention on image. For Crosland, Kennedy's successful use of TV, demonstrated that an individual politician may find in television a powerful vehicle, corresponding to the mass meeting or Midlothian-style campaign in days gone by, for the projection of his oratory or personality.' Labour's dialogue on image' predated Kennedy's victory. Nor was it conducted exclusively amongst revisionists. Bevan told the 1959 conference that having decided what our policy should be', Labour must, put it as attractively as possible to the population'; not change policy opportunistically to the contemporary mood, but .alter its presentation in order to win the suffrage of the population.'[117]

It was Crosland who cautioned, public relations .becomes important only when the underlying reality has been improved.' Otherwise, he insisted that while shortage of money would always be an inhibiting factor' on Labour's use of advertising and PR, the money available could be spent far more professionally and effectively than it is today.' Crosland rehearsed this argument in the 1958 *Co-Operative Independent Commission Report*, which criticized the inefficiency and lack of expert managerial knowledge in the Co-op. Crosland's case for best practice in political communication also exhibited a familiar Fabian belief in the expert. If money is to be spent on TV, posters and advertising', he argued in *Can Labour Win?*, it was no more immoral, and rather more sensible, to spend it wisely.'[118]

Despite the pressures that emanated from 1959 to ensure Labour did not risk losing another election because they presented a blurred or unattractive image' – Crosland stressed the 1959 polls showed .we lost by having a blurred, uncertain, schizophrenic image' – change was slow. It was only in 1962 that Labour leaders (as Koss puts it) overcame their repugnance and resorted to the same techniques' (as the Tories) and appointed professional experts. The new Director of Publicity, John Harris had a background in journalism, was Labour leader on Harlow council and Labour's Parliamentary Press Officer. Percy Clark became deputy director. Among unpaid advisers were American Clive Bradley, responsible for TV and radio, David Kingsley, founder of Kingsley, Manton and Palmer, amongst the 1960s most successful ad agencies and Peter Lovell-Davis.[119]

Harris and Clark had been rebels under the old regime, chafing under the negative.tactics' Labour adopted towards the press.' The bright young men' – Harris was 32 – with pyjama stripe shirts and smart suits' gave their department the air of one of the busier advertising agencies' and caused some unease. In 1963 one elderly Labour MP remarked that the arrival of Harris at Transport House had been a terrible event for the party', adding, by allusion to Packard's critique of advertising, that Labour had no need to resort to *Hidden Persuaders* of their own.'[120]

The process of Harris and Clark's appointment showed the ambiguities of reform. It proved tricky enough to extricate Harris from Bromley CLP (where he was to stand against Macmillan) to accompany Gaitskell during the 1959 election. Key resignations, like that of Broadcasting Officer Ken Peay shortly after the election, aided Harris's incorporation into the party. The post of Director was only designated in May 1962 when Arthur Bax resigned as head of the publicity department. A proposal for creating a similar post was rejected in 1960 on the question of remuneration above the Party's existing salary structure. Barbara Castle told the NEC in 1962 that (for its commercial connotations) the new designation Director' was unfortunate', but also that the current salary scales were not enough to attract suitable applicants.' [121]

The appointment of Harris and his ilk did not indicate then that Labour had shed all amateurism. Crosland attributed to a lingering anti-professionalism that after two years of anguished discussion about the importance of public relations', when Labour finally advertised for a Director of Publicity .to take on .the collective strength of Colman, Prentis and Varley', it was at the farcical salary of £1,650 p.a.' [122]

There were some unlikely applicants – a Nottingham shop porter and ex-CPGB member who admitted to past mental trouble' – but also several impressive candidates. Amongst those not interviewed were Leif Mills, later general secretary of the Banking Union; Winston Fletcher, who would become a leading advertising executive and PR Officers from companies such as Cunard. Those interviewed were all existing Labour officials like Publications Officer, Philip Parry.[123]

Nor would Labour ship out its publicity requirements to an agency as the Conservatives did. It preferred to appoint its own experts, incorporate them into the party structure and continue to use volunteers from TV, advertising and elsewhere (like the *Daily Mirror* journalists who lent a hand in 1959). Neither Harris, Clark nor Abrams were outsiders: Harris was a confirmed Gaitskellite, Clark had worked for *Tribune* and Abrams' first social survey was a Fabian publication.[124]

Morgan Phillips' illness from late 1960 was an added dimension. Phillips was not a barrier to all reform (he had innovated the daily press conference during the election), but his absence did facilitate changes in publicity personnel and structure. Crosland felt that the choice of Morgan's successor is one of the most crucial decisions for many years', and his replacement must have the right attitude to modern public relations techniques'. Yet reformers were thwarted by the choice in 1962 of Len Williams, with Sara Barker replacing Williams as National Agent. Crosland lamented their influence at the Party centre – 'Williams and S. Barker are by no means geniuses,' he had told Gaitskell in 1960. It was significant that modernizers did not have their own way after 1959 and that it was former critics like Phillips and Bacon who were managing Labour's attempts to (as Bacon put it) be publicity conscious.' [125]

For all the fracas of 1959, it was the limits as much as the extent of change ushered in that impressed. In mid-1960 Labour still compared unfavourably to its opponents – the gallup poll people have regular meetings with Tory central office' Crosland told Gaitskell, but have not once been approached by Transport House since the election.' Nor did Wilson's accession in 1963 denote a sea-change. Wilson had himself previously described PR as 'a most degrading profession' and been, according to Tunstall, an outspoken critic' of advertising. It was Wilson's image that a campaign (Labour's first) of national press adverts in May 1963 dwelt upon. Labour's PR team even hoped to portray their leader as a Kennedy-type figure.' But a large part of Wilson's marketability was founded on more traditional Labourist components: his gannex jacket, liking for brown sauce and Huddersfield Town F.C. contrasted with his modernising, scientific rhetoric.[126]

The traditional was evident in Wilson's 1964 campaign – whose success is conventionally ascribed to the efficiency and modernity of its presentation as much as its rhetoric. The opening rally at Wembley featured local Pakistani dancers and a sketch from *Steptoe and Son*'s Harry H. Corbett, but also a Welsh male voice choir and colliery brass band. Wilson borrowed phrases from Kennedy and read Theodore White's *The Making of the President*, but told reporters – 'I am not a Kennedy .I.fly by the seat of my pants.' This was evident in 1964. A car phone Wilson demonstrated to journalists took an age to contact Len Williams at Transport House. Another call found all his aides at lunch. Richard West reported that excepting Wilson, there was the same old Labour Party dullness about his entourage.'[127]

Wilson was reluctant to cede control of party broadcasts and the content of adverts, fearing they could fall beneath the dignity of the

Labour Party.' According to Rosenbaum, this reflected a residual hostility among Labour politicians to the tricks of the advertising trade.' To his eye, during the 1964 campaign Labour's were the more 'respectable' ads, where the Tories employed 'visual gimmicks' in an effort to convey an impression of modernity.'[128] New methods, it seems, contributed little to Wilson's triumph in 1964.

Nor did Wilson's triumph herald the professionalization of the party. 1965's 'Plan for an Efficient Party' called for a paid rather than voluntary PR staff, polling advisers at Transport House and control of broadcasts to be in the hands of experts not the party. It contrasted Party organization with its 1964 election slogan, 'A Modern Britain'. With support from across the party (demonstrating Wilson's ability to unite), it also showed the persistence of the sort of 'penny-farthing' problems diagnosed in 1955.[129] Labour, after all, emerged from 13 years of Tory government with a majority of four. There was no '1997' at the end of the road to 1964 – except, as Jefferys argues, in that it was as much through disenchantment with Conservative administration as embrace of Labour's vision that victory was secured.[130]

Wring has argued the early 1960s saw a shift in Labour's strategy from an 'educationalist' approach ('making socialists') to a 'persuasional' approach (getting votes for Labour rather than winning voters to socialism). This shift was also evident in local canvassing strategies. It was also the product of Labour's disappointment in the people in the 1950s. Changes in Labour's communication methods resulted in part from the dim view it took of popular affluence. Much as Labour felt it 'smacked of paying tribute to the enemy' or was no substitute for active popular support, it was increasingly conscious that, as Rowland argued, the average Labour-inclined ITV viewing-voter has to be got at in the style to which he has become accustomed – simply, repetitively, irrationally.' The very weaknesses Labour perceived in its audience were now to be the axis of its publicity. Benn consistently advocated a more populist approach. As early as 1953 he was recommending to the NEC, fireside chats, the whole lot can be used with great effect for political purposes.' A 1955 Pickles' report was even more explicit in its proposals for beguiling what it saw as the more gullible viewers. 'If properly used', it argued, 'a political figure well over the heads of the audience can give a valuable impression of competence and erudition.' As Garland reluctantly concluded in 1963, good layout and photographs are the only hopes if you are to get an urgent message to a publicity punch-drunk electorate.' Changes in Labour's communication, much as they were a response to new technologies and to addressing voters in ways and they could more readily receive, also expressed Labour's rather circumspect assessment of its audience in the 1950s.[131]

This chapter has stressed the limits of Labour's modernization to 1964. It has outlined a political culture that entertained reservations about modern methods of performing politics, just as it did about the àffluent society'. As with those, its misgivings about TV, advertising and public-opinion research were as much intuitive as drawn from any formal reasoning.

Certainly some Conservatives held a similar suspicion of the press, of Americanism or television. Sampson reported that the vulgarity of the campaign' the Conservatives conducted during the 1959 election horrified many old-school Conservatives.' [132] Just as divisions within the left over communication did not fall into a left-right split, nor was their a clear cleavage between the left and Conservatism. But there were components and values unique to socialist culture, as distinct from the wider political culture, that fuelled these instincts on the left and which cemented a perception of a divide between left and right. As Hopkins noted, where the novelty of TV and opinion-polling made a breakthrough, it was because of the party's old atmosphere of earnestness and faith [that] the change was most striking on the Labour side.'[133]

Socialism in the 1950s was in many ways disinclined to change with the times. There was often an amateurish air to its publicity, where its notion of egalitarianism became equated with anti-professionalism or its ideas of a moral approach precluded an efficient one. For all that socialists cried about the power of the techniques of television and advertising, they contrived to distance themselves from them, in repulse at the ends to which they were being put and the hands that were exercising them (whether in politics or the àffluent society') and also from a fear that it might itself become corrupted by them. In instinct much of the left saw its struggle as *against* these new media rather than *within* debates about their uses. A more cultural angle on politics then goes some way to explaining why the left was reluctant to try out what it recognized were powerful new media, whether to improve its own presentation or in order to promote values with which it was more at ease.

8
Conclusions

Today the moral and mental world of the 1950s left – even of the then modernizers – seems distant. The Lost World' of British Communism looks set to be joined by the remnants of Old Labour' as its characteristic codes are supplanted by New Labour.[1] Mind, New Labour might not be quite so new as it is fond of believing. Its present-mindedness, what critics see as forgetting anything before yesterday, certainly distinguishes it from the left in the 1950s, which was notably historically–minded and reverential towards tradition. Yet echoing this, a pretext for New Labour remains a critical reading of the party's recent history. In the late 1970s and early 1980s', Blair has contended, Labour's ideology and organisation became out of date' and it lost touch with the people.' New Labour has then (effectively) deployed history as a political resource and device by which to construct a distinction between old' and new'. [2]

New Labour also remains attached, like its forebear, to the idea of being The People's Party'. It is to this version of the party's heritage that it avers. Fidelity (as with 1950s revisionists) is cleaved with the values of fellowship and co-operation in Tawney and Morris. Labour's continuing earnestness, its stern discipline, even authoritarianism and that it remains a party of rather puritan persuasions, has attracted comment.[3] If the moderacy of New Labour policy is taken as some estimation of its assessment of the limitations of the electorate, then evidence in this book points to this as a quite characteristic mistrust of the electorate. The 1950s witnessed a similar disenchantment with the people on the part of socialists.

Critics such as *Marxism Today*'s ideologues consider New Labour to be still singing from the old hymn sheet'. They see its project as fuzzy' – lacking clear ideological bearings or espousing values rather than specific policies or theories. This too is a quite traditional critique – the New Left bemoaned the empiricism and piecemeal nature of labourism in the early 1960s, and Tawney, Labour's lack of direction in the inter-war period.[4]

The present book corresponds with other new accounts of post-war British politics. As Francis has done, it stresses Labour's persistently ethical tone – rather then the empirical, non-ideological and state-driven, top-down aspects many commentators have chosen to empha-size. It echoes the limited appeal of socialism, even amongst Labour voters, emphasised in Fielding, Tiratsoo and Thompson's study of popular politics in the 1940s. Zweiniger-Bargielowska's *Austerity in Britain* argues it was the Conservative's ability to convene a popular alliance of consumer support in opposition to rationing and controls that was at the heart of their electoral recovery between 1945 and 1955 and crucial in securing an advantage amongst women voters. Black and Brooke contend Labour by contrast was baffled by questions of gender .indifferent or hostile' and this study suggests much the same of its grasp of affluence in the late 1950s. What is evident is that the left was neither as able nor willing as Conservatism to build a broad constituency of support from affluence.[5]

But this is not to replace the familiar narrative of a post-war political consensus with one of the main parties sharply divided over social change. Jarvis has shown that Conservatives too were uneasy with some of its moral and cultural effects, including those stemming from its own legislation on, notably, commercial television. The Macmillan government was minded to legislate permissively, to modernize and square individual social rights with economic individualism, but also in a more regulatory vein. While the left feared voters were moving away from the start towards socialism made under Attlee and being lured into affluence, it was the erosion of traditional, Christian values that concerned the Conservatives. In addition Conservatives were less than certain that affluence was guaranteed to deliver political and elec-toral benefits to it. Green argues that although electoral results showed the Conservative constituency in the 1950s to be very broad, the party itself was never convinced that its social base was stable.' That both parties were fearful of losing popular support suggests the fluidity and fragility of their electoral support and also parties' limited knowledge of the people.[6]

Far from being the passive beneficiaries of change, Conservative success was worked-for, not inherited from social and economic forces. Likewise the left's hard times under affluence were largely of its own

making. Given change did not have automatic political effects, party
fortunes were contingent upon how the parties perceived and
described it. The difference was that the Conservatives were happier at
the economic individualism of affluence and kept anxieties about
moral and cultural individualism and permissiveness (that flowered in
the 1960s) quieter.

Stuart Hall's verdict on the left in the 1950s seems irresistible:
'whether we knew it or not, we were struggling with a difficult act of
description, trying to find a language in which to map an emergent
'new world'.which defied analysis within the conventional terms of
the left while at the same time deeply undermining them.' Some clung
to established terminology and even those who more readily recognized a need for change, pre-eminently the New Left and revisionists,
worked with a familiar vocabulary. The emphasis upon cultural priorities they revived in the socialist lexicon was a short-lived moment of
the late 1950s, deploying the ethical resources that elsewhere reviled
affluence in a more positive, constructive attempt to build upon it. The
moment was lost, above all, to the economic problems and industrial
strife of the 1970s, which prevailed over revisionist liberalism on social
matters.[7]

It was the limits to change within socialist ranks that impresses
between 1951 and 1964. As the preceding chapter argues, Wilson was
an archetypal 'labourist' figure, whose rhetoric centred heavily upon
economic progress. Where the 1960s Wilson government echoed issues
raised by affluence, its response was not always welcome. The socialists
.really made asses of themselves' in attempts to embrace youth and
British pop culture – awarding the Beatles MBEs and lowering voting
age to 18 in 1969 – one critic argued. The 'permissive' legislation
passed under (more than by) Jenkins' Home ministry was uneasily
received in parts of the party.[8]

The left's engagement with issues that came under the umbrella of
affluence in the 1950s – consumerism, TV, suburbia, popular and
youth culture – was, then, limited and limiting. The left invariably
exhibited what might best be described as an enormous condescension
of prosperity. The dim view it took of affluence meant an equally dim
view was often taken of the newly affluent. That Labour's politicisation
of affluence defined the electorate so critically, meant it was apt to
slight those it was seeking to both better and represent and thus struggled to create a supportive electorate. Where it had more widely shared
criticisms of advertising, the new youth culture or commercial TV's
structure and programme quality, these were undermined by their

undiscriminating tone – often sounding contemptuous of television and televiewers, of the young or painting an unflattering image of the consumer. It also meant the left was seen to be and easily portrayed as being against affluence. As it was the left's critique was not without effect in growing regulation of advertising and television and consumer research and lobbying, but it reaped little political credit from this.

Notwithstanding the gravity of economic concerns in the 1970s, these issues remained a major feature on the social terrain of modern Britain. By contrast with New Labour's populism, the left in the 1950s was in many ways at odds with social change. Its analysis of social change was not necessarily invalid, but disabling and distant from what was popular – say in its preference for folk music over rock'n'roll or just about anything over TV. What can be deduced from voting patterns is the left's failure to articulate its critique or an alternative. Affluence promoted lifestyles and cultural and leisure activities that chafed with those socialists' favoured. The expansion of popular choice and expectations afforded by affluence meant collective provision was no longer so relied upon and the traditional authority of the state could no longer command deference in such matters. A more pluralist and multicultural society required more than ever that parties be able to collate diverse identities and interests.

Socialists were part of a tight-knit community, set in its ways and resistant (in many quarters) to change and which, on the whole, perceived social change in the 1950s negatively. Affluence, whether washing machines, rock'n'roll or home ownership, did not have innate political meaning. Rather, the left contrived to alienate itself from affluence by describing it so unfavourably. By conveying an unease, if not hostility towards many of the social changes of the 1950s, the left, and Labour in particular, confirmed some of the less popular impressions of itself regarding austerity and moralism, and ceded the considerable popular political credit associated with affluence.

The doubts the left entertained about advertising and TV bred scruples about their political uses. With politics itself rapidly changing in the 1950s, this hindered Labour's readiness to adapt. Above all, the left were surprised and disappointed that the foundations Labour had put down after 1945 had given rise to what was felt to be akin to people's capitalism' – something they did not believe in, but feared much of the populace had bought into. Some sought to recast socialism in light of modernity. Others, fearing the people had lost interest in socialism, lost their faith in the people.

The implications of this registered only marginally at the polls. Labour did not forfeit the 1959 election because it was reluctant to rock'n'roll. Nor could the Tory defence of the 'affluence"at which socialists sneer', levelled in its 1964 election manifesto, prevent Labour winning.[9] However, the frequently moralistic rhetoric of branch activists and the left generally could contribute deleteriously to perceptions of socialism. Party members as much as their politics could deter potential support. Local councillors, trade unionists and party leaders often temper this more minority character of socialism, safeguarding electoral fortunes. Wilson could boast in the 1960s that Labour was the 'natural party of government', but relations with activists and their vision of Labour were strained – manifest in the founding of the Campaign for Labour Party Democracy in 1973.[10] What was really at dispute here, much more than any rift between the party's elite and average members, was whether Labour should be a people's or socialist party or how to couple the two.

Different left traditions, this study additionally stresses, had more in common than dividing them. This was partially so for all those who were politically-minded. Conservative activists complained at apathy and harboured reservations about the advent of TV and its use as a political medium. Weiner notes how Macmillan was disparaged across the political elite for his 'vulgar appeal to materialism' in telling the electorate they had 'never had it so good.' Such attitudes were then present in British political culture more generally in the 1950s, if more pervasive on the left.[11] This opens up a broader question of the relationship between political elites and the people and highlights the discrete presence of formal, party politics within British culture in this period.

The 1950s checked socialism's faith – whether Fabian or Marxist – that history itself was progressing towards socialism. The CPGB suffered a blow to this in 1956. As their vision of the popular mood tended towards the conservative, socialists' confidence waned. It was not their own vision that was at fault, most deduced by the close of the 1950s, but rather the people who had fallen short of it. This book argues, conversely, that it was not so much the people as the ways that socialists imagined them, that accounted for the debilitating effect affluence had on the left.

The rudiments of this view of social change were shared across the left. Whether more or less explicit in their denunciation of the affluent society', activists, theorists, Bevanites, revisionists and the New Left were bound to common assumptions. Critically, all detected middle-class values in affluence, registered in support for the Conservatives. This equation was as evident in the measured tones of Crosland and sociological assessment of *Must Labour Lose?* as in the thunder of Bevan's invective. Neither, as they imagined the people under the impact of social change – particularly in the figure of the affluent worker' – provided a particularly useful vocabulary for engaging this constituency.

Labour faced a longstanding progressive dilemma of making a case for reform without insulting (and losing the support of) those they hoped reform would benefit. This problem was more acute with affluence, because the affluent were actively involved in making cultural choices or spending their new prosperity (more so than, say, the poor were in their poverty). The Conservatives were more at ease with the people as they were, not as they *wished* they were. They were more able to pose as defenders of popular pastimes, a sort of reprise of late nineteenth-century popular Conservatism's case against Liberal nonconformism – not so much cakes and ale as ITV and H-P! The left's belief in human perfectibility, their capacity to improve, presupposed current imperfections and need for improvement.

Socialist culture approached the people with an optimism that, disappointed, translated into educating, improving attitudes – fired by philanthropic, moral impulses, but often experienced as condescending or even coercive. These prescriptive attitudes partly accounted for the arresting of the left's development. Labour was not a straightforward upshot of working-class culture. It may have embodied something of the introversion of working-class culture, but from Bevan to Bevin, was often critical of the same 'narrow horizons'. As affluence enlarged popular choice and expectations, the left was often frustrated with new popular horizons – not so much the *lack* of desire as what workers *did* desire concerned socialists. This often remained the case as late as the 1980s with Labour's unease over tenants purchasing council houses. These were not 'interests' they wished to articulate. [12]

For Labour's claim to be the *Voice of the People* (or even the CPGB's to represent workers' true interests') this was problematic. Such claims were always political, rhetorical and aspirant, but how could Labour even sustain the claim if it perceived popular interests to be far removed from (and even contrary to) its own interests? Socialists had always spoken *at* as much as *for* or *with* the people. There was, Lawrence has argued, a tension at the heart of the Labour project from its outset, between speaking for the people and changing them to suit its own remit. And never more so than in affluent, later 1950s Britain, where socialists felt that the prospects for political progress were contingent upon reforming and improving the people themselves.[13]

By the end of this period, this study suggests, it was increasingly uncertain whether Labour even desired to be the conscience of the people finding its expression', as a 1961 pamphlet, *Look Forward*, put it. In *Socialism and the New Society* in 1962 Douglas Jay argued that the central aims of British socialism, if they are intelligently thought out, coincide with the aspirations of the greater part of the nation'. But, Hattersley added, few Party members believed him.' Crosland thought Labour's denigration of affluence and the affluent revealed a priggish self-satisfaction, a contempt for the judgement of ordinary people and an indifference to their interests' that was wholly alien to the party's tradition' as the people's party.[14]

What could Labour do to reconcile its aspiration to be a people's voice with its socialist vision, if the people did not abide by its expectations? This study suggests it blamed them, sought recourse in the state as an agency of change, and incorporated a less idealistic (or more realistic, since its current approach was unpopular) vision of the people into its communication strategy after 1962.

Labour (and the rest of the left for that matter) were confronted with this question during and before the 1950s, but the ensuing years can particularly be read in terms of this tension between Labour as a socialist party and as the people's party'. The hope that the two were compatible, evident in efforts to move the party to the left and to make the leadership more responsive to activists in the early 1970s and 1980s, have given way to a populism based upon an estimation of the limits of political radicalism amongst the mass of the populace. New Labour, in terms of this relationship between socialist reform and wider, popular appeal, would seem to mark a pointed shift in favour of the latter. Making socialist public opinion', as the New Left saw the most awkward but pressing task confronting the left in 1959, has been largely forgone.[15] And if New Labour has attempted to rescue the left from a condescension of popular prosperity, critics argue it has done so by replacing it with an undue esteem for wealth. But it would be a bold historian who declared this tension on the left, and the Labour Party in particular, resolved.

Notes

Chapter 1: Introduction

1. J. K. Galbraith, *The Affluent Society* (1958).
2. P. Gould, *The Unfinished Revolution: How the Modernisers Saved the Labour Party* (1998), pp. 3–4 and 'A Roar from the Suburbs', *Prospect* (Dec. 1998), p. 46.
3. R. H. S. Crossman, *Labour in the Affluent Society* (1960), p. 15. M. Kenny, *The First New Left* (1994), p. 123. V. Bogdanor, 'The Labour Party in Opposition, 1951–64', in V. Bogdanor and R. Skidelsky (eds), *The Age of Affluence, 1951–64* (1970), p. 78.
4. R. P. Formisano, 'The Concept of Political Culture', *Journal of Interdisciplinary History* XXXI: 3 (Winter 2001), pp. 393–426. H. M. Drucker, *Doctrine and Ethos in the Labour Party* (1979), p. vii. R. Samuel, 'The Lost World of British Communism', *New Left Review* 154 (1985), 156 (1986), 165 (1987).
5. R. Desai, *Intellectuals and Socialism: Social Democrats' and the Labour Party* (1994), pp. 102–103. T. Nairn, 'The Nature of the Labour Party – I', *New Left Review* 27 (1964), p. 38.
6. C. Torrie, 'Ideas, Policy and Ideology: the British Labour Party in Opposition, 1951–1959', D. Phil thesis (University of Oxford, 1997), p. 5.
7. M. Francis, 'Labour and Gender' in D. Tanner, P. Thane, N. Tiratsoo (eds), *Labour's First Century* (2000) and 'The Labour Party: Modernisation and the Politics of Restraint' in B. Conekin, F. Mort, C. Waters (eds), *Moments of Modernity: Reconstructing Britain: 1945–1964* (1999). Or in the work of David Jarvis on Conservatism.
8. See D. Wahrman, 'The New Political History: A Review Essay', *Social History* 21:3 (Oct. 1996). J. Lawrence, *Speaking for the People: Party, Language and Popular Politics, 1867–1914* (1998), pp. 26–69.
9. J. Lawrence and M. Taylor (eds), *Party, State and Society: Electoral Behaviour in Britain since 1820* (1997), p. 18.
10. Also N. Kirk, '"Traditional" Working-Class Culture" and the "Rise of Labour"', *Social History* 16:2 (1991).
11. Bogdanor, 'The Labour Party in Opposition, 1951–64', p. 114. G. Stedman Jones, *Languages of Class: Studies in English Working Class History* (1983), pp. 252–3, 241–2.
12. J. Curtice, 'Political Sociology 1945–1992', in P. Catterall and J. Obelkevich (eds), *Understanding Post-War British Society* (1994), argues the importance of political choices rather than social change and how the constitution shields Westminster politics from social change.
13. See J. Turner, 'A Land Fit for Tories to Live In?' The Political Ecology of the British Conservative Party, 1944–94', *Contemporary European History* 4:2 (1995), pp. 190–2; and for debates on the electoral system itself, C. Stevens, 'The Electoral Sociology of Modern Britain Reconsidered', *Contemporary British History* 13:1 (1999).

14 S. Fielding, 'Crisis in Labour History', *Labour History Review* 60:3 (1995), pp. 48–9. *Socialism' and Society since 1951* (1997), pp. 19–20. E. J. Hobsbawm (ed.), *The Forward March of Labour Halted?* (1981). Also R. Samuel and G. Stedman Jones, 'The Labour Party and Social Democracy', in R. Samuel (ed.), *Culture, Ideology and Politics* (1982), p. 321.

15 A. Thorpe, *A History of the British Labour Party* (1997), p. 281. S. Haseler, *The Gaitskellites: Revisionism in the British Labour Party 1951964* (1969); M. Jenkins, *Bevanism: Labour's High Tide* (1979). Notable exceptions are N. Tiratsoo, 'Popular Politics, Affluence and the Labour Party in the 1950s' in A. Gorst, L. Johnmann and W. Scott Lucas (eds), *Contemporary British History 1931–1961* (1991) and S. Fielding, 'Activists against 'Affluence.' Labour Party Culture during the 'Golden Age,"c. 1950–1970', *Journal of British Studies* 40:1 (April 2001).

16 J. Vernon, 'Mirage of Modernity', *Social History* 22:2 (May 1997). p. 209. Fielding, *Socialism' and Society* , pp. 19–20. Also R. Weight and A. Beach (eds), *The Right to Belong: Citizenship and National Identity in Britain, 1930–1960* (1998), pp. 9–10.

17 Drucker, *Doctrine and Ethos in the Labour Party*, pp. 1, vii.

18 R. English and M. Kenny (eds), *Rethinking British Decline* (2000). For an overview, 'Introduction', Conekin, Mort and Waters, *Moments of Modernity*.

19 E. J. Hobsbawm, *Revolutionaries* (1977), p. 12. K. Newton, *The Sociology of British Communism* (1969).

20 R. Hoggart, *The Uses of Literacy* (1957), pp. 15–16.

21 Labour Party, *Facing the Facts* (1952), p. 12; *The Voice of the People* (1956) celebrating the Parliamentary Party's Golden Jubilee. CPGB, *25th Congress Report* (1957), p. 9. Lawrence, *Speaking for the People*, pp. 66, 150. Also B. Schwarz, 'Politics and Rhetoric in the age of Mass Culture', *History Workshop Journal* 46 (1998).

22 G. Eley, Socialism By Any Other Name? Illusions and Renewal in the History of the Western European Left', *New Left Review* 227 (1998), pp. 108–9. On the class debates – J. Goldthorpe, D. Lockwood, F. Bechhofer and J. Platt, *The Afflent Worker* , 3 vols (1968).

23 M. Savage, *The Dynamics of Working-Class Politics: The Labour Movement in Preston 1880–1940* (1987). See Lawrence, *Speaking for the People*, pp. 37, 57. C. Waters, *British Socialists and the Politics of Popular Culture, 1884–1914* (1990). N. Tiratsoo, 'Labour and the Electorate', in Tanner, Thane and Tiratsoo, *Labour's First Century*.

24 S. Fielding, P. Thompson and N. Tiratsoo, *England Arise!: The Labour Party and Popular Politics in 1940s Britain* (1995), p. 211.

25 S. Fielding, 'To make men and women better than they are.' Labour and the Building of Socialism', in J. Fyrth (ed.), *Labour's Promised Land* (1995).

26 J. Hart, 'The Challenge of Politics', *Tribune* (15 April 1960). C. A. R. Crosland, *The Future of Socialism* (1956), p. 12.

27 Bogdanor, 'The Labour Party in Opposition', p. 78.

Chapter 2: Identities

1 R. H. S. Crossman, *Socialist Values in a Changing Civilisation* (Fabian Tract 286, 1950), pp. 11–12. Historians now argue this ethical element was far

from absent under Attlee, see M. Francis, Economics and Ethics: The Nature of Labour's socialism, 1945–51', *Twentieth Century British History* 6:2 (1995).

2 A. Wright (ed.), *British Socialism: Socialist Thought from the 1880s to 1960s* (1983), p. 185.

3 Crossman, *Socialist Values in a Changing Civilisation*, p. 12.

4 Labour Party, *Industry and Society* (1957), *Leisure for Living* (1959).

5 S. Fielding, 'To make men and women better than they are.' Labour and the Building of Socialism', in J. Fyrth (ed.), *Labour's Promised Land* (1995), pp. 24–5. M. Shelden, *Orwell: The Authorised Biography* (1991), pp. 436–437. H. Morrison, *The Peaceful Revolution* (1949).

6 Communist Party of Great Britain (CPGB), *Harry Pollitt –A Tribute* (1960), p. 7. Funeral Orations', in Howard Hill Papers, Brynmor Jones Library (BJL), University of Hull. DHH. 2/16.

7 F. Williams, *Fifty Years' March: The Rise of the Labour Party* (1949), p. 378.

8 R. Hattersley, *A Yorkshire Boyhood* (1991), p. 37. R. H. S. Crossman (ed.), *The God That Failed* (1950). Jack Becow National Sound Archive, British Library (NSA), C/703/01/04.

9 E. Upward, *The Rotten Elements* (1969). pp. 67–9. *Socialist Commentary* (June 1958), p. 22. K. J. W Alexander and A. Hobbs, What Influences Labour MPs?', *New Society* 11 (13 Dec. 1962), pp. 11–14.

10 Philips, *Manchester Guardian* (26 June 1952). *Contact: The Journal of the Lowestoft Labour Party* 7 (Dec. 1958).

11 S. Yeo, 'A New Life: The Religion of Socialism in Britain 1883–1896', *History Workshop Journal* 4 (1977). National Museum of Labour History (NMLH), General Secretary's Papers, GS/SSS/1i–3iii. Also Socialists in Shorts', *The Guardian* (2 Jan. 1996).

12 *The Argus: Journal of the Merton and Morden Labour Party* (June 1953). British Library of Political and Economic Science (BLEPS) Merton and Morden (MM) Papers 1/13. Principles and Objects' (1951). Socialist Union Papers, Modern Records Centre (MRC), Warwick University. MSS. 173 Box 7. S. Townsend, *Mr. Bevan's Dream* (1989), p. 9.

13 R. Samuel, 'A Spiritual Elect? Robert Tressell and the Early Socialists', in D. Alfred (ed.), *The Robert Tressell Lectures 1981–88* (Rochester, 1988), p. 67.

14 D. Kartun, Seeing the trees for the wood', *The Reasoner* 3 (Nov. 1956), p. 6. NMLH, Labour Party NEC minutes (7 Nov. 1951). Labour Party, *Labour Party Annual Conference Report (LPACR)* (1959), p. 155.

15 Gaitskell, *LPACR* (1959), pp. 107–8.

16 M. Abrams and R. Rose, *Must Labour Lose?* (1960), p. 119. C. A. R. Crosland, *Can Labour Win?* (Fabian Tract 324, May 1960), p. 3.

17 CPGB, *London District Bulletin* (3 Dec. 1959). Communist Party Papers, (NMLH). CP/Lon/Circs/3/4. M. Jones, *Chances: An Autobiography* (1987), p. 117. K. Morgan, *Harry Pollitt* (1993), p. 166.

18 D. Lessing, *The Golden Notebook* (1962), pp. 309–10. D. Widgery, *The Left in Britain 1956–1968* (1976), p. 132.

19 H. M. Drucker, *Docrine and Ethos in the Labour Party* (1979), p. 25. Manchester Guardian, *The Future of the Labour Party: A Stocktaking* (Manchester, 1955), pp. 12, 17.

20 T. Jones, 'Taking Genesis Out of the Bible!' Hugh Gaitskell, Clause IV and Labour's Socialist Myth', *Contemporary British History* 11:2 (1997), p. 19. W. Maddocks, *LPACR* (1959), p. 133.

21 N. Wood, *Communism and British Intellectuals* (1959), pp. 212–13. H. McShane and J. Smith, *Harry McShane: No Mean Fighter* (1978), p. 213.

22 E. Martin, 'Blinkers', *The Reasoner* 3 (Nov. 1956), p. 32. 'Taking Stock', p. 4, E. P. Thompson, 'Reply to George Matthews' *The Reasoner* 1 (July 1956), pp. 11–13. H. Levy, 'The Place of Unorthodoxy in Marxism', *The Reasoner* 2 (Sept. 1956), pp. 13–16.

23 Gabriel to Robin Page Arnot (17 May 1956). Page Arnot Papers, (BJL). DAR/2/49.

24 Hall, Oxford University Socialist Discussion Group (OUSDG) (eds), *Out of Apathy: Voices of the New Left Thirty Years On* (1987), p. 153. D. N. Pritt, *The Autobiography of D. N. Pritt, Part Two* (1966), pp. 189–90. M. Jones, *Today the Struggle* (1978), p. 194.

25 Apter, NSA C/703/03/01. T. Davis, 'What Kind of Woman is she?" Women and Communist Party politics 1941–1955', in R. Brunt and C. Rowan (eds), *Feminism, Culture and Politics* (1982), p. 98.

26 M. Saran, *Never Give Up* (1976), p. 52. L. Gardner, *Daily Worker* (23 Aug. 1956). Jones, *Chances*, p. 119.

27 Samuel, 'The Lost World of British Communism III', *New Left Review* 165 (1987), pp. 78–81. M. Foot, *Aneurin Bevan, 1945–1960* (1973), pp. 648–9. Alexander and Hobbs, 'What Influences Labour MPs?', pp. 11–14.

28 I. Waller, 'The Left-Wing Press', in Kaufman, *The Left*, p. 85. On *Tribune* life', P. Duff, *Left, Left, Left* (1971), pp. 25–77. *Tribune* (8 Aug. 1952). Thompson, *Tribune* (22 Aug. 1952). K. Morgan, 'The Communist Party and the *Daily Worker* 1930–1956', in G. Andrews, N. Fishman and K. Morgan, *Opening the Books: Essays in the Cultural and Social History of the British Communist Party* (1995), pp. 154–6.

29 E. Trory, Central Books Ltd', Conservative Party Archive, Bodleian, Oxford. CCO/4/2/13.

30 A. Croft, 'Authors Take Sides: Writers and the Communist Party 1920–1956', in Andrews, Fishman and Morgan, *Opening the Books*, p. 87. B. Brivati, 'Labour's Literary Dominance', in B. Brivati and R. Heffernan (eds), *The Labour Party: A Centenary History* (2000). M. Edelman, *The Minister* (1961). Hawkins, NSA C/609/04/01. Jones, OUSDG (eds), *Out of Apathy* (1987), pp. 135–6.

31 J. Gorman, *Knocking Down Ginger* (1995), pp. 208, 211. McShane, *No Mean Fighter*, p. 264.

32 E. Heffer, *Never a Yes Man* (1991), p. 85. Heardley-Walker, *The Argus* (June 1953).

33 *New Statesman* (1 Dec. 1956), p. 701. CPGB, *25th Congress Report*, p. 24. L. Black, 'British Communism and 1956: Party Culture and Political Identities' (MA thesis, Warwick University, 1994), pp. 63–8.

34 J. Morgan (ed.), *The Backbench Diaries of Richard Crossman* (1981). Nov. 1953, p. 274.

35 Jones, *Chances*, p. 117. CPGB, *25th Congress Report*, p. 25. On Lee, Scott Garnett, NSA C/609/07/01.

36 '1956', E. J. Hobsbawm interviewed by Gareth Stedman-Jones, *Marxism Today* (Nov. 1986), p. 21. Lessing, *The Golden Notebook*, p. 269. Renee Short quoted in N. Tiratsoo, Popular Politics, affluence and the Labour Party in the 1950s', in T. Gorst, L. Johnmann and W. Scott Lucas (eds), *Contemporary British History 1931–1961* (1991), p. 59. Daniels to Gerry Healy (6 Sept. 1959), H. Ratner, *Reluctant Revolutionary* (1994), p. 230.

37 NMLH, General Secretary's Papers, Box 4. CPGB, *Forging the Weapon* (1955), p. 6 Corina, Why I Am a Socialist', *Fabian Journal* 16 (July 1955), p. 21.

38 R. Winstone (ed.), *Tony Benn, Years of Hope: Diaries, Papers and Letters 1940–1962* (1994), 18 Oct. 1958, p. 289. Hodgkinson, *Sent to Coventry*, p. 254. McShane, *No Mean Fighter*, p. 266. R. Tressell, *The Ragged Trousered Philanthropists* (1914, 1991 edn), pp. 428–9.

39 'A Local Labour Party: All Colours of the Political Spectrum', *Manchester Guardian* (9 Nov. 1954).

40 Clem Jones to Phillips, (14 Oct. 1959), GS/Dea/280. Lord Bernard Taylor of Mansfield, *Uphill all the Way* (1972). Saran, *Never Give Up*. B. Castle, *Fighting all the Way* (1993). Autobiographies of Ernie Benson, May Hobbs; Samuel, 'The Lost World III', pp. 62–3

41 R. Hoggart, *The Uses of Literacy* (1957), p. 313. Political Resolution', CPGB, *25th Congress Report*, p. 73.

42 S. Goss, *Local Labour and Local Government: A Study of Changing Interests, Politics and Policy in Southwark from 1919 to 1982* (1988), p. 44. Conference on the work of Branches in Small Towns and Country' (23 Oct. 1955). CP/Loc/Smid/1/1. R. McKibbin, *The Ideologies of Class: Social Relations in Britain 1880–1950* (1990), p. 15. Hawkins, NSA C/609/04/01. Lessing, *The Golden Notebook*, p. 162.

43 Ratner, *Reluctant Revolutionary*, pp. 199–200.

44 M. Jones, 'The Time is Short', in N. Mackenzie (ed.), *Conviction* (1958). Inside Transport House', *Labour Organiser* (Aug. 1952), p. 148. B. Darke, *The Communist Technique in Britain* (1953), p. 113.

45 Jones, *Chances*, p. 164. Gorman, *Knocking Down Ginger*, pp. 255–6. Darke, *Communist Technique*, pp. 8, 149. O. Cannon and J. R. L. Anderson, *The Road From Wigan Pier* (1973), p. 138. D. Hyde, *I Believed: An Autobiography of a Former British Communist* (1950), p. 240.

46 D. Weinbren, *Generating Socialism: Recollections of Life in the Labour Party* (1997), pp. 24–5. J. McGrandle, Organising in the Shadows', *Labour Organiser* (Dec. 1952), p. 236. Hoggart, *The Uses of Literacy*, p. 313. R. Samuel, 'The Lost World of British Communism I', *New Left Review* 154 (Nov.–Dec. 1985), p. 45. H. Pelling *The British Communist Party: A Historical Profle* (1958), pp. 15, 173. McShane, *No Mean Fighter*, p. 250. Darke, *Sunday Express* (3 June 1951); Hyde, *Daily Express* (23 Jan. 1951).

47 M. MacEwen, *The Greening of a Red* (1991), p. 197. Cannon and Anderson, *Road From Wigan Pier*, pp. 135–6. NMLH, CPGB Executive Committee (10, 11 Nov. 1956). Tom Harrisson Mass Observation Archive (THMOA), Sussex University, Topic Collection General Elections 1945–1955', File 4/d – Hendon North (1950).

48 E. Edney, Why be Difficult' (n.d. 1950s), Michaelson papers MRC MSS. 233/3/4/4. Forest, NSA C/703/05/02. P. Clark, Ban Local Election

'Jargon", *Labour Organiser* (Jan. 1961), pp. 11–12. THMOA, General Elections 1945–1955'. File 4/c.

49 R. Williams, *Politics and Letters* (1979), pp. 368–9. Hill in W. Thompson, *The Good Old Cause* (1992), p. 110.

50 Hoggart, *The Uses of Literacy*, pp. 280, 102–3. *Tony Benn: Diaries, 1940–1962* , 23 Oct. 1954, p. 179.

51 THMOA, General Elections 1945–1955', 4/d – Hendon North.

52 *Faversham Times* (27 May 1955). Labour held the seat by 59 votes. The Personal and the Political', Sheila Rowbotham interviewing Dorothy Thompson, *New Left Review* 200 (1993), pp. 89–90.

53 Manchester Guardian, *Future of the Labour Party*, p. 12. J. Gyford, *Local Politics in Britain* (1978), p. 68.

54 Widgery, *The Left in Britain*, p. 44. D. Sassoon, *One Hundred Years of Socialism* (1997), p. 198. R. H. S. Crossman, Draft Memo on the *Daily Herald*' (1955). Crossman papers MSS. 154/3/Be/34–38. W. T. Rodgers, Why I am a Fabian', *Fabian Journal* 12 (April 1954), p. 3

55 THMOA, General Elections 1945–1955', 4/h – Morden (1950). Labour, *The Men Who Failed* (1958), p. 27.

56 Stef Pixner in L. Heron (ed.), *Truth, Dare or Promise: Girls Growing Up in the Fifties* (1985), p. 95. Lessing, *The Golden Notebook*, p. 162. Lindsay in M. Andrews, *Lifetimes of Commitment: Ageing, Politics and Psychology* (1991), p. 154. Hodgkinson, *Sent to Coventry*. E. Upward, *No Home but the Struggle* (1977).

57 L. Gardner, 'A Comrade's Point of Departure', *New Statesman* (29 Oct. 1976), p. 5.

58 E. Upward, *The Rotten Elements*, p. 71. Waters in Andrews, *Lifetimes of Commitment*, p. 155.

59 Mervyn Jones, Interview (23 Feb. 1996). On Ealing, Marieanne Elliot, NSA C/609/17/01. E. Shaw, *Discipline and Discord: The Politics of Managerial Control in the Labour Party 1951–1987* (1988), pp. 72, 78–81. S. Goss, *Local Labour and Local Government*, p. 45.

60 J. Gould, 'Riverside!' A Labour Constituency', *Fabian Journal* 14 (Nov. 1954), p. 15. On family ties in the CPGB see files in CP/Cent/Pers/. Labour Party, *Party Organisation* (1957), p. 27. P. Cohen (ed.), *Children of the Revolution: Communist Childhood in Cold War Britain* (1997). CPGB, *Forging the Weapon* (1961), p. 33.

61 J. Gorman, 'Another East End: A Remembrance', in G. Alderman and C. Holmes (eds), *Outsiders and Outcasts: Essays in Honour of William. J. Fishman* (1993), p. 183. R. Harris, *The Making of Neil Kinnock* (1984), pp. 29–32. Kay in *Children of the Revolution*, p. 42. Weinbren, *Generating Socialism*, p. 29.

62 C. A. R. Crosland, *The Future of Socialism* (1956), pp. 96–8

63 Samuel, 'The Lost World III', p. 53. On the 1947–8 dispute: NMLH, Heffer papers, Correspondence 1947–1954', CP in Hertford'. Upward, *The Rotten Elements*. On the 'third period', letters to *New Statesman* (2 June 1956, 15 Sept. 1956) by 'Marxist' (Brian Pearce). On 1939, J. Saville, On Party History: An Open Letter to Rajani Palme Dutt', *Reasoner* 3 (Nov. 1956), pp. 23–27. Gorman, *Knocking down Ginger*, p. 255.

64 Tucker, NSA C/609/26/01. C. A. R. Crosland, *The Conservative Enemy* (1962), p. 119.

65 *Daily Worker* (1 March 1951). The Haldanes' failed marriage was well known. Correspondence, Mick Jenkins (E. Midlands District Secretary) and Bill Lauchlan (19 Jan., 11 Feb. 1960), CP/Cent/Pers/4/6.

66 Goss, *Local Labour and Local Government*, p. 47. Humber Ward Section, Grimsby, 'Women and the Second Industrial Revolution', *Labour Woman* (Oct.–Nov. 1959), p. 124.

67 Hawkins, NSA C/609/04/01. Davis, 'What Kind of Woman is she'', p. 90. MacEwen, *Greening of a Red*, pp. 156–61. M. Morgan, *Part of the Main* (1990), pp. 73–4.

68 Darke, *Communist Technique*, pp. 103–11. *London District Bulletin* (22 July 1955), CP/Lon/Circ/05/01.

69 Walter White, NSA C/609/24/02. Gorman, 'Another East-End', p. 183.

70 E. Wilson, *Mirror Writing* (1982), p. 30. C. Bryant, *Possible Dreams* (1996), p. 186. Samuel, *Island Stories*, p. 234. D. Thompson, *Outsiders: Gender, Class and Nation* (1993), p. 6. Gorman, *Knocking Down Ginger*, p. 216. W. Fienburgh, *No Love for Johnnie* (1959), pp. 20, 60.

71 On Bevan, P. Hollis, *Jennie Lee: A Life* (1997), p. 218. Upward, *The Rotten Elements*, p. 12. Page Arnot to Gallacher (23 Nov. 1962), BJL DAR. 1/7. John Horner, Labour candidate at Oldbury and Halesowen in 1959 and MP from 1964, told of his dislike of meticulous gardeners, NSA C/609/13/04. John O'Farrell relates similar prejudices in the 1980s, *Things can only get better* (1998), p.59. J. Saville, 'The Twentieth Congress and the British Communist Party', in J. Saville and R. Miliband (eds), *Socialist Register* (1976), p. 7.

72 M. Rees, 'The Social Setting', *Political Quarterly* 31:3 (July–Sept. 1960), pp. 294–5.

73 J. K. Galbraith, *The Affluent Society* (1958). L. Shao-chi, *How to be a Good Communist* (1955), pp. 53–4.

74 Gaitskell in Sampson, *Anatomy of Britain*, pp. 107–8. A. Bevan, 'Whither Labour Now?', *News of the World* (11 Oct. 1959). E. P. Thompson, Socialism and the Intellectuals', *Universities and Left Review* 1 (1957), p. 34. V. Ward, *Daily Herald* (23 May 1960). J. K. Galbraith, *The Affluent Society* (1958, 1973 edn), p. 284.

75 Samuel, 'A Spiritual Elect?', pp. 66–7. Labour Party, *Leisure for Living* (1959), pp. 44–9. Brand, obituary *The Independent* (10 Dec. 1998).

76 Darke, *Communist Technique*, p. 110. Weinbren, *Generating Socialism*, p. 37. Gorman, *Knocking Down Ginger*, p. 210. MacEwen, *Greening of a Red*, p. 90. *Tony Benn, Diaries:1940–1962* , 18 Oct. 1958, p. 289.

77 On Jaywalkers', W. Maddocks, *LPACR* (1959), p. 133. Drucker, *Doctrine and Ethos*, p. 14. A. Thorpe, *A History of the British Labour Party* (1997), p. 150. More recently, Peter Mandelson – who despite his Labour genealogy is warily thought of by party members, because of specializing in political PR and a *bon viveur* lifestyle. More distantly, Jimmy Thomas earned press derision for his sybaritic lifestyle in the inter-war period. That Thomas and Jenkins turned away from Labour (in 1931 and 1981 repectively) was a fillip to such instincts.

78   Mervyn Jones, *The Times* (11 Dec. 1996). G. Thayer, *The British Political Fringe* (1965), pp. 113–15.
79   Wilson on Bevan, *New Statesman* (2 Oct. 1964), p. 484. Hollis, *Jennie Lee*, p. 222. Hattersley, *The Guardian* (12 Oct. 1998). V. Feather, Out in the Cold, Cold Snow', *Labour Organiser* (July 1954), p. 123.
80   S. Crosland, *Tony Crosland* (1982). p. 89. Younger was Grimbsy's first Labour MP, succeeded by Crosland.
81   A Communist Savile Row tailor kitted out party leaders. On this and Cockburn see MacEwen, *The Greening of a Red*, pp. 117–18. Hyde, *I Believed*, p. 155.
82   *Punch* (4 March 1953). Darke, *Communist Technique*, p. 104. Quoted in Tiratsoo, 'Popular Politics, affluence and the Labour Party in the 1950s', p. 59.
83   Samuel, 'The Lost World III', p. 71. Gorman, *Knocking Down Ginger*, pp. 93, 95. Duff, *Left, Left, Left*, p. 132. See also E. Wilson, 'All the Rage', *New Socialist* (Nov.–Dec. 1983), p. 26.
84   Gorman, *Knocking Down Ginger*, pp. 95–6. *Labour's Northern Voice* (June 1961).
85   M. Jones, *Michael Foot* (1994), pp. 222–3.
86   LPRD, R. 151 'Draft of Interim Home Policy Statement' (July 1952). R. Williams, *The Long Revolution* (1961). p. 328. Thompson, 'A Psessay in Ephology', pp. 4–5. Gramsci saw workers' councils as the embryo of socialism'; Bernstein that 'the final aim is nothing; the movement is everything'.
87   R. Blackburn, 'The Politics of Thick Description', *New Left Review* 221 (1997), p. 134. Samuel, 'Lost World I', p. 11.
88   Andrews, *Lifetimes of Commitment*, p. 155. Lessing, *Golden Notebook*, p. 157. Gorman, *Knocking Down Ginger*, p. 215.
89   CPGB, *The Role of the Communist Party: Basis For Branch Education* (1957), p. 19. L. Daly, 'A Letter to My Comrades' (29 Aug. 1956). Daly papers, MRC, MSS. 302/3/10. Statement to EC (March 1956). Michaelson papers, MRC, MSS. 233/3/4/3.
90   B. Potter, 'Special Work', in Widgery, *The Left in Britain*, pp. 76–7. CPGB, *The Report of the Commission on Inner-Party Democracy* (1957). On the Commission, M. MacEwen, 'The Day the Party Had to Stop', in Saville and Miliband (eds), *Socialist Register* (1976).
91   Cannon to M. Cornforth (Jan. 1957). Cannon Papers, MRC, MSS. 137/16. MacEwen, *The Greening of a Red*, p. 190. '1956', Hobsbawm interviewed by Gareth Stedman-Jones, p. 23.
92   T. Dalyell, 'Way of Living', in Labour Party, *HI!* (1959). BLEPS Coll Misc 0730. Labour Party, *Look Forward* (1961), p. 1. 'Quair's Page', *Labour Organiser* (Sept. 1958), p. 165.
93   Mulley, *Socialist Commentary* (Oct. 1953), p. 243. Merton and Morden, *Tote Lottery Bulletin* (12 Dec. 1959). MM Papers 4/1. Darke, *Communist Technique*, p. 100.
94   Crosland, *The Conservative Enemy*, pp. 27, 125, 129. *Labour Women's Conference* (1960), p. 28. C. A. R. Attlee, 'Socialism as I See It', *Socialist Commentary* (Aug. 1952), pp. 192–3.
95   Statement to EC, MSS. 233/3/4/3. *Labour Organiser* (June 1960), p. 103.

96 Samuel, 'The Lost World III', pp. 75, 83. J. Saville, 'The Communist Experience: A Personal Appraisal', in R. Miliband and L. Panitch (eds), *Socialist Register* (1991), p. 12.

97 'A Local Labour Party', *Manchester Guardian*. Lessing, *The Golden Notebook*, p. 162.

98 P. Crane, 'Politics and the Role of the Individual', *Socialist Commentary* (Sept. 1953), pp. 212–13. Mulley, *Socialist Commentary* (Oct. 1953), p. 243.

99 Crossman, *Socialist Values in a Changing Civilisation*, p. 7.

100 Labour Party, *Facing the Facts* (1952), p. 12. In draft, LPRD, R. 151, Draft of Interim Home Policy Statement' (July 1952). See S. Fielding, Labourism in the 1940s', *Twentieth Century British History* 3:2 (1992).

101 Stewart in *Tote Lottery Bulletin* (25 Jan. 1960). MM papers 4/1. Foot in Tiratsoo, 'Popular Politics, Affluence and the Labour Party in the 1950s', p. 58.

102 Crosland, *The Conservative Enemy*, p. 129. 'Socialist Commentary Questionnaire' (1955). MSS. 173 box 9.

103 M. Young, *The Chipped White Cups of Dover* (1960), pp. 12–13. East Midlands Regional Labour Party, Observations from Agents in Marginals' Wellingborough (1959). MRC, MSS. 9/3/3/55. M. Phillips, *Labour in the Sixties* (1960), p. 21. Benn in Conservative Research Department, *Notes on Current Politics* (21 Dec. 1959). Also N. Hayes, *Consensus and Controversy: City Politics in Nottingham 1945–1966* (1996), pp. 117–23.

104 THMOA, General Elections 1945–1955'. Box 9 – General Election 1955' File B – 203 Questionnaires (May 1955)' Nos 5, 34. Johnson, *LPACR* (1959). p. 141.

105 *Socialist Commentary* (March 1954), p. 69. I. Mikardo, *It's a Mug's Game* (1950). *Daily Worker*, (11, 14 Feb. 1956). N. Baker, 'Going to the dogs'' Hostility to Greyhound Racing in Britain: Puritanism, Socialism and Pragmatism', *Journal of Sports History* 23:2 (1996), pp. 99, 119.

106 R. Samuel, 'Lost World III', pp. 70–3. Darke, *Communist Technique*, p. 71. Upward, *Rotten Elements*, p. 30. On Mahon, Hyde, *I Believed*, p. 94. On Gallacher MacEwen, *Greening of a Red*, p. 96. The Labour government was minded to control pubs in the New Towns too.

107 John Williamson's Report (20 Feb. 1958), CP/Cent/Org/6/4. Also CP/Cent/EC/07/07, (Jan. 1961). Cannon to Abbott (29 Oct. 1954). Cannon Papers MSS. 137/10. McKibbin, *Ideologies of Class*, p. 34.

108 Darke, *Communist Technique*, p. 112. Perhaps shedding light on tired and emotional' George Brown.

109 K. O. Morgan, *James Callaghan: A Life* (1997), p. 15. *Daily Worker* (1 March 1951). On Marx, F. Wheen, *Karl Marx* (1999)

110 *Daily Worker* (10 March 1956), E. P. Thompson, 'Why Make Smoking Cheaper?' (20 March 1956). 'Pif"(7 Feb. 1956). M. Allen, 'Keep Britain Tidy', *Labour Woman* (May 1958), p. 69, *Labour Woman* (June 1959).

111 Angus Sinclair, *Socialism and the Individual: Notes on Joining the Labour Party* (1955), p. 167. Bevan, *In Place of Fear*, p. 168. Jones, *Chances*, p. 133. Crosland, *The Future of Socialism*, p. 522.

112 Crosland, *The Future of Socialism*, pp. 521–4. *The Conservative Enemy*, p. 129, 125.

113 Stuart Hall, Memorandum (8 Sept. 1959). In BJL DJS. 51. Samuel in OUSDG (eds), *Out of Apathy*, pp. 51–2. See also Lessing, *Walking in the Shade*, p. 229. Young, *Chipped White Cups of Dover*, p. 16.

114 R. Jenkins, *Pursuit of Progress* (1953), p. 107. Crosland, *The Future of Socialism*, pp. 521–3. D. Potter, *The Glittering Coffi* (1960), p. 10.

115 MacDonald, Plea for Puritanism', in Samuel, *Island Stories*, p. 311. D. Prynn, The Clarion Clubs, Rambling and the Holiday Associations in Britain since the 1890s', *Journal of Contemporary History* 11 (July 1976), pp. 66–7. A. Fox, 'An Old-Fashioned Socialist', *Socialist Commentary* (May 1955), p. 146.

116 S. Crosland, *Tony Crosland*, p. 62. Crosland, *The Future of Socialism*, p. 524.

117 Drucker, *Doctrine and Ethos*, p. 14. *Tony Benn: Diaries, 1940–62*, 29 June 1957, p. 238.

118 J. and M. Postgate, *A Taste for Dissent: The Life of Raymond Postgate* (1994). L. Minkin and P. Seyd, The British Labour Party', in W. Paterson and A. Thomas (eds), *Social Democratic Parties in Western Europe* (1977), pp. 125–6.

119 Littlewood pre-dated the New Left; R. Findlater, Stratford's Left-Wing Stage', *Tribune* (6 March 1953).

120 Hollis, *Jennie Lee: A Life*, pp. 223–4.

121 Gorman, *Knocking Down Ginger*, p. 191. A. Wesker, 'You're Only Living Half a Life', Plans for Centre 42', *Tribune* (12 Feb. 1960, 28 July 1961).

122 E. J. Hobsbawm, Revolution and Sex', in *Revolutionaries* (1973), pp. 218–19 – published as The Revolution is Puritan', *New Society* (22 May 1969). See Chapter 4.

123 We aren't all Eggheads', Labour Party, *Aim: End the Call Up* (1958). A. H. Birch, *Small Town Politics: A Study of Political Life in Glossop* (1959), pp. 76–7.

124 *Daily Mirror* (23 Aug. 1955) – the Red' Dean, Hewlett-Johnson, was a Communist. *Benn: Diaries, 1940–1962*, 8 Dec. 1959, 21 Jan. 1958, pp. 322, 262.

125 Samuel, Lost World III', p. 71. Though Heffer won a YCL dance prize. Heffer, *Never a Yes Man*, p. 22. Gorman, *Knocking Down Ginger*, p. 218. CPGB, *Forging the Weapon* (1961), p. 31.

126 *Rhyming Reasoner* 2 (Nov. 1956), p. 2.

127 R. Samuel, British Marxist Historians, 1880–1980', *New Left Review* 120 (1980), p. 52. Thompson to Saville and Peter Worsley (late Oct. 1959). BJL DJS 51. Samuel used the Webbs' methods, *Island Stories*, pp. xix–xx.

128 G. Orwell, *The Road to Wigan Pier* (1937), pp. 195–6, 151–2. On Socialist Union, L. Black, Social Democracy as a Way of Life: Fellowship and the Socialist Union, 1951–59', *Twentieth Century British History* 10:4 (1999). J. Blumler, Best Face Forward', *Socialist Commentary* (Oct. 1961), p. 24.

Chapter 3: Branch Life

1 It has started to receive attention; see: L. Black, Still at the Penny-Farthing Stage in a Jet-Propelled Era?' Branch Life in 1950s Socialism', *Labour History Review* 65:2 (2000), pp. 202–26 (in which parts of this chapter have appeared); D. Weinbren, Labour's Roots and Branches', *Oral*

History 24:1 (1996) and *Building Communities, Constructing Identities: The Rise of the Labour Party in London'*, *London Journal* 23:1 (1998); S. Fielding, 'The Penny Farthing Machine" Revisited: Labour Party Members and Participation in the 1950s and 1960s', in Pierson and Tormey (eds), *Politics at the Edge* (2000); Microform Academic Publishers, *Local Labour Party Records on Microfin, Series II* (1998).

2 Amongst surveys were: W. Fienburgh and the Manchester Fabian Society, 'Put Policy on the Agenda', *Fabian Journal* 6 (Feb. 1952). J. Gould, 'Riverside: A Labour Constituency', *Fabian Journal* 14 (Nov. 1954). D. V. Donnison and D. E. G. Plowman, 'The Functions of Labour Parties: Experiments in Research Methods', *Political Studies* II:2 (1954). Manchester Guardian, *The Future of the Labour Party: A Stocktaking* (1955). R. T. Mckenzie, 'Labour Party Organisation: A Note on its Future', *Fabian Journal* 16 (July 1955). J. Blondel, 'The Conservative Association and the Labour Party in Reading', *Political Studies* VI:2 (1958).

3 M. Jenkins, *Bevanism: Labour's High Tide* (1979), p. 115. Labour Party Research Department (LPRD) R.322 'Progress Report on Party Education' (Dec. 1953). H. Croft, *Party Organisation* (1950).

4 *Labour Annual Conference Report (LPACR)* (1955), pp. 63–105. NEC minutes, 22 June 1955, Labour Party Papers, National Museum of Labour History (NMLH), Manchester. Harold Wilson was chair and the report researched by Wilson, Margaret Herbison, Arthur Skeffington and J. Cooper between July and Sept. 1955.

5 CPGB, *Report of the Commission on Inner-Party Democracy* (1957). A dissenting minority report was appended.

6 E. P. Thompson, 'A Psessay in Psephology', *New Reasoner* 10 (Autumn 1959), pp. 5–7. M. Kenny, *The First New Left* (1994), pp. 38–40.

7 B. Pimlott, *Harold Wilson* (1992), pp. 195–6.

8 See M. MacEwen, 'The Day the Party had to Stop', in R. Miliband and J. Saville (eds), *Socialist Register* (1976).

9 Wilson Report, pp. 65, 63, 89–92. All 11 Labour Party regions, meeting with regional and women's organizers and 345 party agents; 527 questionnaires were returned by election agents.

10 R. L. Leonard, 'The Co-ops in Politics', in G. Kaufman (ed.), *The Left* (1966). Criticism came from left and right: M. Abrams and R. Rose, *Must Labour Lose?* (1960). D. Potter, *The Glittering Coffin* (1960). And was admitted at the centre, M. Phillips, *Labour in the Sixties* (1960), pp. 15–21.

11 R. Hattersley, *A Yorkshire Boyhood* (1991), p. 37.

12 J. Gould, 'Riverside: A Labour Constituency', p. 18. Merton and Morden, CLP *Annual Report 1960*. British Library of Economic and Political Science (BLEPS) Merton and Morden CLP papers (hereafter MM) 1/13. Bethnal Green CLP *Agents Report 1962*. Bethnal Green Labour Party papers (hereafter BG papers), Tower Hamlets Local Studies Archive, TH/8488/15.

13 Tom Harrisson Mass Observation Archive (hereafter THMOA), University of Sussex, 'Topic Collection General Elections 1945–1955', Box 4 '1950, Reports and Observations', files 4/c – East Ham North, 4/g – Kensington North. EC minutes 21 July 1953, MM papers 1/5.

14 Len Hill, 'Comrade Camera can Help the Party', *Labour Organiser* (Aug. 1952), p. 146. Peter Moyes, 'Bitten by the Property Bug', *Labour Organiser*

(Sept. 1956), pp. 167–8. Roma Waldegrave, Back to the Street Corner', *Labour Organiser* (Oct. 1956), p. 187.

15 J. Gould, Riverside: A Labour Constituency', p. 17. Riverside' was South Hammersmith. THMOA, Topic Collection General Elections 1945–1955', file 4/f – Fulham East.

16 *Labour Organiser* (June 1953), p. 116. Labour Party, *Victories for Labour* (1951).

17 See *Labour Organiser*, June 1961, p. 106 and March 1962, p. 44.

18 On Black (a founder of the Design Research Unit, who worked on the Festival of Britain), Publicity Sub-Committee in NEC minutes, 29 Sept. 1961. C. Hughes Stanton, Brighter Premises Results', *Labour Organiser* (Nov. 1962), pp. 208–9.

19 Letter H. E. Tate (General Secretary Bethnal CLP) to members 4 Aug. 1955. BG papers TH8488/2. Len Hill Comrade Camera can help the Party', p. 146. Phillips, *Labour in the Sixties*. p. 15. *Socialist Commentary* (Dec. 1959), p. 22. Hughes Stanton in *Labour Organiser* (Sept. 1961), p. 166.

20 N. Loewi, *What is Wrong with Ward Organisation?* (1955). Socialist Union papers, Modern Records Centre (MRC), Warwick University. MSS. 173 box 11. N. Tiratsoo introduction to Dulwich Labour Party in *Local Labour Party Records on Microfilm*, p. 2. J. McGrandle, Organising in the Shadows', *Labour Organiser* (Dec. 1952), p. 236. Waldegrave, Back to the Street Corner', p. 187.

21 I. Aitken, *The Guardian* (4 March 1997). Inside Transport House', *Labour Organiser* (Aug. 1952), p. 148. See also Chapter 2 in this volume. For a modern parallel, John O'Farrell, *Things Can Only Get Better* (1998), p. 151.

22 J. Gorman, *Knocking Down Ginger* (1995), p. 209. D. Lessing, *The Golden Notebook* (1962), p. 151. On the *Daily Worker* building, A. J. Davies, *To Build a New Jerusalem* (1992), p. 179. R. Samuel, The Lost World of British Communism III', *New Left Review* 165 (1987), p. 71. B. Darke, *The Communist Technique in Britain* (1953), p. 63. F. Beckett, *Enemy Within: The Rise and Fall of the British Communist Party* (1995), p. 191.

23 F. Bealy, J. Blondel and W. P. McCann, *Constituency Politics: A Study of Newcastle-Under-Lyme* (1965), p. 407. CPGB, Weekly Letter' (14 July 1955). *Labour Organiser* (Dec. 1963), p. 233.

24 Wilson Report, pp. 80, 101. Nottingham, half-yearly report, 1955, NMLH LP/Cons/55/311. E. Shaw, *Discipline and Discord: The Politics of Managerial Control in the Labour Party, 1951–1987* (1987), pp. 78–83.

25 *Labour Organiser* (Dec. 1953), p. 223. Chippenham CLP, Agents' half-year report to Len Williams (National Agent), 20 Jan. 1956. NMLH LP/Cons/55/397. Report, Midlands District Committee to Bill Lauchlan (4 Jan. 1960). Communist Party Papers (NMLH) CP/Cent/Org/1/8. L. Daly, A Letter to My Comrades' (29 Aug. 1956), in Lawrence Daly Papers, MRC MSS. 302/3/10.

26 D. V. Donnison and D. E. G. Plowman, The Functions of Labour Parties', p. 162. Fienburgh and the Manchester Fabian Society, Put Policy on the Agenda', p. 28.

27 D. Jay, *Change and Fortune* (1980), p. 157. V. Feather, Out in the Cold, Cold, Snow', *Labour Organiser* (July 1954), pp. 123–124. Webb in McKenzie, Labour Party Organisation', p. 13.

28 Shaw, *Discipline and Discord*, pp. 144–5. On higher subs', Woolwich is Right', *Labour Organiser* (Feb. 1957), p. 27.

29 NMLH LP/Cons/55/394 Coventry Borough Report of the Sub-Committee to enquire into Organisation and Activities'. Bethnal Green East ward minutes, TH/8488/18.

30 NMLH LP/Cons/55/.394. J. Heardley-Walker in *Labour Organiser* (Aug. 1954), pp. 146–7.

31 Merton and Morden Annual Report 1960, 1/13.

32 H. M. Drucker, *Doctrine and Ethos in the Labour Party* (1979), p. 68. J. Gyford, *National Parties and Local Parties* (1983), pp. 49–50. McKenzie, Labour Party Organisation: A Note on its Future', p. 13. This was an enduring issue for Labour since Ramsay MacDonald and 1931 – and one reprised during the Wilson and Callaghan governments.

33 Wilson Report, p. 81.

34 Work of 21 Districts' (10 Jan. 1953). (Second draft), NMLH CP/Cent/PC/2/11. CPGB, *The Role of the Communist Party (Basis for Branch Education)* (1957), p. 23. J. Gorman, *Knocking Down Ginger*, p. 227.

35 For example John Gollan's Political Report', *25th Congress Report*, pp. 3, 7, to the 1957 Congress talked of a big advance in . . . socialist consciousness' and the tremendous opportunities that now exist.' There was a nation-wide revolt against the government' and the scope of the developing struggle, unprecedented for its determination, for the numbers and sections engaged.' Report of 21 Districts' (first draft, 1953), pp. 12, 17. In CP/Cent/PC/2/11.

36 LPRD, R. 295 Analysis of Replies to Party Education in the Constituencies' (July 1953).

37 S. Lamb, Vitalise Inactive Supporters', *Labour Organiser* (Jan. 1954), p. 14.

38 Poplar Labour Party, Agent's Report' (Jan.–June 1955). BG papers, TH8488/12.

39 G. G. Farner in *Labour Organiser* (Aug. 1956), pp. 153–4.

40 *The Argus: The Journal of Merton and Morden Labour Party* (June 1953). MM papers 4/3.

41 Quair's Page', *Labour Organiser* (Sept. 1958), p. 165.

42 *Labour Organiser* (Aug. 1955), pp. 135–6 and D. Robertson, Agents Leave Because', *Labour Organiser* (Dec. 1961), pp. 230–1. Helen Bastable Eighty Hours a Week!', *Labour Organiser* (April 1952), pp. 66–9.

43 J. Barnes, *Labour Organiser* (May 1952), p. 88. A. H. Birch, *Small Town Politics: A Study of Political Life in Glossop* (1959), p. 65.

44 See Report from John Williamson (20 Feb. 1958). NMLH CP/Cent/Org/6/4.

45 H. Ratner, *Reluctant Revolutionary* (1994), p. 211.

46 *Labour Organiser* (Aug. 1955), p. 136, *Labour Organiser* (June 1960), p. 116. Tory agents were not only better remunerated, but often supplied with accommodation. Wilson Report, p. 76.

47 R. South, *Heights and Depths: Labour in Windsor* (1985), p. 67. D. Tanner, introduction to Swansea Labour Party in *Local Labour Party Records on Microfin* , p. 11. D. Robertson, Agents Leave Because', pp. 230–1.

48 H. R. Underhill, Planning an Election Machine', *Labour Organiser* (March 1954), pp. 46–7.

49 P. Clark, Ban Local Election Jargon'',   *Labour Organiser* (Jan. 1961), pp. 11–12. On Clark see Chapter 7 in this volume.

50 'A Local Labour Party: All Colours of the Political Spectrum', *Manchester Guardian* (9 Nov. 1954).

51 Popular Labour Party, 'Agent's Report' (July–Dec. 1951). BG papers TH/8488/12.

52 Arthur Norris, Our Ward', *Socialist Commentary* (June 1956), pp. 27–8, and see also Sept. 1955, p. 289. Broome in D. Weinbren (ed.), *Generating Socialism: Recollections of Life in the Labour Party* (1997), p. 159.

53 Bethnal Green, GMC minutes (30 June 1950). *LPACR* (1958), p. 46. CPGB, *25th Congress Report* (1957), p. 77.

54 Pollitt, *Daily Worker* (27 Jan. 1956). Also K. Morgan, *Harry Pollitt* (1994), p. 159. N. Wood, *Communism and British Intellectuals* (1959), p. 195. Amongst those that rose through the Labour hierarchy were a number of disciplinarians: Alice Bacon in Yorkshire or Sara Barker.

55 D. Garnett in *Labour Organiser* (Oct. 1952), p. 177. R. Samuel, The Lost World of British Communism I', *New Left Review* 154 (1985), p. 46. Drucker, *Doctrine and Ethos in the Labour Party*, p. 16. See *Labour Organiser* (Sept. 1957), p. 166.

56 *Labour Organiser* (May 1953), pp. 92–3. Leslie Hilliard, Paid Collectors are a Success', *Labour Organiser* (May 1956), p. 85. Morden ward minutes 16 Dec. 1954 (Heardley-Walker lost the vote on payments, 5–1). *The Argus: The Journal of Merton and Morden Labour Party* (June 1953). MM papers 3/5, 1/13.

57 Samuel, The Lost World of British Communism III', *New Left Review* 165 (1987), pp. 80–1. Quair's Page', *Labour Organiser* (July 1953), p. 139. On Dubb, see S. Macintyre, British Labour, Marxism and Working-Class Apathy in the 1920s', *Historical Journal* 20:2 (1977), pp. 487–90. J. Blondel, The Conservative Association and Labour Party in Reading', p. 119.

58 British Library, National Sound Archive (NSA) – C609/13/04. Weinbren, *Generating Socialism*, pp. 173–174.

59 S. Lamb, How to Learn the Canvassing Art', *Labour Organiser* (Oct. 1953), pp. 190–2. Anon, Care will save time', *Labour Organiser* (Feb. 1959), pp. 28–9.

60 Quoted in M. Rosenbaum, *From Soapbox to Soundbite: Party Political Campaigning in Britain since 1945* (1997), p. 227. R. S. Milne and H. C. Mackenzie, *Marginal Seat, 1955: A Study of Voting Behaviour in the Constituency of Bristol North East at the General Election of 1955* (1958), p. 6. S. Watling, Report by a Paid Canvasser', *Labour Organiser* (May 1959), p. 94.

61 S. Lamb, How to Learn the Canvassing Art', pp. 190–2.

62 Morgan, *Harry Pollitt*, p. 159. Lessing, *The Golden Notebook*, p. 159.

63 *Labour Organiser* (Feb. 1959), pp. 28–9.

64 See J. Hinton, 1945 and the Apathy School', *History Workshop Journal* 43 (1997), pp. 266–73.

65 D. Lessing, *In Pursuit of the English* (1960), p. 13. Quair's Page', *Labour Organiser* (Sept. 1958), p. 165. S. Lamb, How to Learn the Canvassing Art', pp. 190–2.

66   D. Potter, *Vote, Vote, Vote for Nigel Barton* (1965). W. Stephen Gilbert, *Fight and Kick and Bite: The Life and Work of Dennis Potter* (1995), pp. 59, 114. Editorial', *Labour Organiser* (Feb. 1960), p. 23.

67   See C. Waters, *British Socialism and the Politics of Popular Culture 1884‒1914* (1990), pp. 51–61.

68   I. Mikardo, New Ideas from Reading South', *Labour Organiser* (Nov.–Dec. 1951), p. 203; Know and Deliver your Vote', *Labour Organiser* (Sept. 1959), pp. 170–1.

69   S. Barker, *How to Build the Postal Vote* (ca. 1962) argued 50 constituencies in 1959 had a majority smaller than the postal votes cast, but warned, don't baffle them with all the official claims forms' (p. 6). Wilson Report, pp. 97–8.

70   R. Wevell, How to Make Socialists', *Labour Organiser* (Sept. 1959), pp. 174–5. Wevell edited *Labour's Western Voice*.

71   R. Samuel, The Lost World of British Communism II', *New Left Review* 156 (1986), p. 97.

72   Work of 21 Districts' (first draft) (10 Jan. 1953), pp. 1–3. CP/Cent/ PC/2/11.

73   For example, Walter White and John Crawford, NSA C/609/24/02, C/609/35/02. Mervyn Jones (interview, 23 Feb. 1996). Around the Regions', *Labour Organiser* (Nov. 1953), p. 218. G. Williams, TV Opens Better Propoganda Prospect', *Labour Organiser* (May 1954), p. 90. Bealy, Blondel and McCann, *Constituency Politics*. p. 406.

74   Jenkins, *Bevanism*, pp. 171–2. D. Alger, Why the Value of Brains Trusts is Limited', *Labour Organiser* (June 1953), p. 111.

75   See NSA, Donald Mattheson C/609/12/01. W. Fienburgh, *No Love for Johnnie* (1959), p. 173.

76   CPGB, *Forging the Weapon: A Handbook for Members of the Communist Party* (1955), p. 17. On Pollitt, see Gorman, *Knocking Down Ginger*, p. 209.

77   CPGB, *Forging the Weapon* (1955), p. 17. Samuel, The Lost World of British Communism II', *New Left Review* 156 (1986), pp. 82–9. See the Yorkshire District Committee (21–2 July 1956) – lengthy but orderly, in Howard Hill papers, Brynmor Jones Library (BJL), University of Hull, DHH. 2/12. CPGB, *Forging the Weapon* (1961), p. 26.

78   How to Prepare the Agenda', *Labour Organiser* (Feb. 1956), p. 36. Lowestoft Labour Party, *Contact* 2:2 (1962). On bureaucracy, NMLH, Labour NEC minutes (28 Oct. 1959), Phillips, *Labour in the Sixties*, p. 24.

79   D. V. Donnison and D. E. G. Plowman, The Functions of Labour Parties', p. 159. NSA – Donald Mattheson C/609/12/01 and Quair in *Labour Organiser* (Nov. 1953), p. 205.

80   R. Huzzard, *Half a Century of Orpington Labour Party* (1993), p. 6. S. Goss, *Labour and Local Government: A Study of Changing Interests, Politics and Policy in Southwark 1919‒82* (1988), p. 45.

81   A Local Labour Party: All Colours of the Political Spectrum', *Manchester Guardian* (9 Nov. 1954).

82   *Labour Organiser*, Oct. 1952, p. 192; May 1954, p. 85. Also E. Randle, Illustrate Meeting Notes', *Labour Organiser* (Feb. 1953), p. 25.

83   Bethnal Green CLP, *Agents Report 1962*, TH/8488/15. NMLH GS/HAS/124–5i, ii, iii for the terms and conference, 25 July 1957. Borough

seat allowances rose from £250 to £350, county's from £300 to £420, though less where there was a full-time agent. Nelson and Colne CLP Circular letter (2 Feb. 1958) in EC mins (27 Jan. 1958). Working Class Movement Library, Salford.

84 Wilson Report, pp. 86–8, 99. Phillips, *Labour in the Sixties*, p. 22.
85 'Around the Regions', *Labour Organiser* (March 1954), p. 57.
86 NMLH LP/Cons/55/378. Birmingham Borough half-yearly report to National Agent (30 Jan. 1956). NMLH LP/Cons/55/375 and D. Howell Thomas, *Socialism in West Sussex* (1983), p. 18
87 See *Labour Organiser* (March 1956), p. 53.
88 Drucker, *Doctrine and Ethos*, p. 15. Wilson Report, p. 87. Dulwich CLP NMLH LP/Cons/55/208.
89 Wilson Report, pp. 84–5, 102–4.
90 *Labour Organiser* (Nov. 1961), p. 206. Evans, *Labour Organiser* (Dec. 1961), pp. 226–7.
91 Wilson Report, pp. 82–3.
92 CPGB, *The Role of the Communist Party (Basis for Branch Education)* (1957), p. 19.
93 See E. Heffer, *Never a Yes Man* (1991), pp. 37–9. E. Upward, *The Rotten Elements* (1969), is a fictional account. Also H. McShane and J. Smith, *No Mean Fighter* (1978). p. 251. Darke, *The Communist Technique in Britain*, p. 96, and the Upwards note in *New Left Review* 155 (1986). The revolt argued the CPGB had absconded from Leninism by supporting Labour's post-war production drive and discouraging strikes.
94 Related in CPGB, *Report of the Commission on Inner Party Democracy*, pp. 59–60.
95 R. Samuel, *Island Stories* (1998), p. 269. Morden was not an appropriate instance. It was a party confronting problems shared by most CLPs – 'apathy' as much as activism. On the area, see S. Bruley, 'A Very Happy Crowd!' Women in Industry in South London in World War Two', *History Workshop Journal* 44 (1997), pp. 58–76. Bevanites did graduate towards such seats. Bob Edwards, editor of *Tribune*, was Merton's PPC in the mid-1950s, Mervyn Jones stood in Chichester and Norman MacKenzie in Hemel Hempstead.
96 For a critique, D. Regan, *The Local Left and its National Pretensions* (1987), p. 25. On Coventry, see Sidney Stringer Papers, MRC MSS. 24/3/1/1–212. St Pancras council raised the red flag over council hall on May Day 1957.
97 *Labour Organiser* (Aug. 1952), p. 143. E. P. Thompson, *Writing by Candlelight* (1980), p. 71.
98 Wilson Report. p. 85. T. Benn, *Out of the Wilderness: Diaries 1963-1967* (1987), p. 114. *Reynolds News* (30 Aug. 1953, 26 Aug. 1956). Fete programmes, *AGM* reports, Faversham CLP Records, Centre for Kentish Studies, County Hall, Maidstone. L. Black, 'The Best Organised Constituency in Britain!' A Short Introduction to the Records of the Faversham Labour Party, 1918–1994', in *Local Labour Party Records on Microfim, Series II* .
99 NMLH LP/Cons/55/228. North Paddington CLP financial statement (16 July 1955).

100 See LP/Cons/55/210/ii. GMC minutes (27 May 1954) BG papers TH8488/15.
101 Manchester Guardian, *The Future of the Labour Party*, p. 16. B. Elliot, 'A House for Young Socialists', *Labour Organiser* (March 1960), p. 54. On Norfolk, correspondence Peter Catterall, 8 Jan. 2002.
102 See *Labour Organiser* (April 1962), p. 76.
103 S. Barker in *Labour Organiser* (Feb. 1954), pp. 32–3. S. Paige, 'Lotteries Can be Dangerous', *Labour Organiser* (Oct. 1957), p. 197. Such as the political" weekly bulletin by agent Heardley-Walker in MM papers 4/1. On the 1958 act *Labour Organiser* (Oct. 1956), pp. 190–1. Chichester had an alternative scheme planned should the act outlaw its present effort, see NMLH LP/Cons/55/375.
104 Manchester Guardian, *The Future of the Labour Party*, pp. 14–16.
105 *Labour Fund Raiser*, vol. 4 (Oct. 1965), pp. 17–18. Maxwell, though Labour MP for Buckingham from 1964, was considered dubious, letter Hinden to Gaitskell (8 June 1954), Gaitskell Papers, University College London A75.
106 'A Local Labour Party', *Manchester Guardian* (9 Nov. 1954). Faversham CLP, *AGM Report* (1959).
107 Huzzard, *Half a Century of Orpington Labour Party*, p. 6. Birch, *Small Town Politics*, pp. 61–3.
108 D. Lessing, *Walking in the Shade: Volume Two of my Autobiography, 1949–1962* (1997), p. 109.
109 *Labour's Northern Voice* (Nov. 1958), p. 4. Fienburgh and the Manchester Fabian Society, 'Put Policy on the Agenda', pp. 28, 32. Birch, *Small Town Politics*, p. 63. Labour Party, *Party Organisation* (1957), p. 53.
110 See the YS plea in Merton and Morden EC minutes (14 June 1960). MM papers 1/8. Elliot, 'A House for Young Socialists', pp. 54–5. See Paul Rose's report in *Labour's Northern Voice* (Aug.–Sept. 1959).
111 Rose in *Labour's Northern Voice* (Aug.–Sept. 1959).
112 *Labour Organiser* (Nov. 1960), p. 217. 'A Local Labour Party', *Manchester Guardian* (9 Nov. 1954).
113 'Quair's Page', *Labour Organiser* (April 1954), p. 65. 'Agents Report' (Jan.–June 1959). BG papers TH8488/12. P. Rose, 'Guts and Fun', *Labour's Northern Voice* (July–Aug. 1959).
114 YS minutes (29 July 1963). MM papers 2/3. And is still the MP today.
115 London YCL District Report (1955). NMLH CP/YCL/16/8.
116 Merton and Morden YS minutes (25 May 1960, 18 March 1963). MM papers 2/1, 2/2. Labour Party, *Hi!* (1959), p. 7. BLEPS Coll Misc 0730, 1950s. P. Rose, 'How to Attract the Young', *Labour Organiser* (Feb. 1960), p. 32.
117 Labour League of Youth, *Me, An Idealist* (n.d. but ca. 1953).
118 Point made by Mervyn Jones (who was in both parties in the 1950s), interview 23 Feb. 1996. CPGB, *The Communist Party and the Role of Branches* (1955), p. 12.
119 Weinbren, *Generating Socialism*; and for the CPGB, P. Cohen (ed.), *Children of the Revolution* (1997).
120 C282. A. Thorpe, *A History of the British Labour Party* (1997), pp. 144–5. See also Chapter 7 in this volume.

121 Our Penny-Farthing Machine', *Socialist Commentary* (Oct. 1965), p. iii; G. Kaufman, Does Labour's Machine need a Shake-Up', *New Statesman* (7 May 1965); D. Leonard, Labour's Agents', *Plebs* (Oct. 1965) and *Tribune* (8 April 1966). Interview Jim Northcott, 14 Feb. 2001.

122 O'Dee, *The Failure and Salvation of the Labour Party* (1938), p. 15.

Chapter 4: Socialism and Social Change I

1 M. Phillips, *Labour in the Sixties* (1960), p. 15. In Modern Accents', *Socialist Commentary* (Oct. 1955), p. 298. *The Times* (13 Sept. 1955) described Labour as 'an aged party'. A. Thorpe, *A History of the British Labour Party* (1997), pp. 140–1.

2 C. A. R. Crosland, *Can Labour Win?* (Fabian Tract 325, 1960), p. 21. Phillips, *Labour in the Sixties*, p. 16.

3 K. Morgan, *Harry Pollitt* (Manchester, 1993), p. 160. Interview, George Matthews (19 May 1994).

4 Phillips, *Labour in the Sixties*, p. 16.

5 *Daily Worker* (23 Aug. 1956). E. P. Thompson, 'A Psessay in Ephology', *New Reasoner* 10 (Autumn 1959), p. 8.

6 N. Mackenzie, 'After the Stalemate State', in N. Mackenzie (ed.), *Conviction* (1958), p. 8. Labour Party Research Department (LPRD), R. 322 Progress Report on Party Education' (Dec. 1953).

7 Phillips, *Labour in the Sixties*, pp. 13, 15, 18. Labour Party, *The Voice of the People* (1956).

8 Labour Party, *Signposts for the Sixties* (1961), p. 7. See also H. Hopkins, *The New Look: A Social History of the Forties and Fifties in Britain* (1963), pp. 372–3.

9 A. Shonfield, *British Economic Performance Since the War* (1958) and 'The Comforts of Stagnation', in A. Koestler (ed.), *Suicide of a Nation* (1963); H. Thomas (ed.), *The Establishment* (1959). P. Anderson, Origins of the Present Crisis', *New Left Review* 23 (1964). See also, R. English and M. Kenny (eds), *Rethinking British Decline* (2000).

10 C. A. R. Crosland, *The Conservative Enemy* (1962), p. 129. H. Wilson, *The New Britain: Labour's Plan* (1964).

11 N. Hayes, *Consensus and Controversy: City Politics in Nottingham 1945–1966* (1996); N. Tiratsoo, *Reconstruction, Affluence and Labour Politics: Coventry 1945–1960* (1990). R. Samuel, Born-again Socialism', in Oxford University Socialist Discussion Group (OUSDG) (eds), *Out of Apathy: Voices of the New Left Thirty Years On* (1989), p. 41.

12 Labour Party, *Festival of Labour Programme* (1962), p. 24. Labour Party, *Leisure for Living* (1959), p. 19. See also R. Jenkins, *The Labour Case* (1959), p. 146. On the *Daily Worker* building: N. Pevsner, *The Buildings of England: London except the Cities of London and Westminster* (1952), p. 224.

13 R. Dallas, Festival was Outstanding Success', *Labour Organiser* (July 1962), pp. 135–6, 123. *Festival of Labour Programme*, pp. 25, 28–30. Labour Party, *Programme for Exhibition of Modern Art* (1962), pp. 6–18. D. Prynn, The Woodcraft Folk and the Labour Movement, 1925–1970', *Journal of Contemporary History* 8 (1983).

14 *New Left Review* 1 (1960), pp. 1–3. R. Samuel, 'Born-again Socialism', in OUSDG (eds.), *Out Of Apathy*, p. 45. Rayner Banham in R. Hewison, *In Anger: Culture in the Cold War, 194560* (1981), p. 183.

15 E. Rickman (Transport House librarian), 'A Rembrandt in Your Attic?', *Labour Organiser* (Sept. 1961), p. 174. 'A Museum of Socialism', *Socialist Commentary* (Jan. 1957), p. 20. On Eaton, M. Foot, *HG –The History of Mr Wells* (1995), p. 162; *Socialist Commentary* (Dec. 1960), p. 29. 1963 saw moves towards a National Museum of Labour History by Reigate Trades Council, J. Gorman, *Images of Labour* (1985), pp. 12–13.

16 Quoted in Labour League of Youth, *Me, An Idealist* (1953). British Library of Economic and Political Science (BLEPS) Coll Misc 0766 – 1950s.

17 'Discussion Statement on Youth', p. 8. Howard Hill papers, Brynmor Jones Library (BJL), University of Hull, DHH. 2/1.

18 Mackenzie, 'After the Stalemate State', in Mackenzie (ed.), *Conviction*, p. 7.

19 J. Gould, 'Riverside: A Labour Constituency', *Fabian Journal* 14 (Nov. 1954), pp. 17–18. W. A. Sinclair, *Socialism and the Individual: Notes on Joining the Labour Party* (1955), pp. 167–8. J. Connell, *Death on the Left: The Moral Decline of the Labour Party* (1958). Also J. Gyford, County Government and Labour Politics in Essex, 1930–1965', *Local Government Studies* (Nov.–Dec. 1989), pp. 41–7.

20 Z. Layton-Henry, 'Labour's Lost Youth', *Journal of Contemporary History* 11 (July 1976), pp. 285–308. Though D. Fowler, *The Teenager in Inter-War Britain* (1996), contends a modern youth culture emerged inter-war.

21 P. Rose, 'How to Attract the Young', *Labour Organiser* (Feb. 1960), p. 32. Richard Marsh, *Labour Party Annual Conference Report* (*LPACR*) (1959), pp. 93–4. Protz, D. Widgery, *The Left in Britain 1956–1968* (1976), p. 203. *LPACR* (1955), p. 205. Hopkins, *The New Look*, p. 373.

22 See M. Waite, Sex and Drugs and Rock'n'Roll (and Communism) in the 1960s', in G. Andrews, N. Fishman and K. Morgan (eds), *Opening the Books: Essays on the Social and Cultural History of British Communism* (1995), p. 211.

23 J. Holroyd-Doveton, *Young Conservatives: A History of the Young Conservative Movement* (1996), p. 62. Labour Party Archive, National Museum of Labour History (NMLH), General Secretary's Papers, GS/YS/50. Press Conference Notes, 21 Jan. 1960. Phillips, *Labour in the Sixties*, p. 17.

24 R. Gosling, *Lady Albemarle's Boys* (1961), pp. 16, 6. Holroyd-Doveton, *Young Conservatives*, p. 4.

25 Gosling, *Lady Albemarle's Boys*, p. 7. Repeated in debates about Labour's communication; see Chapter 7 in this volume.

26 *The Times* (27 April 1959). Labour Party, *Hi!* (1959), p. 8. In BLEPS Coll Misc 0730 – 1950s. Anthony Howard's series in *Manchester Guardian* (3, 4, 6 Feb. 1959). LPRD, RD. 35 Notes on the General Election' (March 1960). In 1955 42 per cent of under-30s voted Labour and 33 per cent Conservative. In 1959, 36 and 35 per cent respectively.

27 'Party and Youth', Communist Party Archive Political Committee (May 1959), NMLH, CP/Cent/PC/18/13.

28 C. MacInnes, 'Labour and Youth', *Socialist Commentary* (Dec. 1959). Macinnes wrote London-based youth novels, p. 20. W. T. Rodgers, 'Politics in the Universities', *Political Quarterly* 30:1 (Jan.–March 1959), p. 85.

M. Abrams and R. Rose, *Must Labour Lose?* (1960), p. 58. J. Gould, Riverside: A Labour Constituency', *Fabian Journal* 14 (Nov. 1954), p. 17.

29 Tiratsoo, *Reconstruction, Affluence and Labour Politics*, pp. 74, 94–7, 116. J. Morgan (ed.), *The Backbench Diaries of Richard Crossman* (1981), pp. 417, 421.

30 NEC minutes (22 April 1959). Phillips, *Labour in the Sixties*, p. 15.

31 S. Fielding, 'White Heat" and White Collars: The Evolution of Wilsonism', in R. Coopey, S. Fielding and N. Tiratsoo, *The Wilson Years* (1993), p. 29. Phillips' notes (Dec. 1959), NMLH, GS/YS/44. Layton-Henry, Labour's Lost Youth', p. 293.

32 See NMLH, GS/Yocom/4i (April 1959). See also C. Ellis, 'The Younger Generation: The Labour Party and the 1959 Youth Commission', *Journal of British Studies* 41.

33 On Gardiner, R. Winstone (ed.), *Tony Benn, Years of Hope: Diaries, Papers and Letter, 1940–62* (1995), p. 359. On Hill's role in abolishing the footballer's maximum wage, S. Wagg, *The Football World: A Contemporary Social History* (1984), pp. 112–17. Serota, National Sound Archive, C609/32/01–03. Willis created *Dixon of Dock Green*. *Expresso Bongo* (1959) co-starred Cliff Richard. T. Willis, *Woman in a Dressing Gown* (1957).

34 Labour Party Youth Commission, *The Younger Generation* (1959), pp. 16, 42, 45. Also NMLH, GS/Yocom/7i–7iv.

35 Labour Party, *Learning to Live* (1958) and *Leisure for Living*, pp. 40–1. See also LPRD, RD. 19 'Report of Youth Commission – Summary of Recommendations' (Jan. 1960). Gosling, *Lady Albemarle's Boys*, pp. 19, 15. The Albemarle Report was published in Feb. 1960. Hoggart was among its members.

36 Letter Arthur Bax to Morgan Phillips (9 Sept. 1959). NMLH, GS/Yocom/12. See LPRD, RD. 17 'Recommendations in Youth Commission Report' (Jan. 1960). MacInnes, 'Labour and Youth', p. 20.

37 MacInnes, 'Labour and Youth', p. 20.

38 R. Gosling, 'Dream Boy', *New Left Review* 3 (1960), p. 33. MacInnes, 'Labour and Youth', p. 20.

39 P. Rose, 'Manchester Labour Club on Youth', *New Left Review* 1 (1960), p. 71. Phillips' comments at the *Labour Women's Conference* (1960), p. 33.

40 MacInnes, 'Labour and Youth', p. 20. Dennis Eisenberg in *Daily Herald* (20 April 1960).

41 *New Left Review* 4 (1960), p. 73. M. Jones, 'Comrades among the Coffee Cups', *Tribune* (18 Dec. 1959). *Socialist Commentary* (Feb. 1960), p. 13. D. Lessing, *Walking in the Shade: Volume Two of My Autobiography, 1949–1962* (1997), pp. 202. It was also non-alcoholic – some on the left (e.g. John Burns) were nicknamed 'old coffee pot' for this reason.

42 A. Kettle, 'How New is the New Left?', *Marxism Today* (Oct. 1960). P. Thompson, 'Raphael Samuel 1934–1996: An Appreciation', *Oral History* 25:1 (Spring 1997), p. 31. 'Memories of the Partisan Club', *Red Pepper* (Feb. 1997), p. 25.

43 Samuel, 'Born-Again Socialism'. p. 87. Interview, Mervyn Jones (28 May 1996). 'Evidence submitted by the *Universities and Left Review*' (July 1959), NMLH, GS/Yocom/29.

44 Labour Party Youth Commission, *The Younger Generation*, p. 38.

45 P. Wilmott, Teddy-Boy', *Socialist Commentary* (Nov. 1955), p. 351.

46 M. Jones, 'A Young New Year to us all', *Tribune* (10 Jan. 1958). D. Potter, *The Glittering Coffin* (1960), p. 113. S. Hall, 'Absolute Beginnings', *Universities and Left Review* 7 (1959), pp. 16–25.

47 Maciness, Labour and Youth', p. 20. E. P. Thompson, Socialism and the Intellectuals', *Universities and Left Review* 1 (1957), p. 34.

48 See D. Marquand, Lucky Jim and the Labour Party', *Universities and Left Review* 1 (1957), p. 57. M. Kenny, *The First New Left* (1994), pp. 99–100 and J. Osborne, *Look Back in Anger* (1956).

49 D. Hill (ed.), *Tribune 40: The First Forty Years of a Socialist Newspaper* (1977), pp. 118–19.

50 S. Hall, 'Absolute Beginnings', R. Gosling, Dream Boy', and B. Prost Solomon, 'America's Age of Innocence', *Socialist Commentary* (Jan. 1959), pp. 4–6. K. Bednarik, *The Young Worker of Today* (1955), described in P. Wilmott, Teddy-Boy'. T. R. Fyvel, Teddy Boys and Politics', *Socialist Commentary* (Feb. 1958), p. 15.

51 Labour Party Youth Commission, *The Younger Generation*, p. 6. Fyvel, Teddy Boys and Politics', p. 15.

52 Labour Party Youth Commission, *The Younger Generation*, p. 40. Gosling, *Lady Albemarle's Boys*, p. 16. B. Davies, Thoughts after Albemarle', *New Left Review* 12 (1961), p. 35.

53 Maciness, Labour and Youth', p. 20.

54 B. Turner, People are beginning to need Jazz', *Daily Worker* (14 Jan. 1956). F. Newton, Rock 'n Roll', *New Statesman and Nation* (22 Sept. 1956). S. Hall, 'Absolute Beginnings', p. 18.

55 Labour Party, *Take it From Here*, p. 6. A. L. Williams, Is This Your Line?', *Labour Press Service* (Sept. 1958), p. 10.

56 C. Waters, *British Socialists and the Politics of Popular Culture, 1884–1914* (1990). Labour Party Youth Commission, *The Younger Generation*, pp. 12–13.

57 Labour Party, *Teamwork's the Answer* (1959). Choice in Sport', *Socialist Commentary* (July 1962), p. 15.

58 Labour Party, *Leisure for Living*, p. 38 and *Take it From Here*, p. 15.

59 H. Jenkins, Entertainment – Is it Necessary to Do Anything About It?', *Co-operative Party Monthly Newsletter* (July 1957), p. 19. On Jenkins as Arts minister see his *The Culture Gap: An Experience of Government and the Arts* (1979). Speech to the 1954 CPGB congress, *Harry Pollitt –A Tribute* (1960), p. 52.

60 Labour Party, *Aim: End the Call Up* (1958), p. 4. Herein lay some explanation for the shock when Dylan went electric' in 1966: see C. P. Lee, *Bob Dylan and the Road to the Manchester Free Trade Hall* (1998).

61 B. Turner, People are Beginning to Need Jazz', *Daily Worker* (14 Jan. 1956). B. Groombridge and P. Whannel, Something Rotten in Denmark Street', *New Left Review* 1 (1960). A. Coram, The Light Music Industry', *Music and Life* 1:2 (1956), p. 14. NMLH, CP/Cent/Cult/11/2. Coram started Why an Industry? Surely music is an art?'

62 Labour Party, *Leisure for Living*, p. 8. *Festival of Labour Programme*, p. 20. F. Newton, *The Jazz Scene* (1959), pp. 163–97. Also R. Bocock, *Consumption* (1993), p. 23.

63 A. Coram, 'The Light Music Industry', p. 14. F. Newton, 'Rock'n'roll'. Presley was from Mississippi not Texas and lived in Tennessee! Rab' Butler in *The Scotsman* (16 Oct. 1956).

64 Labour Party, *Leisure for Living*, p. 8. See A. Munro, *The Folk Music Revival in Scotland* (1984).

65 Labour Party, *Leisure for Living*, p. 28. K. Thompson, Vaughan Williams and the People', *Music and Life* 1:6 (1958), p. 3. A. L. Lloyd, *Folk Song in England* (1967). E. Macoll, *The Shuttle and Cage* (1954), p. 1. Marx Memorial Library (MML), D14 (11)a. Also the conference, 'The Marxist Approach to Folk Music and its Importance for Britain Today', *Daily Worker* (26 Sept. 1953).

66 W. Fienburgh, *No Love for Johnnie* (1959), p. 108. *Socialist Commentary* (Oct. 1956), p. 11. Newton, 'Rock'n'Roll'

67 E. J. Hobsbawm, *The Jazz Scene* (1989), p. xiii. *Daily Worker* (14 July 1956, 12 Jan. 1956). *Socialist Commentary* (Oct. 1956), p. 11.

68 On the pseudonym see Hobsbawm, *The Jazz Scene*. p. vii. Labour Party, *Leisure for Living*, p. 29.

69 Jazz in Britain and America', *Young Chartist* 1:1 (March 1951), p. 3. Labour Party, *Leisure for Living*, pp. 28–9.

70 Living Jazz', *New Left Review* 10 (1961), pp. 40–50. J. Godbolt, *A History of Jazz in Britain, 1950-1970* (1989), p. 263. M. Johnstone, interview (7 July 1994). YCL, NMLH, CP/YCL/2/4. H. Lyttelton, *Second Chorus* (1958), p. 17.

71 Famously for Tony Crosland and Kingsley Amis;   S. Crosland, *Tony Crosland* (1982), p. 85.

72 Labour Party, *Leisure for Living*, p. 28. Newton, *The Jazz Scene*, pp. 287, 289–95.

73 S. Crosland, *Tony Crosland*, p. 84. C. A. R. Crosland, *The Future of Socialism* (1956), p. 246.

74 Labour Party, *Leisure for Living*, pp. 7–8. Labour Party Youth Commisssion, *The Younger Generation*, p. 39.

75 Labour Party, *Leisure for Living*, pp. 9–11, 23. Crosland was also an opera fan. *Music and Life* 1:7 (1959), p. 4. Bush was the composer of operas like *Wat Tyler*.

76 J. Campbell, *Nye Bevan and the Mirage of British Socialism* (1987), p. 69. *LPACR* (1959), pp. 151–5. A. Bevan, *In Place of Fear* (1952), pp. 50–1.

77 Campbell, *Bevan*, pp. 69–70. P. Hollis, *Jennie Lee: A Life* (1997), p. 224. M. Foot, *Anuerin Bevan, 1945-1960* (1975), pp. 74–80.

78 *Tribune* (26 Sept. 1952).

79 Labour Party, *Leisure for Living*, p. 11.

80 J. B. Priestley, *The Arts Under Socialism* (1947), pp. 13, 19. Labour Party, *Leisure for Living*, pp. 43, 26.

81 R. Williams, Culture is Ordinary', in N. Mackenzie (ed.), *Conviction* (1958), pp. 74–92. R. Williams, *Culture and Society 1780-1950* (1958), pp. 318–23. J. Baxendale, 'A Culture for the People?', *Labour History Review* 60:3 (1995), pp. 62–6. See *Daily Worker* (23, 25 Jan. and 5, 10 April 1956).

82 J. B. Priestley, *The Arts Under Socialism*, pp. 18–19.

83 Labour Party, *The Future Labour Offers You* (1958). See also, *Leisure for Living*, p. 52. H. Jenkins, 'What about Entertainment?', *Co-operative Party Monthly Newsletter* (June 1957), pp. 16–17.

84 Labour Party, *Leisure for Living*, p. 5. Potter, *The Glittering Coffin*, p. 51. S. Crosland, *Tony Crosland* (1982), pp. 63, 84.
85 R. Williams, *The Long Revolution* (1961), pp. 131–3.
86 E. P. Thompson (ed.), *Out of Apathy* (1960), pp. x–xi.
87 Williams, *Culture and Society*, pp. 258–75. J. Lindsay, 'Aspects and Problems of Socialist Realism in Literature', in *Arena, Essays on Socialist Realism and the British Cultural Tradition* (1951), p. 76. In MML D14 (1)a.
88 Lessing, *Walking in the Shade*, pp. 80–4, 105–6.
89 J. Klugmann, The *Daily Worker* – Its Policy and Content' (July 1956), EC Minutes (14 July 1956).
90 *Birmingham Post* (20 April 1954). England's 6 to 3 defeat in 1953 was always celebrated by the CPGB – see *Daily Worker* (7 Oct. 1959).
91 Crosland, *The Future of Socialism*, p. 517.
92 S. Hall, The 'First''New Left: Life and Times', and M. Jones, 'A Divided Culture', both in OUSDG (eds.), *Out of Apathy*, pp. 29 (my italics), 135.
93 Whannel, Something Rotten in Denmark Street', p. 52. Samuel, 'Born-Again Socialism'. pp. 51–2. See also Lessing, *Walking in the Shade*, p. 229. E. P. Thompson, 'The Peculiarities of the English' (1965) in E. P. Thompson, *The Poverty of Theory* (1978), p. 35. Though the *Review* maintained some interest in cinema and jazz after 1962 – see R. Hewison, *Culture and Consensus: England, Art and Politics since 1940* (1997), p. 146.
94 CPGB, *The British Road to Socialism* (1958), p. 27. Williams, *The Long Revolution*, p. 131.
95 R. Williams, *Politics and Letters* (1979), p. 115. P. Anderson, Origins of the Present Crisis' (1964), in *English Questions* (1992), p. 15.
96 J. B. Priestley, *Thoughts in the Wilderness* (1957). R. Hoggart, *The Uses of Literacy* (1957), pp. 247–8.
97 F. Mulhern, 'A Welfare Culture? Hoggart and Williams in the Fifties', *Radical Philosophy* 77 (May–June 1996), p. 29–30. Crosland, *The Future of Socialism*, p. 291–2, 522. F. Hope, 'The Intellectual Left', in G. Kaufman (ed.), *The Left* (1966), p. 113. For an overview on Williams and Hoggart, Hewison, *Culture and Consensus*, pp. 95–114.
98 Hoggart, *The Uses of Literacy*, pp. 311–23, 15–16. Kenny, *The First New Left*, p. 94.
99 H. Gavron, 'Hoggartsville and All That', *Socialist Commentary* (May 1962), p. 19.
100 Williams, *Culture and Society*, pp. 288–9.
101 Labour Party, *Leisure for Living*, p. 8. Hoggart, *The Uses of Literacy*, pp. 343, 340. *Leisure for Living* opened with a quotation from Priestley, *The Arts under Socialism*.
102 Hewison, *Culture and Consensus*, p. 115. Quoting from S. Hall and P. Whannel, *The Popular Arts* (1964).
103 Potter, *The Glittering Coffin*, p. 50. H. Gaitskell, 'Understanding the Electorate', *Socialist Commentary* (July 1955), p. 205. A. Bevan, 'Whither Labour Now?', *News of the World* (11 Oct. 1959).
104 Priestley, Our New Society', in *Thoughts in the Wilderness*, pp. 124, 121.
105 J. B. Priestley, J. Hawkes, *Journey down a Rainbow* (1955), pp. 51–2. Priestley, 'Who is Anti-American?', 'A Note on Billy Graham', in *Thoughts in the Wilderness*, pp. 149, 119.

106 Priestley, Who is Anti-American?', Our New Society', They Came from Inner Space', Eros and Logos', in *Thoughts in the Wilderness*, pp. 149, 120–1, 123, 139.

107 Priestley, Mass Communications', in *Thoughts in the Wilderness*, pp. 11–12.

108 A. Croft, Betrayed Spring: The Labour Government and British Literary Culture', in J. Fyrth, *Labour's Promised Land*, p. 219. T. S. Eliot's 1947 Nobel Prize for Literature was also criticized.

109 R. Samuel, Bastard Capitalism', in Thompson (ed.), *Out of Apathy*, p. 57. Priestley, Mass Communications', in *Thoughts in the Wilderness*, pp. 10–11.

110 S. Aaronovitch, 'American Threat to British Culture', *Arena* II:8 (June–July 1951), p. 13. J. Lindsay, 'Aspects and Problems of Socialist Realism', *Arena, Essays on Socialist Realism and the British Cultural Tradition* (1952), p. 60.

111 J. Gorman, *Knocking Down Ginger* (1995), p. 217. Unity Theatre, *Here is Drama!* (1961), p. 17. D. Kartun, *America –Go Home!* (1951), pp. 5, 13–14. Daily Worker, *America –The Facts* (1953), pp. 3–4 in CP/Lon/Circ/7/4.

112 Aaronovitch, The American Threat to British Culture', pp. 16, 21. CP London Bulletin (6 April 1954), NMLH, CP/Lon/Circ/05/01. R. Sear, Youth and the Heritage', in *Arena, Britain's Cultural Heritage* (1952), pp. 60–61.

113 J. B. Priestley's introduction to E. Rickword (ed.), *Soviet Writers Reply* (Society for Cultural Relations with the USSR, 1948). Gorman, *Knocking Down Ginger*, p. 217. *Punch* (4 March 1953). On premature revisionism', Edgell Rickword' in E. P. Thompson, *Persons and Polemics* (1994). The point can be over-made – Thompson's Morris biography was the gift for fraternal delegates at the 1955 CPGB conference.

114 D. Sassoon, *One Hundred Years of Socialism* (1996), p. 196.

115 International Women's Day Committee, *The Lure of the Comics* (1952), pp. 3–5. In MML D10(1).

116 *New Statesman* (1 Jan. 1955), p. 5. P. Mauger, Children's Reading', in *Arena* II:8 (June–July 1951), pp. 45–47.

117 Horror Comics', *Socialist Commentary* (Dec. 1954), p. 349. Labour NEC minutes (26 Jan. 1955). Council for Children's Welfare, *Comics and Your Children* (1954).

118 Horror Comics', p. 349. On the pro-censorship view, Frank Horrabin, *Socialist Commentary* (April 1955), p. 121.

119 B. Shore, 'Americans are Human', *Labour Woman* (May 1952), p. 333. CPGB, *Coronation* (1953), pp. 9–10.

120 Pollitt to Arnot, 5 Dec. 1952. Page Arnot Papers BJL DAR/1/45. J. Gorman, *Knocking Down Ginger*, p. 93.

121 Jenkins, Entertainment – Is it Necessary to Do Anything About It?', p. 19. Labour Party, *Leisure for Living*, p. 32.

122 Godbolt, *A History of British Jazz*, pp. 169–70. Also *Melody Maker* (12 April 1952).

123 Lyttelton, *Second Chorus*, pp. 14–15. Whannel, Lovell, Living Jazz', p. 46. B. Turner, *Hot Air, Cool Music* (1984).

124 R. Jenkins, *The Pursuit of Progress* (1953), p. 11. *Daily Worker* on Robeson (7 Feb. 1956), Seeger (7 Oct. 1959). Aaronovitch, The American Threat to British Culture', p. 3.

125 L. Black, The Bitterest Enemies of Communism!' Labour Revisionists, Atlanticism and the Cold War', *Contemporary British History* 15:3 (2001). Priestley, Eros and Logos', *Thoughts in the Wilderness*, p. 38.

126 J. K. Galbraith, *The Affluent Society* (1958). R. Hattersley, New Blood', in G. Kaufman (ed.), *The Left* (1966), pp. 153–4. See S. Brooke, 'Atlantic Crossing?: American Views of Capitalism and British Socialist Thought, 1932–1962', *Twentieth Century British History* 2:2 (1991), pp. 120–35.

127 D. Riesman, *The Lonely Crowd* (1950). P. Buhle, *Marxism in the United States* (1991), pp. 213–14. C. Wright Mills, *The Power Elite* (1956). Also Letter to the New Left', *New Left Review* 5 (1960). On Sigal, see Lessing, *Walking in the Shade*, pp. 151–62. V. Packard, *The Hidden Persuaders* (1957), *The Waste-Makers* (1960), p. 5.

128 Crosland, *The Future of Socialism*, pp. 244–6, 256, and *The Conservative Enemy*, pp. 125, 11. P. Anderson, Sweden: Mr. Crosland's Dreamland', *New Left Review* 7 (1961), pp. 5–12.

Chapter 5: Socialism and Social Change II

1 See also L. Black, 'Sheep may Safely Gaze?' Socialists, Television and the People in Britain, 1949–64', in L. Black et al., *Consensus or Coercion? The State, the People and Social Cohesion in Post-War Britain* (2001), pp. 28–49.

2 Labour Party, *Leisure for Living* (1959), pp. 9, 29. H. H. Wilson, *Pressure Group: The Campaign for Commercial Television* (1961); J. Corner (ed.), *Popular Television in Britain: Studies in Cultural History* (1991), pp. 1–21.

3 Attlee (13 June 1953), *Keesing's Contemporary Archives*, 13064 (1–8 Aug. 1953). P. Black, *The Mirror in the Corner: People's Television* (1972), p. 49.

4 A. Sampson, *Anatomy of Britain* (1962), pp. 605–7.

5 Black, *The Mirror in the Corner*, p. 47, 53–4, 110. C. Mayhew, *Time to Explain* (1987), pp. 128–30.

6 C. Mayhew, *Dear Viewer...* (1953), pp. 25, 3. *The Argus –Journal of the Merton and Morden Labour Party* (Aug. 1953). In Merton and Morden (MM) papers, British Library of Economic and Political Science (BLEPS) 4/3.

7 Mayhew, *Dear Viewer...* pp. 5, 9, 14, 24 and *Time to Explain*, pp. 123, 127–8.

8 Gordon Walker *House of Commons Debates*, Series 5, vol. 527, col. 2102, 19 May 1954.

9 Pollit to CBS (4 Feb. 1954). CPGB Archive, National Museum of Labour History (NMLH), CP/Ind/Poll/3/12.

10 *Socialist Commentary* (Dec. 1953), p. 275. *The Argus –Journal of the Merton and Morden Labour Party* (Aug. 1953) MM Papers 4/3. Labour Party, *Three Wasted Years* (1955), p. 63.

11 Black, *The Mirror in the Corner*, p. 136. J. Morgan (ed.), *The Backbench Diaries of Richard Crossman* (1981) 26 May 1954, p. 331.

12 M. Allen, 'Future of TV', *Labour Woman* (July 1953), pp. 154–5. D. Lessing, *The Four-Gated City* (1969), p. 140.

13 T. Harrisson, *Britain Revisited* (1961), pp. 208–9. John Heardley Walker in *Weekly Tote Bulletin* (11 May 1959). MM Papers BLEPS 4/1. Labour Party, *Leisure for Living*, pp. 36–7.

14 H. Jenkins, 'Entertainment – is it necessary to do anything to do about it?', *Co-Op Party Monthly Letter* (July 1957). J. B. Priestley, 'Televiewing', in *Thoughts in the Wilderness* (1957), p. 194. H. Hopkins, *The New Look: A Social History of the Forties and Fifties in Britain* (1963), p. 403.

15 Labour Party, *Leisure for Living*, p. 33, 6.
16 Allen, Future of TV', p. 155. *Weekly Tote Bulletin* (11 May 1959). MM Papers BLEPS 4/1. Lindsey Mountford, TV versus the Soapbox', *Revolt* 4 (1955). Horrabin in *Socialist Commentary* (July 1960), p. 29.
17 *Daily Worker* (6 June, 27 Jan. 1956). B. Hogenkamp, *Film, Television and the Left in Britain* (2000), p. 91.
18 Hoggart, *The Uses of Literacy*, p. 169. Hopkins, *The New Look*, p. 229. K. Coppard, Two Television Documentaries', *New Left Review* 3 (May–June 1960), p. 53. F. Hope, TWTWTW', *New Statesman* (29 March 1963), p. 467.
19 Potter, *Daily Herald* (31 Aug. 1962). Diack, *Daily Herald* (11, 18 April 1960).
20 W. Pickles, Political Attitudes in the Television Age', *Political Quarterly* 30:1 (Jan.–March 1959), p. 63. It is symptomatic of Pickles' disinterest in TV that these were both radio programmes.
21 See the New Left's TV Supplement' – Some Proposals' and Tasks for Education', in *New Left Review* 7 (1961), pp. 48, 43. Written by Kit Coppard, Tony Higgins, Paddy Whannel and Raymond Williams.
22 A. Birk, Visit to Hollywood', *Labour Woman* (Jan. 1956), p. 5.
23 C. Mayhew, *Commercial Television –What is to be Done?* (Fabian Tract 318, 1959), p. 15. A. Birk, Let's Talk it Over', *Labour Woman* (Jan. 1958), pp. 6, 12; (Aug. 1958), pp. 111–12.
24 TV Supplement', pp. 43, 39–40.
25 Labour Party Research Department (LPRD), Re. 499, The Financing of a Third Television Programme' (Feb. 1959). Hopkins, *The New Look*, pp. 331, 400.
26 LPRD, R. 482 A. W. Benn Joint Committee on the Future of TV – TV policy draft proposals' (Feb. 1955). Tony Benn, *Out of the Wilderness: Diaries 1963–1967* (1987), p. 440. R. Chapman, *Selling the Sixties: The Pirates and Pop Music Radio* (1992), pp. 35–7, 179.
27 Mayhew, *Commercial Television –What is to be Done?* , pp. 2, 4, 7, 9–10.
28 Mayhew, *Commercial Television –What is to be Done?* , pp. 12, 22, 10. *News Chronicle* (10 March 1959).
29 LPRD Re. 468 Sub-Committee on TV and Radio' (Nov. 1958). Mayhew, *Commercial Television –What is to be Done?* , pp. 22, 24. LPRD Re. 500 Summary of Recommendations (Third Programme)' (Feb. 1959).
30 Press Release, 8 April 1959, CP/Cent/Stat/1/10. Mayhew, *Commercial Television –What is to be Done?* , pp. 22, 24
31 R. Williams, 'An Educated Democracy', *Socialist Commentary* (Oct. 1959), pp. 8–10. *Daily Sketch* (6 Oct. 1959), *Daily Worker* (7 Oct. 1959).
32 *Report of the Committee on Broadcasting*, Cmnd 1753 (1962), p. 245.
33 Black, *The Mirror in the Corner*, p. 154. Hogenkamp, *Film, Television and the Left*, p. 68. R. Hoggart, *An Imagined Life: Life and Times Volume III, 1959–91* (1993), pp. 59–71; Corner, *Popular Television in Britain*, pp. 9–10. M. Kenny *The First New Left: British Intellectuals after Stalin* (1995), pp. 103–8.
34 *Daily Telegraph* (4 April 1962). Mayhew to Gaitskell (3 May, 5 July, 24, 29 Oct. 1962), Hugh Gaitskell Papers, University College London C316. Mayhew, *Time to Explain*, p. 131. Black, *The Mirror in the Corner*, pp. 156–7.
35 C. A. R. Crosland, Pilkington and the Labour Party', *Socialist Commentary* (Aug. 1962), pp. 5–8. Crosland, The Mass Media', *Encounter* (Nov. 1962).

36 Crosland, *The Future of* Socialism, pp. 524, 527. Memo in Black, *Mirror in the Corner*, p. 35. Corner, 'Television and British Society in the 1950s', pp. 10–11.
37 On 'Americanization' see Richard Weight's paper, 'Death to Hollywood!' The Cultural Politics of Anti-Americanism in Post-War Britain', 1998 Institute of Contemporary British History Summer Conference. J. Northcott, *Why Labour?* (1964), pp. 91–2, 176.
38 LPRD, Rd. 412 Joint Working Party on TV and Radio – The Government and the Pilkington Report' (Feb. 1963). 'TV Supplement', p. 48. Mayhew, *Commercial Television –What is to be Done?* , pp. 9–10.
39 Sampson, *Anatomy of Britain*, pp. 609–16. C. Jenkins, *Power Behind the Screen* (1961); Labour Research Department, *Money and Men Behind TV* (1959). B. Baker, *The Communists and TV* (1965), p. 5. 'Lopsided TV', Lowestoft Labour Party, *Contact* 4 (Sept. 1958).
40 Mayhew, *Commercial Television –What is to be Done?* . p. 17. Sampson, *Anatomy of Britain*, p. 611. LPRD Rd. 412 Joint Working Party on TV and Radio – The Government and the Pilkington Report' (Feb. 1963).
41 Notes – The Women's Press' (Feb. 1963). CP/Cent/Wom/1/1, CPGB, Memorandum of Evidence to the Royal Commission on the Press' (June 1961), pp. 5–6, CP/Cent/Stat/1/9. On the *Chronicle* and *Herald*, Murder or Suicide', *New Statesman* (22 Oct. 1960), S. Koss, *The Rise and Fall of the Political Press in Britain* (1984), pp. 1090–1096.
42 T. R. Nevett, *Advertising in Britain: A History* (1982), pp. 184–6. I. Waller, The Left-Wing Press', in G. Kaufman, *The Left* (1966), pp. 79–80. Also on the *Herald* see A. Smith, The Fall and Fall of the Third *Daily Herald*, 1930–64', in P. Catterall, C. Seymour-Ure and A. Smith, (eds), *Northcliffe's Legacy: Aspects of the British Popular Press 1896–1996* (2000)
43 Travel with a Difference', *Socialist Commentary* (Feb. 1960), pp. 22–3. S. Iveson and R. Brown, *Clarion House: A Monument to a Movement* (1987), p. 59. D. Pye, *Fellowship is Life: National Clarion Cycling Club* (1995), pp. 78–82.
44 CPGB, *Forging the Weapon* (1961), p. 31. Priestley, Popular Press', p. 193, and On Education', p. 52, in *Thoughts in the Wilderness*. E. P. Thompson, *The Struggle for a Free Press* (People's Press Printing Society, 1952), pp. 17, 22.
45 Letter, R. Sturgess, *Daily Worker* (4 Feb. 1958). R. H. S. Crossman, Draft memo on the *Daily Herald*' (1955). Crossman Papers, Modern Records Centre, Warwick University (MRC), MSS. 154/Be/3/34–38.
46 Hoggart, *The Uses of Literacy*, pp. 237, 243–4.
47 Priestley, The Popular Press', in *Thoughts in the Wilderness*, p. 191. L. H. Mountford, TV versus the Soapbox'.
48 Nevett, *Advertising in Britain*. p. 177. *Advertising Quarterly* (Summer 1969), pp. 60–1. In 1938 it was 2 per cent.
49 Labour Party, *Signposts for the Sixties* (1960), p. 9. C. Taylor, What's Wrong with Capitalism?', *New Left Review* 2 (1960), p. 8. S. Hall, The Supply of Demand', in E. P. Thompson (ed.), *Out of Apathy* (1960), p. 59.
50 Orwell quoted in *The Guardian* (Media section, 5 June 2000). Bevan in J. Holroyd-Doveton, *Young Conservatives* (1996), p. 47. Edelman in J. Tunstall, *The Advertising Man* (1964), p. 250. K. Garland, Pool Resources

to Obtain Results', *Labour Organiser* (Feb. 1963), p. 32. L. Corina, 'Motivation Research', *Socialist Commentary* (July 1960), pp. 23–4. Hall, 'The Supply of Demand', p. 85, 82.

51 F. Williams, *The American Invasion* (1962), pp. 21–2. V. Packard, *The Hidden Persuaders* (1957), pp. 9–12. A. Offer, 'The Mask of Intimacy: Advertising and the Quality of Life', in A. Offer (ed.), *In Pursuit of the Quality of Life* (1996), p. 246.

52 Corina, 'Motivation Research', pp. 23–4. 'Discussion Notes – The Women's Press' (Feb. 1963). CP/Cent/Wom/1/1. M. Corden, *A Tax on Advertising?* (Fabian Research Series 222, 1961). pp. 9–12. CPGB, 'Memorandum of Evidence to the Royal Commission on the Press', p. 23.

53 CPGB, 'Memorandum of Evidence to the Royal Commission on the Press', p. 23. D. Potter, *The Glittering Coffin* (1960), p. 13. Socialist Union, *Twentieth Century Socialism* (1956), p. 44. LPRD, RD. 169, G. Darling, 'Draft of Consumer Protection', NEC minutes (29 Sept. 1961). E. Burton, *The Battle of the Consumer* (1955), p. 7.

54 *Labour Women's Conference* (1960), p. 15.

55 Crosland, *The Conservative Enemy* (1962), p. 99. Priestley, 'End of a Party', p. 99, and 'The Popular Press', p. 192, in *Thoughts in the Wilderness*. F. Noel-Baker, 'We Need More Light on Advertising', *Labour Woman* (July 1959), p. 99.

56 Crosland, *The Conservative Enemy*, pp. 97–9.

57 R. Williams, *Communications* (1962, 1976 edition), p. 181.

58 Dennis Potter, *Daily Herald* (3 Nov. 1962). Mayhew, *Dear Viewer*, .p. 11.

59 Crosland, *The Conservative Enemy*, pp. 63–4 and 'Advertising – Is It Worth it?', *The Listener* (13 Dec. 1956). Hall, 'The Supply of Demand', p. 86.

60 Crosland, *The Conservative Enemy*, p. 63. CPGB, 'Memorandum of Evidence to the Royal Commission on the Press', p. 20. Corden, *A Tax on Advertising?*, pp. 38–40, 34. Tunstall, *The Advertising Man*, pp. 235–6.

61 F. Noel-Baker, 'Enquiry into Advertising', *Socialist Commentary* (March 1959), p. 8–10. 'We Need More Light on Advertising', pp. 98–9. On Victory for Socialism's interest see 'Advertising Study Group', in letter, Jo Richardson to F. E. Mostyn (8 Aug. 1958), in NMLH Jo Richardson papers, Correspondence, 1958'. Tunstall, *The Advertising Man*, pp. 232–9.

62 Nevett, *Advertising in Britain*, pp. 199–200 and Blythe Labour MP E. J. Milne, *Socialist Commentary* (Jan. 1962), pp. 13–14. Letter, Advertising Commission to Wilson (17 Jan. 1966), NMLH. Terry Pitt Papers D/Pitt/C/1 – 'Advertising'. Labour Party, *Report of a Commission of Enquiry into Advertising* (1966).

63 Labour Party, *Report of a Commission of Enquiry into Advertising*, pp. 162–165, 186–190. LPRD, Rd. 478 (revised) 'Advertising Commission, Public Advertising: A Countervailing Power' (Aug. 1963).

64 LPRD, Re. 169, 'First Draft Report – Advertising Committee' (June 1967). LPRD, R. 176, 'J. H. Wilson – A Consumer Advisory Service' (Nov. 1952).

65 HM Government *Quarterly Bulletin Joint Advisory Council* (July 1960), pp. 11–13. D. Porter, 'Never-Never Land!' Britain under the Conservatives, 1951–1964', in N. Tiratsoo (ed.), *From Blitz to Blair* (1997), pp. 119–20. Harrisson, *Britain Revisited*, p. 207. K. Jefferys, *Retreat From New Jerusalem: British Politics, 1951–1964* (1997), pp. 59–62.

66 N. Mackenzie, 'The Economics of Prosperity', *Universities and Left Review* 5 (1958), p. 63. C. A. R. Crosland, *The Future of Socialism* (1956), pp. 56–76. S. Hall, 'A Sense of Classlessness', *Universities and Left Review* 5 (1958), pp. 27–9, 'The Supply of Demand', p. 73. M. Young, *The Chipped White Cups of Dover* (1960), p. 9.

67 Phillips, *Labour in the Sixties* (1960), p. 13.

68 M. Jones, *Chances* (1987), p. 134.

69 Labour Party, *Labour and the New Society* (1950), p. 3. Gaitskell in Sampson, *Anatomy of Britain*, pp. 108–9.

70 Curran in (London) *Evening News* (7 July 1960). R. Hattersley, 'New Blood', in Kaufman (ed.), *The Left*, p. 153. C. A. R. Hills, *Growing up in the Fifties* (1983), p. 13.

71 J. Baxendale, 'A Culture for the People?', *Labour History Review* 60:3 (1995), pp. 65–6.

72 'Editor's Letter', *Labour Woman* (July 1959), p. 94. Draft (May 1961) of Labour's *Signposts for the Sixties* in Crossman papers, MRC MSS. 154/3/LP/1/56–8. Priestley, 'Our New Society', in *Thoughts in the Wilderness*, p. 122.

73 Rose in M. D. Kandiah, 'Political Science, Ideas and Government in Post-War Britain', *Contemporary Record* 10:2 (1996), p. 181. A. Sampson, *Macmillan: A Study in Ambiguity* (1967), pp. 111, 159, 166. Correspondence with Peter Catterall (8 Jan. 2002) on Macmillan's lifestyle. H. Drinkwater, 'Grand Tale of Endeavour', *Labour Organiser* (March 1956), p. 47. S. Chaplin, 'Apostle from the Pit', *Socialist Commentary* (June 1955), p. 188.

74 T. Fyvel, 'The Age of Participation', *Socialist Commentary* (March 1955), pp. 68–70. Socialist Union, *Twentieth Century Socialism*, p. 144.

75 HM Government, *Quarterly Bulletin Joint Advisory Council* (July 1960), p. 13. D. Porter, 'Never-Never Land'', p. 112. J. Benson, *The Rise of the Consumer Society in Britain 1880–1980* (1994), p. 41. Hopkins, *The New Look*, p. 317. LPRD, Re. 358 Study Group on the Control of Industry – Hire Purchase' (March 1958). Labour Party, *Fair Deal for the Shopper* (1961), p. 16.

76 HM Government, *Quarterly Bulletin Joint Advisory Council* (July 1960), p. 13. D. Porter, 'Never-Never Land'', p. 112. J. Benson, *The Rise of the Consumer Society in Britain 1880–1980* (1994), p. 41. Hopkins, *The New Look*, p. 317. LPRD, Re. 358 Study Group on the Control of Industry – Hire Purchase' (March 1958). Labour Party, *Fair Deal for the Shopper* (1961), p. 16. J. C. Binns, Having it Good', *Socialist Commentary* (Feb. 1960), p. 21.

77 Labour Party, *Fair Deal for the Shopper* (1961), p. 15. R. Small, 'H-P is Alright – its a Question of who runs it', *Daily Worker* (10 Oct. 1959). Small's article was prompted by the accusation that the CPGB was against H-P'.

78 Binns, Having it Good', p. 21.

79 *Labour Women's Conference* (1960), pp. 15–16. C. MacInnes, 'Labour and Youth', *Socialist Commentary* (Dec. 1959), p. 20. LPRD RD 169, Darling Draft of Consumer Protection' (1961). LPRD Re. 358 Study Group on the Control of Industry – Hire Purchase' (March 1958).

80 Hall, 'The Supply of Demand', p. 71. Bevan in Holroyd-Doveton, *Young Conservatives*, p. 47. Labour Party, *Fair Deal for the Shopper*, p. 6. *Labour Women's Conference* (1960), pp. 14–15. LPRD, R. 463, Informal Group on

Party Propoganda' (Jan. 1955). R. 479, Propaganda and the General Election' (March 1955).

81 D. Sassoon, *One Hundred Years of Socialism* (1996), p. 196. D. Lessing, *Walking in the Shade* (1997), p. 90.

82 Boycott South African Goods', Battle of the Boycott', *Tribune* (24 April 1959, 22 Jan. 1960). Ruth Winstone (ed.), *Tony Benn, Diaries, Papers and Letters 1940-1962* (1994), 27 Feb. 1960, p. 325. Weekly Tote Bulletin (29 Feb. 1960, 21 March 1960). MM Papers 4/1.

83 A. Offer, The Mask of Intimacy: Advertising and the Quality of Life', p. 246. Consumers' Association, *Thirty Years of Which?* (1987).

84 Labour Party, *Fair Deal for the Shopper*, p. 6.

85 A. Briggs, *Michael Young: Social Entrepreneur* (2001), p. 96. J. Northcott, *Value for Money? The Case for a Consumers' Advice Service* (1953). See M. Hilton, Consumer Politics in Post-War Britain', in M. Daunton and M. Hilton (eds), *The Politics of Consumption* (2001).

86 *Labour Women's Conference* (1960), p. 15. Crosland, *The Conservative Enemy*, pp. 65–6.

87 Young, *Chipped White Cups of Dover*, pp. 11, 16, 20. *Tony Benn: Diaries, 1940-62*, 19 June 1960, p. 333. Mayhew joined the Liberals, Young the SDP.

88 B. Lancaster and P. Maguire (eds), *Towards the Co-operative Commonwealth: Essays in the History of Co-operation* (1996). D. Ainley, *The Co-ops: The Way Ahead* (1962), p. 4. *Labour Organiser* (Feb. 1957), p. 26. E. Burns, *The Co-ops and the Crisis* (1955), p. 4. J. Gorman, *Knocking Down Ginger* (1995), p. 87. Hoggart, *The Uses of Literacy*, p. 82. R. Crossman, Introduction', G. Hodgkinson, *Sent to Coventry* (1970), p. xxvii.

89 Hattersley, New Blood', p. 152. Crosland, *The Conservative Enemy*, p. 235, and pp. 228–36 from ch. 2 of *Co-operative Independent Commission Report* (1958). G. Ostergaard, Co-operative Democracy', *Socialist Commentary* (July 1958).

90 S. Crosland, *Tony Crosland* (1982), pp. 88, 84. Ainley, *The Co-ops: The Way Ahead*, p. 2. R. Leonard, The Co-ops in Politics', in Kaufman, *The Left*, pp. 51–3. Robert Millar, Why Should Co-ops Ape the Capitalists?', *Tribune* (9 May 1958). Labour Party, *Festival Of Labour Programme* (1962), p. 19.

91 M. Crout, Impressions of America', *Labour Woman* (March 1957), pp. 40–1. M. Johnson, Woo your Customers', *Labour Woman* (July 1960), pp. 82–83. Labour Party, *Fair Deal for the Shopper*, pp. 20–1.

92 A. Black and S. Brooke, The Labour Party, Women and the Problem of Gender, 1951–66', *Journal of British Studies* 36 (Oct. 1997). I. Zweiniger-Bargielowska, *Austerity in Britain: Rationing, Controls and Consumption 1939-55* (2000), pp. 203–55.

93 B. B. Elliot, *A History of English Advertising* (1962), p. 212. Burton to Gaitskell (24 Feb. 1956), Gaitskell Papers, C310. G. W. Rhodes, *LPACR* (1959), pp. 133, 142.

94 S. Rowbotham, *A Century of Women: A History of Women in Britain and the United States* (1997), p. 288. Labour Party, *The High Price of Toryism* (1954), *The Food Fraud* (1954) and *Another Hole in Your Purse* (1954). Editors Letter, *Labour Woman* (Dec. 1952), p. 490.

95 A Charter for Consumers', *New Statesman* (1 Jan. 1955).

96 On rationing, E. Wilson, *Mirror Writing* (1982). pp. 30–1. Burton, *The Battle of the Consumer*, p. 7.

97 LPRD, R. 479, Propaganda and the General Election'. *Labour Organiser* (June–July 1955), p. 123. Wilson, 'TV Election – Round Two', *New Statesman and Nation* (21 May 1955). Phillips', NEC minutes (22 June 1955), p. 6. Mass Observation Archive, University of Sussex, Topic Collection, Labour Campaign – 'Ask Your Dad.''

98 D. Jay, *The Socialist Case* (1937), p. 317. Mass Observation Archive, Topic Collection General Elections 1945–1955', File 6/e Pamphlets for Women'. See R. Toye, 'The Gentleman in Whitehall''Reconsidered: The Evolution of Douglas Jay's Views on Planning and Consumer Choice, 1937–1947', University of Manchester, Working Papers in Economic and Social History, No. 49 (2001).

99 Manchester Guardian, *The Future of the Labour Party: A Stocktaking* (1955), p. 17.

100 Special Meeting, NEC (16 May 1961) In Crossman Papers, MRC MSS. 154/3/LP/1/33. Election Sub-Committee Report. Labour Party NEC minutes (28 Oct. 1959).

101 Crosland, *Can Labour Win?* (Fabian Tract 324, 1960), p. 17. On 'Ask your Dad?', Chapter 4 in this volume.

102 Black, Brooke, Labour Party, Women and the Problem of Gender', p. 439. *Labour Woman* (July 1956), p. 106 for Mrs. Herbert Morrison's egg and tomato fricassee. T. Davies, 'What kind of woman is she?!' Women and Communist Party Politics, 1941–1955', in R. Brunt and C. Rowan (eds), *Feminism, Culture and Politics* (1982), pp. 97, 101.

103 Young, *The Chipped White Cups of Dover*, p. 10. Socialist Union, *Reflections on Social Services* (1958), pp. 18–19.

104 (Quoting E. P. Thompson), E. Wilson, *Only Halfway to Paradise: Women in Post-War Britain, 1945–1968* (1980), p. 12 On the domestic division of labour, N. Tiratsoo, Popular Politics, Affluence and the Labour Party in the 1950s', in A. Gorst, L. Johnmann and W. S. Lucas (eds), *Contemporary British History 1931–1961* (1991), pp. 50–1.

105 This section deals with attitudes, not urban planning or policy, on which there is an extensive literature.

106 P. Gordon-Walker, Butler's Car Trick', *Labour Woman* (Jan. 1959), p. 13. Gorman in R. Samuel, Lost World of British Communism', *New Left Review* 154 (1985), p. 11. See 'April Shanty', *The Car* (April 1951), pp. 24–5.

107 Abrams and Rose, *Must Labour Lose?* (1960), p. 43. H. Gavron, 'Hoggartsville and All That', *Socialist Commentary* (May 1962), p. 21.

108 Crossman, Introduction', p. xi. Wilmott, Young, *Family and Kinship in East London*, p. 159.

109 In *LPACR* (1955), pp. 65, 69, 86–8, 93, 99.

110 'The State of the Party', special NEC (13 July 1960), p. 4. Crossman papers, MRC MSS. 154/3/LP/2/53.

111 M. Young, 'Must we abandon our Cities?', *Socialist Commentary* (Sept. 1954), pp. 253–5.

112 P. Wilmott and M. Young, *Family and Class in a London Suburb* (1960), pp. 131–2, 117–18.

113 Wilmott, Young *Family and Kinship in East London*, pp. 154–5, 159–61.

114 S. Swingler, 'Educate Socialists Now', *Labour's Northern Voice* (Dec. 1959), p. 5.

115 J. G. Watson, 'More Money – More Conservative?', *Socialist Commentary* (April 1962).

116 Potter, *The Glittering Coffin*, p. v. M. Rees, 'The Socal Setting', *Political Quarterly* 31:3 (July–Sept. 1960), p. 294. See also Rees's comments, *LPACR* (1959), p. 123. Jones, *Chances*, p. 133.

117 D. Tanner introduction to Swansea Labour Party in *Local Labour Party Records on Microfilm*, p. 4. J. P. M. Millar, *The Labour College Movement* (1980), pp. 250–1. P. Gordon Walker, 'A New Party Structure', *Socialist Commentary* (Jan. 1956), pp. 18–20.

118 Grove, Rodgers interviews, CPGB Oral History Project. Crawley CPGB, *Rents Can Come Down!* (1952), 'Memo on the Rents Problem' (Feb. 1953), CP/Loc/Misc/1/9. P. Gwynne, *A History of Crawley* (1990), p. 167.

119 J. Drew, 'You Won't be Cold in the House of the Future', *Daily Herald* (9 Jan. 1958).

120 H. Rees and C. Rees, *The History Makers* (1991), pp. 20, 97, 99. See also I. Procter, 'The Privatisation of Working-Class Life: a dissenting view', *British Journal of Sociology* 41:2 (1990).

121 M. Foot, *Aneurin Bevan, 1945–1960* (1975), pp. 365, 375, 438–9. Also Chapter 2 of Orwell's *Coming up for Air.*

122 'Outrage', *Architectural Review* (June 1955). See also *Counter-Attack Against Subtopia* (1957).

123 Labour Party, *Leisure for Living*, pp. 16–17. Review of T. C. Barker and J. R. Harris, *St. Helens, 1750–1900* (1954), *New Statesman* (15 Jan. 1955), p. 83. *Harry Pollitt –A Tribute* (1960), p. 28.

124 Jenkins, *The Labour Case*, pp. 144–6 and Labour Party, *Leisure for Living*, pp. 17, 19.

125 R. Samuel, *Theatres of Memory* (1994), pp. 296–9. D. Weinbren, *Generating Socialism* (1997), pp. 39–46. Labour Party, *Leisure for Living*, p. 44–9. See also M. MacEwen, *The Greening of a Red* (1991), pp. 246–84.

126 Beatrice Webb House, MM Papers 3/16a. S. Crosland, *Tony Crosland*, p. 62. M. Jones, *Michael Foot* (1995), p. 186. Labour Party, *Leisure for Living*, pp. 21–2. Jenkins, *The Labour Case*, p. 144.

127 Castle quoted in Crosland, *The Conservative Enemy*, p. 129.

128 *LPACR* (1959), p. 106.

129 R. Gosling, *Sum Total* (1962), p. 54. E. Wilson, *Mirror Writing* (1982), p. 30.

Chapter 6: Must Labour Lose?

1 F. Inglis, *Radical Earnestness: English Social Theory 1880–1980* (1982), p. 146.

2 R. McKenzie and A. Silver, *Angels in Marble: Working-Class Conservatives in Urban England* (1968); V. Bogdanor, 'The Labour Party in Opposition, 1951–64', in V. Bogdanor and R. Skidelsky (eds), *The Age of Affluence, 1951–1964* (1970). Also K. Jefferys, *Retreat from New Jerusalem: British Politics, 1951–1964* (1997), ch. 7.

3 H. Hopkins, *The New Look: A Social History of the Forties and Fifties in Britain* (1963), p. 313.

4   C. A. R. Crosland, *The Future of Socialism* (1956), p. 76.
5   *New Statesman*, 2 Jan. 1960. Bevan, *Labour Party Annual Conference Report* (1959) (*LPACR*), pp. 151–5. M. Jones, 'The Man From the Labour', *New Left Review* 1 (1960), p. 17.
6   M. Muggeridge, 'Thirteen Years Soft', *New Statesman* (16 Oct. 1964), pp. 571–2.
7   *Tribune*, 16 Oct. 1959. E. P. Thompson, 'A Psessay in Ephology', *New Reasoner* 10 (1959), p. 1.
8   *Reynolds News* (11 Oct. 1959).
9   M. Abrams and R. Rose, *Must Labour Lose?* (1960), p. 119. C. A. R. Crosland, *Can Labour Win?* (1960, Fabian Tract 324) and S. Lipset, Must Tories Always Triumph?', *Socialist Commentary* (Nov. 1960). P. Anderson, 'The Left in the Fifties', *New Left Review* 29 (1965), p. 4.
10 Crosland, *The Future of Socialism*, pp. 286, 68, 76, 79. Jay in *Forward*, 16 Oct. 1959.
11 Election Report by Phillips, p. 5 in Labour Party NEC minutes, 22 June 1955. Election Sub-Committee report, p. 3, NEC minutes, 28 Oct. 1959. East Midlands Regional Labour Party Records, Modern Records Centre (MRC), Warwick University. MSS. 9/3/3/55 Observations of candidates in marginal constituencies'.
12 A. Warde, *Consensus and Beyond: The Development of Labour Party Strategy Since World War Two* (1982), p. 92. F. Zweig, *The Worker in an Affluent Society* (1961). On the sociological debate see J. Goldthorpe, D. Lockwood, F. Bechofer and J. Platt, *The Affluent Worker*, 3 vols (1968); F. Devine, *Affluent Workers Revisited* (1992).
13 E. J. Hobsbawm, 'The Labour Aristocracy in Nineteenth Century Britain', in *Labouring Men* (1964), pp. 272–3, 301–3.
14 Crosland, *The Future of Socialism*, p. 286.
15 E. J. Hobsbawm, 'The Labour Aristocracy'. J. Seabrook and T. Blackwell, *A World Still to Win: The Post-war Reconstruction of the Working Class* (1985), ch. 4.
16 P. Anderson, Origins of the Present Crisis', *New Left Review* 23 (1964), in *English Questions* (1992), pp. 33, 35–7.
17 On 'Admass', J. B. Priestley and J. Hawkes, *Journey Down a Rainbow* (1955), pp. 51–2. J. B. Priestley, *Thoughts in the Wilderness* (1957), pp. 188, 192.
18 See C. Waters, *British Socialists and the Politics of Popular Culture, 1884–1914* (1990), p. 47.
19 E. Hobsbawm, Parliamentary Cretinism?', *New Left Review* 12 (1961), pp. 64–6. R. Hattersley, New Blood', in G. Kaufman (ed.), *The Left* (1966), p. 153.
20 *New Statesman* (17 Oct. 1959).
21 Crosland, *Can Labour Win?*, pp. 24, 7.
22 Ibid., p. 2. H. M. Drucker, 'All the King's Horses and all the King's Men!' The Social Democratic Party in Britain', in W. Paterson and A. Thomas (eds), *The Future of Social Democracy* (1988), p. 109. N. Ellison, *Egalitarian Thought and Labour Politics: Retreating Visions* (1994), p. 134.
23 Crosland, *Can Labour Win?*, p. 10. A. Bevan, Whither Labour Now?', *News of the World* (11 Oct. 1959).
24 G. Matthews, What Next for Labour', *Daily Worker* (13 Oct. 1959). D. Butler and R. Rose, *The British General Election of 1959* (1960), p. 201.

25 Speaker Notes, Who's Having it so Good?' (Feb. 1960), CP/Cent/Spn/2/3. J. Gollan, *What Next?* (1960), pp. 6–7.

26 *Tribune* (19 Sept. 1952). Bevan, Whither Labour Now?'. *LPACR* (1959), p. 154.

27 Bevan, Whither Labour Now?'

28 G. Hogkinson, *Sent to Coventry* (1970), p. 250.

29 R. H. S. Crossman, *Labour in the Affluent Society* (1960, Fabian Tract 325), pp. 15–17. Bevan's 1959 conference speech predicted the challenge is going to come from Russia' which was at long last being able to reap the material fruits of economic planning and of public ownership.' On the left's interest in foreign policy and Soviet economic growth see J. Callaghan, The Left and the Unfinished Revolution.' Bevanites and Soviet Russia in the 1950s', *Contemporary British History* 15:3 (2001) and L. Minkin, P. Seyd, The British Labour Party', in W. Paterson, A. Thomas (eds.), *Social Democratic Parties in Western Europe* (1977), p. 123.

30 *LPACR* (1959), pp. 151–5. See, for example, E. Evans MP, Commons Comment', in *Contact* 6 (Nov. 1958).

31 Labour Party, *Challenge to Britain* (1953). R. H. S. Crossman, Socialism in a Boom', Fabian Society Home Research Committee (Nov. 1954) in Gaitskell Papers, University College London, A74.

32 R. Samuel, The Deference Voter', *New Left Review* 1 (1960), pp. 9–13. Crosland referred to deviant working-class voters', *Can Labour Win?*, p. 7. R. Williams, *The Long Revolution* (1961), p. 358.

33 *LPACR* (1959), pp. 151–5. See Waters, *British Socialists and the Politics of Popular Culture*, pp. 43–64.

34 Crosland, *The Future of Socialism*, pp. 80, 98–100, 193–6. Foot, *Tribune* (3 Jan. 1958). Potter, *The Times* (27 April 1959). Interview, Mervyn Jones (23 Feb. 1996). R. H. S. Crossman, Introduction' to Hodgkinson, *Sent To Coventry*, pp. xi, xxvii, xxviii.

35 Crosland, *Can Labour Win?*, pp. 16–17. C. A. R. Crosland, *The Conservative Enemy* (1962), pp. 11, 22–7.

36 Crosland, *The Future of Socialism*, p. 517. R. Samuel, Born-Again Socialism', in Oxford University Socialist Discussion Group (eds), *Out of Apathy: Voices of the New Left Thirty Years On* (1989). R. Jenkins, *The Labour Case* (1959), pp. 146, 135. Also Jenkins, *Pursuit of Progress* (1953), p. 107. Abrams and Rose, *Must Labour Lose?*, p. 120.

37 Crosland, *The Future of Socialism*, p. 523 (see also p. 242).

38 Bevan, *In Place of Fear*, p. 45. Crosland, *The Future of Socialism*, p. 520.

39 Bevan, *In Place of Fear*, p. 153. Socialist Union, *Socialism, A New Statement of Principles* (1952), p. 11. R. H. S. Crossman, *Socialist Values in a Changing Civilisation* (1950 – Fabian Tract 286), p. 7.

40 Speaker Notes, Who's Having it so Good?'.

41 Labour Party, *Your Personal Guide to the Future Labour Offers You* (1958).

42 Quoted in M. Francis, Mr. Gaitskell's Ganymede? Re-assessing Crosland's *The Future of Socialism*', *Contemporary British History* 11:2 (1997), p. 62.

43 Crosland, *The Conservative Enemy*, p. 8, *The Future of Socialism*, pp. 517, 515.

44 Crosland, *The Future of Socialism*, p. 529. Also *The Conservative Enemy*, p. 103. Marx in P. Anderson, *Arguments within English Marxism* (1980), pp. 22–3. Anderson, The Left in the Fifties', p. 15.

45 Crosland, *The Conservative Enemy*, p. 119. Anderson, Left in the Fifties', p. 6. Crosland's initial verdict on Gaitskell, S. Crosland, *Tony Crosland* (1982), p. 113. T. Nairn, Hugh Gaitskell', *New Left Review* 25 (1964), pp. 63-8.

46 Labour Party, *Industry and Society* (1957), p. 8. Crosland, *The Future of Socialism*, pp. 68-76.

47 Abrams and Rose, *Must Labour Lose?*, pp. 37, 31-36. Anderson, The Left in the Fifties', p. 4. Conservative Party, *They've Got a Little List* (1958).

48 The Insiders', *Universities and Left Review* 3 (1958). C. Jenkins, *Power at the Top* (1959). See also 'A Miner's Life', in R. Fraser (ed.) *Work*, vol. 2 (1968).

49 Crossman, *Socialist Values in a Changing Civilisation*, pp. 11-12.

50 Crosland, *The Conservative Enemy*, pp. 131, 120, jacket. Crosland, *The Future of Socialism*, pp. 195 n. 1, 99.

51 Crosland, *The Future of Socialism*, pp. 96-8. Crosland, *The Conservative Enemy*, p. 126.

52 E. P. Thompson, 'At the Point of Decay', in E. P. Thompson (ed.), *Out Of Apathy* (1960), pp. 3-4.

53 E. Durbin, *The Politics of Democratic Socialism* (1940), pp. 146-7. Abrams and Rose, *Must Labour Lose?*, p. 111.

54 Crosland, *Future of Socialism*, p. 23, *Can Labour Win?*, p. 16. Showing his belief that economic success was now a matter of political will, but also a residual sense that it controlled political fortunes, he continued, full employment would be maintained 'if only because the Conservatives know that a failure here would lead to defeat at the polls.'

55 N. Thompson, *Political Economy and the Labour Party*, p. 150. Crossman, *Socialist Values in a Changing Civilisation*, p. 7. Letter to John Strachey, Crossman Papers, MRC, MSS. 154/3/Pol/1a. S. Hall, The Supply of Demand', p. 74. E. P. Thompson, 'At the Point of Decay', p. 11. and R. Samuel, Bastard Capitalism', in Thompson (ed.), *Out of Apathy*.

56 Crosland, *The Conservative Enemy*, p. 129. J. K. Galbraith, *The Affluent Society* (1958, 1973 edn), p. 284.

57 Crossman, *Socialism and the New Despotism* (1956), p. 2.

58 Crosland, *The Future of Socialism*, pp. 23-4.

59 Crosland, *Can Labour Win?*, pp. 4, 22, 3.

60 M. Young, *The Chipped White Cups of Dover*. (1960), p. 16. Crosland, *Can Labour Win?*, p. 15. Crossman, *Socialist Values in a Changing Civilisation*, p. 11. B. Lancaster and A. Mason, Society and Politics in Twentieth Century Coventry', in *Life and Labour in a Twentieth Century City: The Experience of Coventry* (1986), p. 358.

61 Jenkins, *Pursuit of Progress*, p. 149.

62 Steedman, *Landscape for a Good Woman*, pp. 6-9, 115.

63 Crosland, *Can Labour Win?*, p. 9. Tom Harrisson Mass Observation Archive, University of Sussex, Topic Collection General Elections 1945-1955', 4/h, Morden. G. Stedman Jones, 'Why is the Labour Party in such a mess?', in *Languages of Class: Studies in English Working Class History, 1832-1982* (1983), pp. 247-8.

64 Crosland, *Can Labour Win?*, pp. 15-16, 4.

65 R. Hoggart, Pictures of the People', *Observer* (15 Nov. 1959).

66 Jenkins, *The Labour Case*, pp. 135-146. Crosland, *The Conservative Enemy*, pp. 124-7. Young, *The Chipped White Cups of Dover*.

67 Jenkins, *The Labour Case*, pp. 54–5. Crosland, *The Conservative Enemy*, p. 125, *Future of Socialism*, pp. 278–86.
68 Crosland, *The Future of Socialism*, p. 286.
69 S. Pollard, *The Development of the British Economy, 1914–80* (1983), p. 324. On credit – which lost many of its negative associations and now signalled a desire to improve one's living standards, J. Benson, *The Rise of the Consumer Society in Britain, 1880–1980* (1994), pp. 197–211.
70 Crosland, *The Future of Socialism*. p. 278. N. Davenport, *The Split Society* (1963). On growth, Labour Party, *Plan for Progress* (1958) and Labour Party Research Department, *Twelve Wasted Years* (1963). R. Titmuss, *Income Distribution and Social Change* (1962).
71 D. Lessing, *Walking in the Shade* (1997), pp. 4–5, 276. Crossman, *Socialist Values in a Changing Civilisation*, p. 12.
72 S. Hall, 'The Supply of Demand', pp. 73–4. Hall quotes (pp. 57–8) Farewell to the Fifties', *The Economist* (26 Dec. 1959): 'something began to happen in the field of consumer goods that can only be called a breakthrough.'
73 D. Sassoon, *One Hundred Years of Socialism* (1996), p. 199. 'The materialist escalator', as Lessing describes it, *Walking in the Shade*, p. 317. Crossman, *Socialist Values in a Changing Civilisation*, p. 7. Also R. Samuel, 'British Marxist Historians, 1880–1980: Part One', *New Left Review* 120 (1980), pp. 81–91.
74 W. Thompson, *The Good Old Cause: British Communism 1920–1991* (1992), p. 14.
75 L. Fox to Thompson and Saville (27 Oct. 1956), Brynmor Jones Library (BJL), DJS. 107 'Reasoner 1956–57'.
76 Samuel, 'British Marxist Historians', pp. 91–3. E. P. Thompson, Socialist Humanism, *New Reasoner* 1 (Summer 1957). R. Williams, *Culture and Society* (1958). Williams, *Politics and Letters*, p. 115.
77 M. Kenny, *The First New Left* (1995), p. 64.
78 Samuel, 'British Marxist Historians', pp. 92–3, noted New Left historians were keener on the name change than those in the CPGB. CPGB, *Satellite Special* (1957). The Labour left greeted Sputnik more enthusiastically. *Tribune* (23 Oct. 1959) lauded the Soviet's 'astounding scientific and technical achievement'.
79 CPGB, *The British Road to Socialism* (1958), p. 19. Nicholas, *Daily Herald* (7 Jan. 1958). *Daily Worker* (24 Aug. 1956).
80 R. Hoggart, *The Uses of Literacy* (1957), p. 318.
81 Hoggart, 'Pictures of the People'. M. Phillips, *Labour in the Sixties* (1960), p. 8.
82 E. P. Thompson, 'William Morris and the Moral Issues Today', *Arena* II:8 (1951), p. 29. Hall, 'The Supply of Demand', p. 92. Abrams, 'The Home-Centred Society', *The Listener* (26 Nov. 1959). On 'traditional' working-class culture, E. Hobsbawm, *Worlds of Labour* (1984), p. 191.
83 C. Waters, 'J. B. Priestley: Englishness and the Politics of Nostalgia', in S. Pedersen and P. Mandler (eds), *After the Victorians: Private Conscience and Public Duty in Modern Britain* (1994). J. B. Priestley, *The Writer in a Changing Society* (Herman Ould Memorial Lecture, 1956), pp. 4–5, 14. Priestley, Hawkes, *Journey Down a Rainbow*, pp. 51–2.

84 M. Wiener, *English Culture and the Decline of the Industrial Spirit, 1850-1980* (1981), p. 125. Gaitskell in A. Sampson, *Anatomy of Britain* (1962), pp. 108–9.

85 East Midlands Regional Labour Party, 'Agent's Reports, 1959'. MRC, MSS 9/3/3/55. Butler and Rose, *The British General Election of 1959*, p. 196. Also R. Winstone (ed.), *Tony Benn, Years of Hope: Diaries, Papers and Letters* (1995), 15 Oct. 1959, p. 318.

86 Labour Party, *Personal Freedom* (1956), p. 15. Phillips, *Labour in the Sixties*, p. 8. C. A. R. Attlee, *As it Happened* (1954), p. 140. Crosland, *Can Labour Win?*, p. 12.

87 J. Turner, 'A Land Fit for Tories to Live In.' The Political Ecology of the British Conservative Party, 1944–1994', *Contemporary European History* 4:2 (1995), p. 201. E. H. H. Green, 'The Conservative Party, the State and the electorate, 1945–64', in J. Lawrence and M. Taylor (eds), *Party, State and Society: Electoral Behaviour in Britain since 1820* (1997).

88 Gollan, What Next?', pp. 5–6.

89 Bevan, 'Whither Labour Now?'. R. Miliband, *Parliamentary Socialism* (1961), indicting Labour's parliamentarism, was another product of this moment.

90 See E. J. Hobsbawm, *The Forward March of Labour Halted?* (1979). Bevan, 'Whither Labour Now?'. On Cousins, G. Goodman, *The Awkward Warrior* (1979), p. 134.

91 P. Stead, 'I'm Allright Jack', *History Today* (Jan. 1996). R. Williams, *The Long Revolution*, pp. 328, 355.

92 Hall, 'The Supply of Demand', pp. 95–6. W. Norman, 'Signposts for the 60s', *New Left Review* 11 (1961), pp. 45–6. Labour Party, *Signposts for the Sixties* (1961), p. 28. Miliband, *Parliamentary Socialism*, pp. 339, 348–9.

93 *Tribune* (2 Jan. 1959). S. Swingler, 'Educate Socialists Now', *Labour's Northern Voice* (Dec. 1959).

94 Williams, *The Long Revolution*, p. 328. Samuel, 'Bastard capitalism', p. 55.

95 Hall, 'The Supply of Demand', pp. 73–5.

96 Sassoon, *One Hundred Years of Socialism*, p. 195. Blackwell, Seabrook, *A World Still to Win*, pp. 93, 107. Crosland, *The Conservative Enemy*, p. 130.

97 Bevan in Thompson, *Political Economy and the Labour Party*, p. 167. R. H. Tawney, *The Sickness of an Acquisitive Society* (1920), forerunner to *The Acquisitive Society* (1921).

98 *Daily Herald* (14 Nov. 1958). 'Draft for 1961 Policy Statement', Crossman Papers, MSS. 154/3/LP/1/56–8.

99 Crosland, *The Future of Socialism*, p. 287.

100 Jenkins, *The Labour Case*, pp. 54–5.

101 Arnold's *Essays in Criticism* (1895), Crosland *The Future of Socialism*, pp. 291–2, *Can Labour Win?*, pp. 22–3. See also Priestley, *The Arts Under Socialism* (1947), pp. 18–19.

102 Hoggart, 'Pictures of the People'. R. Miliband, 'Socialism and the Myth of the Golden Past', *Socialist Register* (1964), pp. 101–2.

103 Abrams and Rose, *Must Labour Lose?*, pp. 120–1.

104 Crosland, *Can Labour Win?*, pp. 20–3. Though 'status strains' between economic and social status (together with the 'ideology of class betrayal')

also explained the persistence of militant leftism', *The Future of Socialism*, p. 193–201.

105 Crosland, *The Conservative Enemy*, pp. 66, 27. Jenkins, *The Labour Case*, p. 146. Stedman-Jones, Why is the Labour Party in such a mess?', p. 248.

106 Williams, *The Long Revolution*, p. 354. Abrams, Rose, *Must Labour Lose?*, pp. 42–3, 58 (my italics). Abrams, The Home-Centred Society'.

107 Samuel, Dr. Abrams and the End of Politics', p. 7 Crossman, *Socialist Values in a Changing Civilisation*, p. 4.

108 Abrams and Rose, *Must Labour Lose?*, p. 43. M. Abrams, The Roots of Working-Class Conservatism'. Crosland, *Can Labour Win?*, p. 11.

109 P. Townsend and B. Abel-Smith, *The Poor and the Poorest* (1965). D. Vincent, *Poor Citizens: The State and the Poor in Twentieth Century Britain* (1991), pp. 138–53. Ellison, *Egalitarian Thought and Labour Politics*, p. 134. Crosland, *The Conservative Enemy*, pp. 28–40. V. George and I. Howards, *Poverty amidst Affluence: Britain and the United States* (1991), pp. 22–4. *The Future of Socialism* notes their Fabian pamphlet *New Pensions for Old* (1955), p. 161, but they are absent from *The Conservative Enemy*, by when their work was more established.

110 Labour Party, *National Superannuation* (1957). N. Mackenzie (ed.), *Conviction* (1958). Crosland, *The Future of Socialism*, p. 524.

111 S. Delaney, *A Taste of Honey* (1958), a New Left favourite, directed by Tony Richardson. R. Roberts, *The Classic Slum* (1971). T. Harrison, *Britain Revisited* (1961), p. 42. Jones, *Chances*, p. 133. H. Rees and C. Rees, *The History Makers* (1991), pp. 20, 97, 99, 113. N. Tiratsoo, *Reconstruction, Affluence and Labour Politics: Coventry, 1945–1960* (1990), p. 115.

112 The State of the Party' (Special NEC 13 July 1960). In Crossman papers MRC, MSS. 154/3/LP/2/54.

113 Hoggart, Pictures of the People'.

114 Tiratsoo, *Reconstruction, Affluence and Labour Politics* . p. 120. Cronin quoted in Stephen Brooke, Gender and Working Class Identity in Britain during the 1950s', *Journal of Social History* 34:4 (Summer 2001), p. 773.

115 H. Gavron, Hoggartsville and All That', *Socialist Commentary* (May 1962), p. 21.

116 C. Hodge, The Long Fifties: The Politics of Socialist Programmatic Revision in Britain, France and Germany', *Contemporary European History* 2:1 (1993), p. 17. D. Widgery, *The Left in Britain, 1956–1968* (1976), p. 44.

Chapter 7: Political Communication

1 M. Scammell, *Designer Politics* (1995). P. Gould, *The Unfinished Revolution: How the Modernisers Saved the Labour Party* (1998). C. Powell, *How the Left Learned to Love Advertising* (2000)

2 H. Nicholas, *The British General Election of 1950* (1951), pp. 93–4.

3 See M. Rosenbaum, *From Soapbox to Soundbite: Party Political Campaigning in Britain since 1945* (1997), p. 145.

4 R. Cockett, The Party, Publicity and the Media', in A. Seldon and S. Ball (eds), *Conservative Century: The Conservative Party since 1900* (1994), pp. 576–7.

5 J. Pearson and G. Turner, *The Persuasion Industry* (1965), p. 261. D. Butler and R. Rose, *The British General Election of 1959* (1960), p. 20.

6 M. Foot, *Aneurin Bevan, 1945–1960* (1975), p. 235. H. Hopkins, *The New Look: A Social History of the Forties and Fifties in Britain* (1963), notes (p. 449) that Woolton introduced into [Tory Party] operations the methods of big business merchandising which he knew so well.' Woolton was a leading proponent of Commercial Television.

7 D. Wring, From Mass Propaganda to Political Marketing: The Transformation of Labour Party Election Campaigning', in C. Rallings, D. Farrell, D. Denver and D. Broughton (eds), *British Elections and Parties Review, Volume 5* (1995).

8 F. Teer and J. D. Spence, *Political Opinion Polls* (1973), p. 16.

9 NMLH, Resolutions' to Publicity and Political Education Sub-Committee, NEC minutes (22 July 1959). C. Rowland, Labour Publicity', *Political Quarterly* 31:3 (July–Sept. 1960), p. 350. Rowland was defeated Labour candidate at Eastleigh in 1959 and worked at Transport House and for the B. B. C. R. Hattersley, New Blood', in G. Kaufman (ed.), *The Left* (1966), p. 157.

10 Crosland to Gaitskell (n.d., late 1961, titled 'Appreciation') in Gaitskell Papers, University College London, C282

11 J. Gorman, The Labour Party's Election Posters in 1945', *Labour History Review* 61:3 (1996). P. Duff, *Left, Left, Left: A Personal Account of Six Protest Campaigns, 1945–1965* (1971), pp. 115–17.

12 R. Winstone (ed.), *Tony Benn, Years of Hope: Diaries, Papers and Letters 1940–1962* (1994), 23 Oct. 1956, p. 190. R. Wevell, How to Cultivate Good Press Relations', *Labour Organiser* (Jan. 1956), p. 10.

13 Faversham Labour Party, *Newsletter* 1:3 (Spring 1984). Faversham Labour Party Records, Centre for Kentish Studies, County Hall, Maidstone. Box 11.

14 M. Jones, *Chances* (1987), p. 113. T. Ives, You can Compete with TV', *Labour Organiser* (April 1954), pp. 68–9. Durham Labour Women's Rally, *Labour Organiser* (May 1953), p. 97.

15 J. Blumler and M. Gurevitch, *The Crisis of Public Communication* (1995), p. 207. Rowland, Labour Publicity', pp. 353, 350.

16 E. P. Thompson, Homage to Tom Maguire', in A. Briggs and J. Saville (eds), *Essays in Labour History* (1960), p. 276, and The Segregation of Dissent' (1961) in *Writing by Candlelight* (1980), p. 1. C. A. R. Crosland, *The Conservative Enemy* (1962), p. 130.

17 L. Gardner, Selling the Idea of Socialism', *Daily Worker* (23 Aug. 1956). Davis' and other letters, *Daily Worker* (29 Aug. 1956).

18 R. Waldegrave, Back to the Street Corner?', *Labour Organiser* (Oct. 1956), p. 187. *Labour Organiser* (July 1958), pp. 130–2. BLEPS Merton and Morden (MM) Papers 4/3. Annual Report (1961), 1/13. Jenkins in S. Fielding, *The Labour Party: Socialism' and Society since 1951* (1997), p. 45.

19 B. Williams, What Kind of Noise Annoys?', *Labour Organiser* (March 1961), p. 53.

20 A. Clare, No Holiday Propaganda at Seaside', *Labour Organiser* (July 1961), p. 124. When the 1959 election was declared, Clare reported no evidence of interest from the hundreds of Labour supporters who must have been on holiday in the town'. Also Mervyn Jones' *Today the Struggle* (1978), pp. 240–6.

21 'Wilson Report', *Labour Party Annual Conference Report* (*LPACR*) (1955), p. 99. Hattersley, New Blood', p. 156. J. Maxwell, 'Local Paper Published for Free', *Labour Organiser* (Aug. 1957), p. 145

22 Labour Party, *Party Organisation* (1957), p. 35. A. W. Benn, 'Was this a TV Election?', *Labour Organiser* (June–July 1955), p. 109.

23 Vicky cartoon, *New Statesman* (17 Oct. 1959).

24 Drucker, *Doctrine and Ethos in the Labour Party* (1979), p. 15. 'Wilson Report', *LPACR* (1955), p. 87.

25 Butler and Rose, *The British General Election of 1959*, pp. 28, 21 252–3, 241. M. Phillips, *Labour in the Sixties* (1960), p. 23. *Reynolds News* (13 Sept. 1959). Also Labour Party Research Department (LPRD), RD. 154, 'Political Advertising' (June 1961).

26 K. Garland, 'Pool Resources to Obtain Results', *Labour Organiser* (Feb. 1963), pp. 32–3.

27 R. Miliband, *Parliamentary Socialism: A Study in the Politics of Labour* (1961), pp. 116–20, 301–2, comments on Mr. Cube, 'neither in resources, nor, it may be added in energy and determination, was the Labour Party a match for the business interests and their public relations experts.' On the *Daily Mail*, Michael Foot, *Guardian* (3 Sept. 1998). *Contact: Journal of the Lowestoft Labour Party* 1:4 (Sept. 1958).

28 Phillips to Carol Johnson (10 March 1954). NMLH, General Secretary's Papers, GS/Bcst/237/i–iii, also GS/Bcst/173–6. 'Interim Report on the Monitoring Service', Publicity and Political Education Sub-Committee, NEC Minutes (23 July 1958).

29 Thompson, 'The Segregation of Dissent', pp. 2–3. D. Kartun, *Freedom and the Communists* (1955), p. 6. CPGB, *The Battle For Truth* (1965), p. 1.

30 *LPACR* (1959), p. 133.

31 East Midlands Regional Labour Party Papers, Modern Records Centre (MRC), Warwick University, 'Reports from Agents in Marginals', MSS. 9/3/3/5. Phillips, *Labour in the Sixties*, p. 21. J. Morgan (ed.), *The Backbench Diaries of Richard Crossman* (1981), p. 374 (3 Dec. 1954)

32 J. Saville 'The Communist Experience: A Personal Appraisal', in R. Miliband and L. Panitch (eds), *Socialist Register* (1991), p. 21. Morden ward minutes (20 Oct. 1955), MM Papers 3/5. R. Edwards, *Goodbye Fleet Street* (1988), p. 55.

33 Crosland, *The Conservative Enemy*, p. 34. M. Abrams, 'Public Opinion Polls and Political Parties', *Public Opinion Quarterly* 27 (1963), p. 18. M. Rosenbaum, *From Soapbox to Soundbite*, p. 8.

34 G. Hodgkinson, *Sent to Coventry* (1970), p. 234. See also E. Heffer, *Never a Yes Man* (1991), p. 38, D. Thompson, *Outsiders: Class, Gender and Nation* (1993), pp. 12–13.

35 E. P. Thompson, 'A Psessay in Ephology', *New Reasoner* 10 (Autumn 1959), p. 3. M. Kenny, *The First New Left* (1994), p. 29. Letter, Saville to Ralph Miliband (25 May 1959) and Miliband's reply (bringing an end to the idea), Saville Papers DJS 112 (*New Left Review*, 1959–63). Mervyn Jones, *The Times* (11 Dec. 1996).

36 D. Kartun, 'Seeing the Trees for the Wood', *The Reasoner* 3 (Nov. 1956), p. 5 Crosland, *The Conservative Enemy*, p. 34. Clark quoted in Pearson, Turner, *The Persuasion Industry*, p. 258.

37 Rowland, Labour Publicity', p. 351.
38 NMLH, Public Relations and the Tories' (Oct. 1958) in Chairman's Sub-Committee minutes (21 Oct. 1958). Publicity and Political Education Sub-Committee minutes (11 June 1959), NEC minutes (22 July 1959).
39 Rosenbaum, *From Soapbox to Soundbite*, pp. 140, 285–6. J. Morgan (ed.), *Backbench Diaries of Richard Crossman*, p. 257 (30 July 1953). *Socialist Commentary* (Nov. 1954), p. 307, (Nov. 1958), p. 13
40 H. Campbell, Eavesdropping at Conference', *Co-Operative Party Monthly Letter* (Nov. 1956). p. 12. *LPACR* (1960), p. 195. D. Lessing, *Walking in the Shade: Volume II of my autobiography, 1949–62* (1997), p. 86. Castle in Rosenbaum, *From Soapbox to Soundbite*, p. 95.
41 Pearson, Turner, *The Persuasion Industry*, p. 257. *Labour Organiser* (Aug. 1955), p. 40. Bacon in M. Abrams, Opinion Polls and Party Propaganda', *Public Opinion Quarterly* 28 (1964), p. 13. Hattersley, New Blood', p. 157.
42 Thompson, 'A Psessay in Ephology', p. 3. Hopkins, *The New Look*, pp. 451–2.
43 Heardley-Walker, *Weekly Tote Bulletin* (7 Sept. 1959). MM Papers 4/1. Foot, *Daily Herald* (18 Nov. 1958). Martin Rosenbaum, Betting and the 1997 British General Election', *Politics* 19:1 (Feb. 1999), p. 9.
44 J. Tunstall, *The Advertising Man* (1964), p. 165. Butler and Rose, *British General Election of 1959*, p. 27. R. Pearce (ed.), *Patrick Gordon Walker: Political Diaries, 1932–1971* (1991), p. 35. J. B. Priestley, Mass Communications', in *Thoughts in the Wilderness* (1957), p. 11. Pearson, Turner, *The Persuasion Industry*, p. 261.
45 CPGB, *The Battle for Truth*. p. 1. W. Norman, Signposts for the Sixties', *New Left Review* 11 (1961), p. 47. Hobbs in Kenny, *The First New Left*, p. 27. R. Samuel, Dr. Abrams and the End of Politics', *New Left Review* 5 (1960), p. 3.
46 P. Clark, If I were a Publicity Officer', *Labour Organiser* (Jan. 1962). p. 7, Little Things can Mean a Lot', *Labour Organiser* (Dec. 1961), pp. 228–9.
47 Rowland, Labour Publicity', p. 350. Hattersley, New Blood', p. 157. Morrison in J. Gyford, *National Parties and Local Politics* (1983), p. 47.
48 C. A. R. Crosland, *Can Labour Win?* (Fabian Tract 325, 1960), p. 22. NMLH, Public Relations and the Tories' (Oct. 1958) in Chairman's Sub-Committee minutes (21 Oct. 1958). And Resolutions', in Publicity and Political Education Sub-Committee minutes (11 June 1959). Garland, Pool Resources to Obtain Results'. p. 32.
49 Labour Party, *Your Personal Guide to the Future Labour Offers You* (1958). Hailsham in Butler and Rose, *The British General Election of 1959*. p. 27. *LPACR* (1959), pp. 106–7.
50 R. Hoggart, Pictures of the People', *Observer* (15 Nov. 1959). *Tony Benn, Diaries 1940–62* , 7 Nov. 1958, p. 291. Hopkins, *The New Look*, p. 451. *Contact: Journal of the Lowestoft Labour Party* 1:13 (June 1959). NMLH, Resolutions', to the Publicity and Political Education Sub-Committee, NEC minutes (25 June 1958).
51 Hattersley, New Blood', p. 157. Pearson, Turner, *The Persuasion Industry*, p. 257. G. Roberts, *LPACR* (1959), p. 126.
52 Letter, R. B. Ritchie to R. H. S. Crossman (12 Dec. 1958). Crossman papers (MRC) MSS. 154/3/Pol/179. W. Pickles, Political Attitudes in the Television Age', *Political Quarterly* 30:1 (Jan.–March 1959), p. 57.

53 J. Trenaman and D. McQuail, *Television and the Political Image: A Study of the Impact of Television on the 1959 General Election* (1961), pp. 93–94. *Socialist Commentary* (Feb. 1959), p. 11.

54 Campbell, 'Eavesdropping at Conference', p. 12. J. B. Priestley, 'A Note on Billy Graham', *Thoughts in the Wilderness*, p. 118. A. L. Williams, 'Politics in Greenwich', *Labour Organiser* (Oct. 1956), pp. 183–184. Reviewing M. Benney, A. P. Gray and R. H. Pear, *How People Vote: A Study of Electoral Behaviour in Greenwich* (1956). G. Wallas, *Human Nature in Politics* (1910), p. 5.

55 Phillips, *Labour in the Sixties*, p. 5.

56 Rowland, 'Labour Publicity', p. 358. Also Trenaman and McQuail, *Television and the Political Image*, pp. 162–3. *Tony Benn, Diaries 1940–62*, pp. 159, 183, 201–2, 290–1, 314.

57 *Daily Mail* (30 July 1959).

58 Rowland, 'Labour Publicity', pp. 351–2. Butler and Rose, *The British General Election of 1959*, pp. 24–5.

59 J. B. Priestley, 'Our New Society', in *Thoughts in the Wilderness*, pp. 120–1.

60 R. Hoggart, *The Uses of Literacy* (1957), pp. 103. Orwell *Collected Essays and Journalism* (1981), p. 614.

61 Rowland, 'Labour Publicity', pp. 351–2. Gorman, *Knocking Down Ginger* (1995), p. 208. Rosenbaum, *From Soapbox to Soundbite*, p. 6. LPRD, *Twelve Wasted Years* (1963).

62 A. W. Benn, 'Winning the Next Election – A Problem of Communications' (13 July 1958), MSS. 154/3/Pol/148 and 'The Labour Party and Broadcasting' (23 Feb. 1953). NMLH GS/Bcst/215 ii–xvi.

63 'The State of the Party', p. 15 (13 July 1960). MSS. 154/3/LP/2/64. Rowland, 'Labour Publicity', p. 352.

64 P. Clark, 'Ban Local Election Jargon'', *Labour Organiser* (Jan. 1961), pp. 11–12. Observations from Agents in Marginals – Harborough', MSS 9/3/3/55. D. Widgery, *The Left in Britain, 1956–1968* (1976), p. 513. M. MacEwen, *The Greening of a Red* (1991), p. 207. Jones, *Chances*, p. 185. Kenny, *The First New Left*, p. 200.

65 M. Jenkins, *Bevanism: Labour's High Tide* (1979), pp. 126–7. I. Waller, 'The Left-Wing Press', in Kaufman, *The Left*, pp. 85–8. *Evening Standard* (5, 6 Sept. 1960).

66 Replies to '*Socialist Commentary* Questionnaire' (1955) in MSS. 173 Box 9. *New Statesman* (15 Sept. 1956, 10 Nov. 1956, 1 Dec. 1956). Samuel's letters to *Socialist Commentary* (Sept., Oct. 1960, Jan. 1961).

67 Rowland, 'Labour Publicity', p. 352. Butler and Rose, *The British General Election of 1959*, pp. 56, 26–7.

68 Letter, Crossman to Butler (7 June 1955). MSS. 154/3/Be/29–32.

69 A. Bevan, *In Place of Fear* (1952), p. 15. Rosenbaum, *Soapbox to Soundbite*, p. 151. S. Lamb, 'How to Learn the Canvassing Art', *Labour Organiser* (Oct. 1953), pp. 190–192. Priestley, *Thoughts from the Wilderness*. p. viii.

70 Jones, *Chances*, p. 133. Gaitskell in Butler and Rose, *The British General Election of 1959*, p. 20. K. O. Morgan, *Labour People* (1992), p. 224.

71 E. P. Thompson, 'William Morris and the Moral issues Today', *Arena II:8* (June–July 1951), pp. 27–9 and 'A Psessay in Ephology', pp. 3–4.

72 See A. L. Williams, 'Retreat from Psephology', *Labour Organiser* (Nov. 1955), p. 195.

73 M. Abrams and R. Rose, *Must Labour Lose?* (1960). *Socialist Commentary* May, June, July, Aug. 1960. *Daily Telegraph* (2 May 1960). Phillips, Press Statement (9 May 1960). In MSS. 173 Box 10.
74 Butler and Rose, *The British General Election of 1959*, pp. 244–6. Questionnaire in NMLH, GS/BMR/73. Letter, Deidre Hockton to Wilson (5 Nov. 1958). GS/BMR/2ii–iii
75 Tom Driberg, *Reynolds News* (1 Feb. 1959). Elliot to Morgan Phillips (3 Feb. 1959). GS/BMR/67.
76 *Daily Mail* and *Daily Herald* (31 Jan. 1959). Butler and Rose, *The British General Election of 1959*, p. 245.
77 LPRD, Re. 159 Education Survey' (May 1957).
78 See *Must Labour Lose?* and M. Abrams, 'The Future of the Left: New Roots of Working–Class Conservatism', *Encounter* (May 1960). Samuel, 'Dr. Abrams and the End of Politics', p. 2. R. Samuel, G. Stedman Jones, 'The Labour Party and Social Democracy', in R. Samuel (ed.), *Culture, Ideology and Politics* (1982), p. 323.
79 On funding, letter, Hinden to Gaitskell (5 Feb. 1960). in MSS. 173 Box 7. Samuel, 'Dr. Abrams and the End of Politics', pp. 2, 5. Abrams, *Socialist Commentary* (Sept. 1960), p. 26.
80 R. Samuel, 'The Deference Voter', *New Left Review* 1 (1960), pp. 9–13. Abrams and Rose,, *Must Labour Lose?*, pp. 8–10.
81 LPRD, Re. 47 Memo on Proposed Pilot Scheme for a Public Opinion Survey' (April 1956).
82 Crosland, *Can Labour Win?*, p. 2. Crosland drew heavily on Abrams' work.
83 J. Lawrence and M. Taylor, 'Introduction: Electoral Sociology and the Historians', in J. Lawrence and M. Taylor (eds), *Party, State and Society: Electoral Behaviour in Britain since 1820* (1997), pp. 2–6.
84 R. Samuel, 'The Lost World of British Communism', *New Left Review* 154 (1985), p. 9. Crosland, *Can Labour Win?*, p. 24. Samuel, Stedman-Jones, 'The Labour Party and Social Democracy', pp. 321–2. Lawrence and Taylor, 'Introduction: Electoral Sociology and the Historians', p. 5.
85 Crosland, *Can Labour Win?*, pp. 20–22. Williams, 'Retreat from Psephology', p. 195.
86 LPRD, Re. 68, 'Note on Available Public Opinion Material' (May 1956). R. S. Milne and H. C. Mackenzie, *Straight Fight: A Study of Voting Behaviour in the Constituency of Bristol North-East at the General Election of 1951* (1954); J. Bonham, *The Middle Class Vote* (1954); Benney, Gray, Pear, *How People Vote*; Butler, *The British General Election of 1955*.
87 Morrison cited in Conservative Research Department, *Notes on Current Politics* (2 Nov. 1959), p. 14. Rosenbaum, *From Soapbox to Soundbite*, pp. 151–2. *Economist* (2 April 1966), p. 18.
88 Benn, 'Was this a TV Election?', pp. 108–9. Tony Benn, *Diaries 1940–62* , 27 Jan., 6 Feb. 1958, 7 May 1958, pp. 262–3, 276. Gorman, *Knocking Down Ginger*, p. 192. J. Smith, 'Give up Soap Box for Radio', *Labour Organiser* (Aug. 1953), p. 145.
89 G. Williams, 'Mr. Attlee on Television', *Labour Organiser* (Nov. 1954). *Tony Benn, Diaries 1940–62* , on Bevan, 21 Nov. 1957, 10 Feb. 1958, pp. 254, 264–5. On Gaitskell, 27 Oct. 1958, p. 290.
90 Benn, 'Was this a TV Election?', pp. 108–109. Pickles, 'Political Attitudes in the Television Age', pp. 65–6.

91 Hopkins, *The New Look*, p. 450. On gleam', K. Morgan, *Harry Pollitt* (1994). Upward, *The Rotten Elements*, pp. 116–17.
92 Letter, J. K. O'Hagan to Phillips (20 Dec. 1959). GS/Bcst/291. W. Pickles, Notes on Labour Party Broadcasting and TV', Appendix IV, Phillips' election report to NEC, minutes (22 June 1955).
93 S. Townsend, *Mr. Bevan's Dream*, pp. 8–9.
94 The CPGB stood 259 candidates in general elections between 1945 and 1966, only 15 saved their deposits. But what spurred it on more than anything was success in 1945, when 256 CPGB local councillors were elected.
95 On 1950: CP/Lon/Circ/05/01. A mobile unit showed Pollitt's 1955 broadcast, Widgery, *The Left in Britain*, p. 533. On 1959: Press Release, The Communist Party and General Election Broadcasting' (18 Sept. 1959), detailing correspondence between J. C. Thornton (Deputy Secretary, BBC) and Gollan (General Secretary CPGB), CP/Cent/Stat/1/9. Baker, *The Communists and TV*. p. 3. Dutt, *Luton News* (15 Oct. 1964).
96 LPRD, R. 71, Notes on the Next Election Broadcast Campaign' (Nov. 1951).
97 On costs, LPRD, R. 328, Report on the First Party Political Television', Technical Sub-Committee on Broadcasting (Dec. 1953). *Tony Benn, Diaries 1940062* , 30 Dec. 1958, pp. 295–6.
98 Rosenbaum, *Soapbox to Soundbite*, p. 48. BBC Audience Research Report (28 March 1960), NEC minutes (27 April 1960). Report on Burton, Morrison Broadcasts, NEC minutes (30 March and 23 Nov. 1955).
99 Rosenbaum, *From Soapbox to Soundbite*, p. 49.
100 Crosland to Gaitskell (7 Nov. 1960), Gaitskell Papers C282. *Forward* (27 March 1958).
101 J. Adams, *Tony Benn: A Biography* (1992), pp. 142–6. Tory broadcasts in 1959 came from the ATV studios.
102 R. Samuel, *Island Stories* (1998), p. 273. A. W. Benn, Draft Plan for General Election Broadcasting' (14 Nov. 1958) in Adams, *Tony Benn*, p. 143. Rosenbaum, *From Soapbox to Soundbite*, p. 179.
103 Labour Party, *Leisure for Living* (1959), p. 35.
104 *Tony Benn, Diaries 1940062* , 11, 12, 25 March 1959, pp. 301–2.
105 P. Lucas, Looking Back at the Battle', *Daily Worker* (9 Oct. 1959). *Daily Sketch* (25 Sept. 1959). *The Spectator*, in Trenaman and McQuail, *Television and the Political Image*, p. 120.
106 Trenaman and McQuail, *Television and the Political Image*, pp. 114, 116, 120–1. LPRD, Rd. 7, Further Notes on the General Election', Home-Policy Sub-Committee (Nov. 1959).
107 J. Blumler and D. MacQuail, *TV in Politics: Its Uses and Influence* (1968), pp. 33–6. L. Allaun, TV Roused Voters', *Labour's Northern Voice* (Dec. 1959). P. Black, *The Mirror in the Corner* (1972), p. 47, 53–4.
108 Rosenbaum, *From Soapbox to Soundbite*, pp. 41, 50. LPRD, Rd. 7, Further Notes on the General Election', Home-Policy Sub-Committee (Nov. 1959).
109 *Reynolds News* (11 Oct. 1959). Allaun, TV Roused Voters'.
110 Butler and Rose, *The British General Election of 1959*, pp. 22–7, 136. Rosenbaum, *Soapbox to Soundbite*, p. 7.
111 Hopkins, *The New Look*, p. 450. Butler and Rose, *The British General Election of 1959*, pp. 24, 136, 197.

112   See D. Hennessy, 'The Communication of Conservative Publicity, 1957–1959', *Political Quarterly* 32:3 (July–Sept. 1961), pp. 238–56. Allaun, 'TV Roused Voters'.

113   Butler and Rose, *The British General Election of 1959*, p. 251. Crosland, *Can Labour Win?*, p. 15.

114   Jay in *Forward* (16 Oct. 1959). *Tony Benn, Diaries 1940–62* , 11 Oct. 1959, p. 317.

115   P. Anderson, Origins of the Present Crisis' (1964) in P. Anderson, *English Questions* (1992), p. 37.

116   Crosland, *Can Labour Win?*, p. 8. Wallas, *Human Nature in Politics*, p. 84. LPRD, Rd. 87 'A Note on Dr. Abrams' Survey' (Sept. 1960).

117   See T. H. White, *The Making of the President, 1960* (1962). Crosland, *The Conservative Enemy*, p. 203. *LPACR* (1959), pp. 151–5.

118   Crosland, *Can Labour Win?*, pp. 21–2. Crosland, *The Conservative Enemy*, pp. 229–30.

119   Pearson and Turner, *The Persuasion Industry*, pp. 257–9. Crosland to Gaitskell', 'Appreciation', Gaitskell Papers C282. S. Koss, *The Rise and Fall of the Political Press in Britain* (1984), p. 1101. Rosenbaum, *From Soapbox to Soundbite*, p. 9. On Lord Lovell-Davis, Obituary, *The Guardian* (8 Jan. 2001).

120   Pearson and Turner, *The Persuasion Industry*, pp. 257–8, 261. V. Packard, *The Hidden Persuaders* (1958).

121   See Letter F. Coates (Secretary, Bromley CLP) to Morgan Phillips (6 July 1959), Gaitskell Papers F21. 2 Peay, NEC minutes (14 Jan. 1960). Report of the Staff Salaries Sub-Committee, NEC minutes (27 April 1960); Bax, NEC minutes (24 Jan. 1962) Castle, Campaign Committee NEC minutes (18 April 1962).

122   Crosland, *The Conservative Enemy*, p. 34. £2000–2500 was the going rate for a senior PR post.

123   NEC Minutes, (23 May 1962). See W. Fletcher, *How to Capture the Advertising High Ground* (1994).

124   Rosenbaum, *From Soapbox to Soundbite*, pp. 8–9. Pearson, Turner, *The Persuasion Industry*, pp. 257–8. M. Abrams, *The Condition of the British People 1911–1945* (1946).

125   Crosland to Gaitskell, ('Appreciation', late 1961 and 7 Nov. 1960), Gaitskell Papers C282. Bacon's comments on Future Work', Publicity Sub-Committee (7 Dec. 1961, NEC minutes 20 Dec. 1961)

126   Crosland to Gaitskell (4 May 1960), Gaitskell Papers C282. Wilson quoted in A. Sampson, *Anatomy of Britain* (1962), p. 594. Tunstall, *The Advertising Man*, p. 235. Pearson and Turner, *The Persuasion Industry*. p. 261. Rosenbaum, *From Soapbox to Soundbite*, p. 152. D. Howell, 'Wilson and History', *Twentieth Century British History* 4:2 (1993), p. 182.

127   S. Fielding, 'White Heat and White Collars!' The Evolution of 'Wilsonism'', in R. Coopey, S. Fielding and N. Tiratsoo (eds), *The Wilson Years* (1993), p. 30. A. Sked and C. Cook, *Post-War Britain: A Political History* (1993), pp. 215–19. A. Howard and R. West, *The Making of the Prime Minister* (1965), p. 142. Titled after Theodore White's book. R. West, Campaign Journal', *Encounter* XXIII: 6 (Dec. 1964), pp. 14–15.

128   R. Rose, *Influencing Voters* (1967), p. 81. Rosenbaum, *From Soapbox to Soundbite*, pp. 9–10. Lovell-Davis', obituary, *The Guardian* (8 Jan. 2001).

129 Our Penny-Farthing Machine', *Socialist Commentary* (Oct. 1965), pp. xviii–xx; G. Kaufman, Does Labour's machine need a Shake-Up', *New Statesman* (7 May 1965); D. Leonard, Labour's Agents', *Plebs* (Oct. 1965) and *Tribune* (8 April 1966).
130 K. Jefferys, British Politics and the Road to 1964', *Contemporary Record* 9:1 (Summer 1995), pp. 120–46.
131 D. Wring, Soundbites versus Socialism: The Changing Campaign Philosophy of the British Labour Party', *The Public* 4:3 (1997), pp. 59–67. Koss, *Rise and Fall of the Political Press*, p. 1101. Rowland, Labour Publicity', p. 351. Garland, Pool Resources to Obtain Results', p. 33. A. W. Benn, The Labour Party and Broadcasting' (23 Feb. 1953), NMLH GS/Bcst/215/xi. Pickles, Notes on Labour Party Broadcasting and TV'
132 See Churchill, Conservative Party papers, Bodleian Library CCO4/2/25 and Lord Home, M. Cockrell, Politics – It's a Screen Test', *Independent on Sunday* (23 March 1997). The party had its suspicions about the bias in the BBC, CCO4/1/23. A. Sampson, *Macmillan: A Study in Ambiguity* (1967), p. 163.
133 Hopkins, *The New Look*, p. 451.

Chapter 8: Conclusions

1 See D. Leonard (ed.), *Crosland and New Labour* (1999).
2 M. Jacques, Good to be Back', *Marxism Today* (Nov.–Dec. 1998). T. Blair, *New Britain* (1996), pp. 5, 13, 238–9, and also Blair's comments, *New Statesman* (15 July 1994). See S. Fielding, New Labour and the Past', in D. Tanner, P. Thane and N. Tiratsoo (eds), *Labour's First Century* (2000)
3 T. Wright and M. Carter, *The People's Party: A History of the Labour Party* (1997), p. 7. It's good to be a do-gooder', *Guardian* (22 Jan. 1999). On New Labour's sobriety, Francis Wheen, *Guardian* (16 April 1997).
4 Jacques, Good to be Back', p. 3. T. Nairn, The Nature of the Labour Party – I', *New Left Review* 27 (1964). R. H. Tawney, The Choice before the Labour Party', *Political Quarterly* 3 (July–Sept. 1932).
5 M. Francis, Economics and Ethics: The Nature of Labour's Socialism, 1945–51' *Twentieth Century British History* 6:2 (1995). S. Fielding, P. Thompson and N. Tiratsoo, *England Arise!: The Labour Party and Popular Politics in 1940s Britain* (1995). I. Zweiniger-Bargielowska, *Austerity in Britain: Rationing, Controls and Consumption 1939-55* (2000). A. Black and S. Brooke, The Labour Party, Women and the Problem of Gender, 1951–66', *Journal of British Studies* 36 (Oct. 1997).
6 M. Jarvis, The Conservative Party and the Adaptation to Modernity, 1957–64', Ph.D. thesis (London University, 1998). E. H. H. Green, The Conservative Party, the State and the Electorate, 1945–64', in J. Lawrence and M. Taylor (eds), *Party, State and Society: Electoral Behaviour in Britain since 1820* (1997), p. 196.
7 Hall in Oxford University Socialist Discussion Group (eds), *Out of Apathy: Voices of the New Left 30 Years On* (1989), p. 18. R. Desai, *Intellectuals and Socialism: Social Democrats' and the Labour Party* (1994). pp. 102–6.

8   G. Melly, *Revolt into Style: The Pop Arts in Britain* (1970), p. 77. P. Thompson, 'Labour's Gannex Conscience?' Politics and Popular Attitudes in the Permissive Society', in Coopey, Fielding and Tiratsoo (eds) *The Wilson Governments, 1964-70* (1993).

9   Conservative Party 1964 Election Manifesto, *Prosperity with a Purpose* (1964), p. 26.

10 A. Thorpe, *A History of the British Labour Party* (1997), pp. 180–1.

11 M. Wiener, *English Culture and the Decline of the Industrial Spirit* (1981), p. 126.

12 See Thorpe, *A History of the British Labour Party*, p. 217.

13 Labour Party, *The Voice of the People* (1956). J. Lawrence, *Speaking for the People: Party, Language and Popular Politics in England 1867-1914* (1998), pp. 262–7.

14 Labour Party, *Look Forward* (1961), p. 8. R. Hattersley, 'New Blood', in G. Kaufman (ed.), *The Left* (1966), p. 157. C. A. R. Crosland, *The Conservative Enemy* (1961), p. 129.

15 Press Statement, *New Left Review* launch (Nov. 1959). Brynmor Jones Library, University of Hull, John Saville papers, DJS 51.

Select Bibliography

This bibliography does not include specific articles from contemporary or from historical journals – these are in the endnotes.

Organizational Records and Private Papers and Records

Bodleian Library, Oxford
Conservative Party Archive
CCO/4 – Charman's Office Subject Files

British Film Institute, London
Recording of C.Mayhew MP interviewing H.Shawcross MP (1951), *Challenge to Britain* (1953, LP.20), *Britain Belongs to You* (no.4, 1959, LP.58)

British Library Manuscript Collections
R. Palme Dutt Papers

British Library, National Sound Archive, London
Labour Party Oral History Project (C/609) and CPGB members (C/703)

British Library of Economic and Political Science, London
Records of the Merton and Morden Labour Party, miscellaneous material in Coll Misc 0502, 0730, 0766 and 0789

Brynmor Jones Library, University of Hull
Howard Hill Papers, Robin Page Arnot Papers, John Saville Papers

Centre for Kentish Studies, County Hall, Maidstone
Records of the Faversham Labour Party

Marx Memorial Library, London
Pamphlet collection, boxes A1, A2, A8, A9, D2, D10, D14

Modern Records Centre, Warwick University, Coventry
East Midlands Regional Labour Party Papers, Coventry Borough Labour Party Papers, Sidney Stringer Papers, Les Cannon Papers, Richard Crossman MP Papers, Socialist Union Papers, Dave Michaelson Papers, Lawrence Daly Papers.

National Museum of Labour History, Manchester
Communist Party Papers: Industrial Department, District Records, Organisation Department, Cultural Department, Executive and Political Committee minutes, Young Communist League
Labour Party Papers: National Executive Committee minutes and papers, General Secretary's Papers (Morgan Phillips), Labour Party Research Department Memoranda, Half-Yearly Agents' Reports to National Agent (1955), Terry Pitt (Research Department) Papers, Michael Foot Papers, Eric Heffer Papers, Jo Richardson Papers

Tom Harrisson Mass Observation Archive, University of Sussex
Topic Collections: General Elections 1945–1955', 'Ask Your Dad"

Tower Hamlets Local Studies Library, London
Records of the Bethnal Green Labour Party

Working Class Movement Library, Salford
Nelson and Colne Labour Party Papers

University College London Library
Hugh Gaitskell Papers

Contemporary Newspapers and Journals

Arena
Contact: The Journal of the Lowestoft Labour Party
Co-operative Party Monthly Newsletter
Daily Express
Daily Herald
Daily Mirror
Daily Sketch
Daily Telegraph
Daily Worker
Economist
Encounter
Evening Standard
Fabian Journal
Faversham Times
Forward (both the ILP newspaper and social democratic journal, edited by John
    Harris)
Labour Monthly
Labour Organiser
Labour Press Service
Labour's Northern Voice
Labour's Voice
Labour Woman
Listener
Luton News
Manchester Guardian
Marxism Today
Melody Maker
Music and Life
New Left Review
News Chronicle
New Reasoner
New Society
New Statesman and Nation
Notes on Current Politics
Observer
Political Quarterly

Political Studies
Public Opinion Quarterly
Red Pepper
Revolt
Reynolds News
Rhyming Reasoner
Socialist Commentary
Socialist Register
Sunday Dispatch
Sunday Express
The Argus: The Journal of Merton and Morden Labour Party
The Reasoner
The Scotsman
The Times
Tribune
Universities and Left Review

Contemporary Publications

(Unless stated, place of publication is London)

M. Abrams, R. Rose, *Must Labour Lose?* (Harmondsworth, 1960)
C. A. R. Attlee, *As it Happened* (1954)
D. Ainley, *The Co-ops: The Way Ahead* (CPGB, 1962)
W. Angus Sinclair, *Socialism and the Individual: Notes on Joining the Labour Party* (1955)
B. Baker, *Communists and TV* (CPGB, 1965)
F. Bealy, W. P. McCann, J. Blondel, *Constituency Politics: A Study of Newcastle-Under-Lyme* (1965)
M. Benney, A. P. Gray, R. H. Pear, *How People Vote: A Study of Electoral Behaviour in Greeenwich* (1956)
A. Bevan, *In Place of Fear* (1952)
A. H. Birch, *Small Town Politics: A Study of Political Life in Glossop* (Oxford, 1959)
J. Bonham, *The Middle Class Vote* (1954)
A. Briggs, J. Saville (eds), *Essays in Labour History* (1967)
E. Burns, *The Meaning of Socialism* (1950)
—   *The Co-ops and the Crisis* (1955)
E. Burton, *The Battle of the Consumer* (1955)
D. Butler, *The British General Election of 1955* (1955)
—(with R. Rose),   *The British General Election of 1959* (1960)
CPGB, *Coronation* (1953)
—   *The Communist Party and the Role of Branches* (1955)
—   *Forging the Weapon: A Handbook for Party Members* (1957)
—   *The Role of the Communist Party (Basis for Branch Education)* (1957)
—   *25th Congress Report* (1957)
—   *Report of the Commission on Inner-Party Democracy* (1957)
—   *The British Road to Socialism* (1958)
—   *Our Aim is Socialism* (1959)

—   *Harry Pollitt –A Tribute* (1960)
—   *Forging the Weapon: A Handbook for Party Members* (1961)
—   *The Battle for Truth* (1965)
J. Connell, *Death on the Left: The Moral Decline of the Labour Party* (1958)
Conservative Party, *They've got a Little List* (1958)
—   *Prosperity with a Purpose* (1964)
Co-operative Independent Commission Report (1958)
M. Corden, *A Tax on Advertising?* (Fabian Research Series 222, 1961)
Council for Children's Welfare, *Comics and Your Children* (1954)
Crawley CPGB, *Rents can come down!* (1952)
H. Croft, *Party Organisation* (1950)
C. A. R. Crosland, *The Future of Socialism* (1956)
—   *Can Labour Win?* (Fabian Tract 324, 1960)
—   *The Conservative Enemy* (1962)
R. H. S. Crossman (ed.), *The God that Failed: Six Studies in Communism* (1950)
—(ed.),   *New Fabian Essays* (1952)
—   *Socialist Values in a Changing Civilisation* (Fabian Tract 286, 1950)
—   *Socialism and the New Despotism* (Fabian Tract 298, 1956)
—   *Labour in the Affluent Society* (Fabian Tract 325, 1960)
Daily Worker, *America –The Facts* (1953)
B. Darke, *The Communist Technique in Britain* (1951)
N. Davenport, *The Split Society* (1963)
S. Delaney, *A Taste of Honey* (1958)
E. Durbin, *The Politics of Democratic Socialism* (1940)
M. Edelman, *The Minister* (1961)
B. B. Elliot, *A History of English Advertising* (1962)
Fabian Society, *Where? Five Views on Labour's Future* (Fabian Tract 320, 1959).
W. Fienburgh, *No Love for Johnnie* (1959)
J. K. Galbraith, *The Affluent Society* (first published 1958; Harmondsworth, 1973 edn)
J. Gollan, *What Next?* (CPGB, 1960)
R. Gosling, *Lady Albemarle's Boys* (1961)
—   *Sum Total* (1962)
T. Harrisson, *Britain Revisited* (1961)
E. J. Hobsbawm, *Labouring Men: Studies in the History of Labour* (1964)
R. Hoggart, *The Uses of Literacy: Aspects of working-class life with special reference to publications and entertainments* (first published 1957; Harmondsworth, 1969 edn)
H. Hopkins, *The New Look: A Social History of the Forties and Fifties in Britain* (1963)
A. Howard, R. West, *The Making of the Prime Minister* (1965)
D. Hyde, *I Believed: The Autobiography of a Former British Communist* (1951)
International Women's Day Committee, *The Lure of Comics* (1952)
D. Jay, *The Socialist Case* (1937; 1946 edn)
C. Jenkins, *Power at the Top* (1959)
—   *Power Behind the Screen* (1961)
R. Jenkins, *Pursuit of Progress* (1953)
—   *The Labour Case* (1959)
D. Kartun, *America –Go Home!* (1951)
—   *Freedom and the Communists* (1955)
G. Kaufman (ed.), *The Left* (1966)

Labour League of Youth, *Me, an Idealist* (1953)
Labour Party, *Let Us Face the Future* (1945)
—   *Labour and the New Society* (1950)
—   *Labour Party Annual Conference Report* (1950–60)
—   *Facing the Facts* (1952)
—   *Challenge to Britain* (1953)
—   *Another Hole in Your Purse* (1954)
—   *The Food Fraud* (1954)
—   *The High Price of Toryism* (1954)
—   *Record of the Tory Government –Three Wasted Years* (1955)
—   *Personal Freedom: Labour's Policy for the Individual and Society* (1956)
—   *The Voice of the People* (1956)
—   *Take it From Here* (1956)
—   *Industry and Society* (1957)
—   *National Superannuation* (1957)
—   *Party Organisation* (1957)
—   *Aim: End the Call Up* (1958)
—   *Learning to Live* (1958)
—   *Plan for Progress* (1958)
—   *The Men who Failed* (1958)
—   *Your Personal Guide to the Future Labour Offers You* (1958)
—   *Hi!* (1959)
—   *Leisure for Living* (1959)
—   *Teamwork's the Answer* (1959)
—   *The Tory Swindle, 1951–1959* (1959)
—   *Labour Women's Conference Report* (1960)
—   *Fair Deal for the Shopper* (1961)
—   *Look Forward* (1961)
—   *Signposts for the Sixties* (1961)
—   *Festival of Labour Programme* (1962)
—   *Programme for Exhibition of Modern Art* (1962)
—   *Report of a Commission of Enquiry into Advertising* (1966)
Labour Party Research Department, *Twelve Wasted Years* (1963)
Labour Party Youth Commission, *The Younger Generation* (1959)
Labour Research Department, *Money and Men Behind TV* (1959)
D. Lessing, *In Pursuit of the English* (1960)
—   *The Golden Notebook* (1962; 1993 edn)
H. Lyttelton, *Second Chorus* (1958)
N. MacKenzie (ed.), *Conviction* (1958)
M. MacEwen, *Rents Must Not Go Up* (CPGB, 1955)
Manchester Guardian, *The Future of the Labour Party: A Stocktaking* (1955)
C. Mayhew, *Dear Viewer…* (1953)
—   *Commercial Television –What is to be Done?* (Fabian Tract 318, 1959)
I. Mikardo, *It's a Mug's Game* (1950)
R. Miliband, *Parliamentary Socialism: A Study in the Politics of Labour* (1961)
R. S. Milne, H. C. MacKenzie, *Marginal Seat: A Study of Voting Behaviour in the Constituency of Bristol North East at the General Election of 1955* (1958)
H. Morrison, *The Peaceful Revolution* (1949)
F. Newton, *The Jazz Scene* (1959)
H. Nicholas, *The British General Election of 1950* (1951)

J. Northcott, *Value for Money? The Case for a Consumers' Advice Service* (1953)
— *Why Labour?* (Harmondsworth, 1964)
V. Packard, *The Hidden Persuaders* (Harmondsworth, 1957)
— *The Waste-Makers* (Harmondsworth, 1960)
J. Pearson, G. Turner, *The Persuasion Industry* (1965)
H. Pelling, *The British Communist Party: A Historical Profe* (1958)
M. Phillips, *Labour in the Sixties* (1960)
D. Potter, *The Glittering Coffi* (1960)
J. B. Priestley, *The Arts under Socialism* (1947)
— *The Writer in a Changing Society* (1956)
— *Thoughts in the Wilderness* (1957)
—(with J. Hawkes),   *Journey Down a Rainbow* (1955)
D. Riesman, *The Lonely Crowd* (first published 1953; 1973 edn)
A. Sampson, *Anatomy of Britain* (1962)
— *Macmillan: A Study in Ambiguity* (1967)
L. Shao-Chi, *How to be a Good Communist* (CPGB, 1955)
A. Shonfield, *British Economic Performance Since the War* (Harmondsworth, 1958)
C. Sigal, *Weekend in Dinlock* (1960)
Socialist Union, *Socialism: A New Statement of Principles* (1952)
— *Twentieth Century Socialism* (Harmondsworth, 1956)
G. Thayer, *The British Political Fringe* (1965)
E. P. Thompson, *The Struggle for a Free Press* (1952)
— *William Morris: Romantic to Revolutionary* (first published 1955; 1977 edn)
—(ed.),   *Out of Apathy* (1960)
— *The Making of the English Working Class* (first published 1963; Harmondsworth, 1980 edn)
R. Titmuss, *Income Distribution and Social Change* (1962)
J. Trenaman, D. McQuail, *Television and the Political Image: A Study of the Impact of Television on the 1959 General Election* (1961)
G. Wallas, *Human Nature in Politics* (1910)
A. Wesker, *The Wesker Trilogy* (Harmondsworth, 1964)
T. H. White, *The Making of the President, 1960* (1962)
F. Williams, *Fifty Years' March: The Rise of the Labour Party* (1949)
— *The American Invasion* (1962)
R. Williams, *Culture and Society, 1780-1950* (Harmondsworth, 1958)
— *The Long Revolution* (Harmondsworth, 1961)
— *Communications* (first published 1962; Harmondsworth, 1976 edn)
P. Wilmott, M. Young, *Family and Kinship in East London* (first published 1957; Harmondsworth, 1986 edn)
— *Family and Class in a London Suburb* (1960)
N. Wood, *Communism and British Intellectuals* (1959)
M. Young, *The Chipped White Cups of Dover* (1960)
F. Zweig, *The Worker in an Affluent Society* (1961)

Biographies, Memoirs and Diaries

J. Adams, *Tony Benn: A Biography* (1992)
T. Benn, *Out of the Wilderness: Diaries 1963-1967* (1987)
J. Callaghan, *Rajani Palme Dutt: A Study in British Stalinism* (1993)

J. Campbell, *Nye Bevan and the Mirage of British Socialism* (1987)

O. Cannon, J. R. L. Anderson, *The Road from Wigan Pier* (1973)

B. Castle, *Fighting all the Way* (1993)

S. Crosland, *Tony Crosland* (1982)

R. Crossman, *The Diaries of a Cabinet Minister*, vol. 1 (1975)

P. Duff, *Left, Left, Left: A Personal Account of Six Protest Campaigns, 1945-1971* (1971)

R. Edwards, *Goodbye Fleet Street* (1988)

M. Foot, *Aneurin Bevan 1945-1960* (1979 edn)

G. Goodman, *The Awkward Warrior* (1979)

J. Gorman, *Knocking Down Ginger* (1995)

R. Harris, *The Making of Neil Kinnock* (1984)

R. Hattersley, *A Yorkshire Boyhood* (1991)

E. Heffer, *Never a Yes Man* (1991)

G. Hodgkinson, *Sent to Coventry* (Oxford, 1970)

P. Hollis, *Jennie Lee: A Life* (1997)

D. Jay, *Change and Fortune* (1980)

M. Jones, *Chances: An Autobiography* (1987)

M. Jones, *Michael Foot* (1994)

D. Leonard (ed.), *Crosland and New Labour* (1999)

D. Lessing, *Walking in the Shade: Volume Two of my Autobiography 1949-1962* (1997)

M. MacEwen, *The Greening of a Red* (1991)

H. McShane, J. Smith, *Harry McShane: No Mean Fighter* (1978)

J. Morgan (ed.), *The Backbench Diaries of Richard Crossman* (1981)

K. Morgan, *Harry Pollitt* (Manchester, 1993)

K. O. Morgan, *James Callaghan: A Life* (Oxford, 1997)

M. Morgan, *Part of the Main* (1990)

John O'Farrell, *Things can only get better: Eighteen miserable Years in the Life of a Labour Supporter* (1998)

B. Pimlott, *Harold Wilson* (1992)

H. Pollitt, *Serving My Time* 1940)

J. Postgate, M. Postgate, *A Taste for Dissent: The Life of Raymond Postgate* (Keele, 1994)

D. N. Pritt, *The Autobiography of D. N. Pritt, part two* (1966)

H. Ratner, *Reluctant Revolutionary: Memoirs of a Trotskyist 1936-1960*)

M. Saran, *Never Give Up* (Oxford, 1976)

M. Shelden, *Orwell: The Authorised Biography* (1992)

W. Stephen Gilbert, *Fight and Kick and Bite: The Life and Work of Dennis Potter* (1995)

Lord Bernard Taylor of Mansfield, *Uphill all the Way* (1972)

B. Turner, *Hot Air, Cool Music* (1984)

E. Wilson, *Mirror Writing* (1982)

R. Winstone (ed.), *Tony Benn, Years of Hope: Diaries, Papers and Letters 1940-1962* (1994)

Historical and other works

G. Alderman, C. Holmes (eds), *Outsiders and Outcasts: Essays in Honour of William. J. Fishman* (1993)

D. Alfred (ed.), *The Robert Tressell Lectures 1981-1988* (Rochester, 1988)

P. Anderson, *Arguments within English Marxism* (1980)

— *English Questions* (1992)

G. Andrews, N. Fishman, K. Morgan (eds), *Opening the Books: Essays in the Social and Cultural History of the British Communist Party* (1995)

M. Andrews, *Lifetimes of Commitment: Ageing, Politics and Psychology* (Cambridge, 1991)

F. Beckett, *Enemy Within: The Rise and Fall of the British Communist Party* (1995)

J. Benson, *The Rise of the Consumer Society in Britain, 1880-1980* (1994)

L. Black et. al. , *Consensus or Coercion? The State, the People and Social Cohesion in Post-War Britain* (Cheltenham, 2001)

P. Black, *The Mirror in the Corner: People's Television* (1972)

T. Blair, *New Britain* (1996)

J. Blumler, D. Macquail, *TV in Politics: Its Uses and Inflence* (1968)

J. Blumler, M. Gurevitch, *The Crisis of Public Communication* (1995)

V. Bogdanor, R. Skidelsky (eds), *The Age of Afflence, 1951-1964* (1970)

A. Briggs, *Michael Young: Social Entrepreneur* (Basingstoke, 2001)

B. Brivati, R. Heffernan (eds), *The Labour Party: A Centenary History* (Basingstoke, 2000)

R. Brunt, C. Rowan (eds), *Feminism, Culture and Politics* (1982)

C. Bryant, *Possible Dreams: A Personal History of British Christian Socialists* (1996)

P. Catterall, J. Obelkevich (eds), *Understanding Post-War British Society* (1994)

P. Catterall, C. Seymour-Ure, A. Smith, (eds), *Northcliffe's Legacy: Aspects of the British Popular Press 1896-1996* (Basingstoke, 2000)

C. Chambers, *The Story of Unity Theatre* (1989)

R. Chapman, *Selling the Sixties: The Pirates and Pop Music Radio* (1992)

L. Chun, *The British New Left* (Edinburgh, 1993)

P. Cohen (ed.), *Children of the Revolution: Communist Childhood in Cold War Britain* (1997)

B. Conekin, F. Mort, C. Waters (eds), *Moments of Modernity: Reconstructing Britain 1945-1964* (1999)

Consumers' Association, *Thirty Years of Which?* (1987).

R. Coopey, S. Fielding, N. Tiratsoo (eds), *The Wilson Governments, 1964-70* (1993)

J. Corner (ed.), *Popular Television in Britain: Studies in Cultural History* (1991)

M. Daunton, M. Hilton (eds), *The Politics of Consumption: Material Culture and Citizenship in Europe and America* (Oxford, 2001)

A. J. Davies, *To Build a New Jerusalem* (1992)

R. Desai, *Intellectuals and Socialism: Social Democrats' and the Labour Party* (1994)

F. Devine, *Afflent Workers Revisited* (Edinburgh, 1992)

H. M. Drucker, *Doctrine and Ethos in the Labour Party* (1979)

N. Ellison, *Egalitarian Thought and Labour Politics: Retreating Visions* (1994)

R. English, M. Kenny (eds), *Rethinking British Decline* (Basingstoke, 2000).

S. Fielding, *The Labour Party: Socialism' and Society since 1951* (Manchester, 1997)

S. Fielding, P. Thompson, N. Tiratsoo, *England Arise! The Labour Party and Popular Politics in 1940s Britain* (Manchester, 1995)

N. Fishman, *British Communism and the Trade Unions 1933-1945* (Aldershot, 1997)

R. Fraser (ed.), *Work*, 2 vols (1968)

J. Fyrth (ed.), *Labour's Promised Land: Culture and Society in Labour's Britain* (1995)

V. George, I. Howards, *Poverty amidst Afflence: Britain and the United States* (1991)

J. Godbolt, *A History of Jazz in Britain, 1950–1970* (1989)

J. Goldthorpe, D. Lockwood, F. Bechhofer, J. Platt, *The Afflent Worker*, 3 vols (Cambridge, 1968)

A. Gorst, L. Johnmann, W. Scott Lucas (eds), *Contemporary British History 1931–1961* (1991)

S. Goss, *Local Labour and Local Government: A Study of Changing Interests, Politics and Policy in Southwark from 1919 to 1982* (Edinburgh, 1988)

P. Gould, *The Unfiished Revolution* (1998)

P. Gwynne, *A History of Crawley* (Chichester, 1990)

J. Gyford, *Local Politics in Britain* (1978)

—   *National Parties and Local Parties* (1983)

S. Haseler, *The Gaitskellites: Revisionism in the British Labour Party 1951–1964* (1969)

N. Hayes, *Consensus and Controversy: City Politics in Nottingham 1945–1966* (Liverpool, 1996)

A. Heath, R. Jowell, J. Curtice, *How Britain Votes* (Oxford, 1985)

L. Heron (ed.), *Truth, Dare or Promise: Girls Growing up in the Fifties* (1985)

R. Hewison, *In Anger: Culture and the Cold War* (1981)

D. Hill (ed.), *Tribune 40: The First Forty Years of a Socialist Newspaper* (1977)

J. Hinton, *Labour and Socialism: A History of the British Labour Movement 1867–1974* (Brighton, 1983)

E. J. Hobsbawm, *Revolutionaries* (1977)

—   *Worlds of Labour* (1984)

—   *The Jazz Scene* (new edn, 1989)

B. Hogenkamp, *Film, Television and the Left in Britain, 1950–1970* (2000)

J. Holroyd-Doveton, *Young Conservatives: A History of the Young Conservative Movement* (Bishop-Anckland, 1996)

D. Howell Thomas, *Socialism in West Sussex* (Chichester, 1983)

R. Huzzard, *Half a Century of Orpington Labour Party* (Orpington, 1993)

F. Inglis, *Radical Earnestness: English Social Theory 1880–1980* (Oxford, 1982)

S. Iveson, R. Brown, *Clarion House: A Monument to a Movement* (Preston, 1987)

M. Jacques (ed.), *The Forward March of Labour Halted?* (1981)

K. Jefferys, *Retreat from New Jerusalem: British Politics 1951–1964* (Basingstoke, 1997)

H. Jenkins, *The Culture Gap: An Experience of Government and the Arts* (1979)

M. Jenkins, *Bevanism: Labour's High Tide* (Nottingham, 1979)

M. Jones, *Today the Struggle* (1978)

M. Kenny, *The First New Left* (1994)

S. Koss, *The Rise and Fall of the Political Press in Britain* (1984)

B. Lancaster, A. Mason (eds), *Life and Labour in a Twentieth Century City: The Experience of Coventry* (Coventry, 1986)

B. Lancaster, P. Maguire (eds), *Towards the Co-operative Commonwealth: Essays in the History of Co-operation* (Loughborough, 1996)

J. Lawrence, *Speaking for the People: Party, Language and Popular Politics in England 1867–1914* (Cambridge, 1998)

—(with M. Taylor) (eds),   *Party, State and Society: Electoral Behaviour in Britain since 1820* (Aldershot, 1997)

D. Lessing, *The Four-Gated City* (New York, 1969)

A. L. Lloyd, *Folk Song in England* (1967)

R. MacKenzie, A. Silver, *Angels in Marble: Working-Class Conservatives in Urban England* (1968)

R. McKibbin, *The Ideologies of Class: Social Relations in Britain 1880–1950* (Oxford, 1990)

Microform Academic Publishers, *Local Labour Party Records on Microfin, Series II* (Wakefield, 1998)

J. P. M. Millar, *The Labour College Movement* (1980)

T. R. Nevett, *Advertising in Britain: A History* (1982)

K. Newton, *The Sociology of British Communism* (1969)

O'Dee, *The Failure and Salvation of the Labour Party* (Manchester, 1938)

A. Offer (ed.), *In Pursuit of the Quality of Life* (Oxford, 1996)

G. Orwell, *Collected Essays and Journalism of George Orwell* (1981)

Oxford University Socialist Discussion Group (eds), *Out of Apathy: Voices of the New Left Thirty Years On* (1987)

W. Paterson, A. Thomas (eds), *Social Democratic Parties in Western Europe* (1977)

W. Paterson, A. Thomas (eds), *The Future of Social Democracy* (Oxford, 1988)

S. Pedersen, P. Mandler (eds), *After the Victorians: Private Conscience and Public Duty in Modern Britain* (1994)

C. Pierson, S. Tormey (eds), *Politics at the Edge* (Basingstoke, 2000)

C. Ponting, *Breach of Promise: Labour in Power 1964–1970* (1989)

C. Powell, *How the Left Learned to love Advertising* (1998)

A. Prost, G. Vincent (eds), *A History of Private Life Vol. V: Riddles of Identity in Modern Times* (Cambridge, MA, 1991)

D. Pye, *Fellowship is Life: The National Clarion Cycling Club* (Bolton, 1995)

C. Rallings, D. Farrell, D. Denver, D. Broughton (eds), *British Elections and Parties Review, Volume 5* (1995)

H. Rees, C. Rees, *The History Makers* (Stevenage, 1991)

D. Regan, *The Local Left and its National Pretensions* (1987)

M. Rosenbaum, *From Soapbox to Soundbite: Party Political Campaigning in Britain since 1945* (Basingstoke, 1997)

R. Samuel (ed.), *Culture, Ideology and Politics* (1982)

—— *Theatres of Memory: Past and Present in Contemporary Culture* (1994)

—— *Island Stories: Unravelling Britain, Theatres of Memory vol. 2* (1998)

D. Sassoon, *One Hundred Years of Socialism: The Western European Left in the Twentieth Century* (1997)

M. Savage, *The Dynamics of Working-Class Politics: The Labour Movement in Preston 1880–1940* (Cambridge, 1987)

J. Seabrook, T. Blackwell, *A World Still to Win: The Post-War Reconstruction of the Working Class* (1985)

A. Seldon, S. Ball (eds), *Conservative Century: The Conservative Party since 1900* (Oxford, 1994)

E. Shaw, *Discipline and Discord: The Politics of Managerial Control in the Labour Party 1951–1987* (Manchester, 1988)

A. Sked, C. Cook, *Post-War Britain: A Political History* (Harmondsworth, 1993)

D. Smith, *Socialist Propaganda in the Twentieth Century British Novel* (1979)

R. South, *Heights and Depths: Labour in Windsor* (Windsor, 1985)

G. Stedman Jones, *Languages of Class: Studies in English Working-Class History 1832–1982* (Cambridge, 1983)

C. Steedman, *Landscape for a Good Woman: A Story of Two Lives* (1986)

D. Tanner, P. Thane, N. Tiratsoo (eds), *Labour's First Century* (Cambridge, 2000)

F. Teer, J. D. Spence, *Political Opinion Polls* (1973)

D. Thompson, *Outsiders: Gender, Class and Nation* (1993)

E. P. Thompson, *Writing by Candlelight* (1980)

—   *Persons and Polemics* (1994)

N. Thompson, *Political Economy and the Labour Party* (1996)

W. Thompson, *The Good Old Cause: British Communism 1920–1991* (1992)

A. Thorpe, *A History of the British Labour Party* (Basingstoke, 1997).

N. Tiratsoo, *Reconstruction, Affluence and Labour Politics: Coventry 1945–1960* (1990)

N. Tiratsoo (ed.), *From Blitz to Blair: A New History of Britain Since 1939* (1997)

S. Townsend, *Mr. Bevan's Dream* (1989)

R. Toye, 'The Gentleman in Whitehall" Reconsidered: The Evolution of Douglas Jay's Views on Planning and Consumer Choice, 1937–1947', University of Manchester, Working Papers in Economic and Social History, No. 49 (2001)

R. Tressell, *The Ragged Trousered Philanthropists* (1914; 1991 edn)

J. Tunstall, *The Advertising Man in London Advertising Agencies* (1964)

E. Upward, *The Rotten Elements* (1969)

—   *No Home but the Struggle* (1977)

M. Veldman, *Fantasy, the Bomb and the Greening of Britain: Romantic Protest 1945–1980* (Cambridge, 1994)

D. Vincent, *Poor Citizens: The State and the Poor in Twentieth Century Britain* (1991)

A. Warde, *Consensus and Beyond: The Development of Labour Party Strategy since World War Two* (Manchester, 1982)

C. Waters, *British Socialists and the Politics of Popular Culture 1884–1914* (Manchester, 1990)

R. Weight, A. Beach (eds), *The Right to Belong: Citizenship and National Identity in Britain 1930–1960* (1998)

D. Weinbren (ed.), *Generating Socialism: Recollections of Life in the Labour Party* (Stroud, 1997)

D. Widgery, *The Left in Britain 1956–1968* (Harmondsworth, 1976)

M. Wiener, *English Culture and the Decline of the Industrial Spirit, 1850–1980* (Cambridge, 1981)

R. Williams, *Politics and Letters* (1979)

E. Wilson, *Only Halfway to Paradise: Women in Post-War Britain 1945–1968* (1980)

A. Wright (ed.), *British Socialism: Socialist Thought from the 1880s to 1960s* (Harlow, 1983)

T. Wright, M. Carter, *The People's Party: A History of the Labour Party* (1997)

I. Zweiniger-Bargielowska, *Austerity in Britain: Rationing, Controls and Consumption 1939–55* (Oxford, 2000)

I. Zweiniger-Bargielowska, M. Francis (eds), *The Conservatives and British Society 1880–1960* (Cardiff, 1996)

Unpublished Material

L. Black, 'British Communism and 1956: Party Culture and Political Identities', MA, (University of Warwick, 1994)

M. Donnelly, Labour Politics and the Affluent Society, 1951–1964', Ph.D. thesis (University of Surrey, 1995)

M. Jarvis, The Conservative Party and the Adaptation to Modernity, 1957–64', Ph.D. thesis (University of London, 1998)

C. Torrie, Ideas, Policy and Ideology: the British Labour Party in Opposition, 1951–1959', D.Phil. thesis (University of Oxford, 1997)

R. Weight, Death to Hollywood?'The Cultural Politics of Anti-Americanism in Post-War Britain', paper delivered to tenth Institute of Contemporary British History Summer Conference (July 1998)

Interviews

Recorded interviews with Ted Rodgers, David Grove (CPGB Oral History Project).

Mervyn Jones (23 Feb., 28 May 1996); George Matthews (19 May 1994), Jim Northcott (14 Feb. 2001)

Index